PURSUIT OF JUSTICES

PURSUIT
OF
JUSTICES

PRESIDENTIAL POLITICS
AND THE SELECTION OF
SUPREME COURT
NOMINEES

DAVID ALISTAIR YALOF

THE UNIVERSITY OF CHICAGO PRESS
CHICAGO AND LONDON

DAVID ALISTAIR YALOF is assistant professor of political
science at the University of Connecticut, Storrs.

The University of Chicago Press, Chicago 60637
The University of Chicago Press, Ltd., London
© 1999 by The University of Chicago
All rights reserved. Published 1999
Printed in the United States of America
08 07 06 05 04 03 02 01 00 99   1 2 3 4 5

ISBN: 0-226-94545-6 (cloth)

Library of Congress Cataloging-in-Publication Data

Yalof, David Alistair.
    Pursuit of justices : presidential politics and the selection of
Supreme Court nominees / David Alistair Yalof.
        p.   cm.
    Includes bibliographical references and index.
    ISBN 0-226-94545-6 (cloth : alk. paper)
    1. United States. Supreme Court.—Officials and employees—
Selection and appointment. 2. Judges—Selection and appointment—
United States. 3. Law and politics. I. Title.
KF8742.Y35   1999
347.73'14—dc21   99-27979
                                                           CIP

♾ The paper used in this publication meets the minimum
requirements of the American National Standard for
Information Sciences—Permanence of Paper for Printed
Library Materials, ANSI Z39.48-1992.

Contents

Preface and Acknowledgments

This book relates how presidents since World War II have selected nominees to serve on the United States Supreme Court. During the past half-century, Supreme Court appointments have become high-stakes political events. Intense interest group activity, heightened media attention, and the regular occurrence of divided party government have all significantly constrained the degree to which a president may control the politics of the selection process. The president's ability to influence this highly charged nomination environment thus increasingly depends on his individual management style, the relative capabilities of White House subordinates who enjoy delegated authority, and the unique political circumstances surrounding each vacancy. A number of important questions arise in this context. How do individuals come to be considered for the Supreme Court? Why do presidents select certain candidates over others? Have changes in the institution of the presidency during the past half-century affected the consideration and vetting of Supreme Court candidates? In particular, how have modern presidents fared in pursuing their own goals through the appointment process?

Executive branch decisionmaking concerning potential Supreme Court nominees constitutes a critical stage in the Supreme Court appointment process as a whole. Yet recent controversies surrounding the nominations of Robert Bork and Clarence Thomas have focused scholarly attention to a large degree on the vagaries of the Senate confirmation process. This book's focus on aspects of presidential decisionmaking that occur *prior* to the formal submission of a nominee's name for Senate consideration reflects another reality: candidates who emerge from this initial stage of the decisionmaking process become justices in all but a handful of cases. Indeed, the Senate has confirmed 89 percent of the president's nominees during this century.[1] Such deference has continued in recent years, as twelve of fourteen nominees between 1970 and 1994 have garnered Senate approval. In overemphasizing the confirmation process we may be neglecting the most critical decisionmaking stage in most Supreme Court appointments.

In truth, a seamless web links *both* phases of the appointment process.[2] Just as a quick, successful confirmation process may be attributed to careful and strategic selection decisions, so may a contentious confirmation battle arise from missteps in the selection process that preceded it. While the confirmation of Supreme Court nominees is not the immediate focus of this work, I have tried to take account of any changes in the confirmation process that may have influenced modern presidents' approaches to nominee selection. Of course there already exist a large number of excellent studies of the confirmation process that focus primarily on failed or controversial nominees to the Court.[3] By contrast, nomination politics that precedes the confirmation process remains the central concern of this work.

I have drawn on a variety of sources for the information and data found in this book. Primarily, I have utilized documents found in seven presidential libraries and numerous other archives. My interpretations of those documents benefited greatly when I could corroborate them with information gleaned from interviews with actual participants in the selection process. Naturally, I am grateful to all the former White House and Justice Department officials who granted interviews and shared their remembrances with me. Several of them asked that they not be identified by name in this manuscript. Some did speak on the record, however, and their contributions to this research are quite evident. The late Herbert Brownell met with me twice at his home in New York City, devoting a large amount of his personal time to this project. Ramsey Clark, William P. Rogers, Theodore Sorenson, Nicholas Katzenbach, Fred Fielding, Peter Wallison, Howard Baker, and Edwin Meese all generously volunteered to talk to me about their experiences with the process. President Gerald Ford also extended to me considerable time from his schedule; his unique perspectives on the selection process proved invaluable.

Generous research grants from the Harry S. Truman Library Institute, the Dwight D. Eisenhower World Affairs Institute, and the

Lyndon Baines Johnson Institute facilitated primary research at their respective presidential libraries in Independence, Missouri; Abilene, Kansas; and Austin, Texas. I conducted additional research at the Ronald Reagan Library in Simi Valley, California; the Gerald R. Ford Library in Ann Arbor, Michigan; the John F. Kennedy Library in Boston, Massachusetts; and the Nixon Presidential Materials Project at the National Archives in College Park, Maryland. The staff at each of those research collections provided considerable assistance to me. I would especially like to thank Randy Sowell and Elizabeth Safley of the Truman Library; David Haight of the Eisenhower Library; John Wilson, Allen Fisher, and Claudia Anderson of the Johnson Library; Pat Anderson of the Nixon Project; and Diane Barrie of the Reagan Library, who often went beyond the call of her official duties to track down documents and information for this project.

A large number of people directly assisted me in the preparation of this book. My dissertation advisors, J. Woodford Howard Jr. and Joel B. Grossman, carefully read the manuscript this work drew from, and each contributed thoughtful criticisms and advice. I am by no means the first scholar to credit those two individuals with providing the ideal conditions for the study of public law and the development of original research ideas. Each has proven to be a trusted mentor and faithful friend. John A. Maltese generously gave of his time and energy to review this manuscript in its various stages, and his comments were invaluable. John Tryneski of the University of Chicago Press has been a supportive editor and a fine critic, commenting on numerous issues of style and substance for this book. Leslie Keros and Robert Caceres went over every inch of this manuscript in preparing it for publication.

Others played indirect roles in this book's preparation, but their contributions were no less significant. John T. Tierney provided immeasurable encouragement and advice during the past four years. Sheldon Goldman and Benjamin Ginsberg offered many useful suggestions. Suzette Hemberger was always willing to listen to my ideas, and she usually provided me with some necessary perspective. My new colleagues at the University of Connecticut have all been supportive of this project, furnishing me with the perfect environment for preparing a book for publication. Bob Gilmour, Martha Gibson, Carol Lewis, and Howard Reiter deserve special mention: each of them patiently answered the endless number of questions I posed to them about issues in American politics and public administration that cropped up while writing this book. As department chairman, John Rourke always kept my eye focused on the ball. And I especially want to thank David J. Danelski, who has been a special source of inspiration to me throughout my short career; I will be forever grateful to him for taking an ongoing interest in this work.

Among the many others to whom I owe a personal thanks are: Michael Cornfield, a trusted friend for over a decade who (along with Steven Finkel) sparked my interest in the field of political science when I was an undergraduate at the University of Virginia; Donald B. Ayer, who never stopped encouraging me in this endeavor; Patrick D. Schmidt, a close friend and companion, with whom I shared all the joys and frustrations of being a doctoral student; my other fellow graduate students—especially Margie Brassil, Mark Cushman, Douglas Dow, Douglas Harris, Rob Kahn, Char Miller, Tracy Roof, Ward Thomas, and Pamela Winston—who provided considerable friendship and intellectual support; and Evelyn Stoller, Esther Abe, Lisa Williams, and Jim Gillespie, for always taking time to help me on numerous and varied administrative matters at Johns Hopkins University. Without knowing it, Henry Abraham provided a professional model for me to emulate; Barbara Perry often lifted my spirits with reassurance when I needed it most. I also cannot begin to express my appreciation for Stephanie Lindquist, whose optimism about all matters large and small has been a godsend. Dwayne Leslie, John Boyle, Mike Schiavo, and Robert Hardie knew little of the details of this project, but their friendships got me through many difficult times working on it. Of course my family's encouragement has also been critical. I am indebted to my parents, Harvey and Marion Yalof, for their constant support; and to Velma Metusevich Pierce, for her willingness to go the extra mile (literally) to make my life easier.

But most of all I am indebted to my wife, Andrea, for her abundant love and faith. When I am with Andrea and our daughter Rachel, I am reminded of just how lucky I am. I dedicate this to them.

January 1999
Storrs, Connecticut

ONE

INTRODUCTION

On June 27, 1992, the Supreme Court inserted itself once again into the national debate over abortion with its surprising decision in *Planned Parenthood v. Casey*.[1] Specifically, five of the nine justices refused to cast aside *Roe v. Wade*,[2] the Court's controversial 1973 opinion establishing a constitutional right to abortion. Included among *Roe*'s saviors that day were Sandra Day O'Connor and Anthony Kennedy, both appointees of former President Ronald Reagan. As a candidate for the presidency in 1980 and 1984, Reagan had supported a constitutional amendment to overturn *Roe*, a ruling considered to be among the most vilified of public targets for social conservatives in his party. As president, Reagan had publicly promised to appoint justices to the Supreme Court willing to reverse *Roe v. Wade*. Yet just the opposite occurred in *Casey*: a majority of the Court reaffirmed the core right to privacy first discovered in *Roe*.[3] And in a touch of irony, two of President Reagan's own nominees had played significant roles in safeguarding the decision from the Court's conservatives.

Obviously the selection of Supreme Court nominees is among the president's most significant duties. Yet as the outcome in *Casey* demonstrates, it is a task beset with difficulties and potential frustrations. On one hand, a president ordinarily tries to choose a nominee whose influence will reach beyond the current political environment. As a beneficiary of life tenure, a justice may well extend that president's legacy on judicial matters long into the future. Yet in selecting a nominee the president must also successfully maneuver through that immediate environment, lest he suffer politically or (as in some cases) see his nominee rejected by the Senate outright.

In recent years internal strife and factionalism within the executive branch have only further complicated what was already a delicate undertaking.

Beyond merely overcoming the constitutional requirement of Senate approval, Ronald Reagan confronted numerous obstacles in selecting his nominees for the Supreme Court. During the 1980s a disjunction eventually arose within his administration between the ardently conservative "Reagan revolutionaries" in the Justice Department, who were campaigning to transform the constitutional landscape at all costs, and the pragmatic White House officials concerned with protecting the president's more immediate political interests. Certainly the U.S. Senate deserves some of the credit for *Roe*'s last-minute resuscitation. President Reagan's first choice for the Court in 1987 had been Court of Appeals Judge Robert Bork, an admitted opponent of *Roe;* the Senate's defeat of Bork by a 58–42 vote set the stage for Anthony Kennedy's ultimate appointment to the Court in January 1988. Still, all of the president's nominees (including Kennedy) first had to survive political struggles within the administration itself. High-level advisors to the president waged these civil wars long before the Senate had its say in the appointment process.

Prior to the respective nominations of O'Connor and Kennedy, various officials in the Reagan administration became aware that each had evidenced some ambiguity on the critical issue of abortion rights.[4] Despite such clear warnings, a select group of high-level officials mustered enough support in each case to ensure that its favored candidate remained high on the administration's "shortlists." A combination of assets in O'Connor's case, including youth (she was just fifty-one years old) and a conservative record on law enforcement issues, convinced Attorney General William French Smith to look past troubling ambiguities about her abortion position. Similarly, Anthony Kennedy's youth (he was also just fifty), his stature in the legal community, and his eminent confirmability made him a top candidate for a Supreme Court vacancy as early as 1986. After witnessing two consecutive nominations to the Supreme Court go awry (Robert Bork and Douglas Ginsburg), Chief of Staff Howard Baker and White House Counsel Arthur B. Culvahouse were able to seize the upper hand from Reagan's other chief advisor, Attorney General Edwin Meese III, in November 1987. Kennedy's star thus rose despite Justice Department officials' qualms over his judicial record on privacy rights. Few of these same

officials could have been surprised five years later ɯ
joined the controlling opinion in *Casey*.

A central question remains: why were these partic
chosen over others possessing similar—and in so
rior—qualifications? The classic "textbook" portɯ
preme Court nomination process depicts presidents as choosing
Supreme Court justices more for their judicial politics than for their
judicial talents. By this version of events, presidents, by nominating
justices whose political views appear compatible with their own, try
to gain increased influence over the Supreme Court. Once on the
Court, a justice may then satisfy or disappoint the appointing president by his decisions. Such an oversimplified view of nomination
politics usually ignores the more complex political environment in
which modern presidents must act, including the various intricacies
and nuances of executive branch politics.

In this book I contend that modern presidents are often forced
to arbitrate among factions within their own administrations, each
pursuing its own interests and agendas in the selection process. At
first glance, presidential reliance on numerous high-level officials
equipped with a variety of perspectives might seem a logical response to the often hostile and unpredictable political environment
that surrounds modern appointments to the Court. Yet conflicts
within the administration itself may have a debilitating effect on
that president's overall interests. High-level advisors may be sincerely pursuing their own conceptions of what makes up the administration's best interests; but to achieve their own maximum preferred outcomes, they may feel compelled to skew the presentation
of critical information, if not leave it out altogether. In recent administrations the final choice of a nominee has usually reflected one
advisor's hard-won victory over his rivals, without necessarily ac-
counting for the president's other political interests. Analysis of
these intra-executive branch conflicts, and the role such conflicts
play in the Supreme Court selection process as a whole, constitutes
the central aspect of this work.

EVALUATING THE POLITICAL LANDSCAPE
THAT SHAPES NOMINEE SELECTIONS

In studying the various pathways that lead to a Supreme Court
nomination, my assumption throughout is that presidents enjoy

considerable discretion in considering and selecting candidates for the Supreme Court. No candidate ever forces himself or herself upon a president of the United States. Even if a Supreme Court seat is offered in fulfillment of a promise, political or otherwise, it remains the case that the president originally exercised his discretion when issuing that promise in the first place. Certainly he could have showed his appreciation by some means other than a Supreme Court bid. One must nevertheless distinguish between the discretion a president technically enjoys as a matter of constitutional prerogative from that which he can realistically wield without causing undue political hardship to his presidency. As to the latter, a president's personal prestige and ability to influence other public matters suffer when the selection of a Supreme Court nominee fails to adequately account for the hostile forces at work in the immediate political context.

The *timing* of a vacancy usually plays a critical role in the selection of a nominee. When a vacancy arises just before a pending presidential election, the president may be forced to nominate a noncontroversial moderate as a means of achieving the requisite support in the Senate. The nominations of Benjamin Cardozo by President Hoover in 1932 and John Paul Stevens by President Ford in late 1975 were each heavily influenced by such political reality. A Supreme Court vacancy may also occur when public attention to issues surrounding the Supreme Court is relatively high. In those cases, a president must take careful account of public perceptions. Having tried to sell his 1937 "court-packing" plan as a means of reducing the workload for older justices, Franklin D. Roosevelt was understandably reluctant to nominate an older justice to the Court in subsequent years; the seventy-one-year-old Learned Hand thus stood little chance of landing a Supreme Court nomination in 1943 despite enjoying considerable support in some legal circles.[5] After the abortion issue rocketed into the national spotlight during the late 1970s, the Reagan administration was forced to consider abortion politics in its evaluation of Supreme Court nominees throughout the following decade.

The *composition of the Senate* will constrain presidential discretion in this context. The Democrats' comfortable twelve-seat advantage in the Senate made it easier for President Truman to name two close personal associates to the bench in 1949. Truman suffered some harsh criticism initially for his nominations of Tom Clark and Sherman Minton, but each candidate was confirmed handily. More than anyone, Ronald Reagan saw first-hand what a difference a year makes. The Republicans' 53–47 edge in the Senate during the summer of 1986 eased the confirmation paths for two ardently conservative Supreme Court nominees, Antonin Scalia and William Rehnquist. In fact, Rehnquist was confirmed as chief justice by a thirty-two-vote margin despite some harsh allegations by Democrats. By contrast, a year later, after the Republicans had lost their Senate majority, the nomination of Robert Bork ran into more serious resistance from newly empowered Senate Democrats.

Public approval of the president similarly shapes the setting for each Supreme Court nomination. A president who enjoys high public support may comfortably submit almost any nominee of his choosing. By contrast, an unpopular president stands little chance of seeing any nominee confirmed easily, if at all. One scholar doubts "the Senate would have approved God himself" had he been nominated by the highly unpopular Andrew Johnson after the Civil War.[6] (Even Johnson's cautious selection of Attorney General Henry Stanbury, a well-respected Ohio Republican and Unionist, stood little real chance of success in 1865.) Sophisticated new polling techniques today give presidents yet another tool in deciding whether to choose a controversial nominee. Rising poll ratings in early 1970 actually may have spurred President Nixon to respond to the defeat of his second nominee to the Court, Court of Appeals Judge Clement Haynsworth, with an even more controversial candidate for the Court, G. Harrold Carswell.

Attributes of the outgoing justice, including his or her status in the legal community and perceived position on the Court's ideological spectrum, may also influence expectations for a prospective replacement. In seeking a nominee for the seat vacated by the legendary Justice Oliver Wendell Holmes in 1932, President Hoover fully realized that the highly esteemed Court of Appeals judge from New York, Benjamin Cardozo, was one of few candidates in the country capable of filling such lofty shoes. Perhaps Robert Bork's strong opinions on abortion, affirmative action, and other social issues would have resonated less with senators and the public had he been selected to replace a fellow conservative on the Court instead of the critical "swing" justice, Lewis F. Powell Jr.

In all cases *the realistic pool of candidates* available to the president necessarily restricts his selection of Supreme Court nominees. This field has been winnowed in advance by traditional norms of political and professional advancement. Richard Watson and Rondal

Downing have employed a "progressive winnowing theory" to explain the phenomenon of judicial recruitment in general.[7] At one end of the process lies the "particular subculture" from which judges are drawn, especially the legal community of persons admitted to the bar. Additional stages eliminate more and more candidates on the basis of acceptability to interest groups, personal desire, and other factors.[8] Finally, at the other end a chosen few emerge as the final products of the entire process: the pool of those eligible for nomination.

Although the Constitution does not specify qualifications for a justice of the Supreme Court, even the most daring president would find it difficult to ignore de facto norms of advancement that define the pool of candidates available to him. Historically, every justice has been a lawyer. Since 1943, every justice has formally graduated from an accredited law school. Some limited participation in politics, however broadly defined, colors the background of nearly all Supreme Court justices. Many carry past partisanship as a badge of honor, having risen through the ranks of a political party before catching the attention of a senator, governor, presidential advisor, or even the president himself. Others were themselves governors, members of Congress, or high-level executives before appointment to the Supreme Court. Still others were active in local bar association politics or interest groups such as the AFL-CIO, the ACLU, and the NAACP. As J. Woodford Howard Jr. remarked, even the final stages of judicial recruitment involve "an intricate web of vocational and political contacts developed long before the denouement."[9]

How do modern presidents go about the complicated task of selecting Supreme Court nominees? Presidents since 1945 have tended to utilize one of three decisional frameworks in considering candidates: (1) an *"open"* selection framework, in which all critical decisions about the next Supreme Court nominee are rendered *after* a particular vacancy arises; (2) *a single-candidate focused* framework, in which the identity of the next justice has been decided in advance of a vacancy (usually based on previous political promises, commitments, or other such circumstances); and (3) a *criteria-driven* framework for selection in which—prior to any actual vacancy arising— the president and his advisors set forth specific criteria to be met by prospective nominees (without settling on any specific candidate). Under the more flexible "open" framework, the president (with or without the assistance of advisors) may respond quickly and effectively to changes in the immediate political environment and adjust his goals accordingly. On the other hand, the president's long-term goals for the Court (to the extent he has any) may be obscured in his efforts to achieve more immediate gains. That risk is reduced whenever a criteria-driven framework for selection is utilized.

Key decisionmakers and the roles they play in executing these frameworks must also be identified. Modern presidents may utilize any of a number of approaches to structuring their administration's selection processes. On one end of a continuum lies a strictly personal approach to selection, in which the president primarily keeps his own counsel in considering and selecting nominees. On the other end lies a more bureaucratic approach, in which presidential advisors and subordinates make many critical selection decisions about Supreme Court nominations on behalf of the president. Some presidents hope to draw on positive aspects of both approaches: the final product may thus emerge from a dialogue between the president and the decisionmaking bureaucracy beneath him.

Regardless of the precise balance struck, during the past thirty years some form of delegation to bureaucratic structures has become a defining characteristic of the selection process. Both the Nixon and Reagan administrations—together responsible for filling eight of nine vacancies that arose on the Court between 1969 and 1987—established more bureaucratic, subordinate-driven mechanisms for vetting Supreme Court candidates. These systems featured (1) the promulgation of political and/or legal criteria for nominees that administration officials could interpret and apply, and (2) the participation of multiple officials and/or agencies in the process of choosing nominees. Both presidents hoped such a system would identify a broader pool of candidates. In fact, these innovations often failed to serve the president's overall interests. Officials forced to compete for influence within the administration often assume alternate roles as advocates of their *own* political agendas or causes in the selection process. And those concerns do not always represent those of their boss.

In providing a comprehensive look at the modern politics of choosing Supreme Court nominees, I utilize research and data depicting the selection politics practiced in seven administrations spanning from 1945 through 1987. These case studies lay an ample foundation from which to judge how the various decisional frameworks outlined above actually fared in practice. First, however, I briefly review the history of Supreme Court recruitment practices up to and including the New Deal, in order to provide a richer perspective from which to judge more modern practices. The transition to nominations in the post–World War II era is then captured in a survey of the ten most significant developments that have shaped the modern landscape of Supreme Court recruitment. Together, these introductory sections set the stage for more fruitful analysis of the case studies that follow.

THE NOMINEE SELECTION PROCESS IN HISTORICAL PERSPECTIVE

Consensus on the most appropriate method of selecting justices proved "elusive" at first to the drafters of the Constitution.[10] William Paterson's "New Jersey Plan" provided for judicial appointment by an executive elected by the legislature. A later resolution placed the appointment of judges exclusively in the hands of the Senate. James Madison's alternative would have required appointment by the president subject to two-thirds of the Senate's disapproval. Finally, after three months of debate, the Committee on Postponed Matters proposed the language that eventually was adopted in the Constitution: "the president shall nominate, and by and with the advice and consent of the Senate shall appoint . . . Judges of the Supreme Court."

As the debate over the Constitution was waged in state ratifying conventions, the delegates' primary concern with the judicial appointment clause was that it gave too much influence to the Senate.[11] They worried that the Senate's veto power—if wielded too often—might translate into a de facto legislative power to choose nominees. Their worst fears were soon realized in the context of lower federal court nominations. During the nineteenth century, the practice of appointing federal district judges evolved into a quite elaborate system of bargaining between the executive and the legislature grounded in political rather than constitutional norms.[12] Many individual senators assumed a near-absolute veto power over judicial selection in their home states. The president meanwhile enjoyed relatively greater discretion when choosing nominees for the U.S. Supreme Court, although the Senate of course was able to exercise its authority to challenge nominees during the subsequent confirmation process. And for well over a century, the upper chamber often did exactly that—between 1789 and 1900, the Senate rejected, postponed action, or took no action at all on nearly a quarter of the president's Supreme Court nominees.

Early American presidents thus faced a set of daunting challenges in selecting suitable Supreme Court justices. The Senate stood ready as a combatant in the confirmation process. Resources for researching and analyzing prospective Supreme Court nominees were scarce. Who (if anyone) counseled early presidents in the consideration and selection of Supreme Court nominees?

As the nation's chief legal officer, the attorney general might have seemed a logical source for such advice. Under the Judiciary Act of 1789, Congress authorized the new position, assigning the attorney general two principal responsibilities: (1) to conduct "all suits in the Supreme Court in which the United States shall be concerned"; and (2) to give "advice and opinion upon questions of law when required by the president . . . [or] by the heads of any of the departments."[13] From the outset, most attorneys general spent the bulk of their official time serving as the government's advocate in the Supreme Court. Until 1870, there was no Department of Justice, and the attorney general had few resources or staff. Indeed, because the office was conceived as a part-time government position, early attorneys general felt compelled to maintain their own private practices for most of the calendar year.[14] Only one of the first twenty-two attorneys general even resided in the capital city when the Supreme Court was not in session.[15] Leonard White captured well the attorney general's tenuous position at the beginning of the republic: "He had no establishment, . . . [H]e received no reports and was in a curious way disconnected from the actual conduct of the government's everyday business."[16]

There were some notable exceptions. Edmund Randolph's close friendship with George Washington made him an especially powerful figure in the capital.[17] William Wirt, who served for a record twelve years from 1817 through 1828, left as his lasting legacy a volume of "printed opinions of the attorney general." Yet even these relatively powerful figures apparently exerted little influence over the selection of Supreme Court nominees.[18] And while the newly created Justice Department began to expand steadily in the late nineteenth century,[19] the attorney general's role in this context remained limited, at least until the New Deal. For example, Woodrow Wilson's attorney general, T. W. Gregory, played only a limited part in the nomination of Louis Brandeis to the Court in

1916.[20] According to Brandeis's biographer, it was more likely Dr. Cary Grayson, the president's personal physician, who first suggested Brandeis's name to the president: "Gregory's part was limited to agreeing and earnestly fighting for confirmation."[21]

The White House staff also offered little in the way of political advisors who might aid the president in selecting nominees. Throughout the nineteenth century most White House aides and servants were either clerical helpers or junior aides "paid from the president's own pocketbook."[22] Not until the twentieth century did the White House staff begin to include political officers, including liaisons with Congress and other power centers in Washington. With a weak attorney general and a Spartan White House operation in place, many early presidents on their own sorted through the multitude of names suggested to them, personally canvassing the field for possible nominees. For example, George Washington worked virtually alone to staff the newly formed Supreme Court.[23] Benjamin Harrison's selection of David Brewer in 1889 came after an especially long period of private contemplation by the president.[24] Indeed, Harrison so deeply resented any outside attempts to influence his selection that one supporter's determined campaign on Brewer's behalf nearly derailed his nomination.[25]

Other than the president himself, members of Congress, the Cabinet, and even some Supreme Court justices represented occasional participants in the initial stages of selection. Given the strength of sectionalism in the nineteenth century, early presidents usually adhered to rough notions of geographical diversity in staffing the Supreme Court. The "advice" portion of the "advice and consent" clause never really carried much bite in the context of high court appointments. Still, some early presidents voluntarily chose to rely on senators and congressmen for counsel and to suggest possible candidates from their home states or regions. Thomas Jefferson in particular was famous for his reliance on senators and House members to scout out legal talent for the Court. When ill health prompted Justice Alfred Moore of North Carolina to resign in 1804, Jefferson looked to South Carolina for a replacement; he asked two members of the state's congressional delegation (Senator Thomas Sumter and Congressman Wade Hampton) to prepare a statement of the "Characters of the lawyers of S.C."[26] Nearly a century later the retirement of Justice Horace Gray, a native of Massachusetts, presented Senator Henry Cabot Lodge (R-Mass.) with a unique opportunity to exert influence in choosing his successor.

Lodge, speaking with Theodore Roosevelt directly, urged the president to nominate Oliver Wendell Holmes Jr., then chief justice of the Supreme Judicial Court of Massachusetts, to replace Gray.[27] Lodge's support proved critical, as the Massachusetts senator assured Roosevelt that Holmes was a true Republican ("not a Mugwump") and that he was "safe on imperialism." The president reportedly told Lodge, "I would not appoint my best beloved . . . unless he held the position you describe."[28]

Cabinet members only occasionally counseled presidents concerning prospective high court nominees. Chief Justice Salmon Chase's death in 1873 set off a chain of tragicomic events, as President Ulysses Grant attempted to name a new chief justice. Among a series of missteps,[29] Grant considered giving a "temporary appointment" to seventy-four-year-old Caleb Cushing. But Secretary of State Hamilton Fish openly questioned the move, and with the support of the rest of the Cabinet, he convinced Grant to drop the plan.[30] Months later, Fish joined Interior Secretary Columbus Delano in successfully urging Morrison R. Waite's appointment as chief justice.[31] After Charles Evans Hughes resigned from the Court in 1916, Secretary of War Newton Baker was the first to bring District Judge John H. Clarke's name to Woodrow Wilson's attention.[32] Serving as the president's emissary to his prospective nominee, Baker met with Clarke at length, quizzing him on a variety of subjects including his position on the all-important "trusts" question. Baker's enthusiastic support for Clarke apparently convinced Wilson that the nominee could be depended upon for "a liberal and enlightened interpretation of the law."[33]

Finally, sitting and former justices occasionally influenced deliberations over prospective nominees. Some justices tried in vain to secure seats on the Court for close friends or colleagues. Justice Samuel Miller, long coveting a Supreme Court seat for his brother-in-law, pressed his case (unsuccessfully, as it turns out) to President Rutherford B. Hayes in May 1877.[34] In the 1920s, Chief Justice William Howard Taft wielded unprecedented influence over the selection process. A strong proponent of property rights, the former president had argued during the 1920 presidential campaign that the chief issue in the upcoming election was in fact the future control of the Supreme Court.[35] After President Warren G. Harding appointed him chief justice in 1921, Taft became the new administration's prime clearing house for all appointments to the federal bench. Ultimately, Taft exercised considerable influence in Har-

ding's subsequent nominations of George Sutherland, Pierce Butler, and Edward T. Sanford to the Supreme Court.[36]

TEN FACTORS SHAPING MODERN
RECRUITMENT TO THE SUPREME COURT

The New Deal marked the beginning of a fundamental transforma-
tion in American politics. A national economic crisis demanded
national solutions, and the government in Washington grew ex-
ponentially to meet these new demands. Beginning in the 1930s,
the federal government entered one policy area after another that
had previously been the exclusive province of state governments.
Emergency conditions required quick institutional responses, and
the executive branch in particular was drawn into critical aspects
of national policymaking. Just as the character of national politics
changed dramatically, the Supreme Court was undergoing a trans-
formation of its own. Fundamental changes in the political landscape affecting Supreme Court appointments were a by-product of
these changes. At least ten critical developments in American politics substantially altered the character of the modern selection process for justices:

   1. The *growth and bureaucratization of the Justice Department* facilitated the investment of considerable manpower and other resources towards the consideration of prospective Supreme Court
candidates. As the size of the national government grew dramatically during the early twentieth century, the government's overall
legal responsibilities quickly expanded. Congress reacted by increasing the size of the Justice Department and transferring to it
most litigating functions from other federal agencies. Armed with
a full staff of attorneys and more extensive bureaucratic support,
attorneys general in modern times have enjoyed more regular input
into the selection of Supreme Court nominees, often consulting
with the president well before a vacancy on the Court even arises.

   The Justice Department under Franklin Roosevelt underwent a
minor reorganization that affected the politics of the nomination
process. Attorney General Homer Cummings merged the Division
of Admiralty into the Civil Division and established the Office of
Legal Counsel ("OLC").[37] In its infancy, the OLC served primarily
as a means of supporting the attorney general in his role as legal
advisor to the president. Yet like most other executive branch of-

fices, the OLC grew steadily over time, and eventually its mission changed to meet new administration demands. Headed today by an assistant attorney general with a staff of nearly twenty lawyers, the OLC has become responsible for developing legal positions to support the administration's policy initiatives and for resolving disputes over legal policy within the executive branch. Since 1964, the OLC has been considered one of the most politicized units in the department. And in the late 1980s the Reagan administration opted to rely principally on OLC lawyers for comprehensive research and analysis of prospective Supreme Court candidates.

2. The *growth and bureaucratization of the White House* has also had an impact on the nomination process. The White House staff, once limited to a handful of personal assistants, was barely a factor in political decisionmaking for most of the nineteenth and early twentieth centuries. Starting with Franklin Roosevelt's administration, however, the White House staff experienced prodigious growth, expanding from just thirty-seven employees in the early 1930s to more than nine hundred by the late 1980s.[38] As the modern presidency has brought more policymaking activities within the White House, the White House staff has increasingly figured in matters of high presidential priority.

Modern presidents often rely on the White House Counsel's Office to assist them in screening and selecting prospective Supreme Court nominees. Thus, increasingly, the attorney general's most constant and genuine competitor for influence has been the White House Counsel. Theodore Sorenson, John Kennedy's special counsel, asserted that his duties did not overlap with the attorney general's; rather he was involved "as a policy advisor to the president with respect to legislation, with respect to his programs and messages, with respect to executive orders, and with respect to those few formally legal problems, which come to the White House."[39] But those supposed lines of demarcation have blurred considerably during the past thirty years. Today, a president has at his disposal two distinct organizations, each with its own bureaucratic resources; the president may rely on either or both offices for counsel concerning the selection of Supreme Court nominees.

3. Paralleling the increased role for national political institutions in American life has been the *growth in size and influence of federal courts*. Congress's willingness in the past to meet increased caseloads with new judgeships has steadily multiplied the president's opportunities to place his imprint on lower court policymaking.

The total number of district and circuit judgeships rose from under two hundred in 1930 to well over seven hundred by the late 1980s.[40] Thus between thirty and forty vacancies may occur annually on the federal bench. These federal judges must be counted on to interpret, enforce, and in some cases limit the expansion of federal governmental authority. At times federal courts have even fashioned national law and policy, serving as key facilitators of social, economic, and political growth.

Senatorial courtesy, to be sure, remains the dominant factor in lower court selections, but the steady increase in the number of judgeships has provided presidents with more than an occasional opportunity to nominate candidates of their own choosing after the preferences of individual senators have been satisfied. The growing size and prestige of the D.C. Circuit have given presidents additional opportunities to hand out plum assignments: because senatorial courtesy does not apply to those seats, presidents may freely nominate ideologically compatible law professors, former administration officials, and others to positions of considerable prestige in the federal judicial system. Thus more than ever before, the federal courts today provide an especially useful "proving ground" for candidates who might one day be considered for a seat on the high court.

4. *Divided party government* has become a recurring theme in American government since World War II. Between 1896 and 1946, opposing parties controlled the White House and the Senate during just two sessions of Congress.[41] By contrast, split party conditions now seem almost routine. In all, the president has confronted a hostile U.S. Senate in fourteen separate Congresses since World War II. When a Democratic-led Senate considered Eisenhower's nomination of John Harlan in March 1955, it represented the first time in sixty years that a president's nominee had to undergo review in an upper chamber controlled by the opposition. Since then, fifteen of twenty-six nominees to the Court have faced an opposition-led Senate, a condition that has severely constrained presidential discretion in this context.

5. *The confirmation process has become increasingly public.* For much of our nation's history the confirmation process unfolded largely behind closed doors. Though the Senate Judiciary Committee often met and offered recommendations on nominees during the nineteenth century, closed investigative hearings were not conducted until 1873 when President Ulysses Grant unsuccessfully

nominated George Williams to be chief justice.[42] Open hearings were held for the first time only in 1916, when the Senate considered Louis Brandeis's candidacy. Nine years later Harlan Fiske Stone became the first nominee in history to appear before the committee personally.[43] Full-fledged public hearings were finally instituted on a regular basis beginning in 1930 with President Hoover's nomination of John J. Parker.

Since 1955, virtually all Supreme Court nominees have formally testified before the Senate Judiciary committee.[44] Hearings have been televised live since 1981, insuring heightened public access to the process. The increasingly public nature of confirmation-stage politics has placed added strain on senators, many of whom may be reluctant to spend their time and political capital on an arduous process that will only create enemies back home.[45] Meanwhile, the president must now find nominees who, aside from meeting ideological or professional criteria, will fare well in front of television cameras when facing a barrage of senators' questions.

6. *The rise in power of the organized bar* has figured significantly in recent Supreme Court selections. The American Bar Association's Special Committee on the (federal) Judiciary (later renamed the "Standing Committee on Federal Judiciary") was founded in 1947 to "promote the nomination of competent persons and to oppose the nomination of unfit persons" to the federal courts.[46] During the past half-century that committee has played a significant if uneven role in the appointment of lower federal court judges.[47] Not surprisingly, the ABA has taken an especially strong interest in the nomination of Supreme Court justices as well. Beginning with Eisenhower's nomination of Harlan in 1954, the ABA has formally reviewed all Supreme Court nominees for the Senate Judiciary Committee.[48] Thus in selecting nominees, presidents must incorporate into their calculations the possibility that a less-than-exceptional rating from the ABA could serve as a rallying point for opposition during the subsequent confirmation process.[49] Still, the bar's actual influence over the choice of nominees has varied largely depending upon the administration in power. In 1956, the Eisenhower administration began to submit names of potential Supreme Court nominees to the ABA at the same time that the FBI began its background check.[50] During this period the ABA exerted little direct influence during initial deliberations over prospective candidates. By contrast, subsequent administrations have often enlisted the committee's services during much earlier stages of the process.

High-ranking officials in the Justice Department have consulted with committee members to gauge potential support for and opposition to a prospective candidate. In 1962, for instance, committee chairman Bernard G. Segal informed Kennedy administration officials that the ABA would react favorably to Byron White's nomination if it came before the Senate.

In 1971, the Nixon administration formalized this advisory relationship for a limited period, agreeing to submit a slate of candidates to the ABA for consideration prior to its public designation of that nominee. Although the arrangement soon broke down amid allegations that the ABA had leaked the names of prospective candidates to the press, the Ford administration reinstituted the procedure in 1975. Thus, immediately following Justice Douglas's retirement in November 1975, Attorney General Edward Levi furnished the ABA with a list of prospective nominees for its review. Apparently, the ABA's positive evaluation of Judge John Paul Stevens figured heavily in the final outcome. Yet Ford remains the last president to have afforded the ABA such a degree of influence during initial selection deliberations; during the past twenty years the ABA's role has again been reduced to rating nominees only *after* the president has formally submitted their names to the Senate. Conservative disenchantment with the ABA in the years following Bork's defeat may diminish the group's role even further, especially if a Republican-controlled Senate Judiciary Committee gets an opportunity to review the qualifications of a Supreme Court nominee (an event that has not occurred since 1986).

7. *Increased participation by interest groups* has also altered the character of the Supreme Court nomination process. This is not an entirely new phenomenon. Organized interests (including the National Grange and the Anti-Monopoly League) figured significantly in defeating Stanley Matthews's nomination to the Court in 1881.[51] Almost fifty years later, an unlikely coalition of labor interests and civil rights groups joined together to defeat the nomination of John Parker.[52] Since World War II, interest groups have extended their influence into the early stages of nominee selection by virtue of their increased numbers and political power. Groups such as the Alliance for Justice, People for the American Way, and the Leadership Conference on Civil Rights have made Supreme Court appointments a high priority in their respective organizations. Many interest groups now conduct their own research into the back-

grounds of prospective nominees and inundate the administration with information and analysis about various individual candidates.

8. *Increased media attention* has further transformed nominee selection politics. Presidents in the nineteenth and early twentieth centuries, working outside the media's glare, could often delay the selection of a nominee for many months while suffering few political repercussions.[53] By contrast, contemporary presidents must contend with daily coverage of their aides' ruminations concerning a Supreme Court vacancy. Reporters assigned to the "Supreme Court beat" often provide their readership with the most recent "shortlists" of candidates under consideration by the president. A long delay in naming a replacement may be viewed by the press as a sign of indecision and uncertainty on the part of the president. Delay may also work to an administration's benefit, especially if media outlets expend their own resources investigating prospective candidates and airing potential political liabilities prior to any formal commitment by the administration.

9. *Advances in legal research technology* have had a pronounced effect on the selection process. All modern participants in the appointment process, including officials within the White House and the Justice Department, enjoy access to sophisticated tools for researching the backgrounds of prospective Supreme Court candidates. Legal software programs such as LEXIS/NEXIS and WESTLAW allow officials to quickly gather all of a prospective candidate's past judicial opinions, scholarship, and other public commentary as part of an increasingly elaborate screening process. Computer searches may be either tailored around narrow subject issues or they may be comprehensive in scope. The prevalence of C-SPAN and other cable and video outlets has made it possible to analyze prospective candidates' speeches and activities that would have otherwise gone unnoticed. Of course, advanced research technology is a double-edged sword: media outlets and interest groups may just as effectively publicize negative information about prospective candidates, undermining the president's carefully laid plans for a particular vacancy.

10. Finally, the *more visible role the Supreme Court has assumed in American political life* has increased the perceived stakes of the nomination process for everyone involved. Several of the critical developments listed above, including increased media attention and interest group influence in the nominee selection process, stem

from a larger political development involving the Court itself: during this century the Supreme Court has entrenched itself at the forefront of American politics. Prior to the New Deal, the Court only occasionally tried to compete with other governmental institutions for national influence. For example, the Taney Court inserted itself into the debate over slavery with its decision in *Dred Scott v. Sanford* (1857).[54] The Court's aggressive protection of property rights in the late nineteenth century pitted it first against state governments, and then later against Congress and the president during the early part of the twentieth century. In each instance the judiciary usually represented a political ideology in decline; after a period of time the Court eventually returned to its role as an essentially reaffirming institution.

Since the early 1940s, however, the Supreme Court has positioned itself at the center of major political controversies on a nearly continuous basis. Driven by a primarily rights-based agenda, the Court has found itself wrestling with matters embedded in the American psyche: desegregation, privacy rights, affirmative action, and law enforcement. With the Court's continuously high visibility in the American political system, each appointment of a new justice now draws the attention of nearly all segments of society. The stakes of Supreme Court appointments may only seem higher than before, but that perception alone has caused a veritable sea change in the way presidents in the late twentieth century must treat the selection of Supreme Court nominees.

These changes in the political landscape have had a profound impact on the process by which Supreme Court nominees are chosen, including the determination of who will participate in the early stages of the decisionmaking process and what type of candidates will be favored. The growth and bureaucratization of both the White House and the Justice Department have provided the president with considerable administrative resources to conduct an elaborate and comprehensive search for candidates. Still, the president's interests have not always been served by the above-described developments. The increased role the judiciary now plays in national policymaking has encouraged interest groups to increasingly assert their own distinct (and often competing) interests in the nominee selection process. Forces within the administration itself may also take a special interest in the process and its outcome. The Justice Department's preference for federal appeals judges, for example, may undermine the president's more immediate political interests by unnecessarily restricting the pool of candidates under consideration.

Certainly presidential objectives may be sacrificed whenever an ill-equipped associate or subordinate is charged with carrying out significant responsibilities in the selection process. At the same time, too many cooks may also spoil the broth, as internal strife carries its own set of negative consequences. The president's interests have often been compromised by the shift to a more bureaucratic selection process featuring multiple advisors with overlapping responsibilities. These advisors have often become advocates, striving to enlarge their own "turf" or influence over the selection process. As these competing advocates engage in conflict within the confines of the administration itself, information may be distorted; the "advice" a president receives will be based on erroneously optimistic projections about a particular outcome. Ultimately it is the president who suffers most when the full impact of negative information about candidates is not realized until after the fact, such as during a confirmation process that turns unexpectedly hostile, or later, after that individual has become a sitting justice.

The effect these various developments have had on the selection process for Supreme Court nominees will be explored more fully in the chapters that follow. Chapters 2 through 6 portray this decisionmaking process as it unfolded during seven presidential administrations from 1945 through 1987. In chapter 7, I draw on the case studies provided to analyze relevant shifts in the politics of Supreme Court recruitment over the past half century. The recent phenomenon of increased conflict within the executive branch will be examined in light of evidence that presidential aides do not always work to pursue their boss's political interests. Finally, this book briefly considers (from the more limited data available) how the selection practices of the Bush and Clinton administrations fit within the broad theoretical framework already described.

TWO

TRUMAN REWARDS
LOYALTY AND FRIENDSHIP

Thrust into the White House by Franklin Roosevelt's sudden
death in April 1945, Harry Truman never had the opportunity
to articulate a clear agenda for the Supreme Court prior to his becoming president. Nor did he plan to set forth such an agenda after
spending time in office. Yet while the Court certainly was not des-
tined to play any *positive* role in Truman's plans for governing the
nation, the new president did come to fear its ability to resist or
even veto some of his more ambitious projects. Specifically, he worried about high court interference with his administration's anti-
Communist loyalty program and any other executive branch efforts
to exercise broad power in the management of economic and foreign affairs. To address that challenge, the president was determined to nominate justices who came directly from his own tight-
knit political circle. Truman wanted to feel a sense of "personal
comfort" with each of his nominees, in part because he believed
those who knew him well would be more understanding about such
forays outside the traditionally enumerated powers of his office.
Naturally, the president would also revel in rendering the nation's
highest court yet another governmental outpost for his administration, filled with his close friends and long-time colleagues. And
since only Harry Truman himself could apply such a subjective approach to recruitment, even his most trusted advisors would wield
little or no authority in Truman's selection process.

Truman's highly personal approach to nominee selections
clearly had its up-sides. The president effectively eliminated the infighting and internal conflicts over nominations that would plague
later administrations. Additionally, Truman was willing to employ

an "open" framework for selecting nominees; avoiding advance commitments to candidates or political criteria left him considerable discretion and flexibility in addressing vacancies. Unfortunately, the president also proved so close-minded to others' input that he often failed to comprehend the political consequences of his actions. By the time he left office in January 1953, Truman's approval ratings had sunk to a low of 32 percent. He had spent the previous year fending off mounting charges of corruption within his administration. And Truman's four nominees to the Court— all close friends and loyalists of the president—were seen as emblematic of his unfortunate tendency to reward "cronies" with positions of high public trust. Truman's "open" mechanism for filling vacancies thus proved a mixed blessing for him in the end: perhaps this president exercised *too* much personal discretion when considering justices for the nation's highest court.

THE BURTON NOMINATION:
AN OLIVE BRANCH TO THE REPUBLICANS

July 1945 was a busy month for Harry Truman. The war in Europe was over, and the president was preparing for the upcoming conference of Allied leaders at Potsdam. American military officials had initiated discussions with Truman concerning the timing of an atomic strike on Japan. Domestically, the president faced heightened labor unrest; union spokesmen had promised a "wave of strikes" after V-J day. All the problems of post-war reconversion now reared themselves. Then on July 5, 1945, Justice Owen J. Roberts announced his plans to retire from the Supreme Court.[1] To a president who was already apathetic about judicial matters, the selection of a new Supreme Court nominee understandably resided low on his list of priorities.

Truman would give little thought to the matter until his return from Europe in early August. In his absence, Attorney General Tom Clark assumed responsibility for keeping track of a growing list of candidates recommended by others. Justice Department officials in July actually compiled two formal lists. The initial list of candidates, dated July 23, 1945, contained forty-seven names, including a wide spectrum of prominent senators, jurists, and administration officials.[2] A revised list of "applicants" was generated eight days later, this time with fifty-three names.[3] This second list included all forty-seven original candidates plus six newcomers: Joseph E. Casey Jr., Will Davis, Judge Henry W. Edgerton of the U.S. Court of Appeals for the D.C. Circuit, Robert Guinthier, Judge George H. Moore of the U.S. district court in St. Louis, and Harold H. Burton, a senator from Ohio.

From these names Clark culled his own personal list divided into four categories, which he entitled "Supreme Court Possibilities":[4]

REPUBLICANS
Warren R. Austin, Senator, age 67
Harold H. Burton, Senator, age 57

U.S. CIRCUIT COURTS
John J. Parker, judge (Fourth Circuit), age 59
Orie L. Phillips, judge (Tenth Circuit), age 59
John B. Sanborn, judge (Eighth Circuit), age 61

U.S. DISTRICT COURTS
Paul J. McCormack [sic], judge (S.D. Cal.), age 66

DEMOCRATS
Sherman Minton, judge (Seventh Circuit), age 54
Robert P. Patterson, undersecretary of war, age 54
Samuel G. Bratton, judge (Tenth Circuit), age 57
John Biggs Jr., judge (Third Circuit), age 49

But Clark never submitted his full list to the president. Sworn in as the new attorney general the previous month,[5] Clark had dutifully followed Truman's instructions for filling lower federal court vacancies by generating a list of three possibilities for each (including one senator or House member); he then submitted each list to the president for his consideration. Clark mistakenly assumed that this practice would also apply to vacancies on the Supreme Court.[6] Weeks later Clark would submit to the president a list with just three names: Burton, Patterson, and McCormick.[7]

Unknown to Clark, the president was busy ruminating on his own about the nomination once he returned from Europe. Apparently, Truman had informally promised the first Supreme Court vacancy of his administration to Lewis B. Schwellenbach, the newly appointed secretary of labor, long before Roberts even announced his retirement.[8] Edged out in 1939 for the nomination that went to fellow Washington state native William O. Douglas, Schwellenbach had apprised then-Senator Truman of his frustrations. He had remained a loyal friend to the Missouri senator, actively campaigning for Truman during his hard-fought 1940 Senate reelection contest.[9] All things being equal, the president probably would have liked to have satisfied his close friend's long-held ambition to be a justice.[10]

Unfortunately for Schwellenbach, all things were not equal on the Supreme Court as it stood in 1945. With Justice Roberts's retirement, Chief Justice Harlan F. Stone was now the only remaining Republican on the Court. Not since 1887 had less than two members of a major party been represented on the high tribunal. Thus in late July Senate minority leader Wallace White and House minority leader Joseph Martin Jr. called publicly for a "halt to the policy of packing our courts with judges of one political faith."[11] Pressure for a Republican nominee continued to mount during the first two weeks of August. Once Truman returned from Europe, a bevy of Republican senators and party leaders directly urged him to nominate a Republican. Even some Democratic senators joined the call for a Republican nominee.[12] Still new to the presidency, Truman was clearly susceptible to such pleas at this point in time. In the wake of Burton's resignation, Truman had privately admitted to one aide that he would in all likelihood be forced to name a Republican to the newly vacated seat.[13] By the second week in August, Truman had fully accepted the logic of a politically balanced court and appeared to abandon any thought of appointing Schwellenbach (or any other Democrat)[14] to Roberts's seat.

Even with this astute nod to political reality, Truman still maintained tight control over the actual selection process. Senator Warren Austin (R-Vt.), sixty-seven, was the Republican most often mentioned in the press and elsewhere for the post. A consistent supporter of the new administration's foreign policy, Austin had gained admiration from both sides of the aisle for his bipartisan advocacy of internationalism. Another highly respected Republican senator, Carl Hatch of New Mexico, declared that "the appointment of Senator Austin would meet with universal approval throughout the country."[15] Hatch then personally pressed the case for Austin at a meeting with Truman.[16] But concerns about Austin's age discouraged the president from seriously considering the senior senator for a high court bid.

Another favorite of Republicans was Judge John J. Parker of the U.S Court of Appeals for the Fourth Circuit. Nominated to the high bench by President Hoover in 1930, Parker had been rejected then by the Senate because of his alleged hostility to labor unions and minorities. Now Parker's reputation was enjoying a renaissance by virtue of his widely respected, moderate judicial record. Even many Democrats had bemoaned the unfortunate events of fifteen years earlier. From mid-August through early September, Truman met with a number of visitors who pressed Parker's case, including Willis D. Smith, the president of the ABA, and the two Democratic senators from North Carolina, Josiah Bailey and Claude Hoey.[17] Yet Parker was now fifty-nine years old, and more significantly, the president did not know him personally. Continued lobbying from Parker's supporters convinced Truman that at least some show of appreciation for the appeals judge was in order,[18] but the president was determined to nominate someone he knew and trusted. Parker's candidacy was quickly dismissed,[19] as was that of Judge Orie L. Phillips, a Colorado Republican with no ties at all to the president.

Ultimately, the president focused his attention on two Republicans he did know well: Undersecretary of War Robert Patterson and Senator Harold Burton of Ohio. Technically a Republican, Patterson, fifty-four, had been a judge on the U.S. Court of Appeals for the Second Circuit. He had also served with distinction in two Democratic administrations.[20] The fifty-seven-year-old Burton, a former mayor of Cleveland who held moderate political views, had served in the Senate since 1941. During the war Burton had been an energetic member of the famed "Truman Committee" charged with investigating the National Defense Program. The two men had remained close friends ever since.

Of the two, Truman felt more comfortable with Patterson. Accordingly, during the first week of September he met with the undersecretary to sound out his interest in the Supreme Court vacancy. Patterson was indeed interested, and Truman nearly went ahead with the nomination that same day.[21] Holding Truman back, however, was the growing concern that he'd be losing a valued member of the War Department at a time when the 80th Congress was already gearing up to investigate war-time procurement. The widely respected Patterson had handled virtually all such procurement matters during the war.

On September 8, Attorney General Clark presented Truman with his original list of three candidates: Patterson, Burton, and Judge Paul McCormick.[22] Yet even before consulting with Clark, the president had already been weighing the merits of Patterson and Burton's candidacies. Still concerned about the impact a Patterson appointment would have on defense matters, Truman asked Clark to talk with the undersecretary about whether he would be foreclosed from at least testifying to Congress as a justice. In a conversation with the attorney general, Patterson allayed the president's fears about his ability to testify; Clark thus prepared to report the matter favorably to the president the following Monday. But Truman was moving more quickly than he let on, and had already decided that Patterson would remain in the administration. Truman so informed Clark of his decision on Saturday, September 15. As Clark recalled of their final conversation, the president asked, "Have you seen Patterson?" "Yes," replied Clark. "I wished you hadn't seen him," Truman said, "I have about changed my mind. . . . I've decided on Senator Burton."[23]

After informing Chief Justice Stone of his plans, Truman met with Burton at the White House on the evening of Monday, September 17 and stunned his friend with the news of his nomination.[24] According to Burton's diary, the Ohio senator said: "Harry, I would not ask for it." "I know that, I would not appoint you if you did," Truman responded. "But I will appoint you and you will take it." Dismissing Burton's trepidation about not having practiced law in ten years, Truman reassured his friend: "I have canvassed the whole field and I believed you are the best. . . . I started with you and I considered all the others, Parker, Phillips, Patterson and you know all the rest and I came back to you." After exchanging further pleasantries, the future nominee excused himself at 5:30 P.M. to catch a train to Cincinnati.

The next day, at his second largest press conference to date, the president began by announcing that he was reorganizing the Department of Labor, bringing under its control both the War Labor Board and the U.S. Employment Service. Each division would now report to Secretary of Labor Schwellenbach, the candidate Truman had spurned in the name of partisan balance.[25] He also announced the resignation of Secretary of War Henry L. Stimson and the nomination of his successor, Robert P. Patterson, another candidate who was nearly offered the post ten days earlier. Finally, the president announced the nomination of Senator Burton to serve as associate justice. When Truman finished, reporters asked just a few questions about the appointments before Merriman Smith of UPI shouted the traditional, "Thank You Mr. President" and the president made a dive for the door.[26] Truman was pleased with himself. He had rewarded several close friends, kept partisan politics at bay, and still managed to appoint a personal and trusted friend to the Supreme Court.

The Senate confirmed Burton's appointment by acclamation the very next day. His nomination was the culmination of a very personal selection process for Truman. Pushing to one side his previous commitment to Schwellenbach, the president utilized a more open framework for decisionmaking, taking careful note of the political winds that swirled around him. But in the end it was Truman alone who had made every critical selection decision. Meanwhile, the attorney general and other key administration advisors had been left on the outer fringes of the selection process.

THE VINSON NOMINATION: A PEACEMAKER . . . AND A FRIEND

Ironically, Truman's own personal commitments and understandings again had to be put on hold when a second vacancy on the Court arose the following year. On April 23, 1946, while cruising near Washington, D.C., aboard the presidential yacht, the S.S. *Williamsburg*, the president first learned of the death of Chief Justice Stone. Truman attended Stone's funeral on the morning of August 25, but then returned to his cruise immediately. Although the trip had begun as an opportunity to view naval exercises, Washington reporters connected the remainder of the cruise with a more pressing concern: the search for a new chief justice of the United States.

On April 27, Truman confessed both to John Snyder, the director of war mobilization and reconversion, and to his press secretary, Charles Ross, that his "first impulse" was to promote Justice Robert H. Jackson to chief justice and put Secretary of Labor Schwellenbach on the Court in his place.[27] Upon closer examination, it is easy to understand what led the president to reach those tentative conclusions. Like most of official Washington, Truman was aware that Roosevelt had promised the chief justiceship to Jackson five years earlier. And according to one observer, Truman had always valued continuity and loyalty, and he sincerely "hoped to honor" his predecessor's earlier commitment.[28] Moreover, Truman respected Jackson; the two had been on mutually friendly terms ever since Truman first arrived in Washington in 1935. After the war Truman had even tapped Jackson to be the chief U.S. prosecutor of Nazi war criminals at Nuremberg.

As for the vacancy opened up by Jackson's promotion, Truman knew it was "now-or-never time" for Schwellenbach to go on the Court.[29] According to the well-connected political columnists Joseph and Stewart Alsop, Schwellenbach had "all but fell sick of desire from the moment when he learned of Stone's death."[30] Truman remained sensitive to the hopes of his former Senate colleague and long-time friend. Schwellenbach had lost out on a Supreme Court seat the previous year when politics dictated the selection of a Republican. Having succumbed to that argument once, Truman seemed inclined to name a Democrat to the Court this time around.

Still, Truman remained cautious about both candidacies for several reasons. Schwellenbach had lacked initiative in his year-long stint as secretary of labor, as serious illness had hampered his performance in that position. Although most of the country's labor problems were clearly not his fault, Schwellenbach still had reaped much of the public blame.[31] As early as October 1945, his weakness in the post had forced Truman to bring John R. Steelman into the White House as a "special assistant" in charge of reconversion operations.[32] If Schwellenbach was not up to the job as secretary of labor, it was difficult to imagine him facing the daily rigors of the Supreme Court. Thus if the president was prepared to honor his friend's claim to the Court, it was not without some serious misgivings.[33]

Jackson's claim to the chief justiceship posed a trickier dilemma for Truman. By 1946, harsh infighting among the Court's various factions had become a matter of growing public concern. Certainly the most fiery combatants on the Court—Justices Hugo Black, William O. Douglas, Felix Frankfurter, and Jackson—were all New Dealers of the strictest sect: each had been energetic and active supporters of Roosevelt during the judicial "counterrevolution" of 1937–38. Yet as colleagues on the Supreme Court, critical legal fissures had developed among them in recent years.

Accepting self-restraint as a guiding principle for judging all commercial legislation, several justices (Stone, Black, Douglas, and later, Murphy) began propounding the notion of a "preferred position" for civil liberties, including freedom of speech. By contrast, Justices Frankfurter and Reed (and on occasion Jackson) firmly believed that civil liberties cases should equally conform to the principle that "we are not legislators . . . [and] that direct policy making is not our province."[34] Symbolic of this division was *West Virginia State Board of Education v. Barnette* (1943),[35] in which the Court

dramatically reversed a controversial three-year-old decision upholding a flag salute in public schools.[36] In an impassioned dissent, Justice Frankfurter accused the six justices in the majority of enforcing
their own "private notions of policy into the Constitution."[37] During this period the Roosevelt Court "clearly broke the aura of Olym-
pian objectivity on which judicial power in good part depends."[38]

Part of the problem lay with the Court's weak leadership. President Roosevelt had named Harlan Fiske Stone as chief justice in
1941 to succeed Charles Evans Hughes, the "consummate leader
of the high bench" and a jurist of "unchallengeable command."[39]
Unfortunately, Stone's clumsy administration of the Court had
only exacerbated the growing factionalism. According to Alpheus
Mason:

> [Stone] refused to use the high-pressure tactics of Taft and Hughes.
> Nor would he resort to ingenious reasoning, good fellowship, the cau-
> cus, or other familiar political devices useful in keeping the Court
> united; much less would he try to create that impression.[40]

Whereas Hughes's Saturday case conferences usually required four
hours to complete, under Stone they dragged on for days.[41]

Nor were the justices' barbs and criticisms of each other always
limited to the merits of individual cases. In 1945, against the background of a national coal strike, the Court reinterpreted the Federal
Wages and Hours Act to benefit union workers in *Jewell Ridge Coal
Corporation v. Local No. 6167, United Mine Workers.*[42] The Court
had initially split in the case, with Hugo Black providing the deciding vote in favor of the mineworkers. The union's lawyer in the case
had originally been one of Black's law partners back in Alabama.
In conference, Jackson argued that Black should disqualify himself,
but Black refused to do so. Incensed, Jackson insisted on writing
a dissenting opinion that quoted statements Black allegedly made
as a senator debating the fair wages bill; according to Jackson,
Black's own words seemed to contradict the *Jewell Ridge* decision.[43]
Soon after the case was decided Jackson departed for Nuremberg,
his squabble with Black unresolved.

Until 1945, most of this feuding had remained behind closed
doors, surfacing only occasionally in the written opinions of the
justices.[44] Yet over the next year or so, the conflict would enter
the public sphere. Newspaper and magazine columnists, including Arthur Krock of the *New York Times,* provided lurid details

of the justices' antagonisms.[45] Scholars Herman Pritchett, Carl Swisher, and Walter Dodd even conducted a roundtable radio discussion addressing the topic, "Is the Supreme Court Becoming Unstable?"[46] Pritchett, who offered the most strident comments, compared the justices to the Hatfields and McCoys taking potshots at each other "from behind the marble columns."

Aware of the turbulent and bitter factionalism dividing the Court, Truman feared that the elevation of Jackson might now irrevocably tear it apart.[47] Friend and columnist Irving Brant echoed the president's fears, warning Truman in an April 29 letter that Jackson's promotion would "be a demoralizing blow to the Court."[48] There had even been unconfirmed reports of Justices Douglas and Black threatening to resign from the Court if Truman named Jackson as the new chief justice.[49] At this critical juncture Jackson seemed an especially poor choice to pacify a quarrelsome bench. Hence early in the selection process, Truman shifted the focus of his attention to Fred M. Vinson, the current secretary of treasury. Known as Truman's "favorite poker companion,"[50] Vinson had won the president's favor in recent years by his down-to-earth, unpretentious style and his loyal support for the administration's causes. Although only fifty-six, Vinson had achieved a record of distinction in all three branches of government—as a Kentucky congressman, a judge on the U.S. Court of Appeals for the D.C. Circuit, and most recently as secretary of the treasury. Moreover, Vinson's affable personality had made him a popular figure around Washington. As early as April 25, Arthur Krock had predicted that the chief justiceship would ultimately go to Vinson, who could then "exercise his celebrated diplomatic talents to soothe the Court's ruffled feathers."[51] Truman hesitated, however, because of the prior "promises" that had been made to Jackson and Schwellenbach. Truman also had some personal interest in retaining Vinson in his role as a valued administration advisor.

The momentum may have swung permanently in favor of Vinson's candidacy near the end of Truman's cruise when Postmaster General Robert E. Hannegan, an influential presidential advisor and Democratic party leader, revealed to Truman that he had been hearing complaints from anti-Jackson forces in Washington. Disliking Jackson himself, Hannegan had become the "main conduit for the various protests against Jackson reaching the White House within the Court."[52] The postmaster general also reinforced Truman's own perception that the Court was in turmoil. John W. Snyder, the director of war conversion and another of Truman's top advisors, echoed Hannegan's sentiments. More and more the president saw Vinson, a son of the quintessential border state of Kentucky, as someone who could best make peace among the high court's quarreling factions.[53]

The president returned to the White House on April 28, certain that the next chief justice would come from outside the Court, and that Fred Vinson was the most suitable candidate for the task. The next afternoon Truman placed a telephone call to former Chief Justice Hughes, asking if he could visit with him about the nomination.[54] Truman in effect wanted a distinguished legal authority to confirm the state of instability on the Court and echo his own sentiment that Vinson would indeed make an ideal peacemaker. A simple phone conversation would not have served Truman's purposes; he wanted the press to take special note of their consultation. Truman thus urged Hughes to come see him at the White House that afternoon.[55]

The contents of their meeting would later become the subject of some controversy.[56] According to Hughes, he recommended that the president nominate Jackson for the position of chief justice, largely because he knew Roosevelt had promised him the post in 1941.[57] For the record, Truman remembered the meeting differently. The president recalled that he and Hughes discussed "every member of the Supreme Court, a number of federal circuit judges and several members of the state supreme courts," and that while Hughes "spoke highly of Justice Jackson," the conversation ended with Hughes's recommendation that Vinson become the next chief justice.[58]

In retrospect, Hughes's account appears closer to the truth.[59] While Hughes was not personally close to Vinson, as the official "circuit justice" for the D.C. Circuit, Hughes certainly knew of Vinson's work on the appeals court under his jurisdiction between 1938 and 1941. Ever the diplomat, Hughes probably spoke well of Vinson, as he did of most of the candidates under serious consideration. Truman interpreted Hughes's comments about factionalism on the Court and praise for Vinson in light of his own personal interest in seeing Vinson appointed, and remembered their meeting accordingly. But Truman was mistaken when he later described Hughes's "final recommendation" as being for Vinson, unless he was trying to imply that Hughes had simply deferred to the president's own steadfast conclusions on the matter.

Truman then sought additional support for Vinson's nomination. He telephoned retired Justice Owen J. Roberts and asked him to drop by the White House, which Roberts did on the morning of May 2. Truman and Roberts reviewed the names of various members of state supreme courts and federal appellate courts; they also discussed Vinson's fitness to serve as chief justice. While Roberts was as noncommittal as Hughes was on the subject of Vinson's candidacy, Truman believed he was building a public case for his close friend and colleague.

Although the die was still not quite cast, Vinson was now the presumptive nominee in Truman's mind. On May 11, Truman met briefly with Attorney General Clark and Charles Ross, his press secretary. Although Clark had dutifully served as the president's sounding board during the search for Roberts's replacement the previous year, the attorney general was rendered a virtual outsider this time around. Like Ross, Clark loyally concurred with Truman's choice of Vinson as chief justice. Why then did the president wait another twenty-six days to nominate Vinson? In all likelihood, Truman needed all the help he could get that spring from his trusted secretary of the treasury. Every major industry at that time seemed to be either enduring or recuperating from a strike. With Lewis Schwellenbach rendered ineffective by illness, Truman was relying heavily on Steelman and Vinson for solutions to the labor strife. The president also wanted time to select an effective replacement for Vinson at the Treasury Department.

Meanwhile, Justice Roberts had grown more uncomfortable with Truman's quick rush to a Vinson candidacy. He penned a letter to the president asking for another meeting to discuss the vacancy, which the president finally granted to him on May 21.[60] Handwritten notes from this second meeting indicate that they discussed at least six candidates that day, including three Republicans and three Democrats:[61]

Robert P. Patterson, secretary of war
Fred M. Vinson, secretary of treasury
Peter Woodbury, judge (First Circuit)
Harrie Brigham Chase, judge (Second Circuit)
Orie L. Phillips, judge (Tenth Circuit)
Sam G. Bratton, judge (Tenth Circuit)

Roberts described Woodbury and Chase as writing "good opinions" but reserved special praise for Phillips, whom he described as a "diplomatic" person with "all other qualities needed for a good chief justice." He offered that Bratton, a Democrat from New Mexico, was "not as able a judge as Phillips." Truman asked Roberts about the four jurists' personal qualities. The former justice said he knew Phillips for a long time, and that he was "strong and able," but that the others required further inquiry. The meeting lasted just twenty-five minutes, but Roberts left with a clear impression that Truman cared more about the candidates' "personal qualities" than anything else. In truth, the president was unwilling to be swayed on his commitment to nominate Vinson.

Truman maintained a public silence regarding the Supreme Court vacancy throughout May. By the end of the month, the myth that Hughes had unsettled Truman's "determination" to appoint a sitting member of the Court had firmly taken hold; even Truman's closest friends feared that Hughes had unduly influenced the president in the nomination process.[62] Truman now sought the right moment to spring his news on Vinson. That moment came on June 6 at a White House luncheon for the president-elect of Columbia. Only the day before Truman had met with Vinson to discuss Treasury Department matters without so much as mentioning the nomination.[63] Now the president asked Vinson privately whether he would like to be the next chief justice. "That would be quite an honor," Vinson reportedly replied. Truman slapped him on the back and said, "Well maybe you will be," before walking back into the reception.[64] An hour-and-a-half later Truman announced at a hastily called press conference that he planned to nominate Vinson to be chief justice, and that John W. Snyder would replace him as the new secretary of treasury.

The morning after Vinson's nomination, the *Washington Post* recalled how "Jackson's nomination was believed to be imminent in late April" before Truman consulted with Hughes.[65] The *New York Times* account was even more explicit:

> The case for Jackson was understood to have been lost when Mr. Truman called in the former chief justice. . . . Mr. Vinson, a friend of the president, was suggested to him as one who could do much to smooth over the discords on the highest bench.[66]

Truman was thus depicted as a cautious protector of the Court, yielding to the calls of distinguished jurists to nominate a peacemaker. Rumors of strife on the Court may explain Truman's rejection of Justice Jackson for the post, but it does not fully explain his choice of Vinson over others equally capable of pacifying the quarrelsome bench. The answer lies squarely with the president himself and the limited scope of his open selection process. Truman was flexible enough to read the political environment on the Court and adjust his priorities accordingly, yet once he settled on those priorities, input had been welcome only from the yes-men who surrounded him.

Vinson was in every sense Truman's personal choice for the Court. Attorney General Clark, to whom the president turned routinely for advice on other legal matters, had been practically excluded from the selection process. There had been no formal selection process to speak of: no lists generated by the Department of Justice or elsewhere, no formal criteria established for prospective candidates, and no sustained vetting by advisors. On June 20, 1946, Vinson was confirmed by Senate acclamation. He was sworn in as chief justice later that summer.

THE CLARK AND MINTON NOMINATIONS: KEEPING IT IN THE FAMILY

Bolstered by his miraculous, come-from-behind election victory in 1948, as well as by the support of new Democratic majorities in both houses, Truman returned to the White House for a second term brimming with confidence. However, even with close friend Fred Vinson sitting at its helm for the past three years, the Court remained a source of at least mild concern for the president. Since 1943, Justices Black, Douglas, Murphy, and Rutledge had formed a powerful liberal bloc that needed just one more vote to exert effective control over the Court's decisionmaking. This voting bloc now threatened elements of Truman's loyalty program, as well as some controversial prosecutions of communists by the Department of Justice. Even more troubling for Truman was the possibility that the Court might block his ability to exercise executive power when dealing with national emergencies, including those resulting from labor disputes. Although the Court's senior justice, Felix Frankfurter, was still an energetic sixty-six years old, Truman held out hope that he would receive at least one more opportunity to influence the makeup of the Court.

Frank Murphy's unexpected death on July 19, 1949, presented

Truman with that opportunity. Many assumed that Truman would endeavor to preserve what was assumed to be the Court's "Catholic seat": both Murphy and his predecessor in that seat, Pierce Butler, had been Roman-Catholics. At the time of his nomination in 1940, some reporters had speculated that Murphy might hesitate to accept an appointment dictated by his religion.[67] But Murphy had accepted the offer, and the tradition of the so-called Catholic seat had continued.

Without any prompting from Truman, Justice Department officials initiated their own elaborate selection process, compiling a list of candidates including a number of Catholic lawyers and jurists. On July 26, Assistant Attorney General Peyton Ford met at the Justice Department with J. Howard McGrath, the Democratic National Committee chairman, and Donald Dawson, a White House administrative assistant, to discuss candidates for a wide range of judicial vacancies, including the open Supreme Court seat.[68] Six candidates for the Supreme Court received mention, including three Catholics: Judge John W. Delehant of the U.S. district court in Nebraska, Chief Justice Paul Farthing of the Illinois Supreme Court, and McGrath himself.[69] The list also included Robert Patterson, Judge Raymond W. Starr of the U.S. district court in western Michigan, and Judge Herbert F. Goodrich of the U.S. Court of Appeals for the Third Circuit. Because FBI reports were available only for Delehant and Starr, a final report to the attorney general would have to wait. Ironically, Attorney General Clark was independently developing his own list of Catholic nominees that he might recommend to the president. Clark settled on two frontrunners of his own: Joseph B. Keenan, the former Allied Forces' chief prosecutor before the Tokyo war crimes tribunal, and Charles Fahy, a former solicitor general in the Roosevelt administration.[70]

Clark and his colleagues were apparently unaware that the president was moving on his own to fill this particular vacancy. Aboard the S.S. *Williamsburg* during the weekend of July 23, Truman considered just two candidates for the Court: Judge Sherman Minton of the U.S. Court of Appeals for the Seventh Circuit, and Clark. The president resented the fact that Cardinal Francis Spellman, the influential Archbishop of New York, had decided to attack Eleanor Roosevelt for what he termed her "anti-Catholic" utterances about an education bill. Truman thus felt little compulsion to continue the "Catholic seat" out of principle.[71] Minton, fifty-eight, had been a close friend of Truman's since their days serving together as freshmen Democratic senators in 1935. He also possessed over eight years' experience on the court of appeals. Still, as a senator Minton had been a vocal leader of the "extreme left wing"[72] and his voting record in Congress suggested that he might now join his old colleague Hugo Black to resolidify the liberal bloc of the Court.

Clark proved to be a more appealing candidate for a number of reasons. The Court had just completed a term marked by numerous 5–4 decisions, a factor that weighed heavily in the president's mind. And on issues important to Truman, his attorney general had established himself as an unwavering supporter.[73] Throughout his career Clark had been a firm believer in the inherent power of the president to act in emergencies. Only five months earlier he had written a Justice Department memo asserting that such presidential power was "exceedingly great," even apart from any specific statutory authority.[74] Clark had energetically employed the government's power in the antitrust field, in civil rights litigation and in developing the administration's controversial internal security program.[75] Although some observers later claimed that Truman was dissatisfied with his attorney general and looking to "bump him upstairs,"[76] the weight of the evidence suggests otherwise. In fact, Clark earned Truman's accolades for having done an "excellent job" as attorney general.[77]

Moreover, Truman believed in rewarding loyalty. Tom Clark had been the "moving leader" in the 1944 Democratic convention to nominate Truman as vice president. During the summer of 1948, when leading Democrats were deserting Truman during his reelection campaign, Clark was one of few Cabinet members who stumped the country; he contributed hard-earned dollars to the campaign, and "never lost faith in the chief."[78] Truman had offered Clark the attorney generalship in 1945 on the basis of recommendations from Speaker Sam Rayburn, Senator Tom Connally of Texas, and Bob Hannegan, each of whom convinced the president that the Texan would be an asset to his administration.[79] Since then Clark had developed into one of Truman's close circle of poker-playing companions and was now a trusted advisor on substantive policy matters.

Finally, Truman believed that the choice of Clark, unlike Minton, might provide at least some defense against the expected outcry from Catholic groups. Four years earlier the president had sought Clark's suggestion for a solicitor general who—in the event Clark ever departed—could effectively assume the attorney generalship.[80] Clark then had recommended J. Howard McGrath, a Catholic, for the post. Although McGrath resigned from the Justice Department in 1946 to run for the U.S. Senate, Truman now planned to nominate McGrath to be attorney general, giving the president a second Catholic official for his Cabinet.[81] The president hoped this final step would "placate the howls" that would undoubtedly come for not appointing a Catholic to Murphy's seat.[82]

By the morning of July 26, the same day that Justice Department officials were readying lists of potential nominees for the president, Truman had already settled on Clark. The president met that afternoon with Minton, who arrived through the west basement door to avoid the notice of the press.[83] Minton probably expected to receive the nomination himself at that meeting. The two men discussed recent Supreme Court decisions, with Minton indicating that he felt only Vinson and Black wrote consistently lucid opinions.[84] Truman then stunned his friend with the news that he planned to appoint Clark to Murphy's seat. Although Minton received no hard or fast promises from the president, he had good reason to believe that the next available vacancy would be his.

Two days later, on July 28, 1949, Truman called McGrath and Clark into his office for a brief conference. It was the first time that the president had met with either of them since Murphy's death nine days earlier. Clark, assuming they would be going over names of prospective candidates, had brought his own list of prominent Catholic lawyers and jurists, including Fahy and Keenan. McGrath fully expected that Truman would offer him the Supreme Court seat.[85] Instead, the president offered the two men a package job: McGrath as attorney general and Clark to the Supreme Court.[86] While Clark accepted right away, a devastated McGrath initially declined, although he eventually agreed to think over the offer. McGrath finally accepted the nomination a few days later in the hope that his loyalty might eventually garner him consideration for the Court.[87]

At a press conference later that day, Truman hoped to avoid discussing the Supreme Court nomination; he had wanted to announce both nominations together to soothe any injured feelings among Catholics. In fact, his prepared statement made no reference to the Court, but when radio commentator Earl Godwin asked whether the president had made up his mind on the Supreme Court seat, Truman could not resist. He informed the press of his two proposed nominations.[88] Truman jumped on the reporters' inevitable questions about the Catholic seat: "If he is qualified, I wouldn't care what his faith is, whether it's Catholic, Baptist or Jewish."[89] Despite serious questions raised in the media about Clark's relatively slim legal credentials, the Senate confirmed his appointment less than a month later by a 73–8 vote.

Truman aide Donald S. Dawson later depicted the president's appointment of Clark as "purely personal with *him.*"[90] Unlike before, Truman made no pretense at all of consulting others. He looked among his close set of personal friends and advisors and weighed his options privately. Columnist Harold Ickes's reference to Clark as a "second-rate political hack who has known what backs to slap and when" echoed widespread sentiment that Clark's appointment must have been the result of extremely poor counsel. In fact, the president had received no counsel at all.

The announcement of fifty-five-year-old Justice Wiley Rutledge's death on September 10, 1949, set into motion a single-candidate-focused selection mechanism for the first time during Truman's presidency. Although one justice later claimed that Secretary of War Bob Patterson had been high on the president's list,[91] the weight of the evidence suggests there was no such "list" to speak of: Truman was simply not willing to pass over his close friend Sherman Minton once again. In effect, Truman ruled out discussion of any candidate other than Minton by his very actions. Following Rutledge's death, two overriding issues were raised in the press and elsewhere in conjunction with the search for his successor: (1) the continued absence of a Catholic justice, and (2) the Court's striking partisan imbalance, with Justice Burton now the sole Republican justice serving. A more open framework for selection might have addressed at least one (if not both) of those concerns. But Truman was determined this time to appoint Minton— a Protestant and a Democrat—who had been disappointed in his bid for the Court only two months earlier.

The swiftness with which Truman moved on the Minton nomination adds further weight to the notion that Minton's appointment was a fait accompli. Minton had contacted the president twice that year, urging him to appoint Walter C. Lindley, a Republican and U.S. district court judge for the eastern district of Illinois, to a seat on the U.S. Court of Appeals for the Seventh Circuit.[92] With Minton slated for the vacant Supreme Court seat, Truman quickly settled on Lindley as Minton's successor. Within two days of Rutledge's death, Truman was already conferring with Senator Scott

Lucas of Illinois about a possible successor for Lindley's district court seat. Just three days later, on September 15, Truman announced at a news conference that he would nominate Minton to the high court, Lindley to the Seventh Circuit, and Illinois state judge Casper Platt (a close friend of Senator Lucas) to the district court. Truman later confided to columnist Harold Ickes that it was a "good arrangement" for all concerned.[93] And it was accomplished in less than a week—a testament to Truman's quick decision on Minton.

The selection of Minton was praised by many who had criticized the appointment of Clark, including Ickes himself.[94] On paper Minton seemed eminently qualified for the Court. He had received a master's degree from Yale University and a law degree from Indiana University. After a six-year stint as U.S. senator from Indiana, Minton had served with distinction for nearly a decade on the Seventh Circuit Court of Appeals. Even though Minton refused an invitation by anti–New Deal Republicans to testify before the Senate Judiciary Committee, he was still confirmed handily by the Senate on October 4 by a 48–16 vote. Like Burton, Clark and Vinson, Minton's Supreme Court appointment had been a product of his loyalty and dedication to the president.

CONCLUSION

Harry Truman molded the Supreme Court selection process to meet a number of personal objectives. His unique brand of personal selection politics limited others' influence over the decisionmaking process, whether it came from within or outside his administration. Even when the public and media clamored for breaking news of the selection process—such as when Truman was choosing the next chief justice in 1946—he managed to exert such absolute control over the process that even his closest aides were left in the dark.

Truman's initial two opportunities to name a justice arose during just the first fourteen months of his presidency. In this early period Truman was a new president who lacked any electoral mandate; the Senate remained in Democratic hands, but senators stood wary of their former colleague. In each case, Truman's open framework for decisionmaking proved flexible enough to adjust to shifting political winds, even though he remained generally closed to others' suggestions about specific candidates. Senators from both sides of the aisle demanded a more favorable partisan balance on the Court in 1945; the following summer, speculation about a quarrelsome bench led Truman outside the Court for a "peacemaker." Within those carefully established political boundaries, Truman exercised nearly absolute control over the nominee selection process. Burton was Truman's favorite Republican: a former colleague and trusted friend. Vinson was Truman's kind of peacemaker: a poker companion whom he trusted without reservation. There were no other stifling criteria or filters that unduly restrained his discretion in these matters; in each case Truman was able to find a nominee from within his own closed political circle.

The president exercised even greater discretion in filling two more vacancies in 1949. Truman now enjoyed his own electoral mandate, having only recently won his first presidential election. The Senate, temporarily under Republican control during the 80th Congress, had now reverted back to more friendly Democratic hands. Emboldened, Truman pushed the limits of his own personal discretion even further. He ignored calls for a "Catholic seat" in both instances. Unlike in 1945, demands for a Republican nominee also fell on deaf ears. Clark's nomination was spurred primarily by the president's interest in shoring up support for Vinson on the Court, while Minton's was more the product of simple, unadulterated cronyism.

Unfortunately, Truman's near total domination of the selection process did not translate into the nomination of superlative justices. His administration's judicial recruitment mechanism was a relatively peaceful one, with advisors' influence limited. The Court itself may have paid a price, however: by most scholars' assessments, Harry Truman's four Supreme Court justices rank as a "mediocre" group at best. Of the four, Burton and Clark's abilities may have been somewhat underestimated by legal scholars. Clark in particular matured as a justice during his thirteen years on the bench, proving himself to be "a determined, if cautious craftsmen of the law."[95] Still, neither jurist influenced the law to any great degree; both tended to be more or less uncertain followers of one bloc or another on both the Vinson and Warren Courts. Meanwhile, court experts regard Minton and Vinson as unmitigated Supreme Court failures.[96] Minton arrived on the Court armed with substantial appellate court experience, but he wrote few opinions of any lasting significance in his seven years as a justice.[97] Vinson proved an even greater disappointment in his role as chief justice. The new chief justice enjoyed relatively limited influence over doctrinal matters that came before the Court. The ideological factions that waged war during Stone's tenure as chief justice only hardened their positions under Vinson, divided both by ideology and personality. And Vinson's most famous decision—his opinion sustaining the convictions of eleven Communist Party leaders in *Dennis v. United States* (1951)[98]—has been reversed both by the force of history and the Warren Court, which rendered the *Dennis* doctrine obsolete within two decades.[99]

Was the president himself disappointed with his four nominees? The record on this score is mixed. In considering candidates for chief justice, Truman wanted a leader who would pacify a Court torn apart by internal bickering. In that respect Truman should have been disappointed indeed at his results. Additionally, there would be no lasting "Truman Court" cast in the image of the chief executive. The president was pleased with many of his appointees' decisions upholding federal convictions of communists. At the same time, he was outraged by the Court's Steel Seizure decision, where Clark and Burton joined the majority in rejecting his exercise of presidential authority.

Personally, Truman stayed close to each of the four justices he appointed to the Court. Vinson kept a direct phone line to Truman, advising him on a number of important matters. Reportedly, in 1952 Truman even ran the idea of seizing the steel industry past his former secretary of the treasury. Truman's relationships with Burton and Minton, which had been formed in the U.S. Senate decades earlier, also continued. And while some believe Clark and Truman suffered stormy relations after the Steel Seizure case, their correspondence in fact continued on friendly terms for years afterward. Never again would one president successfully fill nearly half the bench with his close friends and associates. To a president with only limited interest in most of the Court's docket, that constituted no small measure of personal success.

THREE

EISENHOWER TAKES ON "CRONYISM"

If Harry Truman's method of selecting nominees epitomized the personal approach to Supreme Court recruitment, Dwight Eisenhower's practices epitomized the impersonal. From the outset, Eisenhower planned to delegate the bulk of responsibility for choosing Supreme Court nominees to a single advisor: Herbert Brownell, his attorney general. The new president's propensity to delegate in this fashion was hardly surprising; as a former commander of the Allied Forces in Europe and of NATO, General Eisenhower had proven himself a sophisticated and skillful leader of large organizations. And while he occasionally refrained from deferring in certain other policymaking areas,[1] the president's immense respect for Brownell encouraged him to delegate considerable authority in this particular context. Everything seemed in place for his administration to conduct a truly comprehensive search for Supreme Court nominees.

Unfortunately, the administration's recruitment process was hampered first by personal promises, and later by the president's overt attempts to force Brownell (and his successor, William Rogers) to work within a set of overly restrictive criteria. Eisenhower's occasional missteps in choosing nominees were at least partially a result of his decision to rigidly adhere to such criteria. In doing so, he all but negated the benefit of charging one supremely qualified and competent aide with carrying out these broad responsibilities in the first place.

The president's heavy reliance on Brownell first developed during the latter's stint as Eisenhower's campaign manager in 1952. Then, during the pre-inaugural period the president-elect entrusted in Brownell and another aide, Lucius Clay, the primary responsibility of filling most positions in the Cabinet, a truly "remarkable grant of power."[2] By the middle of his first year in office, Eisenhower was praising Brownell as a "man of consummate honesty, incapable of an unethical practice," a "lawyer of the first rank," and an "outstanding leader."[3] Of all of Eisenhower's Cabinet members, perhaps only Secretary of State John Foster Dulles enjoyed the same level of unrestricted power and influence afforded to Brownell.

Eisenhower resisted politicizing the appointment process by refusing to make the Court a central issue in either of his two presidential campaigns. Privately, though, he believed that the meaning of the Constitution was "what the Supreme Court says it is,"[4] and thus as president he took seriously his duty to appoint qualified justices. At a minimum, Eisenhower wanted to distinguish his administration's method of judicial selection from that of his two Democratic predecessors. Criticizing what he viewed as the Democrats' unfortunate policy of awarding judgeships on the basis of "patronage" and "partisanship," the new president wanted to appoint only "individuals of the highest possible standing."[5] He was particularly critical of so-called liberal justices like Frank Murphy and Wiley Rutledge, confiding to friends that judicial vacancies should not be filled by such "left-wingers."[6] Instead, Eisenhower sought candidates for the bench who shared his own "middle of the road" philosophy of government.[7] While Republicans could still expect the lion's share of judicial appointments during his tenure, Eisenhower encouraged the perception that they would at least be "highly qualified, moderate" Republicans.[8]

How specifically did Eisenhower recruit nominees for Supreme Court vacancies? Some clues may be found in his administration's mechanism for appointing lower court nominees. Early in his first term, the administration set forth certain age and health requirements to be met by prospective district and circuit court judges. (As to the former criteria, Eisenhower hoped that few if any candidates for lower court judgeships would be over sixty-two years of age.) In addition, the president wanted to establish some measure of "quality control" for his appointees. Thus at Eisenhower's urging, Brownell's Justice Department became the first to regularly consult with the ABA's Standing Committee on Federal Judiciary concerning all lower court nominees.[9] As part of this arrangement, Eisenhower agreed to appoint no one to a lower court unless that individual was "enthusiastically recommended by the American

Bar Association."[10] In return, the ABA agreed to discontinue its practice of suggesting names of its own in advance of being asked by the administration to evaluate a particular candidate. Finally, before formal announcement of any nomination by the administration, the FBI would perform a confidential check to determine that there was "nothing in [a candidate's] record which could be brought up to diminish his effectiveness as a judge."[11]

During Eisenhower's presidency, several rigid criteria also came to dominate the administration's mechanism for choosing Supreme Court nominees. Age would eventually become a strict consideration. Beginning in 1954, the president made known his intention to enforce a rigid sixty-two-year age limit in the case of any future Supreme Court nominees.[12] For Eisenhower, the risk that he might be succeeded in 1956 or 1960 by a "New Deal president" compelled him to seek "relatively young men" for any subsequent vacancies that might occur on the Court. Ideally, he hoped to find "a number of outstanding jurists in the low 50's."[13]

An emphasis on candidates with previous experience on the bench was also a dominant theme in the recruitment of Supreme Court nominees during his administration. Perhaps Eisenhower's emphasis on judicial training reflected his belief that it would be "completely futile to try to use a Supreme Court vacancy as a mere reward for long and brilliant service."[14] More likely, the president hoped to benefit politically from publicly establishing such a requirement. The policy appeared outwardly to be a conscious rejection of New Deal and Fair Deal patterns of selecting justices: six of Roosevelt's nine appointments and two of Truman's four appointees had never before served in any judicial capacity. Some, like Felix Frankfurter, had been left-leaning academicians prior to arriving on the high court.[15] According to historians Gunther Bischof and Stephen Ambrose, with a single stroke the Eisenhower administration in effect had pledged to the public: "No senators with a somewhat radical reputation (Black), no allegedly radical college professors (Frankfurter), no bright young lawyer-professor types who rose to fame as tamers of Wall Street (Douglas), no governors noted for tolerating such radical notions as sit-down strikes (Murphy), and no old political cronies."[16]

Responding to claims that Chief Justice Earl Warren lacked such experience, the president declared in late 1953 that, except in unusual circumstances, no one in the future would be appointed to any appellate court, including the Supreme Court, without previous judicial experience.[17] In practice, his administration would especially favor nominees from the ranks of the federal courts of appeals and state supreme courts; as a military man, such a hierarchical promotion system struck Eisenhower as the most logical progression.[18] The administration came to apply this criterion so rigidly that by 1959 Attorney General William Rogers felt compelled to respond to especially heavy criticism of the practice that had been leveled at the administration by Justice Felix Frankfurter.[19]

Naturally, the president expected Brownell to initiate the decisionmaking process for all vacancies.[20] The attorney general (usually working with his deputy attorney general, William Rogers[21]) would formulate a list of names to be investigated and submit a list of finalists to the president for his consideration. While Brownell (and later Rogers) appeared to possess considerable discretion in suggesting potential nominees to the president, their influence was in fact limited by Eisenhower's expectation that they adhere strictly to criteria he established in advance. At times this made for a truly stilted and inflexible selection process.

THE WARREN NOMINATION:
"PROMISES, PROMISES . . ."

Eisenhower had to forego most of those carefully developed criteria when he nominated Earl Warren to serve as chief justice in 1953. During a visit to his transition headquarters in December 1952, the president-elect had concluded that he would not be able to offer Earl Warren, the governor of California, a position of appropriate stature in the new administration.[22] As Brownell recalls:

> Ike was worried that Warren might feel sort of hurt or left out. . . . [H]e said "we want to keep him enthusiastic for the Eisenhower administration and if we go ahead and announce the whole Cabinet without any mention of Warren, I'm afraid he will misunderstand and feel he wasn't a top-ranking Republican." He told me that he wanted to call Warren up on the phone, and offer him the first available vacancy on the Supreme Court.[23]

The president's interest in Warren stemmed in part from events that had transpired at the national Republican convention five months earlier. Warren, the favorite-son candidate of the formidable seventy-vote California delegation, found himself at the center of a neck-and-neck battle for the presidential nomination between Eisenhower and Senator Robert Taft of Ohio. Warren could have clinched Taft's victory at the convention either by (1) throwing his sizeable contingent to the senator early in the convention or (2) casting his votes against the so-called Fair Play Amendment,[24] thus allowing Taft's delegates with contested credentials to vote themselves into permanent seats. Instead, Warren yielded to the Eisenhower forces' arguments in both instances, and his actions proved critical in helping Eisenhower to victory.

While Warren's actions in facilitating Eisenhower's nomination are a matter of historical record, the California governor's motives in taking those actions are not so easy to discern. Certainly Warren's moderate policy positions fit Eisenhower's agenda better than Taft's. Many scholars have accepted the conventional wisdom that Warren received some type of commitment about a high position in government in return for his support.[25] But even assuming Eisenhower's floor leaders did make such promises, the shrewd Warren was also playing his own hand that day. Warren's refusal to support Taft may have been part of his own independent plan to emerge as a late-ballot alternative in a deadlocked convention. Warren's stance in favor of the Fair Play Amendment was already a matter of public record even before the convention had begun.[26] Moreover, while the California governor had been publicly supportive of Eisenhower, privately he harbored resentment of the general for refusing to support Warren's opposition to loyalty oaths in California two years earlier.[27] As it was, the California contingent remained neutral throughout the convention, casting its votes for Eisenhower only after he had already secured the nomination.

Both publicly and privately, Eisenhower refused to see himself as "indebted" to Warren. But as Brownell conceded many years later, the president was not naive: "Eisenhower understood who had helped him at a crucial moment in the convention . . . *he knew what the score was.*"[28] During the campaign, Eisenhower's affection for the California governor grew as Warren played loyal soldier for the party's ticket despite the personal animosity he harbored toward the vice presidential candidate, Richard M. Nixon. Eisenhower often referred to Warren, who had a calming influence over Ike's campaign in California, as "the big man."[29] Eisenhower also aspired to Warren's lofty status as a "statesman." To him, Warren epitomized such statesmanship, having been nominated for his third term by both the Republican and Democratic parties in 1950.

By December 1952, the president-elect's respect for Warren had grown into a real "crush," and Eisenhower desperately wanted to insure that he and his administration stayed in the governor's good graces. So, having already tapped Brownell to head the Justice Department, Eisenhower now suggested to his top advisor that Warren might also make a good Supreme Court justice. Brownell was equally impressed by Warren's bearing, character, and stature, and he responded to the suggestion with enthusiasm. Reassured, Eisenhower phoned from his transition headquarters in New York and extended him his "personal promise" that he would appoint him to the "first vacancy on the Supreme Court."[30]

A decade earlier President Franklin D. Roosevelt had developed a reputation for routinely tossing out such promises, only to renege later whenever it became politically expedient to do so.[31] Eisenhower, by contrast, had every intention of standing behind his promise, even though he soon began to develop some second thoughts. Specifically, the president was troubled by Warren's absence from daily legal work during the past decade and, more importantly, by his lack of judicial experience. Although he knew Warren would shun a lower court appointment as preparation for the high court, Eisenhower suggested to Brownell in July 1953 that he offer Warren the vacant solicitor generalship, ostensibly as a chance to "brush up on the law" in preparation for going on to the Court. The third-ranking post at the Justice Department might have seemed a step down for the governor of California, but Warren viewed it positively in light of the previous commitment of a Supreme Court seat. While traveling in Europe that August, he cabled his acceptance to the president, remarking that he "could return to work with enthusiasm.[32] Once he arrived back on the West Coast, Warren began preparing for his imminent departure to Washington.

Chief Justice Fred Vinson's death from a heart attack on September 8, 1953, stunned Eisenhower and Brownell. When he had talked to Warren a year earlier, the president had never imagined that the "first vacancy" would be the chief justiceship. He felt his promise was for the first *associate justice* vacancy, not the center seat on the high court. Assuming that Warren shared this understanding, the president asked Brownell to launch a formal selection process for Vinson's successor.

While vacationing in Colorado the week after Vinson's funeral, the president dictated a letter to his brother Milton that provides a window into his thinking about the next chief justice.[33] "As far as the Supreme Court vacancy is concerned," Eisenhower wrote,

> my problem is to get a man (a) of known and recognized integrity, (b) of wide experience in government, (c) of competence in the law, (d) of national stature in reputation so as to be useful in my effort to restore the Court to the high position of prestige that it once enjoyed.[34]

Even more than the appointment of an associate justice, Eisenhower believed the selection of a chief justice provided a clear test of his commitment to restore prestige to the Court. In a letter to the dean of the Columbia Law School, Young B. Smith, Eisenhower already found himself worrying about the implications of his promise to Warren. The president conceded that an experienced jurist might have both an "unimpeachable record" and a "reputation for integrity," but he was also quick to argue that "the same can be said of a number of others *whose experience is of a somewhat different type.*"[35]

Eisenhower and Brownell did not meet face-to-face to discuss the nomination until mid-September. At that time they discussed several names from outside the court, including three prominent Republican jurists: Arthur T. Vanderbilt, chief justice of the New Jersey Supreme Court, sixty-five; Orie L. Phillips of the U.S. Court of Appeals for the Tenth Circuit, sixty-seven; and John J. Parker of the U.S. Court of Appeals for the Fourth Circuit, sixty-seven.[36] Vanderbilt had been a former dean of the New York University Law School and a former president of the American Bar Association. He had also been the leader of New Jersey's Supreme Court since 1948, and had earned a national reputation as a reformer of the state courts. Orie Phillips had served with distinction on the court of appeals in Denver for nearly a quarter of a century. Since the defeat of his initial nomination to the Court in 1930, Parker too had established himself as a leading federal jurist, receiving the ABA's medal for conspicuous service to jurisprudence in 1943. Both Vanderbilt and Phillips were close friends of the president; in fact, Phillips had spent a day fishing with Eisenhower during a visit to Colorado earlier that summer.[37] Because Vanderbilt (the youngest of the three) had only recently suffered a heart attack, Brownell planned to investigate his health further during the coming weeks.

As he had promised Dean Smith, Eisenhower also considered national figures without judicial experience. When first hearing of

Vinson's death, the president briefly contemplated naming Secretary of State John Foster Dulles to the vacancy. Because Dulles expressed no interest in serving on the Court at that time, his name never came up in discussions with Brownell.[38] The president also considered Earl Warren for the post. Both Brownell and Eisenhower agreed that the California governor, now sixty-two years old, possessed the requisite national stature. Thomas E. Dewey, Brownell's mentor in the late 1940s,[39] was also identified on a number of lists appearing in the media.[40] In truth, Eisenhower considered the two-time presidential candidate "so political in his outlook" that he could scarcely imagine him serving as a federal judge at any level.[41] Although the president himself recalled in his memoirs having considered former presidential candidate John W. Davis for the post,[42] it is hard to imagine that Davis, by then seventy-nine years old, received any serious attention.[43]

Finally, Eisenhower and Brownell discussed promoting a sitting member of the Court to chief justice. (Warren would then receive the vacant associate justice seat as promised.) Like Truman, the president assumed the most viable justice for promotion was sixty-one-year-old Robert Jackson.[44] Once a stalwart New Dealer, Jackson had moderated his views on the bench during the last decade, siding infrequently with the liberal bloc that included Justices Black and Douglas. After his stint as chief U.S. prosecutor at the Nuremberg trials, Jackson had grown more and more willing to balance competing values of freedom and public order, sustaining federal efforts to fight communism both in *Dennis v. United States* (1951)[45] and *American Communications Association v. Douds* (1950).[46] One Republican on the bench was also available for promotion: sixty-five-year-old Harold Burton. But neither Eisenhower nor Brownell viewed Burton as sufficiently distinguished to serve as chief justice.[47]

Several obstacles lay in the path of Jackson's candidacy. First, Jackson was a Democrat. After twenty years of Democratic control over judicial appointments, it would have offended many supporters of a new Republican president to see the top post in the American judiciary ceded to a member of the other party. To be sure, Roosevelt had nominated a Republican, Harlan Fiske Stone, as chief justice in 1941 as a bipartisan gesture on the eve of the war. And Jackson's recent opinions on the Court escaped any clear partisan characterization. If Eisenhower wanted to transcend purely political considerations in naming a new chief justice, the appointment of a Democrat would have provided powerful proof of his sincerity. Other objections to Jackson were more serious. As solicitor general in 1937, he had championed Roosevelt's infamous "court-packing plan." Jackson's subsequent writings on the subject,[48] which cast him as a symbol of that earlier attack on the integrity of the Court, made him unacceptable to many Senate Republicans. In addition, as Brownell warned Eisenhower, the well-publicized Jackson-Black feud of seven years earlier[49] had rendered Jackson an unlikely figure to harmonize a still fractious Court or to offer fresh leadership in the post-war era.

Still going through the motions of a more open-ended and flexible selection process, Brownell and Eisenhower had narrowed the chief justice list to four candidates: Vanderbilt, Phillips, Parker, and Warren. With no sitting justices still in contention, there would be no second seat to fill. But at this point, the president and the attorney general were forced to bring the formal selection process to a grinding halt. Before considering the matter further, Eisenhower wanted assurances from Warren that he would be willing to wait for the next available vacancy. Technically, Eisenhower's promise to Warren had been for the "first vacancy" on the Court. So Eisenhower sent Brownell on a mission to California to sound out the governor's interpretation of their original commitment.

The attorney general flew to the West Coast on September 27 and met Warren at McClellan Air Force Base, ten miles from Sacramento. Already preparing to fly to Washington for the opening of the Court's session, Warren was determined to hold the president to his promise for this first vacancy. As Brownell later recalled:

> Warren told me, "If there's any hesitation on the president's part, he can appoint someone from the Court to chief justice and me to the new vacancy." It was clear to me then that Warren would think the president was breaking his word if he wasn't named to the Court immediately.[50]

With Jackson and the other sitting justices all but eliminated from consideration, Warren's interpretation of the commitment left the president compelled to nominate the California governor to be chief justice. Brownell knew as he flew back from California that the open selection process had been transformed into one targeting Warren alone. Eisenhower would be especially reluctant to betray his commitment in Warren's eyes.

Just three days later the president announced that he would give

Warren a recess appointment as chief justice, which allowed him to begin serving immediately. Eisenhower's resort to a recess Supreme Court appointment in this instance was the first by a president in over a century. Article II, Section 2 of the Constitution authorizes the president to fill vacancies even when the Senate is in recess—the nominee can legally serve until the Senate returns to act on that nomination. With Congress in session less frequently during the late eighteenth and early nineteenth centuries, a number of earlier justices had received recess appointments in this manner, although few took their seats on the Court formally until *after* the Senate had confirmed their respective nominations. Of course, individuals who take their seats *in advance* of Senate confirmation run the risk of having to publicly defend decisions in which they have already participated. Prior to Warren, only two justices in history fit that category, having served on the high court for a period without Senate approval: John Rutledge, who served as chief justice for four months until the Senate rejected his nomination in 1795, and Benjamin Curtis, who served as associate justice for two months prior to his successful confirmation in 1851. Eisenhower's apparent determination to have Warren serve immediately was spurred in part by practical considerations: the Court needed a chief justice to operate effectively, especially with rearguments in the contentious desegregation cases scheduled for that December. (By contrast, Eisenhower would later utilize recess appointments under more questionable circumstances, such as in the cases of William Brennan and Potter Stewart's appointments.) Warren served as chief justice for a total of five months prior to the Senate's formal consideration of his candidacy. After some forceful questioning from senators at his confirmation hearings, the Senate finally approved Warren for the post by acclamation on March 1, 1954.

In the months that followed Warren's nomination to the Court, Eisenhower earnestly campaigned to convince family, friends, and associates that the selection of Warren had been justified on the merits. To his brother Edgar, who had urged the president not to make a "political appointment," he defended Warren as a "man of national stature" and "unimpeachable integrity" with "a splendid record during his years in active law work."[51] To brother Milton, the president argued that "statesmanship" was developed through the hard knocks of general experience and that Warren had a "national name for integrity, uprightness and courage."[52] To boyhood friend Edward "Swede" Hazlett he stressed that Warren was "emphatically not a political appointment" and that he was particularly well-suited for the administrative tasks of a chief justice "as well as obvious responsibilities involving personal leadership."[53] Finally, to special counsel Bernard Shanley, Eisenhower discussed the similarities between Warren's background and that of John Marshall, who had also gained valuable experience off the bench in public service.[54]

However, the key to unlocking Eisenhower's thinking lies in his personal diary entry of October 8, 1953. Just a week after choosing Warren, Eisenhower desperately tried to justify the decision to himself—and for history. Once again Eisenhower's defensiveness spoke volumes. Convinced that the prestige of the Court had suffered in recent years, Eisenhower said that he wanted a man of "nationwide reputation for integrity."[55] Fending off charges that Warren's appointment was political, Eisenhower offered that at the Republican convention Warren had never consented to turn over his delegates to any candidate until after the nomination had been decided. He further noted that senior judges Phillips, Parker, and Vanderbilt had been eliminated only because they failed his test of "physical fitness." Thus, he had made up his mind that sixty-four was to be "the absolute limit for anyone that I would consider."[56]

But this arbitrary age limit had never come up during any of his discussions with Brownell. Indeed, by his own admission the president had personally sought out John Foster Dulles, then sixty-five years old, for the post. In later years the president's own reflections on the particular age requirement to be enforced would shift, a reflection of his own confusion on the matter.[57] Eisenhower had actually downplayed most concerns of age in considering candidates for chief justice, just as numerous presidents had done before him.[58] Warren had been one of four finalists for the post, and the promise tendered to him by the president the previous December had vaulted him above the other candidates before any more serious consideration of their candidacies could occur.

Eisenhower clearly tied his own hands for this first Supreme Court nomination of his presidency. A president desperate to be seen as apolitical was confined by a political promise he had tendered to mend fences with a leader in his party. On balance, Warren was a formidable candidate who might well have prevailed amid more searching scrutiny of the four finalists. Yet as befits a single-candidate selection framework, no such scrutiny was ever forthcoming.

THE HARLAN NOMINATION:
AN ATTORNEY GENERAL REALIZES HIS DREAM

What began as an open and comprehensive search for Vinson's successor in 1953 had quickly reverted into the simple fulfillment of a political promise. In form, the following year's search for a successor to the late Justice Jackson was only barely distinguishable. Again there was an unwritten promise of a Supreme Court seat, this time issued by the attorney general, Herbert Brownell, to his longtime friend and colleague of the bar, John Marshall Harlan II. Again, the Eisenhower administration stood by its promise: no serious consideration was given to candidates other than Harlan in the months following Justice Jackson's death in 1954. Brownell's influence was never so obvious as it was in this instance—the president's hesitance about Harlan was quickly overborne by the attorney general's persistent determination to see him appointed. As it turned out, Brownell did well by his president: Harlan emerged to become the consummate moderate-to-conservative jurist Eisenhower was hoping for in the first place.

The attorney general first became acquainted with the grandson of former Supreme Court justice John Marshall Harlan when Brownell joined the New York law firm of Root, Clark, Buckner & Ballantine in 1927. As an associate of the firm, Harlan had already become a protégé of the firm's chief litigator, Emory Buckner. Under Buckner's watchful eye, Harlan honed his litigation skills, becoming a "lawyer's lawyer" in the eyes of his contemporaries. When the elder attorney was named chief federal prosecutor for New York's southern district in 1925, Harlan joined his staff as one of "Buckner's boy scouts," vigorously enforcing the Prohibition law and prosecuting local officials charged with corruption. Upon returning once again to private practice, Harlan stood second only to Buckner as his firm's principal trial advocate. By the 1950s he had amassed an impressive array of corporate clients and was considered one of the nation's foremost litigators in antitrust law.[59]

Five years younger than Harlan, Brownell looked up to his senior colleague; even after Brownell moved to Lord Day & Lord in 1929, the two attorneys remained close friends.[60] Thus when Brownell ran for the New York State assembly in the early 1930s, Harlan actively supported his friend both with personal financial contributions[61] and whatever political influence he had to offer.[62] Though Harlan maintained close ties with Thomas Dewey,[63] his friendship with Brownell eventually linked him to the Eisenhower administration as well.

Brownell had always thought Harlan would make an excellent Supreme Court justice. More important, the new attorney general was prepared to use every means at his disposal to put Harlan on the Court. Brownell knew that Harlan's lack of judicial experience would be a strike against him with the president. Thus to enhance Harlan's prospects, Brownell tried to secure him an appointment to the U.S. Court of Appeals for the Second Circuit. The retirements of Judges Thomas Swan and Augustus Hand from that tribunal in June 1953 presented Brownell with just that opportunity. Yet the most imposing obstacle to Harlan's circuit court appointment appeared to be Harlan himself, who by all accounts enjoyed his lucrative private practice. Knowing this, Brownell estimated his chances of getting Harlan to give up his practice as "very, very small."[64] Harlan's fellow partners, especially Arthur Ballantine, were not eager to see him leave their firm, either.[65] Thus beginning in the summer of 1953 Brownell pulled out "all the stops" to get Harlan to leave private practice.[66] At an August meeting of the ABA, Brownell pleaded with Harlan to accept the circuit court judgeship.[67] Faced with a reluctant nominee, Brownell enlisted help from members of the bar, suggesting that the Federal Bar Association review Harlan's qualifications. At Brownell's urging, one FBA Judiciary Committee member even informed Harlan that he was "quite confident" his nomination would be judged "eminently qualified" by his organization.[68] But Harlan requested that no such action be taken on his behalf, as he was "in no sense seeking judicial office."[69] These entreaties nevertheless continued throughout the fall.

Brownell eventually convinced Harlan that the Second Circuit would be just a temporary way-station; that with some appellate judicial experience, he would soon land an appointment to the Supreme Court. As Brownell recalled, "I had told him at the time that it was my personal 'dream' for him to go on the Supreme Court . . . and while he knew that wasn't completely within my powers, it made a big difference to him."[70] Harlan's decision to accept the circuit court appointment became easier once Thomas Dewey joined Root, Clark as a name partner, reducing any uncertainty Harlan's departure might have caused for the firm's future.[71] The FBI launched a full investigation of Harlan in mid-November, and Eisenhower formally forwarded his nomination to the Senate on January 13, 1954.

Two weeks after Harlan's circuit court nomination was forwarded to the Senate, Brownell remarked that he "took as much
pleasure" recommending Harlan's name to the president "as anything I have done since I became attorney general."[72] Just ten
months later, on October 9, 1954, Justice Jackson died of a heart
attack at the age of sixty-two. Now Brownell had the opportunity
to fulfill his "dream" of seeing Harlan on the U.S. Supreme Court.
Although he had served less than a year to that point on the court
of appeals, the fifty-five-year-old Harlan otherwise seemed well-
suited for the position. A New Yorker like Jackson, Harlan could
expect strong support from the entire New York legal community.

Meanwhile Eisenhower, with an eye towards the approaching
midterm elections, briefly considered using this second vacancy to
appease a critical political constituency. Special Counsel Bernard
Shanley reminded the president of Cardinal Spellman's previous
suggestions that he appoint a Catholic to the next vacancy.[73] None
had sat on the Court since Frank Murphy's death in 1949. Yet
when Eisenhower first spoke to Brownell about the nomination on
October 12, no Catholic candidates were even discussed. The attorney general's sole candidate was Harlan. Although the president's initial reaction was positive, he asked Brownell to suggest
other names for consideration, reminding him once again of the
firm condition that all candidates be sixty-two years of age or
younger.[74]

Determined that Harlan fill the vacancy, Brownell refused to
open up the selection process, providing no additional names for
the president's consideration. Instead, Brownell arranged a meeting
between Eisenhower and Harlan during a presidential visit to New
York City in mid-October.[75] Sensitive to the attorney general's personal commitment to his friend, Eisenhower quickly yielded to his
pleas. In doing so, he was resisting an increasingly furious lobbying campaign in favor of naming a Catholic to Jackson's seat.[76] Accordingly, Brownell advised the president to hold off publicizing
Harlan's appointment until after the election in order not to offend Catholic groups during the campaign.[77] Eisenhower finally
announced Harlan's appointment on November 9, 1954. The
Washington Post described it as "the culmination of a search for an
eminent lawyer with a judicial temperament and some judicial experience."[78] In fact, the search had been both short and sweet: short
in scope, and sweet for Herbert Brownell, who had made good on

his promise to a friend. The Senate confirmed Harlan's nomination on March 16, 1955, by a vote of 71–11.

THE BRENNAN NOMINATION:
A JUSTICE FOR ALL PURPOSES

In his first two opportunities to name a justice, Eisenhower essentially abandoned the administration's carefully constructed criteria for judicial appointments. Earl Warren possessed no judicial experience and was over sixty-two years old at the time of his appointment as chief justice. John Marshall Harlan enjoyed less than a year's experience on the U.S. Court of Appeals. Loyally fulfilling promises made by himself and Brownell, the president's discretion had been qualified in each instance by these commitments. Indeed, the single-candidate framework appeared to sweep aside all other administration objectives.

By the time Harlan's appointment was confirmed by the Senate in early 1955, Eisenhower was already giving thought to how he might strategically fill the next Supreme Court vacancy that might arise.[79] His interest in reinstating the "Catholic seat" on the Court had never diminished: the Catholic vote was to become a critically important target of Eisenhower's 1956 re-election campaign.[80] Not wanting to offend Cardinal Spellman or his constituency again before the next election, Eisenhower decided early on that his next appointee would be a Catholic. Accordingly, the president asked Brownell for "the name of some fine prominent Catholic to nominate to the bench" even before another vacancy was imminent.[81]

Catholics were not the only group that Eisenhower sought to placate. The Association of State Court Judges had become as "nettlesome" a critic of his judicial appointments as had the Catholic hierarchy, urging the president on past occasions to appoint the first justice from the state courts since Benjamin Cardozo.[82] As Brownell recalled, "Eisenhower had been told by several state chief justices that nobody currently on the Court understood the proper relation between the federal government and the states . . . and the president asked me to keep that in mind for the next vacancy that arose."[83]

As his campaign for reelection began to gain steam, the president also hoped to distinguish himself further from the Democrats by demonstrating that his judicial appointments, even to the Supreme Court, were nonpartisan. This issue had become a sensitive one for the president. Eisenhower had campaigned in 1952 against the Democrats' practice of turning judgeships into mere party handouts, but halfway through his first term his administration's record was little better. Both Supreme Court vacancies and all but a handful of lower court vacancies had gone to Republicans. Eisenhower was aware of his administration's questionable record on this point. Thus after the 1954 midterm elections he urged Brownell to consider "anti–New Deal" Democrats for judicial posts, noting that "we should appoint an occasional Democrat even though our ration from that party is already overwhelming."[84] If a vacancy on the Supreme Court were to arise prior to the November 1956 election, Eisenhower could deliver an especially forceful blow for bipartisanship by appointing a Democrat.

With no obvious candidate waiting in the wings, civil rights issues also figured significantly into the administration's decision-making calculus. The Supreme Court's decision in *Brown* was now two years old; a political moderate, Brownell had so far insisted that all prospective lower court appointees, especially from the South, be willing to faithfully enforce that controversial precedent. In a similar spirit, would Brownell now try to use his influence over the Supreme Court selection process as well to promote a civil rights agenda? Southern conservative leaders who opposed civil rights legislation of all types had urged Eisenhower to run for president in 1952, and the president had tried to stay sensitive to their interests whenever possible. Thus while the president had shown a willingness to support the *Brown* decision on the one hand, he had also squelched a number of civil rights initiatives offered by Brownell and others, including a proposal to more closely monitor minority housing problems in early 1955.[85] Brownell believed Eisenhower's heart was in the right place on civil rights, but he also knew Ike's administration would not "lead the charge to change race relations fundamentally in the United States."[86] Eager to avoid being labeled the administration's "chief architect of intervention," the attorney general had also learned to temper his own initiatives so that they would not unnecessarily provoke southern resistance.

Shrewd in cultivating his relationship with the president, Brownell clearly wanted to avoid outright conflict with Eisenhower over the selection of Supreme Court nominees. Accordingly, there is no evidence that the attorney general ever used his considerable influence to place more liberal justices on the Supreme Court. Nor did Brownell try to enforce any ideological litmus upon prospective high court nominees. Privately, civil rights advocates hoped that this moderate attorney general would at least steer the president away from choosing ardent segregationists for the bench. In point of fact, Brownell's determination to safeguard the president's political interests meant he would be equally willing to steer the president away from vocal civil rights advocates as well.

On September 7, 1956, Associate Justice Sherman Minton wrote the president of his plans to retire effective October 15.[87] Eisenhower immediately informed Brownell of Minton's letter; the president's secretary, Ann C. Whitman, listening on the extension phone,[88] took the following notes of their discussion:

> President suggests that attorney general start thinking again about a very good Catholic, even a conservative Democrat—thinks we really would be better off to appoint a Democrat to show that we mean our declaration that the Court should be nonpartisan (in spite of the fact that the ratio now is Democrat 6, Republican 3). Some discussion of Judge Danaher. Brownell said he was a good practicing Catholic. But the president asked the attorney general to canvass the field, to try to find an outstanding man, with court experience, regardless of his political affiliation.[89]

Judge John A. Danaher was a member of the U.S. Court of Appeals for the D.C. Circuit and had been active within the Republican Party during an earlier stint as a U.S. senator from Connecticut. But the president seemed more interested in appointing a Democrat to Minton's seat. Later that day he repeated his case to the chairman of the Republican National Committee, Leonard Hall. According to Ann Whitman's account:

> Chairman Hall called. He just heard of Justice Minton's letter of retirement. Makes room for Catholic. President said he called Brownell about it this noon. Thought of a good conservative Democrat, particularly if he has been on the bench for some time—politics would be of no moment. Hall said if the area could be Midwest, that would be wonderful. . . .[90]

Hall was duly concerned by the loss of eight Republican House seats from the Midwest during the most recent congressional elections; he feared that trend might spread to the presidential election that fall. (Hall's fears were not entirely unfounded: although Eisenhower later finished with fifteen more electoral votes in 1956, the

Republicans failed to capture Missouri, a state they had won from Stevenson in 1952.) Whatever Eisenhower's reaction to Chairman Hall's geographic argument was at the time, that issue never came up again in further discussions between him and the attorney general.

Brownell met with his deputy, William Rogers, to pass on the president's marching orders: canvass the field for a candidate who was a Catholic, a Democrat, and who possessed substantial experience as a judge. The attorney general also knew Eisenhower wanted to appoint a justice below the age of sixty-two, preferably with some background in the state courts. "This was a tall order," Brownell later remembered, "as there weren't that many judges out there that would fit all of Eisenhower's instructions."[91] Rogers may have been the first to suggest the name of William J. Brennan Jr., a fifty-year-old justice of the New Jersey Supreme Court.[92]

Brennan was a Catholic, a Democrat, and had served as a judge in the New Jersey courts since 1949. Less than four months earlier he had impressed Brownell and Rogers with a rousing speech at the attorney general's "Conference on Court Congestion and Delay in Litigation" held in Washington. Whether Brennan's speech truly deserved the plaudits it later received from both Brownell and Rogers is a subject of some historical debate. By one version of events, Arthur Vanderbilt—who had asked his junior colleague to substitute for him at the conference at the last minute—provided Brennan with the text of his own speech, ostensibly so that Brennan could read it at the conference. However, Brennan's biographer, Stephen Wermiel, has found substantial evidence to contradict this well-circulated myth.[93] Specifically, Wermiel discovered in previously closed FBI files a copy of the original speech prepared by Brennan, the text of which matches nearly verbatim the lecture Brennan gave at the conference.[94] Of course Brennan drew at least in part on Vanderbilt's notes in preparing his own material. Regardless, standing alone that speech could hardly account for Brennan's nomination. More likely, it helped to fix his name in the minds of both Brownell and Rogers when the two men were searching for a candidate four months later. In the final analysis, Brennan's name emerged from the pack because he was one of few candidates in the country able to satisfy each of the president's elaborate criteria.

On September 10, Eisenhower urged Brownell to investigate Brennan's record as a jurist more fully. Danaher was now ignored, presumably because of his Republican credentials. Besides,

Brownell had never viewed Danaher as genuine "Supreme Court caliber" in the first place.[95] Who else might the president have realistically considered, given the strict political and demographic filters he had imposed on the nomination? At the time of Minton's retirement, there was only one Catholic federal judge (other than Danaher) below the age of sixty-three: Paul C. Leahy, a fifty-two-year-old Roosevelt appointee sitting on the U.S. District Court of Delaware. Leahy lacked any appellate court experience. As for state judges, Brennan was a full ten years younger than the next youngest Catholic on a state supreme court, the distinguished Charles Desmond, sixty, of the New York Court of Appeals. This was a slim pool indeed for selecting the next Supreme Court justice, but the combination of election-year politics and the president's own political commitments seemed to rule out any alternatives.[96]

If Brennan's speech four months earlier had given Brownell and Rogers a false impression of his judicial philosophy, Brownell now had the opportunity to learn more about the New Jersey justice. The attorney general later claimed to have read all of Brennan's opinions written for the state supreme court.[97] If so, he would have identified at least a handful of liberal decisions (including several vitriolic dissents) written by the young judge. More likely, Brownell read most of these opinions for their clarity and intellect; up to that point Eisenhower had avoided imposing any specific ideological criteria on the nomination process.[98] The moderate Brownell would not have taken offense from an occasional liberal opinion in any event. The attorney general eventually concluded that despite a lack of constitutional opinions, Brennan's "legal and judicial experience were not only adequate but really outstanding."[99] Duly impressed, he unequivocally recommended Brennan to Eisenhower.

Most accounts of Brennan's nomination also give undue credit to Bernard Shanley and Chief Justice Vanderbilt for intervening on Brennan's behalf. While both men played some role in the process of Brennan's appointment, they were really only supporting players, smoothing the waters for a candidate already touted highly by Brownell and Rogers. Shanley was Brennan's childhood friend. He had reminded the president of Cardinal Spellman's continuing interest in seeing a Catholic on the Supreme Court; once the White House spotlight was focused squarely on Brennan, Shanley then contacted Spellman and other Catholic officials to verify Brennan's fitness as a Catholic.[100] Spellman confirmed for Shanley that Brennan was a legitimate practicing Catholic, although the cardinal was noticeably frustrated that the administration had chosen a Catholic whom he had never met.[101] Still, it was likely Rogers and not Shanley who first suggested Brennan as a candidate to Brownell. Brennan's speech on court congestion, not Shanley's endorsement, had encouraged Brownell to investigate Brennan's record further. Brennan himself never realized that Shanley had merely followed the lead of the Justice Department in supporting the nomination.[102]

Arthur Vanderbilt, a contender for the chief justiceship three years earlier, also played only a supporting role in the selection process. Now sixty-eight years old, Vanderbilt had already given up any realistic hope of sitting on the Supreme Court himself. To be sure, Eisenhower's memoirs give full credit to Vanderbilt for actively suggesting Brennan for the seat.[103] Yet the records and recollections of other key participants point to a more passive role. Indeed, the New Jersey chief justice recommended Brennan only after realizing that he was the administration's leading choice.[104] Ten years later the president recalled: "Judge Vanderbilt said that, in his opinion, Brennan possessed the finest 'judicial mind' that he had known in a long experience, and was of the highest character."[105] Eisenhower may have feared that his friend Vanderbilt would take offense at the appointment of a junior colleague. Vanderbilt's unequivocal endorsement now removed this potential obstacle to Brennan's nomination.

With the presidential election now just five weeks away, Eisenhower and Brownell moved quickly. The attorney general phoned Brennan on September 28 and asked him to come to Washington immediately. The next morning Brownell and Brennan met with the president and his chief of staff, Sherman Adams, in the Oval Office, where Brennan was formally offered the nomination.[106] Later that afternoon, the president publicly announced that he would appoint Brennan to Minton's seat. Two weeks later, on October 16, 1956, Brennan was sworn in as a recess appointment to the Court. On March 19, 1957, the Senate confirmed Brennan for the post by acclamation.

Brennan's selection could not be linked to the efforts of just one sponsor. Brownell and Rogers had met Brennan a few months earlier. Others who knew Brennan better, such as Bernard Shanley and Arthur Vanderbilt, were as surprised as anyone to learn that the relatively new justice of the New Jersey Supreme Court had leapfrogged over so many more experienced men for the post. But criteria defined this appointment. For the administration, the selection process was never about simply finding the "best possible person" for the job; rather, it was about finding a candidate who could survive all of the president's various political and demographic filters. In that sense Brennan's criteria-driven nomination was not so "unlikely" as some of his biographers suggest.[107] Indeed, the choice was all but preordained from the moment that Eisenhower decided to exploit the vacancy to pursue a number of immediate but unrelated political ends.

THE WHITTAKER NOMINATION:
A ONE-MAN CAMPAIGN

Eisenhower's second inauguration was less than a week old when Associate Justice Stanley Reed informed the president of his intention to retire on January 28, 1957. With the 1956 election behind him, the president no longer felt compelled to satisfy frustrated constituencies or make a grand show of bipartisanship. Unhampered by the unusual combination of circumstances and political pressures that had produced Brennan's appointment, Brownell hoped to utilize a more open selection process to survey a wider range of qualified jurists than had been considered during the administration's first term. Unfortunately for Brownell, Eisenhower remained adamant that any candidate for the Supreme Court both possess prior judicial experience and not exceed sixty-two years of age. And the president continued to demand that only federal court of appeals judges and state supreme court justices be considered. With a Democratic state judge receiving the nod for the previous vacancy, Eisenhower was apparently hoping for a Republican federal judge this time around. The attorney general's task was thus greatly simplified: canvass the pool of federal circuit judges for an experienced Republican jurist, sixty-two years of age or younger.

Concerns about candidates' policy views now entered the political equation for the first time. Specifically, Eisenhower and Brownell both wanted a candidate with verifiably moderate-to-conservative views. Liberal decisions regarding school desegregation, criminal law, and labor relations had produced widespread criticism of the Supreme Court. Although Brownell remained a moderate-to-liberal on civil rights issues, he had publicly challenged some of the Court's decisions in law enforcement, including those that unduly protected communists.[108] Even the normally discreet Eisenhower was beginning to openly criticize the chief justice in front of friends and close associates.[109]

Brownell and Rogers quickly surveyed all Republican appointees then sitting on the federal courts of appeals and as Brownell recalled, "we didn't find many who met Eisenhower's stringent age requirements."[110] At the time there were only fourteen federal appeals judges who possessed Republican credentials and were sixty-two years of age or younger.[111] None struck either Brownell or Rogers as being a step above the rest.[112] One possibility was fifty-nine-year-old Elbert Tuttle of the Fifth Circuit, whose name had arisen when Brownell and Eisenhower first met to discuss the nomination on January 28. Brownell was lukewarm on Tuttle, ironically because he may have feared the political ramifications of nominating a southern moderate who had loyally enforced the recent desegregation decision. Still, the attorney general agreed to give Tuttle a second look.[113] Qualified individuals from outside the federal circuit courts were not even considered during this initial stage of review.

With no obvious frontrunner emerging, the circumstances now seemed ripe for deft sponsorship to vault one person ahead of the pack. To be successful, that sponsor would have to enjoy ready access to either the president or Brownell. As Brownell himself recalled, Roy Roberts, an executive editor with the *Kansas City Star*, was the ideal suitor in this regard. Papers on file at the Eisenhower Library provide evidence of a close, personal friendship between Roberts and the president; the two men had corresponded frequently in the past, often exchanging intimate details about each other's personal lives.[114] Roberts was hardly a neutral bystander in the nation's political wars. His newspaper had been a strong advocate of President Eisenhower's administration. Roberts also supported the Republican Party in a number of ways, including working with Leonard W. Hall to create briefing material for Eisenhower and other Republican candidates in 1956.[115]

Roberts was also a direct and loyal promoter of Charles Whittaker, then a judge on the U.S. Court of Appeals for the Eighth Circuit. The fifty-six-year-old Whittaker had reached the top ranks of the Kansas City bar during the early 1950s. Impressed by the lawyer's capable representation of the *Kansas City Star*, Roberts soon became "very keen on Whittaker."[116] Eisenhower appointed Whittaker to serve as U.S. district judge in 1954, and then promoted him to the Eighth Circuit Court of Appeals in 1956. Each appointment derived in no small part out of Roberts's persistent efforts on his behalf.[117] Although Whittaker also benefited from the support of former U.S. Senator Harry Darby and others in his rise through the federal judiciary, Roberts had been the most influential person of all in paving Whittaker's path to successive federal court nominations.[118] Now Roberts jumped at the opportunity to place his friend on the nation's highest court and extend his own influence in the process.

During the first week of February 1957, Roberts began to literally "pester" Brownell about a Whittaker candidacy.[119] To assist him in this effort, Roberts enlisted the services of his paper's Washington correspondent, Duke Shoop. Shoop, who had previously assisted Roberts's efforts to promote Whittaker to the Eighth Circuit, now pressed his candidacy for the high court directly to Brownell and Rogers throughout the month of February.[120] Rogers eventually agreed to review the opinions Whittaker had written both on the district court and in his brief service on the court of appeals. Although there is no written record of Rogers's reaction, any such review would have painted Whittaker as introspective, conservative, and "most unlikely to transform the Warren-Black-Douglas-Brennan minority into a solid liberal majority."[121] Brownell and Rogers were both unexcited about Whittaker, whom they viewed as a good judge, though not "outstanding."[122]

Despite these mixed reviews, Whittaker still emerged as the leading candidate to replace Reed, because he had influential sponsors and because his candidacy posed no obvious disadvantages to the administration. Though Brownell and Rogers were unenthusiastic about Whittaker, neither was willing to muster the necessary energy or interest that would have been required to fight off his persistent supporters. Roy Roberts also knew Whittaker's nomination might carry some geographical appeal for Eisenhower. Since the president had assumed office in 1953, the Court had lost two Kentuckians (Vinson and Reed), a New Yorker (Jackson), and a native of Indiana (Minton). They had so far been replaced by a Californian (Warren), a New Jerseyite (Brennan), and another New Yorker (Harlan). Minton's retirement had left Harold Burton as the only Midwesterner on the Court. The president could thus justifiably favor a neighboring "Kansan" without appearing to unduly favor his home region.

With no other candidate in sight, Eisenhower nominated Whittaker to the Supreme Court on March 2, 1957. The Senate confirmed
his appointment less than three weeks later by acclamation. The
nominee's political credentials were as strong as his legal credentials were thin. Unfortunately, the president's original criteria had
narrowed the field considerably. Instead of expanding the search
to find an outstanding potential justice, the Eisenhower administration remained wedded to its own predetermined filters.

THE STEWART NOMINATION:
PUTTING ASIDE THE AGE ISSUE

As Brownell's successor in the fall of 1957, Attorney General William Rogers quickly arrived at the conclusion that the Whittaker
nomination had been a mistake.[123] Rogers had never been particularly keen on Whittaker, and during only his first term on the Court
the justice was already showing signs of being overwhelmed by the
job. On two separate occasions in early 1958 the new justice called
Rogers, complaining that he wanted to quit.[124] Rogers refused to
take Whittaker's complaint to the president; he convinced the justice to give the position more time. All the while, Rogers knew that
potentially outstanding candidates had been ignored prior to Whittaker's selection for want of judicial experience, the right age, or
some other carefully defined guideline. With Brownell back in private practice, Rogers would serve as Eisenhower's primary advisor
for any future Supreme Court nominations, and he was determined
to avoid a repeat of the Whittaker debacle.

Rogers's opportunity came quickly. Some time during June
1958, Justice Harold Burton decided to retire from the Court. Burton informed Rogers of his plans about a month before he was
scheduled to meet with the president, giving the new attorney general ample time to consider possible replacements before receiving
any strict guidance from Eisenhower.[125] Rogers briefly surveyed the
field of candidates available to the administration. Only forty-five
years old himself, the attorney general was perhaps more inclined
than Eisenhower to favor some of his contemporaries on the federal
circuit courts, including possibly Judge Warren Burger, fifty, a D.C.
Circuit judge and Rogers's former associate at the Justice Department, or Judge Potter Stewart, forty-three, of the U.S. Court of
Appeals for the Sixth Circuit. Rogers's survey of federal district
courts also identified William Jameson, fifty-nine, of Maine and

George Boldt, fifty-four, of Tacoma, Washington, as strong possibilities.[126] Finally, Rogers reviewed a number of candidates now in private practice, including his predecessor at the Justice Department, Herbert Brownell (now fifty-four).

Once the president got involved in the process, the same overly restrictive criteria that had produced Whittaker's nomination began rearing its restrictive power again. On July 17, Rogers joined Justice Burton at the White House for his meeting with the president. Burton's notes from that meeting, preserved in his own carefully kept diary, provide a unique behind-the-scenes glimpse into the selection process. The president formally accepted Burton's resignation, "expressed disappointment" at the recent decisions of Warren and Brennan, and instructed the attorney general to be "most careful" in this choice.[127] Eisenhower criticized Warren in particular and heaped praise on Justice Clark's dissent in the recent *Watkins* decision regarding congressional investigations of alleged Communists.[128] He indicated generally that he "wanted a conservative attitude for justices of the Supreme Court."

Rogers suggested Stewart, a federal judge who was from Burton's home state of Ohio, as a possible replacement. He believed that Stewart would appeal to the president's desire to maintain geographical balance on the Court. Burton recorded in his diary: "Both the A.G. and I spoke highly of him (Stewart). The president asked the A.G. to be especially careful because Stewart's age is forty-three."[129]

Perhaps Eisenhower doubted that such a young man could be qualified to sit on the nation's highest Court.[130] Rogers also praised Jameson and Boldt as worthy candidates, but the president was uninterested and quickly changed the subject. Already evident at this first meeting was the tug of war developing between the president and his new attorney general over the framework to be employed in filling this particular vacancy. Rogers, hoping to utilize a more open framework of decisionmaking, raised the name of a budding legal star and two well-respected trial judges; Eisenhower wanted Rogers to stick to the more criteria-driven list of federal circuit court and state supreme court judges between the ages of fifty and sixty.

With the news of Burton's retirement still not public, the search for a new justice continued over the summer. Both the president and the attorney general were eager to see Burton stay on the Court for the duration of the Little Rock school desegregation case.[131] Neither wanted the looming confirmation of his successor to distract from these proceedings.[132] When the Court finally ruled against the Little Rock school board on September 12, Eisenhower and Rogers resumed their search in earnest.

Rogers eventually provided the president with a long list of candidates for the Court, which included (in addition to those already discussed) a wide variety of individuals from state and federal courts, government agencies, and private practice. The president responded by identifying three of Rogers's listed candidates as the "most satisfactory judges": Herbert Brownell, a private practitioner; Warren Burger, a judge on the D.C. Circuit; and Elbert Tuttle, a judge on the Fifth Circuit.[133] The president also identified his close friend Kenneth Royall as being "almost ideally fitted for my conception of the kind of man we now need," but noted his reluctance to replace Burton with a Democrat.[134] Again the president brushed aside Stewart for his relative youth, and ignored Jameson and Boldt for their lack of appellate experience. Still, there were signs that the president was retreating slightly from his strict criteria of the past: Eisenhower had openly raised the possibility of appointing Brownell, who was a lawyer from private practice.[135] (In truth, the president's eagerness to see Brownell on the high court would have justified him as an exception in Eisenhower's mind, no matter the circumstances.)

But Rogers feared Brownell's appointment would cause "political complications" as to his confirmation and he related these concerns to the president.[136] Convinced that Eisenhower would never consider a trial judge for the high court, Rogers turned his efforts to challenging the president's minimum age requirement of fifty, and he pushed Stewart for the post. This was not much of a stretch. Stewart fit the president's stated criteria for a Supreme Court justice in every other way. He had federal appellate court experience, was a Republican, hailed from Burton's home state, and lacked any political enemies that might complicate his confirmation. Even Ohio's maverick senator, Republican John Bricker, heartily approved of Stewart's candidacy.[137]

Eisenhower finally yielded to Rogers's recommendation and announced Burton's retirement and Stewart's recess appointment on October 7 and 8, respectively. Despite misgivings about Stewart's youth, the president deferred in the end to his attorney general's judgment. The criteria established for the vacancy had been relaxed slightly, but the process was still a far cry from the more open framework Rogers might have desired. The following May the Senate confirmed Stewart by a vote of 70–17.

CONCLUSION

During the 1950s, a number of important political developments threatened to intensify the political environment surrounding Supreme Court nominations. The Supreme Court's decision in *Brown* had placed the federal judiciary at the center of American politics. For most of his two terms Eisenhower faced a Senate controlled by Democrats. And beginning with John Marshall Harlan in 1955, nominees began testifying before the Senate Judiciary Committee. In 1956, William Brennan was subject to especially harsh questioning from a number of hostile senators, including Joseph McCarthy of Wisconsin.

Yet few of these developments manifested themselves in the form of threats to the president's decisionmaking authority. Eisenhower's criteria-driven framework for choosing nominees generally confined the arena of selection conflict. The president relied heavily on the expertise of his attorney general, rather than allowing competing interests within the administration to battle over each nomination. Brownell (and later Rogers) served admirably in their respective roles, although the president's heavy emphasis on criteria-based decisionmaking gave them limited freedom to advise the president.

Unlike some future presidents, Eisenhower did not employ unduly restrictive ideological criteria. He aspired to choose moderate-to-conservative justices, but there were no ideological "litmus tests" for candidates on any hot-button issues like school desegregation. Unfortunately, the administration's other filters excluded a large number of qualified candidates from consideration either because they were too young, held jobs in private practice, served on trial courts, or worked for the administration. If Eisenhower wanted to distinguish his method of selecting Supreme Court justices from that of Truman, he for the most part succeeded. Instead of conducting an open and free-wheeling search for a trusted friend or associate, Eisenhower brought sometimes militant order to the process. In the case of his first two appointments, this highly structured selection process was placed on hold, as Eisenhower honored political promises made to Earl Warren and John Marshall Harlan. But for the president's final three appointments, a highly bureaucratic selection process prevailed. In 1956, political criteria dominated the deliberations over choosing a successor to Sherman Minton. With a presidential election fast approaching, Eisenhower felt compelled to address several immediate political needs. By contrast, Charles Whittaker's nomination fit all of the administration's requirements for a Supreme Court candidate established several years earlier: the nominee was in his fifties and possessed adequate experience as an appellate court judge. With his final appointment of Potter Stewart, the president showed only minimal flexibility in applying those exact same criteria.

As time went by, the president grew more and more frustrated with the decisions of Earl Warren and William Brennan, especially as the Warren Court expanded protections for criminal defendants in the 1960s. It was surely a source of disappointment for Eisenhower when his Democratic successor, President John F. Kennedy, named Whittaker's replacement barely five years after the retiring justice had arrived. By contrast, Harlan and Stewart, both moderate-to-conservative justices on the Supreme Court, met most if not all of the president's lofty expectations. As an indication of the acclaim each of the two justices later received from Eisenhower and other high-level Republicans, President Nixon would eventually consider both men for the chief justiceship after Warren's retirement in 1969.[138]

History would prove much kinder to the Eisenhower legacy than he himself would be. In 1990, court-experts ranked Warren and Brennan, the two justices Eisenhower later disavowed, as two of the five greatest justices ever to serve on the Supreme Court.[139] John Marshall Harlan's reputation as a distinguished "jurist's jurist" made him a revered figure in American law schools. Potter Stewart's standing as an independent legal craftsman continues untarnished. Save for Charles Whittaker, Eisenhower's nominees may rank historically as among the finest group ever to be appointed by one president.

President Eisenhower aspired to substitute a more strategic brand of political discretion for Truman's loyalty-based politics. The president consulted regularly with the Justice Department and took advantage of its resources, but rather than simply hand the decisionmaking power over to these political actors, he limited their own discretion by his prescribed criteria. Certainly the attorney general remained an influential actor in the process: Eisenhower's two favorite appointments, Harlan and Stewart, became nominees precisely because in each case the attorney general wielded especially strong influence over the process. Meanwhile, the nominations of Brennan and Whittaker emerged out of discrete political criteria that filtered away many otherwise qualified alternatives. And there was no formal selection process at all for the selection of Warren, who had been promised his Supreme Court seat even before Eisenhower's inauguration. Republicans who sought a more conservative judicial legacy would soon long for a little more of Truman's excess discretion, the type that focused more on personal friends and party loyalists than on highly specific political objectives.

FOUR

KENNEDY AND JOHNSON RESTORE THE POLITICS OF PATRONAGE

Presidents John F. Kennedy and Lyndon B. Johnson each took a strong personal interest in the consideration and selection of prospective Supreme Court justices during their respective administrations. Both chief executives assumed an active role throughout the selection process, from the early consideration of candidates to the final selection of a nominee. Each turned ultimately to candidates they knew personally—individuals who had earned their trust and confidence in the recent past. For much of his tenure Eisenhower had labored to rid his own administration's judicial recruitment practices of strictly personal considerations; by all appearances, his two Democratic successors set to work restoring the politics of patronage to its traditionally important role in the selection calculus. Those appearances may have obscured a more significant truth, however: despite some similarities in recruitment philosophy, the actual process utilized by Johnson and Kennedy in identifying and selecting Supreme Court nominees could not have been more different.

President Kennedy felt Eisenhower's style of operating government discouraged "new and innovative policies," forcing agreement on the "lowest common denominator."[1] Accordingly, he rejected his predecessor's highly structured and rigid model for selecting Supreme Court nominees. Certainly Kennedy was not above living up to political promises himself: in August 1962, he faithfully stood behind his promise of a Supreme Court seat to Arthur Goldberg. But when Kennedy did have the opportunity to conduct a full-fledged search for justices earlier that same year, the president encouraged an open-ended and flexible give-and-take between himself and numerous other high-level officials. He refused to impose any rigid criteria or narrowly defined filters during the initial stages of canvassing and selection. More importantly, while staying actively involved in the selection process, Kennedy passed on a considerable amount of decisionmaking authority to his subordinates.

The bulk of responsibility for screening candidates fell to the president's brother and top advisor, Attorney General Robert Kennedy. The failed Bay of Pigs invasion in April 1961 had caused dramatic shifts in the structure of power in the White House. Recovering slowly from his administration's first public foreign policy disaster, the president began to turn to those he trusted most, and "conversely, to trust little in those he knew least."[2] Under the new regime, Robert Kennedy came to enjoy increased power in numerous areas of policymaking. And when two vacancies arose on the Supreme Court within a six-month period in 1962, the young attorney general was prepared to exert his already considerable influence on the process.

Whereas President Kennedy took interest in a winnowing process that was being conducted primarily within the Justice Department, Lyndon Johnson's personal domination of Supreme Court selections surpassed even Truman's tight control over the same process two decades earlier. Johnson dispensed with formal selection processes and advice from counsel in all but the most perfunctory sense. On those rare occasions when he did sound out advisors concerning a vacancy, Johnson was looking more for their approval than independent advice. Unlike Truman, Johnson proved stubbornly inflexible even when drastically shifting political circumstances should have dictated a different approach to nominations. While Truman relied on a free-wheeling and open selection framework that could adjust to new and unforeseen circumstances, Johnson's approach remained focused on the one or two candidates that he had already targeted long before. This stubborn adherence to pre-identified candidates proved especially costly to him and his administration during the summer and fall of 1968.

THE WHITE NOMINATION:
LOYALTY FIRST, CREDENTIALS SECOND

On March 16, 1962, Justice Charles Whittaker informed President Kennedy that he intended to retire from the Court for "health rea-

sons."[3] Whittaker's letter took the president and his advisors somewhat by surprise. Although the justice had recently checked into a
hospital complaining of physical and mental exhaustion, Whittaker
was still just sixty-one years old, making him the third youngest
sitting justice after Potter Stewart (forty-seven) and William Brennan (fifty-six). In fact, Whittaker's relative youth had been a key
factor in Eisenhower's decision to appoint him five years earlier.
Initially, there seemed little need for any drawn-out formal selection
process. Within the Justice Department it was common knowledge
that Kennedy had already promised the seat to Secretary of Labor
Arthur J. Goldberg. President Kennedy admitted as much to Assistant Attorney General Nicholas Katzenbach on at least "a half
dozen" occasions.[4]

A graduate of Northwestern Law School, Goldberg was a former
general counsel for the Steelworkers' Union, the CIO, and later the
AFL-CIO. He had first made Kennedy's acquaintance during the
senator's tenure on the Senate's permanent investigations subcommittee investigating union corruption in the 1950s.[5] Goldberg
quickly established himself as the Kennedys' invaluable liaison to
the labor movement. Occasionally he even backed Senator Kennedy in causes that offended traditional union interests.[6] Goldberg
campaigned hard for Senator Kennedy during his 1960 presidential
race; perhaps his greatest contribution to Kennedy's political for-
tunes came at the 1960 Democratic convention when Kennedy had
first suggested the possibility of naming Lyndon Johnson as his running mate.[7] Working to soothe the adamant opposition of George
Meany and other union leaders to Johnson's candidacy, Goldberg
eventually managed to ensure labor's unconditional support for a
Kennedy-Johnson ticket.[8]

After Kennedy's victory in November, Goldberg let the president-elect know that he was interested in serving as either attorney
general or solicitor general for his new administration. Goldberg
made no attempt to hide the fact that his ultimate objective was to
serve on the Supreme Court; he believed that, strategically speaking, either of those two positions at the Justice Department would
provide the logical first step to a high court nomination.[9] However,
the president tapped Robert Kennedy to head the Justice Department and sought a law professor (first Paul Freund and later Archibald Cox) to serve as solicitor general. A disappointed Goldberg
was offered the top spot at the Labor Department instead.[10] His
first instinct had been to decline; as Alan Adams observed, for

Goldberg "the law, not labor, was his career."[11] But he dutifully accepted the assignment anyway, overcoming a legion of protests from Meany and other labor officials about his proposed nomination.[12]

Both the president-elect and his brother knew that Goldberg had accepted a cabinet position which he neither sought nor desired. Goldberg's willingness to be a good soldier for the administration would not go unrewarded. Once Goldberg came into the fold as labor secretary, John Kennedy promised him consideration for a Supreme Court post some time in the future. As Assistant Attorney General Nicholas Katzenbach recalled, "The 'promise' was more simply in the casual sense of the word, that the Supreme Court had come up [in their discussions] and he said to Arthur that Arthur would have a good crack at this when a vacancy came up."[13] When news of Whittaker's retirement first reached the administration in March 1962, Robert Kennedy confirmed to his aides that Goldberg had indeed been promised a Supreme Court seat.[14]

At least one significant obstacle to Goldberg's nomination remained, however: Goldberg had become so valuable to the administration as labor secretary that the president was now reluctant to part with him. President Kennedy's campaign for a "noninflationary" steel settlement was coming to a head that spring,[15] and Goldberg had already met twice with Roger Blough of the U.S. Steel Corporation and the Steelworkers' Union chief, David McDonald. Three more sets of meetings with Blough and McDonald were scheduled for the next six weeks to meet a new contract deadline in June.[16] The administration could not easily spare Goldberg, now actively managing the steel negotiations, at such a critical juncture.[17] To their credit, neither the president nor his brother proved so inflexible that they were willing to risk suffering political costs in the name of a personal promise. As Robert Kennedy summed up the situation to one aide: "It's just too early . . . and we need him."[18]

Deferring Goldberg's candidacy for the time being, the Kennedys soon launched a more comprehensive search for Whittaker's replacement. Robert Kennedy's Justice Department played a critical role in this process. During the previous year the attorney general had relied on his top deputy, Byron R. White, to oversee appointments to lower federal courts. White was now the logical choice to head the search for potential high court candidates.[19] But just as the administration was gearing up to initiate a comprehensive search for Whittaker's successor, White was preparing to depart for Colorado to attend a prescheduled meeting at the University of Denver.[20] Before leaving Washington, White instructed his two assistant attorneys general, Joseph F. Dolan and Katzenbach, to "get cracking on the search" right away. He asked both men to talk to Philadelphia lawyer Bernard G. Segal, then chair of the ABA's Standing Committee on Federal Judiciary,[21] and directed each to report his findings directly to the attorney general.

On a completely separate front, White House official Theodore Sorenson, the special counsel to the president, offered to prepare his own list of potential Supreme Court nominees for the president's perusal (see table below).[22] After consulting with Clark Clifford and the deputy special counsel, Mike Feldman, Sorenson compiled a first-class list of nineteen names "deserving of consideration for the court vacancy."[23]

In an attached memorandum, Sorenson argued that Kennedy's first appointment "should be one hailed by all for his judicial mien—not primarily known as a politician—not subject to con-

Sorenson's List of Potential Supreme Court Candidates, March 21, 1962

I.	Members of Administration	Age	Party
	1. Arthur Goldberg	53	Dem.
	2. Nick Katzenbach	40	Dem.
	3. Byron White	44	Dem.
	4. Adlai Stevenson	62	Dem.
	5. H. H. Fowler	53	Dem.
	6. Archibald Cox	49	Dem.
II.	Members of the Judiciary		
A.	Federal Judiciary		
	1. Hastie	57	Dem.
	2. Friendly	58	Rep.
	3. Washington	53	Dem.
	4. Bazelon	52	Dem.
B.	State Judiciary		
	1. Traynor, California	62	Rep.
	2. Fuld, New York	59	Dem.
	3. Schaefer, Illinois	57	Dem.
III.	Members of Bar, Academics		
	1. Paul Freund	54	Dem.
	2. Bethuel Webster	61	Rep.
	3. Clark Clifford	55	Dem.
	4. Herbert Wechsler	52	Dem.
	5. Edward Levi	50	Dem.
	6. Whitney North Seymour	61	Rep.

firmation delays because of controversial associations."[24] Sorenson called Goldberg the ablest nominee, "if a politician is to be chosen." However, he recommended that Kennedy appoint "the highly respected" Paul Freund, save Goldberg for the vacancy of chief justice, and appoint William Henry Hastie to any subsequent associate justice vacancy that might arise.[25] Freund, a longtime Harvard Law School professor and student of Felix Frankfurter's, was at the time a leading scholar in American constitutional law. Hastie, the only black candidate on Sorenson's list, had served as dean of Howard Law School and governor of the Virgin Islands before Harry Truman appointed him to the Court of Appeals for the Third Circuit in 1949. Sorenson opposed Hastie's nomination this early because the president was already considering another black (Robert C. Weaver) for a Cabinet post, and Sorenson feared charges of reverse racism against the administration.[26] During the 1960 campaign Kennedy had weathered charges that as the first Catholic president his allegiance would be split between the interests of America and those of the politically powerful Catholic Church. Clearly Kennedy wanted to avoid naming a fellow Catholic to this first vacancy. What about the nomination of a Jewish candidate such as Freund? Given the president's previous commitment to Arthur Goldberg (who was also Jewish), the president was equally wary about nominating a Jewish candidate to replace Whittaker.

Meanwhile, Katzenbach and Dolan were busy compiling their own lists of candidates at the Justice Department.[27] Dolan spoke several times with Segal, polling the ABA committee chair for his impressions about various jurists and practicing lawyers around the country. Dolan was also interested in gauging the organized bar's reaction to the candidacy of his own boss, Byron White. Specifically, Segal feared that White's relative youth (he was just forty-four years old) and inexperience might cost him support from certain legal circles.[28] But Byron "Whizzer" White, a former Rhodes Scholar and Heisman Trophy–winning football player at the University of Colorado, had quickly established himself as a top mind in the Denver legal community after graduating from Yale Law School. Segal confidently assured Dolan that White's nomination would enjoy the bar's overwhelming support.

Dolan's enthusiasm for White's candidacy seems natural in hindsight. The two men had worked closely together on the Kennedy campaign in their home state of Colorado, and then again for the past fifteen months at the Department of Justice.[29] Dolan also knew the president had admired White ever since they first met in 1939 while touring in Europe. White and Kennedy had then worked together as fellow naval officers in the Pacific during World War II. In preparing to assume the presidency, Kennedy had a firm grasp of the importance of subcabinet appointments—his administration actively sought "action intellectuals" for this second level of posts.[30] Thus in staffing the Justice Department, the president-elect had urged his brother to hire White as his second in command. At first, Robert Kennedy discouraged any talk of White as a Supreme Court candidate. He told Dolan that White had already declined interest in the position before leaving for his trip to Colorado.[31] White's value to the Justice Department may have also discouraged Kennedy from enthusiastically supporting White's candidacy at this stage of the process. In fact, Theodore Sorenson recalls leaving White's name off his own shortened list of prospects for that very reason: he believed the Kennedy administration could not afford to lose him.[32]

Katzenbach settled on his own list of candidates, which included Traynor, Schaefer, Hastie, Freund, White, and Levi. He also listed one female candidate as a possibility: Soia Mentschikoff, fifty, a law professor from the University of Chicago. Mentschikoff was a distinguished and pathbreaking legal scholar, as well as being Katzenbach's personal friend. White was a late addition to Katzenbach's list. Speaking by phone from Denver, White repeated to Katzenbach what he had told Robert Kennedy: that he wanted his name left off all lists of high court possibilities. But Katzenbach sensed some hesitation on White's part and left White's name on his list anyway.[33] Despite the candidate's repeated expressions of reluctance at being considered for the high court, momentum seemed to be building in favor of White's candidacy.

Before leaving for Colorado, White had also expressed concern that rumors of "left-wing" connections might cause some difficulties with Hastie's confirmation. At White's request, Katzenbach drafted an eight-page memorandum to Robert Kennedy in which he dismissed as baseless those charges concerning Hastie's former political connections and background.[34] Hastie, fifty-seven, possessed sterling credentials for the high court. Katzenbach's review of Hastie's judicial writings was not so glowing, however, concluding that the judge's opinions, while "good" and "competent," were certainly not "brilliant."[35]

By the final week of March no consensus on the nomination had yet been reached. Sorenson was on record in support of Freund. Clark Clifford seemed disposed to Freund as well. Robert Kennedy still favored the historic appointment of Hastie, who would have become the first black justice in the nation's history.[36] The attorney general's top priority, however, was to blunt any possible interest in Freund. During the 1950s Freund had provided valuable counsel to Senator John Kennedy on pending legislation, including the controversial jury trial amendment in voting rights cases.[37] Then, beginning in 1959, Freund became an avid supporter of the Kennedy campaign.[38] But immediately after Kennedy's narrow election victory in 1960, Freund had refused the president-elect's request that he serve the administration as its new solicitor general. According to his colleague at Harvard, Abram Chayes, Freund had little interest in returning to the solicitor general's office where he had served as chief assistant from 1935 to 1939.[39] Although he understood that serving as solicitor general would improve his chances of being chosen for the next Court vacancy, Freund was reluctant to take the position simply as a "stepping stone" to something else.[40] Freund was also persuaded by the arguments of his mentor, Justice Felix Frankfurter, who himself had turned down an offer of the solicitor generalship from Franklin Roosevelt. Frankfurter reportedly had told his friend not to leave Harvard Law School *except* for a seat on the high court.

Freund was busy wrestling with Kennedy's offer in late 1960 just as speculation was rising in Washington about Kennedy's plan to name his brother as the next attorney general. Opposition to Robert Kennedy's candidacy quietly grew among academics and lawyers, many of whom believed he lacked sufficient legal credentials for the position. To Freund, Robert Kennedy's expected appointment made the position of solicitor general (just the third-ranking position at the Justice Department) even less attractive. When Freund finally turned down the position in December, Robert Kennedy took the rejection personally; he perceived—perhaps accurately— that Freund did not want to work under his command.

To be sure, Freund's decision would seriously diminish his Supreme Court prospects sixteen months later. Learning of Sorenson and Katzenbach's support for Freund, Robert Kennedy now aggressively lobbied his brother against such a nomination. The attorney general's stated complaint was that Freund had not been active enough in the administration. As Robert Kennedy later recalled of his feelings at the time:

Paul Freund was asked to come down and be solicitor general, and he
turned it down. And that was a factor, obviously; when President Kennedy wanted him, he didn't want to do it. And then why appoint him
when, you know, I mean, Arch Cox had done very well [as solicitor
general]. I mean, the logical person would be . . . Archie Cox. . . .[41]

Of course the attorney general had never once suggested Cox for
the current vacancy. Meanwhile, Hastie, still his top choice for the
moment, had never served the administration in any capacity whatsoever.[42]

Hastie's nomination would also pose a number of political difficulties for the administration. The nomination of the nation's first
black justice (even one with moderate views) was sure to set off a
furor among Southern senators on the Senate Judiciary Committee.
Kennedy had nominated another well-known black lawyer, Thurgood Marshall, to a recess appointment on the U.S. Court of Appeals in New York during the previous September. Nearly six
months later, the full Judiciary Committee still had not considered
Marshall's nomination formally, and Chairman James Eastland (D-
Miss.) was threatening further delays.[43] Moreover, even if Hastie's
confirmation somehow could be secured, it would happen only at
great political cost to the administration. President Kennedy only
recently had introduced to Congress a major package of economic
reforms, including tax credits. A version of the administration's
proposal had been approved by the House Ways and Means Committee as recently as March 22. The support of Senate Finance
Committee Chairman Robert Byrd (D-W.Va.) and other southern
senators was considered critical to the bill's passage in the Senate.
Hastie's nomination might well endanger these and other legislative
efforts. Finally, Hastie's potential candidacy had already encountered resistance within a number of influential liberal quarters.[44]

Robert Kennedy invited Katzenbach and Dolan to the White
House on March 29 to consider the current list of candidates. Their
discussions focused on seven individuals: Freund, Hastie, White,
Traynor, Schaefer, Cox, and Edward Levi. Dolan strenuously objected to Hastie's nomination, fearing it would "blow everything
we've got going on the Hill."[45] Katzenbach favored Freund, though
he noted that appointment of "another Harvard Professor" might
be a problem.[46] Both Dolan and Katzenbach then spoke enthusiastically of Byron White. Meanwhile, the two state judges received
short shrift in the discussion—Schaefer, because he had been born

a Catholic, and Traynor, because his opinions were thought to align too closely with those of the extreme liberal on the Court, Justice Black.[47] Afterwards, Katzenbach and Dolan tried to use the attorney general's own vanity to benefit White's cause: Katzenbach's suggestion that the Justice Department might suffer substantially in White's absence may have helped move Robert Kennedy over to White's camp.

The few substantive discussions in the days that followed revolved around two candidates: White and Hastie. Given the immediate political environment, President Kennedy appeared unwilling to risk his legislative agenda to secure Hastie's confirmation. Robert Kennedy seemed to back off Hastie as well. Even though White was now the presumptive nominee by default, another high-level official in the administration, McGeorge Bundy, tried to revive Paul Freund's candidacy on March 30. Before joining the administration as Kennedy's special assistant for national security affairs, Bundy had been a professor of government at Harvard for ten years, where he had established close ties to many in the academic community, including Freund. In a memorandum to the president, Bundy campaigned hard for his former colleague, arguing that "Freund is a great scholar . . . a Brandeis in conviction, but a Cardozo in temperament."[48] "Of all the men you might choose, he is the most likely to be a great judge," Bundy concluded, "and he is ripe for appointment now."[49]

But these last-minute efforts could not overcome Robert Kennedy's strenuous objections to Freund. In fact, even with numerous advisors swirling around the president with advice, Robert Kennedy was still the main conduit for the president in the selection process. The attorney general's steadfast efforts buried Freund's candidacy even while it enjoyed the support of at least four other high-level advisors. Despite clear political disadvantages to his candidacy, Hastie's name remained in the mix only through Robert Kennedy's urging. But once Katzenbach and Dolan had convinced the attorney general of White's advantages, his nomination became all but inevitable. On the afternoon of March 30, John Kennedy formally submitted White's nomination to the Senate. The Senate confirmed White to the post by acclamation just twelve days later.

Ironically, in considering a successor to Whittaker, Kennedy's associates had paid little attention to the leading candidates' ideologies or positions on particular legal issues. The Court issued its watershed reapportionment decision in *Baker v. Carr*[50] on March 26,

1962, just days before Kennedy formally nominated White. The decision laid bare the Warren Court's various ideological cleavages and drove home the potential impact a new justice might have in shaping the future landscape of constitutional law. Yet the landmark ruling played little or no role in any of the deliberations between the president and his advisors that led to White's selection. Kennedy was not wedded to any one candidate or any strict set of criteria, ideological or otherwise. Before him was a nominee the president felt "comfortable" with, but also one who possessed sparkling legal credentials. Even more important, Byron White had emerged as the favorite candidate of the Justice Department, whose counsel the president principally relied upon. Unlike Herbert Brownell, Robert Kennedy was able to leave his mark on the process because the open framework for decisionmaking facilitated a free and open discussion of all available candidates. It was a marked contrast indeed from the rigid, stilted selection mechanism at work during the previous decade.

THE GOLDBERG NOMINATION: ANOTHER LOYAL SOLDIER GOES REWARDED

Justice Felix Frankfurter was hospitalized during the summer of 1962 with a mild stroke. In late August, the seventy-nine-year-old justice notified the president that he planned to retire immediately. This time around there would be no open consideration of candidates within the administration. "There was no discussion for the seat, no list . . . no anything," Katzenbach admitted later.[51] From the outset the president focused on just one candidate for the vacancy: Arthur Goldberg. The threat of a serious steel strike had now passed, and Goldberg remained very much interested in a nomination to the Court.[52] And Frankfurter's status as the lone Jewish justice only added to the logic of replacing him with Goldberg, who was also Jewish.

Goldberg biographer Victor Lasky has suggested that the president and the attorney general, so reluctant to part with Goldberg in March, were actually eager to see him leave five months later. According to Lasky, the secretary of labor had violated a central tenet of the Kennedy administration: that the only visible idea man and house spokesman for the president should be Robert Kennedy.[53] Goldberg had emerged as a "loquacious and well-publicized gadfly of the Cabinet";[54] his success in the recently concluded steel negotiations encouraged him to assume a more public presence. Perhaps the Kennedys, with a sigh of relief, now viewed Goldberg's looming Supreme Court nomination as a political reward to a supporter whose style of politics was beginning to wear a bit thin within the administration.

On August 29, 1962, Robert Kennedy asked Bernard Segal to canvass members of the ABA Committee for a tentative rating of Goldberg. The results were favorable, and the president acted immediately. Frankfurter's impending retirement so far had remained a secret to the press. Later that day the president released the news of Frankfurter's retirement and announced his plans to nominate Arthur Goldberg in his place. Like Byron White, the highly qualified Goldberg breezed to confirmation, garnering a unanimous vote of approval from the Senate on September 23, 1962.

THE FIRST FORTAS NOMINATION: THE "ONLY MAN" FOR THE JOB

Even before beginning his first full term as president in January 1965, Lyndon Johnson had already settled on his first nominee to the U.S. Supreme Court: his close friend and confidante, attorney Abe Fortas. A brilliant legal strategist, the fifty-five-year-old Fortas had gone directly from Yale Law School to Washington, D.C., where he had served the Roosevelt administration during the New Deal. Later, Fortas built his own law firm, Arnold, Fortas & Porter, into one of Washington's most successful practices.

Fortas had rescued the future president from electoral defeat in 1948; thanks in part to Fortas's forceful legal counsel, Johnson secured what at the time was a highly disputed Senate primary victory. In subsequent years Fortas had emerged as one of his most trusted advisors. When Johnson first assumed the presidency in late 1963, Fortas continued to advise him on a variety of matters, drafting speeches and executive orders. Throughout that period Fortas held no official title on Johnson's staff or in his administration, even refusing Johnson's offer that he head the Justice Department in early 1964.[55] Fresh off his landslide victory in the 1964 general election, Johnson now wanted to place his close friend and advisor on the U.S. Supreme Court.[56]

Unfortunately for the president, there was no vacant Supreme Court seat to be filled. So in the spring of 1965 Johnson began scheming to convince Arthur Goldberg, the newest justice, to step down from the Court and accept a role in his administration.[57] The president offered Goldberg the position of attorney general not long after Fortas turned down the same job.[58] Although Goldberg resisted this initial invitation, Johnson remained convinced that he could tempt Goldberg with some other government post. As early as May 1965, the White House ordered the FBI to conduct name checks for both Goldberg and Fortas, as each was then "being considered for presidential appointment."[59] Later the president sounded out Goldberg's interest in heading the Department of Health, Education, and Welfare.[60] As an extra inducement, he even hinted that Goldberg might eventually become the first Jewish vice president.[61]

Certainly Johnson had Goldberg in mind for any of a number of administration positions even before U.N. Ambassador Adlai Stevenson's unexpected death on July 14, 1965. Scholars credit Harvard economist John Kenneth Galbraith with suggesting Goldberg for Stevenson's old post, essentially to preclude the possibility that the president might tap him instead for the U.N. assignment.[62] Galbraith reportedly told Johnson that Goldberg was dissatisfied with the Court and might accept the United Nations post.[63] Johnson spoke with Goldberg about the U.N. post (and other matters) on as many as five different occasions between July 17 and 20, 1965.[64] Although the junior justice indicated that he was happy on the Court, the president steadfastly insisted that it was in Goldberg's and the nation's best interests that he leave the Court immediately. Spurred perhaps by his own vain belief that he might positively influence policy toward peace in Vietnam, Goldberg eventually succumbed to Johnson's entreaties on July 20. Later that day Johnson announced his plans to nominate Goldberg to succeed Stevenson at the United Nations.

In all this time the president never once wavered from his private determination to name Fortas to Goldberg's seat. Johnson offered the seat to Fortas on two occasions even before Goldberg resigned from the Court. At a White House dinner with Fortas and his wife on July 16 the president speculated aloud that Goldberg might resign and asked Fortas whether he would take the vacant seat.[65] Fortas immediately declined the offer without spelling out specific reasons. Privately, Fortas had three principal reservations to accepting such a nomination: (1) he had only recently assumed a number of extensive financial commitments;[66] (2) he was personally committed to the continued growth and development of his own law firm;[67] and (3) his wife strenuously objected to the nomination.[68]

Undaunted, the president phoned Fortas from Air Force One while flying back from Stevenson's funeral on July 19. Again, Johnson forthrightly told his trusted advisor that he planned to nominate him to the Supreme Court.[69] But Fortas asked the president to hold off making any specific announcement. Writing the president later that day to reject the renewed offer, Fortas cited commitments to his law firm and his desire "to be of service to you and the Johnson family for a few more years."[70] Thus Fortas had unequivocally declined Johnson's offer at least twice even before Goldberg's resignation was even made public.

Nicholas Katzenbach, now Johnson's attorney general, had no specific knowledge of either offer when he first met with the president to discuss the Supreme Court vacancy on July 21. Johnson believed that Fortas would ultimately accept the nomination, but he asked Katzenbach to generate a list of names for the vacancy just in case. Katzenbach recalled telling the president: "Why bother with a list? The person who you really want to appoint to the Court, the one who is closest to you and who is eminently qualified to be on the Court, is Abe Fortas."[71] But Johnson urged Katzenbach to investigate "all possible options."[72]

Katzenbach left the meeting convinced that Fortas was the presumptive nominee. Still, on July 23, 1965, he dutifully submitted a six-page memorandum to the president describing various other candidates worthy of consideration.[73] Katzenbach addressed a number of factors to be considered in choosing a successor to Goldberg, including: the Court's partisan balance (at the time there were five Democrats and three Republicans on the Court); geography (the candidate "should come from the middle, mountain states, border states or New England"); religion ("I think it undesirable for there to be no Jew on the Court for too long"); and age ("Ideally, the appointee should be between 50 and 60 years of age"). He also touched on issues of "judicial philosophy" ("The appointee should reflect you . . . an open-minded, judicious liberal") and background ("[You are] free to choose from the federal and state judiciary, private practice, or the academic world"). Fortas fit most of the criteria quite comfortably; he was a native son of Memphis, a Jew, and fifty-five years old. Before proceeding to other candidates, Katzenbach declared that "from a completely objective viewpoint Abe Fortas has every qualification for the Court. If you did not know him he would be my first recommendation—and still is."[74]

In addition to Fortas, Katzenbach identified eleven other candidates for the president's consideration:

A. Paul Freund, professor (Harvard)
W. Willard Wirtz, secretary of labor
Edward H. Levi, professor (University of Chicago)
Henry Friendly, judge (Second Circuit)
Soia Mentschikoff, professor (Yale)
Eugene Rostow, dean (Yale)
Roger Traynor, chief justice (Cal.)
Joseph Weintraub, chief justice (N.J.)
Walter V. Schaefer, justice (Ill.)
Frank Kenison, justice (N.H.)
Charles Breitel, judge (Second Circuit)

Katzenbach also raised three additional possibilities: (1) Erwin Griswold (dean of the Harvard Law School), (2) Leo Levin (a professor of law at the University of Pennsylvania), and (3) Robert Stern, a former acting solicitor general in the Eisenhower administration and expert on Supreme Court procedure. Describing the three as "able people," Katzenbach still doubted that Johnson would want to "consider any of [the three] seriously at this time."[75] For all fourteen names other than Friendly, the attorney general attached a brief biographical sheet listing their accomplishments, education, and experience.

Katzenbach was clearly seeking a justice in the mold of Felix Frankfurter. Of the eleven names listed, four (Freund, Levi, Mentschikoff, and Rostow) were academics and six (Freund, Levi, Friendly, Rostow, Weintraub, and Breitel) were Jewish. Noteworthy was the near total absence of candidates from federal courts of appeals. While Eisenhower had focused three of his five searches exclusively on judges from those courts, Friendly was the only federal judge at any level to appear on Katzenbach's list. Katzenbach wrote in his memo to Johnson:

> I do not believe there is any present member of the courts of appeals (except for Judge Friendly) who would be regarded as an exceptional appointment. The same, in my judgment, is true of the U.S. district courts.[76]

Judge Friendly was an Eisenhower appointee, named to the Second Circuit in 1959. Remarkably, after four years of Democratic control of the appointment process, not one such judge would merit serious consideration for the Supreme Court. To Katzenbach, who had personally participated in lower court selections during both the Kennedy and Johnson administrations, the most qualified candidates still resided elsewhere: in academic circles, the state courts, and in private practice.

As Katzenbach suspected, Johnson had no intention of considering his lengthy memorandum. Instead, the president planned to use every means at his disposal to persuade Fortas to accept the nomination. As Goldberg summed up the situation to his increasingly anxious group of clerks: "The president says he's going to appoint Abe and Abe says no. *The president won't even consider other names. He's going to wear him down. He'll wait until the end of time.*"[77] The president sought help in this effort from Fortas's original mentor at Yale and in Washington, D.C., Justice William O. Douglas.[78] But Douglas also had little luck persuading Fortas. Issuing yet another "firm refusal," Fortas told Douglas that his "personal affairs would not permit him to leave private law practice at that time."[79] Just as Johnson remained steadfast in his choice, Fortas's refusal seemed equally inflexible.

Finally, Johnson literally "ambushed" Fortas with the nomination on July 28. That same day the president was scheduled to announce plans to escalate dramatically the war effort in Asia. On the way to his press conference, Johnson stated his case simply to Fortas: "I'm going to send your name to the Supreme Court, and I'm sending fifty thousand boys to Vietnam, and I'm not going to hear any argument on either of them."[80] Under the gun, even Fortas was unable to resist the president's powerful appeal. The president had kept his plan to surprise Fortas a secret from even his top aides. Only the day before Katzenbach reported that the Fortas nomination was "not firm" because there was "no consent."[81] Two of Johnson's top aides, Bill Moyers and Joe Califano, had also been left in the dark about Johnson's plan. Hours before the announcement Johnson had ordered Califano to draft a statement announcing the nomination of a new Supreme Court justice, but he refused to be more specific.[82] "Just write a statement that will fit any truly distinguished lawyer and scholar," the president said, "Someone like Clark Clifford, but make it general and leave it blank."[83]

Only in this way did Johnson successfully snare Fortas, the one candidate seriously considered for the vacancy. Replacing one Jewish justice with another made for convenient politics, but religion was hardly a determining factor in this instance. Like Truman, Johnson had gone through the motions of a more formal Supreme Court search. Privately, however, Johnson refused to consider anyone but Fortas, and he executed his single-candidate focused strategy accordingly. The man best equipped to counsel the president on this issue was perhaps Fortas himself. Yet in selecting his first Supreme Court nominee, Abe Fortas's opinion had counted the least of all. On August 11, 1965, the Senate confirmed Fortas's appointment by acclamation.

THE MARSHALL NOMINATION:
MAKING HISTORY . . . ON LBJ'S TERMS

When Archibald Cox announced his plans to retire as solicitor general during the summer of 1965, Judge Thurgood Marshall of the U.S. Court of Appeals for the Second Circuit was one of a handful of candidates the administration considered to replace him. A graduate of Howard Law School, Marshall had risen through the ranks of the NAACP to become one of the most visible legal advocates for the civil rights movement. He ultimately had been responsible for achieving twenty-nine victories in the Supreme Court, including unanimous decisions in the landmark cases of *Brown v. Board of Education* (1954)[84] and *Cooper v. Aaron* (1958).[85]

But Marshall's performance in nearly four years on the federal bench in New York had garnered only mixed reviews. One conservative journalist offered that as a circuit judge Marshall left a record that was "less than awe-inspiring."[86] Others have criticized Marshall for failing to carry his share of the court's load.[87] In fact, despite a lack of familiarity with business and tax issues that made up much of the second circuit's docket, Marshall had written more than one hundred and thirty opinions during his four years on the court. Additionally, none of Marshall's ninety-eight majority opinions had been reversed by the U.S. Supreme Court. Thus more accurately, Marshall had established a reputation as a "solid though unspectacular appellate judge."[88] Yet in recommending Marshall to Johnson, Katzenbach barely made reference to Marshall's judicial service, remarking only that he had served as a judge in "one of the most difficult circuits in the country."[89] Instead, the attorney general placed heavy emphasis on Marshall's background as an attorney for the NAACP. In that role, Katzenbach argued, Marshall might be considered "one of the most distinguished advocates in the nation."[90]

In truth, Marshall's shift to the Justice Department would represent just the first step in President Johnson's carefully conceived plan to make him the first black justice in the nation's history. Exercising uncharacteristic discretion, the president never made any express promise to that effect to Marshall or anyone else. Indeed, by Marshall's account, the president made it clear "over and over again" that there was no connection between his agreement to serve as solicitor general and a future Supreme Court seat.[91] Only after leaving the White House did Johnson admit that while he never told Marshall of his intentions, he had "fully intended to eventually appoint him to the Court."[92] Certainly Johnson could not ignore the personal sacrifice Thurgood Marshall would have to make in accepting his new position. By 1965 Marshall had few financial reserves left over from his relatively meager NAACP salary. Then, after patiently serving for a year in an interim capacity on the federal appeals court, Marshall had finally been confirmed by the Senate for a lifetime appointment with a guaranteed salary of $33,000 per year. As solicitor general, he would have to accept a $4,500 pay cut, and he would be forced to serve effectively at the president's pleasure. Faced with an arguably less severe sacrifice, Paul Freund had declined the same exact offer four-and-a-half years earlier.

At the same time, the solicitor generalship was a prestigious government position. As chief advocate for the United States before the Supreme Court, Marshall would assume responsibility for most federal appeals to the nation's highest tribunal. He would have at his disposal a skilled staff of ten extremely able lawyers. Although no one in the administration had made any express promise of a future Supreme Court seat, Marshall and his wife Cissy carefully surveyed the recent history of the position.[93] According to friend and columnist Carl Rowan, they clearly "smelt a bouquet of opportunities, including a powerful Supreme Court seat."[94] Accordingly, on July 13, 1965, President Johnson announced that his new solicitor general would be Marshall.

According to Randall Bland, in two years of service in the post Marshall at least established a "creditable" record as solicitor general. Unlike some of his predecessors, he refused to farm out clear "losers" to his associates; even so, Marshall won nine of the first fourteen cases he argued. He even proved himself a successful advocate outside of his area of expertise in civil rights. Marshall prevailed in cases involving the SEC and the Clayton Act, in a civil libel action, and in cases involving federal income tax laws.[95]

Even though no high court vacancies appeared imminent, by early 1967 Johnson was again scheming to create one for Marshall. Nicholas Katzenbach had left the Justice Department the previous year to become undersecretary of state. That left Ramsey Clark, son of Justice Tom Clark, as next in line at the Justice Department. Johnson did not rush to promote Clark to be the new attorney general; while Clark served as acting attorney general, the president carefully weighed his options. Among them was the possibility that he might elevate Clark to attorney generalship in hopes of forcing his father off the Supreme Court due to a perceived "conflict of interest."

The president raised that possibility directly to Ramsey Clark during a telephone conversation on January 25, 1967.[96] "You think you could be attorney general with your daddy on the Court?" Johnson asked. "Well, I think that other people ought to judge that," Clark replied, "but I know as far as I'm concerned that would not affect my judgment. I don't think it would affect daddy's judgment." Ramsey Clark believed that—even at the age of sixty-seven—his father was still performing at the peak of his abilities. Under no condition did he want him to resign. Ramsey Clark appealed to the president's political instincts: "In the police community and some other conservative areas dad ranks awfully high . . . for you to replace him with a liberal would hurt you." Yet as was so often the case, the president would not budge. Johnson replied:

> if my judgment is that you become attorney general, he [Tom Clark] would have to leave the Court. For no other reason than the public appearance of an old man sitting on his boy's case. Every taxi driver in the country, he'd tell me that the old man couldn't judge fairly what his old boy is sending up (laughter).[97]

Later in their conversation, Johnson also addressed the subject of appointing a successor to Justice Clark. At this point Ramsey Clark had not yet been named attorney general, and Tom Clark had not resigned. Even so, the president's single-candidate-focused framework was churning away, and it had targeted its one name for consideration: Solicitor General Thurgood Marshall.

Johnson was especially interested in determining how Marshall might line up with the Court's various competing factions.[98] The president viewed Marshall in simplified terms as a "liberal . . . chalk it up there 100 percent of the time." Ramsey Clark disagreed: "There's no doubt as to how he'd vote on civil rights cases, but on crime and other cases he reflects an older generation's attitude." Clark insisted that compared to Black, Marshall would be "considerably less liberal on everything except civil rights . . . he would be more liberal on civil rights than [Hugo] Black has been for two years now."[99] But none of Clark's comments swayed Johnson. In fact, the president seemed almost to delight in Marshall's potential for extreme liberalism. He told Clark, "I think we'd have to put Marshall on the Court. . . . And my judgment is with Hugo Black, Bill Douglas, the Chief, Abe Fortas . . . they'll just have a field day."[100]

The president announced Ramsey Clark's nomination as attorney general on February 28, 1965. Justice Tom Clark immediately announced that he would resign at the end of the current term—he cited a letter he had written to Earl Warren the previous October stating that he would do so under exactly these circumstances.[101] Justice Clark's delayed retirement gave Johnson several more months to reconsider his selection of Marshall. Katzenbach, now an official at the State Department, recalled Johnson expressing some limited doubts about Marshall later that spring.[102] Abe Fortas reportedly suggested that William Hastie would make a better black candidate for the Court. But Katzenbach was no fan of Hastie's and he brought the president back to political reality: "If you're thinking of not putting Marshall on the Court, don't put a black on the Court at all because you'll get absolutely nothing but criticism from the black community if you put Hastie on the Court rather than the hero of black liberals."[103] Katzenbach assured the president that while "Hastie has a better legal mind than Marshall . . . I can also guarantee you that Thurgood Marshall will never, ever disgrace that Court."

Marshall biographers Michael Davis and Hunter Clark report that Johnson also expressed some reservations about Marshall in conversations that March with Joseph Califano, the special assistant to the president.[104] Apparently, the president rattled off the names of other possibilities, including one female, California jurist Shirley Hufstedler. But in the end Johnson always returned to Thurgood Marshall as his first choice for the vacant seat. Months later, on June 13, 1967, Johnson introduced Marshall to the press as his next nominee. The president declared, "I believe he earned the appointment, he deserves the appointment. . . . I believe it is the right thing to do, the right time to do it, the right man and the right place." In fact, Marshall was more than simply in the right place at the right time; he had endeared himself to the president by his service to the administration. Given Johnson's personal approach to Supreme Court selections, it was those personal considerations that mattered most. Although Marshall's nomination ran into some protracted opposition from southern Democrats, the candidate was eventually confirmed by a comfortable 69–11 margin on August 30, 1967.

THE FORTAS AND THORNBERRY NOMINATIONS: ONE LAST GASP FOR PERSONAL POLITICS

At the Court's last conference of the term during the spring of 1968, Chief Justice Earl Warren informed his colleagues that he had made plans to retire that summer. On June 11, Warren sent word through Justice Fortas that he hoped to meet with the president as soon as possible.[105] When the two met on June 13, the chief justice told Johnson that although he remained in fine health, he was seventy-nine years old and had served long enough.[106] In truth, Warren desperately wanted Johnson to appoint his successor; the chief justice did not want to risk leaving that opportunity to his former arch rival and now likely Republican presidential nominee, Richard M. Nixon.

During the course of their meeting only one candidate's name was ever mentioned. The president asked Warren forthrightly, "What do you think about Abe Fortas?" "I think Abe would be a good chief justice," Warren reportedly replied.[107] Johnson's choice of a chief justice thus followed the pattern of his first two nominations: the president never seriously considered more than one candidate for the pending vacancy. During his four years on the bench Fortas had continued to act as a top adviser to the president, attending high-level meetings and drafting speeches and executive orders for Johnson.[108] Thus Fortas had continued to serve the administration, allaying his own original fears that he would not be around to help "if the president were faced with any real troubles."[109] Those same considerations of loyalty, service, and friendship that made Fortas the most compelling nominee in 1965 were equally at force three years later.

Even if Johnson viewed the chief justiceship as somehow transcending personal considerations, he believed he could make a strong case for promoting Fortas on ideological grounds as well. According to Califano, Johnson viewed the Court as a means both of perpetuating his social reforms and of upholding various legislative compromises he had reached on controversial issues ranging from aid for parochial schools to consumer, health, and environmental legislation.[110] Who better to protect the president's legacy than Fortas, who had played a key role in drafting much of that legislation in the first place? By all accounts, the president settled on Fortas immediately after learning of Warren's retirement.[111]

Johnson quickly pushed to shore up key congressional support for his prospective nominee. By the president's thinking, Fortas's confirmation appeared all but certain.[112] After all, the Senate had not rejected a Supreme Court nominee in nearly four decades, and Fortas had been confirmed by acclamation just three years earlier.[113] Still, with this nomination Johnson wanted to play it safe: he feared that even a handful of Republican senators might balk at a Supreme Court nomination so late in the term of a lame duck president. Johnson met with Everett Dirksen (R-Ill.), the Senate minority leader, on the afternoon of June 13. The two men discussed several candidates for chief justice, including Cyrus Vance, Secretary of the Treasury Henry Fowler, and Dirksen's personal favorite for the post, William Campbell, a senior district judge in Chicago. When the president then mentioned Fortas, Dirksen told him, "I could certainly support Abe Fortas on the basis of his record."[114] As far as the president was concerned, Dirksen's approval had effectively eliminated the greatest threat to Fortas's nomination: a minority-led filibuster. Less than a week later Johnson phoned Fortas and told him of his plans to tap him as the next chief justice.[115]

The question of who would replace Fortas as associate justice also received little discussion. Here, too, the president had already identified one candidate alone for the position: Judge William "Homer" Thornberry of the U.S. Court of Appeals for the Fifth Circuit. Johnson had been Thornberry's friend and benefactor for nearly forty years. While campaigning for the Senate in 1948, Johnson had provided helpful political advice to Thornberry, a childhood friend and mayor of Austin who eventually won the House seat Johnson vacated.[116] Then as vice president he had been largely responsible for Thornberry's appointment to the U.S. district court in Texas in 1963.[117] Johnson was so intent on appointing Thornberry to the Fifth Circuit in 1965 that he rushed his name to the Senate without even providing advance notice of the nomination to the ABA's Standing Committee on Federal Judiciary.[118] Later, Thornberry took the oath for his new judicial office at Johnson's Texas ranch. Here was a political clone of LBJ: a moderate-liberal Texan, now fifty-nine years old, who supported civil rights for minorities and liberal protections for free speech.[119]

To Johnson's narrow way of thinking, the choice of Thornberry was also smart politics. The Senate, having twice before approved Thornberry to judicial posts in the past five years, would again be disposed to approve an alumnus of Capitol Hill. He would enjoy the support of a key Democratic southerner, Richard Russell (D-Ga.). (In fact, when told of Thornberry's candidacy, Russell remarked, "that's a man I can enthuse about."[120]) With Texan Tom Clark retiring only the year before, Thornberry's appointment would also restore some geographic balance by bringing a fellow Texan back to the bench. Fortas had been confirmed without trouble in 1965 despite being a close friend and associate of the president. It never even occurred to Johnson that Thornberry (or for that matter, Fortas) could now be rejected on those same grounds.

As with Fortas's prospective nomination, Johnson leaned so heavily towards Thornberry that he barely listened to others' suggestions. On June 22 the president met with Fortas and Secretary of Defense Clark Clifford, two advisors who were normally influential in such matters.[121] Volunteering his plan to choose Fortas, the president indicated his interest in seeing Thornberry replace Fortas as associate justice. Clifford, fearful that charges of cronyism would bury such a ticket, raised warning flags about Thornberry. "The Republicans are convinced they are going to elect the next president," Clifford reportedly warned. "They would probably accept Abe on his own . . . but if his nomination is tied up with Thornberry's I am afraid that they will find some way to sidetrack it."[122] Clifford surely recognized that Fortas's promotion would be Johnson's top priority. As such, he tried to persuade Johnson to replace Thornberry as a means of saving Fortas.[123]

But any persuasive authority Clifford might have wielded with the president disappeared once he suggested that the president nominate a well-qualified, nonpolitical Republican for Fortas's old seat. Clifford identified as one possibility Albert Jenner, a moderate Republican lawyer who was then chairman of the ABA's Standing Committee on Federal Judiciary.[124] The president responded harshly to the suggestion, stating that he wouldn't put any "damned Republican" on the Court.[125] Fortas, who had thus far remained silent during the discussion, endorsed the president's position that a Fortas-Thornberry ticket would survive notwithstanding the upcoming presidential election. Rather than turning to a Republican, Johnson stuck with Thornberry.

That afternoon Johnson met with Attorney General Ramsey Clark to discuss the matter. When word of Warren's retirement first reached the attorney general, he had dutifully worked with Deputy Attorney General Warren Christopher to draw up a list of candidates for the Supreme Court seat.[126] But the president had waited nearly a week before even discussing the nomination with Clark, by which time all crucial decisions had already been made. On the subject of the chief justiceship, the president asked Clark to prepare a memo justifying the appointment of a chief justice so late in the president's term.[127] Regarding the associate justiceship, Clark then suggested four names he had discussed with Christopher:[128] Cyrus Vance; Senator Edmond Muskie of Maine; Henry Fowler, the secretary of treasury; and Albert Jenner, a private practitioner. Clark's list included three prominent Democrats along with Jenner, a Republican. But the president remained committed to Fortas and Thornberry.

Thornberry's nomination ran into more vocal resistance from Larry Temple, the White House special counsel, who now openly challenged his selection to the president. Temple essentially restated Clifford's argument that a Fortas-Thornberry ticket would invite charges of cronyism and cause confirmation difficulties. Johnson now sharply rebuffed Temple, reportedly snapping, "What political office did you ever get elected to?"[129] Apparently, it was Lady Bird Johnson who then rushed to Temple's defense. The First Lady persuaded the president to at least take the temperature of key Senate Democrats concerning potential problems with the Fortas-Thornberry ticket.

Abiding the First Lady's wishes, Johnson sent word of his plan to the two most powerful southern Democrats in the Senate, James Eastland of Mississippi and Richard Russell of Georgia. Like Dirksen, each gave Johnson a response favorable enough so that the president felt he could count on their support.[130] Yet even before Johnson announced the two nominations on June 26, a contingent of senators from outside the Republican leadership had already prepared a bitter attack against the president's selections. Opposition leaders Robert Griffin (R-Mich.) and George Murphy (R-Cal.) drafted a petition opposing any attempt to replace Warren before the November elections. Their document was circulating in the Senate cloakroom at the time of Johnson's public announcement of the appointments.[131]

Notwithstanding his earlier support for Fortas, Dirksen quickly sensed that the president might be opening himself up to charges of cronyism.[132] In fact, those charges soon cast an ominous shadow over the Senate's proceedings, just as Clifford and Temple had predicted. The president had anticipated some objections to the timing of the nominations so near to a presidential election. But no one foresaw the mountain of additional issues that would arise during the Fortas hearings: the harsh criticism of Warren Court rulings that were placed at Fortas's feet; the potential impropriety of Fortas providing continued counsel to the president; and what would became the final nail in the coffin, revelations that Fortas had accepted improper lecture fees for participating in several college seminars. After Democrats' efforts to kill a Senate filibuster failed decisively, on October 2, 1968, Fortas asked Johnson to withdraw his nomination for chief justice, an action that effectively ended Thornberry's candidacy as well. A week later the president announced that he would leave the nomination of a new chief justice to his presidential successor.

A more thorough investigation of the pros and cons of Fortas's candidacy might have foreshadowed the degree to which his nomination was a potential firestorm in the making. But Johnson never instructed his aides to conduct any such investigation, and they had little incentive to research such issues on their own. If Johnson had substituted Thornberry with a prominent Republican attorney, Republican senators would have had the olive branch they were looking for. Instead, the president focused on only two candidates from the outset, and he committed to them both early and decisively. His style of preselecting nominees effectively foreclosed analysis and effective deliberation concerning the range of alternative candidates available to him. It also blinded him to all the potential confirmation difficulties that lay ahead.

CONCLUSIONS

During the 1960s, the political conditions shaping the Supreme Court appointment process continued to undergo dramatic change.

Liberal interest groups, including the NAACP, increasingly demanded that their voices be heard in the nomination process. Democratic control of both Congress and the White House presented a misleading front of united party government: in truth, the New Deal coalition was beginning to split apart. Democrats were suffering from a deep ideological rift between northern liberals and more conservative party members from the South. The Warren Court's liberal activism made it a natural target for conservative politicians of every stripe, including some Democrats. And starting in the late 1960s the confirmation process itself began to serve as a public forum by which opposing interests could air their grievances.

To successfully maneuver through this changing political environment, a president would have to utilize a framework for choosing nominees that was both comprehensive and flexible. The selection mechanisms utilized by Presidents Kennedy and Johnson favored candidates that were well-connected with the highest levels of government. But Kennedy heavily relied on a handful of trusted advisors for advice, and in the case of Byron White's nomination, he appeared open and flexible to a range of possibilities. Even the candidacy of Paul Freund, who had insulted Robert Kennedy by refusing the position of solicitor general, garnered serious discussion. By contrast, Johnson's single-candidate-focused framework was closed in two significant ways. Johnson arrived at decisions on nominees without the benefit of objective counsel from within his own administration. And to make matters worse, he arrived at those decisions so early in the process that he could not account for important shifts in the political winds. This inflexible nomination strategy seemed to work well enough in 1965 and 1967 when the president's political standing remained strong, but it haunted him in 1968 when his own personal agenda was no longer backed by an invincible base of support.

Byron White would serve for thirty-one years on the high court and establish an admirable record as a moderate, nondoctrinaire jurist, frustrating liberals on some issues and conservatives on others. It was Kennedy's nomination of Arthur Goldberg to replace Felix Frankfurter that shifted the Supreme Court's ideological balance decisively in favor of the liberals. Goldberg's tenure was brief, however, as President Johnson enticed him to accept the post of U.S. Ambassador to the United Nations after he served just three years on the Court. In that short time Goldberg made a name for himself with innovative approaches to the law. His concurrence in

NIXON AND FORD

The "Southern Strategy" and
Political Reality

Richard Nixon sought to duplicate the model for Supreme Court selections utilized by his former boss and political mentor, Dwight Eisenhower. Like Eisenhower, Nixon established restrictive criteria in advance that he planned to apply to each vacancy. He also relied heavily on his attorney general and the Department of Justice to canvass the field for candidates who might meet the administration's criteria. Unfortunately for Nixon, his administration confronted a far more contentious political environment than that faced by Eisenhower. Prior to 1967, objections to Supreme Court nominations generally stemmed from problems with the candidate himself: his meager qualifications, questionable political associations, ethical lapses, or some combination of the above. During the confirmation hearings for Thurgood Marshall, however, witnesses got a taste of the new challenge facing nominees, as Marshall was quizzed about his views on the rights of criminal defendants and other hot-button issues. The following year resentment against the Supreme Court as a whole spilled over into Senate hearings considering Abe Fortas's nomination as chief justice. During several days of questioning by senators, Fortas not only had to defend his own questionable activities in office, he was taken to task for the controversial opinions of his Warren Court brethren. On several occasions Fortas was even asked to defend rulings issued before he had arrived on the Court in 1965.

Nixon effectively increased the stakes for all subsequent Supreme Court nominations by making the Supreme Court a central issue in his 1968 presidential campaign against Hubert Humphrey. Blaming the Warren Court for civil unrest, Nixon promised to ap-

point only conservative "law and order" judges who would strictly
interpret the Constitution and not "make law." This law-and-order
theme dovetailed nicely with his campaign's "Southern strategy."
Nixon had already linked his candidacy to southern resentment
against the federal government by furiously opposing busing and
avoiding overt alliances with liberal Republican senators. In emphasizing law enforcement issues during the general election, Nixon
believed he was appealing further to a southern constituency fed
up with liberal Warren Court opinions that had illegitimately expanded defendants' rights. Once he became president, Nixon then
tried to tailor his selection of Supreme Court candidates to further
solidify southern support of his presidency. In particular, Nixon
sought out younger candidates (if possible from the South) with
proven judicial records as "strict constructionists." At the same
time, the president had little interest in appointing close friends or
associates to the Court. Following a path carved out by Eisenhower,
Nixon hoped to distance himself from the emphasis on personal
patronage that appeared to play such a prominent role in the Truman, Kennedy, and Johnson administrations. Nixon was especially
concerned that he not be perceived as awarding close friends or
associates with Supreme Court seats.[1]

Nixon's attorney general, John N. Mitchell, oversaw the nominee selection process during the administration's first term in office.
Mitchell was poorly suited, however, to fill this crucial role for the
president. Nixon's former law partner and campaign manager had
made his name as a bond attorney, providing legal advice on bond
issues to state and local governments,[2] but he had little experience
beyond this immediate area of expertise. Before becoming attorney
general, Mitchell had never worked on issues of criminal law enforcement or any other Justice Department matters.[3] In fact, Nixon's 1968 presidential campaign represented Mitchell's first real
foray into national politics. Although Nixon admired his colleague's
tough, no-nonsense attitude,[4] Mitchell's lack of political instincts
and weak diplomatic skills did his boss more harm than good in
this heated political context.

Not surprisingly, Mitchell and his aides struggled during Nixon's
first term to satisfy the president's numerous political and policy objectives through the appointment process. Initially, they had great
difficulty even finding qualified young Republican judges able to fulfill the president's myriad requirements. Together, the Kennedy and
Johnson administrations had appointed 7 federal judges, more than

twice the number Eisenhower named (322) during a comparable eight-year period. Consequently, when Nixon first came to office there existed a depressingly shallow pool of attractive conservative nominees sitting on the federal bench. In January 1969 there were only four Republicans under sixty years of age serving on U.S. courts of appeals: Francis Van Dusen of the Third Circuit (a fifty-six-year-old Johnson appointee); John Brown of the Fifth Circuit (fifty-nine); Oliver Koelsch of the Ninth Circuit (fifty-six); and David Lewis of the Tenth Circuit (fifty-six). And of the many Republicans then serving on state supreme courts around the country, only two came from southern states, as patronage in the South continued to reside largely with Democratic state party machines.[5] If Nixon truly intended to nominate an experienced Republican jurist from the South, there would be few real options available to him and his administration. Additionally, Mitchell was not willing to accept help from the organized bar in any such canvassing efforts: early in Nixon's first term, the attorney general declared that he would not consult with the ABA about pending Supreme Court nominations.[6]

Thus the obstacles facing Nixon in this decisionmaking context were formidable indeed: Southern constituencies needed to be rewarded; charges of cronyism had to be avoided; a hostile Congress lay in wait, with numerous Democratic senators eager to avenge the Fortas affair; few Republican jurists were available for promotion. Worse still, an attorney general unseasoned in the ways of Washington politics would have to navigate the administration through this increasingly complex political maze. Ironically, the president's selection of Warren Burger as chief justice in 1969 may have gone off too smoothly—the president was perhaps lulled into a false sense of confidence about his own power over the nomination process. If so, by the spring of 1970, much (if not all) of that confidence had dissipated. Soon Nixon would turn for answers to others in the administration besides Mitchell. And the free-for-all that resulted among those advisors proved a far cry from Eisenhower's highly efficient (if unduly streamlined) selection process.

THE BURGER NOMINATION:
A "MEAT AND POTATOES,"
LAW-AND-ORDER CONSERVATIVE

Chief Justice Warren had written to President Johnson on June 13, 1968, that he was retiring from the Court "effective at [his] pleasure."[7] But the political circumstances that surrounded his initial retirement offer soon changed dramatically. Republican senators successfully filibustered Fortas's nomination to succeed Warren, and Nixon won a narrow election victory that fall. Warren remained steadfast in his plans to retire as chief justice,[8] but on December 4, 1968, he agreed to President-Elect Nixon's request that his retirement be delayed until the following June. Nixon thus enjoyed ample time with which to select a new chief justice confirmable by the start of the fall 1969 term.

Dwight Eisenhower actually offered the president his own opinion about the pending vacancy: the former president urged Nixon to nominate Herbert Brownell to the Court's top post, or alternatively, to elevate Potter Stewart to the chief justiceship and nominate William Rogers in his place. Eisenhower's appeal on behalf of his two former aides did not fall on deaf ears. In fact, it appears that despite concerns about Brownell's advancing age (he was now sixty-four years old) and lack of judicial experience, Nixon actually favored nominating Brownell to the post of chief justice.[9] His candidacy encountered opposition, however, from other officials within the new administration. Some feared southern senators would react negatively to Brownell, who as Eisenhower's chief counselor on civil rights had urged the president to send troops to enforce school integration in Little Rock, Arkansas. Indeed, Brownell had gone "out of his way to appoint judges who did not have a record of support for segregation."[10] The point was moot, however, as Brownell quickly declined interest in the position.[11] Throughout December and January he consistently disavowed any interest in joining the Court, just as he had on previous occasions during the Eisenhower administration. Not even the lure of the chief justiceship could pull Brownell away from his lucrative private practice in 1969.

Once Brownell took his name out of the running, Nixon relied on a criteria-driven framework for selection, instructing Mitchell to look for young conservative nominees from "the meat-and-potatoes law schools" located in areas of the country Nixon thought of as his core constituency: the South, the Midwest, and the Far West.[12] For Nixon this would be the first of many attempts to "stick it" to the Ivy League. Mitchell, working with Deputy Attorney General Richard Kleindienst, generated a list of 150 candidates who "merited consideration" for the post based on suggestions from law school deans, powerful constituents, and numerous congressional sources.[13] Mitchell then hand-carried the list over to the White

House, where he and the president pared it down to ten names. Included on the shortlist were two Republican circuit judges from Minnesota—Warren Burger, sixty-one, of the D.C. Circuit and Harry Blackmun, sixty, of the Eighth Circuit—and two southern Democrats: Lewis Powell, sixty-one, of Virginia, a former ABA president from Virginia, and Judge Clement Haynsworth, fifty-six, a South Carolinian sitting on the U.S. Court of Appeals for the Fourth Circuit.[14]

Of these names, Burger's was by far the best known within the administration. Appointed to the federal bench in 1956, Burger was currently the chief judge of the prestigious U.S. Court of Appeals for the D.C. Circuit. He had risen quickly through the Republican ranks in Minnesota after graduating from St. Paul College of Law in Minnesota. To Nixon these strong local ties were an asset to his candidacy. Nor was Burger a product of the northeast intellectual establishment Nixon so despised. Even more important, Burger had cultivated a reputation as an outspoken critic of the Warren Court's decisions favoring the accused, including the controversial 1966 *Miranda* decision. In a well-publicized 1967 speech at Ripon College in Wisconsin, Burger had charged that criminal trials were often unfairly delayed and that courts had become bogged down with excessive appeals and gratuitous defense tactics. Nixon later contacted Burger to inform him that the Ripon speech would provide a basis for some of his campaign positions the following year.[15]

Burger also benefited from his own long-standing friendship with Herbert Brownell. In 1956, Eisenhower's attorney general had helped place Burger, at the time an assistant attorney general, on the D.C. Circuit, and the two men had remained in close contact ever since.[16] Brownell also fully subscribed to Burger's conservative judging philosophy. In a 1965 letter to former president Eisenhower, Brownell called Burger "a leader among federal judges" in espousing two fundamental positions: (1) that federal courts should not interfere with the judgments of elected representatives in matters of national security, and (2) that federal courts should not "cripple the power of law enforcement agencies in obtaining confessions from suspected criminals."[17]

No shrinking violet, Burger had commented occasionally to Brownell about the possibility of his one day receiving a Supreme Court nomination. In fact, with Nixon leading in the polls in October 1968, Burger launched a full-fledged campaign on his own behalf. He wrote Brownell:[18]

I know you have many loyalties and demands on you and I shall never embarrass you with any request of mine. But the Midwest (from Ohio to the Rockies is a hell of a lot of USA!) is not represented on the "top-side" & ought to be. [*sic*]¹⁹ Before RN gets firmly fixed I hope that thought will be put to him. I have never known him well and probably suffer some guilt by association. But last year he wrote me spontane-ously on my Ripon College criminal justice speech . . . hence he is not unfriendly. . . .

The following spring Burger learned for the first time that Justice Potter Stewart was receiving serious consideration for the chief justiceship. Of his perceived rival Burger now wrote:[20]

> If the news stories on Potter have any basis at all, someone ought to do a close check on *all* the bad 5–4 holdings and take note of how many of those had him in the 5 and sometimes 6. *Witherspoon*[21] and the Cali-fornia pornography case are just two recent examples. It just *can't* be that they could be serious. . . .

Burger insisted that the only sure way to predict future votes was to name a judge who had already served long enough for a "philo-sophic pattern" to be discerned.[22] Reviewing the potential pool of judges available to Nixon, Burger concluded: "there is really far too small a list of real prospects. . . . There do not seem to be many Arthur Vanderbilts in the state system."[23]

Astutely, Burger began to carve out a substantial role for himself as an advisor to the Nixon administration on matters of judicial administration. In February 1969 he met with Richard Kleindienst to recommend nominees for two vacancies on the D.C. Circuit.[24] Burger also met with the president's top aide, John Ehrlichman, to discuss new proposals for the federal courts. Showing little hu-mility, Burger even provided Nixon with another copy of his now famous Ripon College speech.

To be sure, other candidates enjoyed their own influential sources of support. Senator Ernest Hollings (D-S.C.) personally urged Mitchell to consider Clement Haynsworth for the chief jus-ticeship.[25] Lewis Powell's candidacy was touted by the influential Senator Harry Byrd (D-Va.) among others. Yet Burger enjoyed the critical support of Brownell, whose opinion carried great weight with Nixon. In early May both Mitchell and Nixon had sought Brownell's comments on a number of candidates then under con-sideration for the chief justiceship. But Brownell reserved special praise for his friend and former Justice Department colleague, Warren Burger.[26]

In May, suggestions for alternative candidates flooded in from all sides. White House aide Pat Buchanan urged Nixon to name Justice Harlan, now sixty-nine, to the Court's top spot despite rumors of his failing health.[27] Leonard Garment urged Nixon to elevate Byron White to chief justice and then nominate Burger or Judge Henry Friendly to the vacant associate justice seat. Garment believed this strategy would benefit Nixon the most "from the standpoint of symbolism and drama."[28] Yet to Nixon and Mitchell, Burger and Stewart remained the most compelling candidates for chief justice.[29] The tide turned irrevocable in Burger's favor on April 30 when Stewart asked Nixon to remove his name from consideration for the post of chief justice. Given the circumstances of Fortas's recent withdrawal, Stewart told Nixon "this was simply not the time for a sitting justice to be appointed chief justice."[30] Burger's nomination became a virtual certainty on May 15 when Abe Fortas—suffering beneath a new ethical cloud[31]—announced his decision to retire from the Court. With an additional vacancy at hand, Nixon was assured that he could also name a southerner soon enough to replace Fortas.

On May 19, 1969, Nixon and Mitchell formally settled on Burger as chief justice. The president told his staff that he intended to make the announcement some time that week.[32] Nixon had already decided against addressing the two vacancies at once.[33] Instead, the president planned to dramatize Burger's appointment alone with a live, evening-time announcement.[34] Once all FBI and other security checks were complete, Mitchell and Nixon met separately with Burger on the afternoon of May 21. Later that evening the president introduced Warren Burger to the press as his nominee to be chief justice.

The nomination proved a surprise to some. Although Burger had been mentioned prominently as a candidate in most media reports, several leading congressmen continued to believe that Stewart would be promoted to the Court's top post.[35] The announcement also took ABA officials by surprise; as Mitchell promised, the country's leading organization of lawyers had played no role whatsoever in the administration's prenomination screening process.[36] In his press announcement Nixon stressed Burger's background and his "unquestioned integrity throughout his private and public life,"[37] which was perhaps an attempt to zing Fortas for his recent ethical difficulties. Burger himself termed the nomination "a tribute to all of the sitting judges of the federal and state systems. . . ."[38]

In reality, Warren Burger had carefully nurtured his ties to the Republican Party since the early 1950s. He had campaigned to fill the vacant seat, flooding Herbert Brownell with suggestions about his interest in the post, then cultivated a high profile with key administration officials. Burger was not just in the right place at the right time after Warren's retirement: he was the beneficiary of his own strategically formed political relationships and associations. Nixon, fresh off victory in a national election, wanted to nominate a strict ideological conservative. The ardently conservative Burger enjoyed the enthusiastic support of White House officials and outside advisors.

On June 9, 1969, the full Senate confirmed Burger as the new chief justice by an overwhelming 74–3 vote. Nixon and Mitchell may have misinterpreted his easy confirmation as a sign that any nominee with proper judicial credentials and some personal distance from the president would enjoy smooth sailing in the Senate. As both men soon learned, nothing could be further from the truth.

THE HAYNSWORTH NOMINATION:
THE "SOUTHERN STRATEGY," PART ONE

When Abe Fortas announced that he would resign from the Court on May 15, Nixon immediately set his sights on nominating a conservative from the South as his replacement. As a sign of his steadfast commitment to that principle, the president privately refused to even consider a northerner for the new vacancy.[39] Youth would also be a more important consideration than it had been in Burger's case. The president informed his aides that he hoped to pair the sixty-one-year-old Burger with a younger nominee, hopefully "someone in their late forties and no older than sixty."[40]

A faithful adherence to the president's instructions would in all likelihood bring an end to the so-called Jewish seat on the Court.[41] In reality, there was little support within the administration for continuing this tradition, which dated back to Brandeis's appointment in 1916.[42] Speechwriter William Safire was one of several Jews on the White House staff urging Nixon *not* to make religion an issue in the appointment process.[43] Given Nixon's interest in shoring up support among conservatives, an emphasis on Jewish candidates also might backfire politically. As conservative columnist James J. Kilpatrick warned, merely considering a large number of Jewish candidates might cause the administration to be charged with perpetuating a form of reverse discrimination.[44]

In June Mitchell returned to the same ten-person shortlist he had dutifully compiled when considering the chief justice vacancy. Ironically, the two most prominent southerners on the list were both Democrats: Lewis Powell and Clement Haynsworth Jr.[45] Yet both men epitomized the conservative bona fides Nixon claimed to be seeking. Powell had made the attorney general's shortlist despite a lack of judging experience, in large part due to his impeccable credentials. A name partner in the Richmond, Virginia firm of Hunton, Williams, Gay, Powell & Gibson, he had served at one time as president of the American Bar Association and as president of the American College of Trial Lawyers. As chairman of the Richmond School Board Association, he had won a reputation as a moderate accommodationist after crafting a peaceful resolution to the thorny problem of school desegregation. More recently, Powell had decried the "crisis in law observance" and thus had established himself as a tough proponent of public order. As a member of President Johnson's Commission on Law Enforcement and the Administration of Justice,[46] Powell had openly criticized Supreme Court decisions such as *Miranda,* which he felt unduly limited reasonable law enforcement activities. Unfortunately, Powell's age represented a significant obstacle: like Burger he was sixty-one years old.

Haynsworth was five years younger than Powell. Although nominally a member of the Democratic Party, Haynsworth had openly supported every Republican candidate for president beginning with Eisenhower in 1952. Since receiving his nomination to the Fourth Circuit in 1956 he had amassed a generally conservative record on the bench. Haynsworth enjoyed the enthusiastic support of Harry Dent, a South Carolinian who had moved from Senator Strom Thurmond's staff to the White House in order to provide a "white southerner's perspective."[47] Additionally, Senator Ernest Hollings (D-S.C.) was prepared to act as Haynsworth's prime sponsor on the Hill.[48] At a meeting with the president on May 28, Hollings argued that Haynsworth "had brought the Fourth Circuit to the highest degree of administrative efficiency that the court has ever enjoyed."

Despite his age, Powell may have been the president's first choice for the seat. The point was rendered moot, however, when the Virginia lawyer informed the administration in early June that he no longer wished to be considered for a Supreme Court nomination. Lacking any other viable alternatives, Mitchell endorsed Haynsworth's candidacy, and Nixon's approval of the choice soon followed. Here was a candidate who met Nixon's strict request for a conservative federal appeals judge from the South, and he was still young enough to serve on the Court for another two decades. As Nixon would later explain, Haynsworth was quite simply the "best judge of that age group."[49]

The Justice Department stepped up its investigation of Haynsworth, reviewing his tax returns and other potential sources of conflict. At the end of June, Mitchell met with Haynsworth at a Fourth Circuit conference in Virginia to discuss the state of his financial investments.[50] As it had done with Burger, the FBI also conducted its own investigation of the candidate, reporting back that the judge had been an ardent supporter of the FBI and was "definitely in favor of law and order."[51] But Mitchell's policy against prenomination involvement by the ABA remained firm: the administration refused to submit Haynsworth's name to the ABA for prior consideration. Justice Department records revealed one source of concern about Haynsworth: the Textile Workers' Union had raised a conflict of interest charge against the judge in 1963 based on his participation in a case involving Deering Milliken & Co.[52] Mitchell notified Nixon of the problem in early August, just as the screening process for Haynsworth was nearing its conclusion. Mitchell himself decided that the allegations were overblown. The chief judge of the Fourth Circuit had cleared Haynsworth of all charges, and Attorney General Robert Kennedy had decided at the time that the charges were without foundation. Select members of the Democratic leadership also offered shows of support for Haynsworth. Senator James Eastland (D-Miss.), chairman of the Senate Judiciary Committee, assured the president that if nominated, Haynsworth would be confirmed. Senator Hollings added his own assurances on the matter.[53] Nixon also checked with key Republican senators about Haynsworth and concluded that the GOP was "fully locked" to support him.[54] Senate Minority Leader Everett Dirksen (R-Ill.) lent his own critical support. Nixon fully expected that once he had submitted Haynsworth's name to the Senate, an alliance of Republicans and southern Democrats would guarantee him a quick, carefree confirmation.[55]

The president called Haynsworth on August 16, 1969, to formally offer him the post. He told the judge not to worry about the conflict of interest inquiry, offering that he would "kill that bird" at the time of his nomination announcement.[56] Nixon was at the time unaware that the AFL-CIO had been amassing a large file on Haynsworth ever since the Deering Milliken case. Labor lawyers were actively preparing to make a case against the judge on ideological grounds, contending that he had shown an anti-labor bias on the bench. For Haynsworth's opponents, Deering Milliken was to be "Exhibit 1." On August 18, two days after his conversation with Haynsworth, Nixon confirmed for the press that he planned to nominate Haynsworth to serve as associate justice of the Supreme Court. Almost immediately, Haynsworth's nomination drew fire not only from labor groups, but also from the NAACP and other civil rights organizations that criticized the judge's allegedly anti-liberal and anti-civil-rights stands. Such attacks had been anticipated by the administration, although few in the Justice Department expected them to stand in the way of confirmation.

Despite the ideological objections offered, opponents of Haynsworth's confirmation made the most headway by trotting out evidence that he had *twice* as a judge shown a lack of propriety by participating in cases where he had a financial interest: first, in the Deering-Milliken case and second, in a case involving the Brunswick Corporation.[57] In neither case did the judge commit any technical legal violations; but the pattern of ethical insensitivity reeked too much of the charges that the Justice Department had offered against Fortas just a few months earlier. Political scientist Henry Abraham summarized the dilemma of many senators: "How could the Senate confirm Haynsworth when it had played such an admirable activist-moral role in causing Fortas's resignation?"[58] The opposition included Democrats led by Senator Birch Bayh (D-Ind.) and Senator Joseph Tydings (D-Md.). But Republican senators were also instrumental in defeating Haynsworth. Among them were Robert Griffin (R-Mich.), Fortas's arch-nemesis from a year earlier, and Jack Miller (R-Iowa). On November 21, 1969, the Senate rejected Haynsworth's nomination by a 55–45 vote.

In the post mortems on Haynsworth's nomination, Nixon placed principal blame on Mitchell for mistakes made in the early selection stages, while blaming Bryce Harlow for his ineffective handling of the confirmation process.[59] Nixon faulted his attorney general in particular for "not having all the facts" and "for coasting on assurances from Eastland and Hollings instead of really working. . . ."[60]

Certainly the administration's poor management of the confirmation process harmed Haynsworth's confirmation chances in the end. After forwarding the nomination to the Senate, the White House had failed to provide pro-Haynsworth and undecided senators with the necessary information to counter charges of ethical insensitivity in the press. A belated shift to aggressive hardball tactics also may have proved counterproductive.[61] But flaws in the selection process also doomed Haynsworth, as Nixon correctly suggested. Mitchell did have the facts, at least with regard to the Deering-Milliken case; his mistake was to minimize their significance in light of how ethical conflicts had so recently forced Fortas's resignation. In the final analysis, the propriety issue forged a public link between the Haynsworth and Fortas cases that was certain to redound unfavorably for the administration in the confirmation process. No less than thirteen senators who voted against the Haynsworth nomination publicly attributed their opposition to the events surrounding Fortas.[62] The administration's next nominee would have to be ethically pure, not just legally above board.

In defense of Mitchell, the attorney general was also hamstrung by the president's insistence on a rigid, criteria-driven framework for nominee selections. The pool of candidates able to meet all the president's criteria was a strikingly small one. Mitchell's insensitivity to the political backlash that might greet Haynsworth was in part spurred by the precarious position in which the administration found itself. Powell's decision to withdraw his own name from consideration had left Haynsworth as one of the few candidates left who could meet all of Nixon's various and sundry requirements. Other qualified candidates were neglected simply because they could not measure up to any one of Nixon's filters for geography, age, judging experience, and conservatism. To expect a candidate to meet all those requirements—and then meet heightened ethical standards—may have been too much for the administration to expect.

THE CARSWELL NOMINATION: FURTHER SOUTH AND FURTHER TO THE RIGHT

As the Haynsworth affair drew to its unsuccessful conclusion in November 1969, the Nixon administration was already trying to reap some political benefits in its aftermath. In campaigning for

Haynsworth, the Nixon administration had publicly demonstrated its loyalty to the South, and southern senators from both parties had rallied to the administration's side. Nixon could have responded to the Haynsworth debacle by loosening the rigid demographic criteria that had propelled forward Haynsworth's candidacy in the first place. Instead, Nixon chose to dig his heels in further. Apparently the president was now committed to finding a good federal judge from "even further South" and who was further to the right.[63] History seemed to be in Nixon's favor, as no president had seen two consecutive Supreme Court nominees defeated in nearly seventy-five years.[64]

It is not clear who in the administration first recommended fifty-year-old G. Harrold Carswell, a newly minted judge on the U.S. Court of Appeals for the Fifth Circuit, for the reopened vacancy. A native of Georgia, Carswell had been a federal district judge in Northern Florida for eleven years before being promoted to the federal appeals bench in May 1969. One noted legal scholar credits endorsements from Chief Justice Burger and William Rogers, Nixon's new secretary of state, as propelling Carswell's name to the top of administration lists.[65] Carswell had once served as U.S. Attorney for Northern Florida in the 1950s. From that position in the Justice Department, he had reported to both Burger and Rogers. Attorney General Mitchell also backed Carswell's candidacy. In truth, the administration's remaining shortlist had grown bare of suitable southern candidates. Besides, Mitchell saw in Carswell everything the president wanted: a young, conservative southerner with ample judging experience, including a brief stint on the U.S. Court of Appeals. And as a former prosecutor and trial judge, Carswell seemed ideally suited to sell the president's "law and order" theme.

Asked to review Carswell's file, the Justice Department turned up no ethical controversies of the type that had buried Fortas and Haynsworth. Officials were also encouraged that Carswell had survived Senate scrutiny as a judicial candidate less than a year earlier. In truth, Carswell's appointment to the Fifth Circuit had been far from carefree. His promotion had caused "substantial rumblings from civil rights sources,"[66] including the Leadership Conference on Civil Rights, a coalition of over one hundred labor and civil rights organizations. The Conference submitted a memorandum to a Senate subcommittee in June 1969 asserting that Judge Carswell had displayed a "strong bias against Negroes asserting civil rights claims."[67] Mitchell surely was aware that civil rights groups might again challenge some of his rulings concerning school desegregation.[68]

Despite these early warning signs, the Justice Department conducted a hasty investigation of Carswell. Mitchell asked Assistant Attorney General William Rehnquist to only briefly screen Carswell's legal work. Hoping to make the case for Carswell, Mitchell ordered Rehnquist to gather any evidence that Carswell had demonstrated at least a "balanced view" on civil rights and labor issues.[69] Rehnquist's final memorandum was hardly persuasive on this point.[70] Yet amazingly, Nixon's prenomination screening of Carswell's legal and political record proceeded no further. In the White House, Egil "Bud" Krogh, a special deputy assistant to the president, met briefly with Carswell in mid-January.[71] In light of the recent investigation of Carswell for his Fifth Circuit nomination, the candidate's name was never resubmitted to the FBI for another political clearance. Still recovering from the Haynsworth fiasco, Justice Department officials had focused all of their energies on finding evidence of any possible ethical lapse by Carswell. Convinced that his record was unstained in that regard, Nixon forwarded Carswell's nomination to the Senate on January 19, 1969.

White House aide William Safire later called the Carswell nomination "one of the most ill-advised public acts" of Nixon's early presidency.[72] Opponents of Carswell discovered a damaging statement Carswell made to a meeting of the American Legion on August 2, 1948, while running for a seat in the Georgia legislature. Carswell had at that time declared, "I yield to no man as a fellow candidate or as a fellow citizen in the firm, vigorous belief in the principles of White supremacy, and I shall always be so governed."[73] Although the nominee now disavowed the statement, other incidents soon cast doubt on Carswell's objectivity in racial matters. While a U.S. attorney in Florida, Carswell had been involved in the transfer of a public, municipally owned Tallahassee golf course built with federal funds—a transfer designed to circumvent a contemporary Supreme Court decision proscribing segregation in municipal recreation facilities. Carswell had also signed an affidavit chartering a booster club for the Florida State University football team limited in membership to any "white person."

Thus the selection of Carswell did little to lessen feelings of hostility toward the White House that were already simmering in the Senate. One GOP senator saw the Carswell nomination as Nixon's attempt to belittle the Court and to "rub the Senate's nose in the mess it has made of the Haynsworth nomination."[74] In this growing atmosphere of hostility, false rumors and misunderstandings only fed the opposition's frenzy.[75] And the administration's careless screening procedures allowed each revelation to take the administration by surprise. Mitchell's investigation apparently failed to turn up Carswell's damaging 1948 campaign speech. The Justice Department was also unaware of both the country club incident and the booster club affidavit. As John Massaro noted, "the discovery and disclosure of these incidents by opponents of the nomination rather than by the Justice Department further embarrassed the White House and contributed to undermining the nomination effort."[76]

Finally, Republican senators resented being urged to support a controversial nomination by an administration that had not carefully checked out the nominee's background. Carswell's unsure standing in the legal community did not provide them with much reassurance. The ABA's inquiry of Carswell—initiated only at the request of the Senate Judiciary Committee—resulted in the ABA Committee rating him merely "qualified." Even some legal scholars who had backed Haynsworth refused to support Carswell on strictly professional grounds. These included Professor William Van Alstyne of the Duke Law School, one of the foremost constitutional experts in the country. Moreover, as a district court judge Carswell's reversal rate had been among the worst in the country. The overwhelmed Mitchell viewed Carswell's reversals as a sign of principled conservatism; Van Alstyne read the same statistics as evidence of inadequate legal reasoning. Whether justified or not, senators from both sides of the aisle soon conceded that Carswell possessed only mediocre credentials for the Court.[77] On April 8, 1970, the Senate rejected Carswell's nomination by a 51–45 vote.

At least one scholar would later characterize Nixon's choice of Carswell as one in a series of so-called spite nominations that had followed the defeat of presidents' first-choice nominees.[78] (Owen Roberts and Douglas Ginsburg were the others.) Under this theory, Nixon used the nomination to pursue a strategy of vengeance intended to (1) "hold the constituency that had mobilized behind the initial nominee" (in this case the conservative South); and (2) "force the Senate into a posture of ironic acceptance of a second-choice nominee possessing professional credentials widely perceived as inferior to those of the original nominee."[79] In retrospect, Carswell's nomination would have been ridiculed had it been the administration's first choice; when viewed in the wake of Haynsworth's rejection, it now seemed like an act of political suicide by a frustrated administration.

This "spite" interpretation seems misleading, however, when applied to Carswell's case in particular. Notwithstanding Nixon's fiery rhetoric, Justice Department officials may not have understood that Carswell's credentials were so far inferior to Haynsworth's. Before them stood a long-time federal district court judge, with substantial experience as a federal prosecutor in Florida. In fact, Carswell's nomination to the federal appeals court in 1969 rounded out what appeared on the surface to be a sterling career in the law. Mitchell and his aides certainly could be faulted for not going far enough below the surface. However, claims that Carswell's credentials were "inferior" or "mediocre" came to Nixon's attention only later, after the nomination had already been placed before the U.S. Senate. Additionally, the Justice Department did not accidentally "stumble" upon Carswell as part of a search designed to recruit "controversial" or "provocative" candidates. In truth, he was one of only a handful of candidates in existence who was able to meet each of Nixon's stringent requirements for nominees. Carswell was young, conservative, a federal judge, and from the South. And on several critical legal issues—busing, the rights of the accused and civil rights—his positions seemed perfectly in line with those held by the administration.

In essence, Carswell's nomination followed in the tradition of the Whittaker nomination, facilitated by a litany of hoops and rigid political filters defined in advance by the administration in power. Unfortunately for Nixon, his own administration's criteria for nominees had stunted what should have been a comprehensive and effective selection process. Once again, the attorney general had been exposed for his lack of political savvy and sensitivity in dealing with an increasingly hostile political environment.

THE BLACKMUN NOMINATION: A COMPROMISE FROM THE NORTH

Following Carswell's defeat, a bitter President Nixon declared on April 9, 1970, that the Senate as "presently constituted" would not approve a southern conservative. Nixon considered waiting to nominate an even more conservative southerner after the midterm elections that fall, but ultimately he yielded to political reality and public cries for a Supreme Court acting at full capacity.[80] Nixon still promised to nominate a strict constructionist, preferably from a federal court. This time, however, he promised to seek only candidates from outside the South.[81] It was Nixon's obvious attempt to link the administration with southern political interests as shared victims of a politicized confirmation process.

If the Senate subsequently rejected a nominee hailing from the North, the president's charges of regional discrimination might ring false. Accordingly, Nixon sought a northern judge who posed little risk of confirmation failure. Among the ten finalists on Mitchell's original list had been Harry Blackmun, sixty-one, a judge on the U.S. Court of Appeals for the Eighth Circuit. Others included two federal district judges: Edward T. Gignoux, fifty-three, of Maine and Alfred T. Goodwin, forty-seven, of Oregon. Blackmun's candidacy enjoyed several advantages over the others. Of the three jurists mentioned, only Blackmun had served on an appellate court. Blackmun also enjoyed the hearty endorsement of his childhood friend, Chief Justice Warren Burger. Burger and Blackmun had grown up together in St. Paul, and each had served in key advisory capacities with the Mayo Clinic during the early 1950s. Blackmun had even been the best man at Burger's wedding. Finally, Blackmun had the support of two of Mitchell's closest friends, Herschel Friday, a bond lawyer from Little Rock, and Pat Mahafey, a fellow judge with Blackmun on the U.S. Court of Appeals.[82] The attorney general spoke to Blackmun on April 9, the day after Carswell's defeat.

Nixon wanted Burger's assurances that Blackmun was at bottom a strict constructionist. Blackmun's record on the Eighth Circuit provided ample evidence of a conservative judicial philosophy. His most visible and controversial ruling on civil rights had come in *Jones v. Alfred Mayer Co.* (1965),[83] a civil rights case pitting a black couple against a subdivision developer who had refused to sell them a house because of their race. Writing for the majority, Blackmun refused to view the 1866 Civil Rights Act as effectively creating an "open housing guarantee." Judge Blackmun had also issued tough rulings in a number of high-profile, criminal cases. In 1960, he ruled that prosecutors need not show criminal intent for charges involving only a light penalty.[84] Three years later Blackmun became the first circuit judge in the country to uphold the constitutionality of the 1961 federal antiracketeering law.[85]

Blackmun was not a rigid conservative, however. Thus liberals too could find comfort in some of his opinions. Unlike Carswell and Haynsworth, Blackmun consistently upheld district court orders demanding that school officials in Arkansas move forward with desegregation measures. In the controversial *Mayer* case Blackmun had spoken in a measured tone: confessing that he was tempted to find in the plaintiff's favor, he reasoned only that an "inferior tribunal" was not entitled to make such a complete doctrinal break from the past. Blackmun had even suggested that the Supreme Court might later find merit in the black couple's claim.[86] And in law enforcement matters, where he had forged an overwhelmingly conservative record, Judge Blackmun had drawn the line against the harsh treatment of prisoners. In one opinion he struck down as unconstitutional the use of a leather strap as a disciplinary device in Arkansas prisons.[87]

Mitchell met with Blackmun on April 10 to discuss his views and background and to root out any potential sources of conflict.[88] In this case it appeared that "the sheer exhaustion of the Senate after two draining rejections of prospective justices, coupled with the perceived ideological compromise evident in the choice of Blackmun," would assure him a relatively easy confirmation.[89] This time, Mitchell's instincts proved correct. On April 13, Nixon announced his nomination of Blackmun to the Supreme Court, his third attempt at filling Fortas's vacated seat. Blackmun's hearings before the Judiciary Committee lasted less than a day, as no organizations or interest groups actively opposed him before the Senate.[90] Finally on June 9, 1970, a tired Senate confirmed Blackmun's appointment to become the nation's 102d Supreme Court justice by a 94–0 vote.

THE POWELL AND REHNQUIST NOMINATIONS: A TUSSLE WITH THE ABA, AND SOME LAST-MINUTE SCRAMBLING

Hospitalized by a fatal blood disorder, Justice Hugo Black of Alabama informed Nixon on September 17, 1971, that he planned to retire from the Supreme Court effective immediately. The case for the nomination of a southern conservative nominee now appeared more compelling than ever: Black's departure left the South without representation on the Supreme Court for the first time in the twentieth century. Yet to nominate a conservative from the South, Nixon would again have to confront many of the same political obstacles that had frustrated him before. Senate Republicans had gained just two seats in the 1970 election, leaving the party at least five votes short of a majority.[91] With only fourteen months until the next presidential election, another delay in confirmation might prove fatal to the administration's efforts to appoint a southern conservative. Pat Buchanan warned Nixon that his failure to move fast might even encourage Democrats to reprise Senator Robert Griffin's argument from 1968, that a "new president should name the Court's new members."[92]

A welcome surprise for Nixon came three days later when Chief Justice Burger informed Mitchell that Justice Harlan also planned to announce his retirement from the Court within the week.[93] Mitchell urged Nixon to consider both vacancies together. As a matter of confirmation strategy, the administration could perhaps balance a consensus "heavyweight" nominee with a more controversial southern conservative.[94] By contrast, White House aides urged the president to submit the more controversial nominee (presumably the southern conservative) first for consideration. As Bud Krogh argued:

> this strategy would avoid the Senate being able to go with the easiest nominee and delaying action on the weak one, thus making it more difficult for us to refute allegations of racism or, quite bluntly, from denying them the *time* necessary to make a public case against a man. The longer these procedures drag out, the more difficult it is for us to get our man through.[95]

Based on postmortems conducted after the Carswell affair, the Nixon administration had already taken steps to revamp its nominee selection process. Specifically, the president was determined to avoid the embarrassment of continued last-minute disclosures. After Carswell's defeat, Lawrence Walsh, a well-known ABA official, traded correspondence with Mitchell in the hope of avoiding such mishaps in the future.[96] Eventually, Mitchell agreed for the first time to send a final list of candidates to the ABA for its comments and opinions before the formal nomination was announced.[97] In a memo to John Ehrlichman, Bud Krogh had also proposed expanded screening procedures for nominees. He assumed the Justice Department would continue to take the lead on all "substantive selection matters," including the generation of all names, review of opinions or speeches, and FBI background checks. Krogh worried, however, that those investigations were insufficient to elicit all the information necessary to ensure a smooth confirmation process. He thus proposed the creation of a White House committee to "debrief" each prospective candidate, probing every facet of his or her "professional life, personal life, trips, etc."[98]

Nixon adopted most of Krogh's proposals during the fall of 1971. White House aide John Ehrlichman assumed the task of overseeing White House prenomination screening procedures. Field interviews would be conducted by former Domestic Council member David Young and the current counselor to the president, John Dean. As a protégé of Henry Kissinger, Young had only recently become commander of the White House special investigative unit known as the "plumbers."[99] Dean, a former official in the Justice Department, was perhaps ideally suited to coordinate efforts with the attorney general and his staff. Under this new regime, both the White House and the Justice Department would share responsibility for the screening of Supreme Court prospects.

Once Harlan's retirement was confirmed, Nixon targeted nominees for two distinct Supreme Court vacancies. The president wanted another hard-line southern conservative for the first vacancy—a law-and-order, strict constructionist who would appeal directly to the old segregationist South. But Nixon was now willing to forego the requirement of judicial experience, as long as that nominee could still be confirmed. Freed of that rigid filter, a number of new candidates emerged as administration favorites.

Representative Richard Poff (D-Va.) seemed "made to order" for the first vacancy. Poff had cultivated for himself a strict law-and-order reputation while serving on the House Judiciary Committee. In 1956 he had signed the "Southern Manifesto" opposing desegregation, a sure sign of his appeal to his Nixon's southern base of support.[100] Yet unlike Carswell and Haynsworth, Poff also stood to benefit from his position as a member of Congress; in particular, he enjoyed the support of many moderate congressmen who had worked closely with him on the Hill.[101] And at forty-seven years of age, he was young enough to serve for the remainder of the century and beyond. Poff was already being considered by the administration for a seat on the U.S. Court of Appeals for the Fourth Circuit[102] and had so far received clearance for the lower court judgeship by both the FBI and the ABA right before Hugo Black tendered his resignation.

Pat Buchanan was Poff's chief supporter in the White House.

On September 20, Buchanan presented his case to Nixon in strictly political terms:

Poff has already gone through the laborious clearances; it would be exceedingly difficult for Democrats in the Senate to reject one of their own from the Hill. Indeed, if they did, it would clearly put the Democrats in the position of anti-southern bias—fix them in that posture for the coming election. The president might even be able to get a massive bipartisan House resolution endorsing Dick Poff's nomination—to pressure the Senate.[103]

But rumors of Poff's potential candidacy elicited mixed reviews in Congress. Senator Hubert Humphrey (D-Minn.) told reporters that he did not think much of the qualifications of "anyone" who had signed the Southern Manifesto. Buchanan belittled Humphrey's comments, noting that such a rule would eliminate "Sam Ervin, Bill Fulbright, Russell, etc. and some 50 others."[104] He told the president that "Poff has gotten a good review from the *New Republic,* and is getting some fairly good ink from responsible liberals."[105] Then, with rumors of Poff's appointment circulating around Washington in late September, civil rights leaders began to mobilize against his prospective candidacy. Clarence Mitchell of the NAACP and Joseph Rauh of the Leadership Conference on Civil Rights publicly declared their opposition to Poff, citing his record of hostility to civil rights legislation.[106] Another liberal interest group, the Americans for Democratic Action, charged that Poff had failed to meet the criteria of legislation he himself proposed in every Congress since 1959, which would have required five years of prior judicial experience or ten years of law practice before service on the Supreme Court.[107] Such a large degree of mobilization against a candidate who had still not been formally designated as a nominee was unprecedented.

To deflect unwanted attention away from Poff, administration officials encouraged speculation about candidates for the other open seat. Buchanan urged Nixon to name to this second seat a conservative who is a "Judiciary Committee type . . . the most distinguished strict constructionist we can find, a real heavyweight in everyone's eyes."[108] One possibility was Elliot Richardson, the well-respected secretary of health, education, and welfare. Richardson, fifty-one, boasted sufficiently impressive credentials for the Supreme Court. A former attorney general of Massachusetts, he had clerked both for Learned Hand and Felix Frankfurter. Irving Kristol suggested Edward H. Levi, who was then the president of the University of Chicago. A renowned legal scholar, the sixty-year-old Levi had the support of highly respected moderates in the administration, including Patrick Moynihan and Peter Peterson.[109] The president meanwhile had other ideas for the second vacancy. With Poff's name percolating as a possibility for the "southern seat," Nixon hoped also to satisfy additional demographic groups before the 1972 election. Levi was Jewish, but Nixon still showed little interest in restoring the Jewish seat.[110] He also spurned Buchanan's suggestion that he nominate an Italian-American.[111] Instead, Nixon was eyeing a place in American history as the first president to nominate a female justice to the U.S. Supreme Court. Such an idea may have first originated with First Lady Pat Nixon, who had been urging her husband to appoint a woman to the Court since 1969.[112] The president seemed almost to delight in the dilemma a female nominee would cause for liberals in the Senate. Nixon first told H. R. Haldeman that he wanted to find a "good, tough, conservative" woman for the Court: "while many people would be opposed to it, nobody would vote against [us] because of it."[113] Then on September 26 Nixon instructed Mitchell to find a conservative woman judge for the Court.[114]

Already frustrated by Nixon's rigid criteria for the other vacancies, Mitchell reluctantly pressed ahead to fill these strict new orders. Within just two days he had produced a tentative list of thirteen female candidates:[115]

Sylvia Bacon, judge (D.C. Superior Court), Republican
Constance E. Cook, assemblywoman (N.Y.), Republican
Martha Griffiths, U.S. representative, Democrat
Margaret Heckler, U.S. representative, Republican
Shirley Hufstedler, judge (Ninth Circuit), Democrat
Cornelia Kennedy, judge (district of Michigan), Republican
Jewel Lafontant, private practitioner, Republican
Mildred Lillie, judge (California Court of Appeals), Democrat
Soia Mentschikoff, professor (University of Chicago), Democrat
Constance Baker Motley, judge (southern district of New York),
    Democrat
Dorothy W. Nelson, dean (University of Southern California),
    Democrat
Ellen Peters, professor (Yale), Democrat
Susie M. Sharp, justice (North Carolina Supreme Court), Democrat

Clearly Mitchell had not limited the pool to ardent conservatives. The list featured eight Democrats, including two (Hufstedler and Peters) whom he described as having "mixed political leanings" and three (Mentschikoff, Motley, and Nelson) that he termed "very liberal."[116] Only two Democrats on the list (Sharp and Lillie) were deemed true "conservatives." And of the five Republicans listed, only Cornelia Kennedy possessed even minimal judicial experience.

By the end of September the selection process was proceeding along two separate fronts: a "southern front" and a "female front." As to the former, Nixon was still leaning towards Poff, although he awaited the ABA's more extensive review of Poff's credentials. On September 28 Nixon met with the Republican congressional leadership to plot strategy. Hugh Scott (R-Pa.), the Senate minority leader, estimated that Poff would lose between thirty-one and twenty-six votes.[117] The president admitted only that Poff was still under investigation by his aides; while the nominations remained an "open question," he assured them that "one will be a southerner." Regarding the second vacancy, Scott indicated his belief that a female candidate would be readily approved. The president did not hide his distaste for the pool of female candidates under investigation, referring to those on the current list as "a bag of bags." Still, he echoed Scott's sentiments, suggesting that no senator would oppose a female candidate so long as she could "read or write." The president speculated that Chief Justice Burger might object to a female justice given the "close and tight" court life. Perhaps in jest, he also asked whether a female justice would even be safe around Justice Douglas.[118]

Poff's candidacy encountered considerable trouble even before he had been formally offered the nomination. Near the end of September critics began to question Poff's limited legal experience. Fearing a lukewarm endorsement from the ABA, Deputy Attorney General Kleindienst submitted a ten-page letter to the ABA's Committee on Federal Judiciary, arguing that Poff's experience as a congressmen qualified him professionally for the Supreme Court.[119] The early mobilization of interest groups against Poff had not phased Bud Krogh, who viewed the tactic as a sign that the opposition was "leading from a position of weakness."[120] Others in the administration were not so sure. Leonard Garment warned Nixon that Democrats and various interest groups could find a number of effective rallying points against Poff, including his support of the Southern Manifesto, his opposition to civil rights legislation, and his "very limited legal experience."[121] Appealing to the president's political instincts, Garment told Nixon:

> A far more basic danger results from the wholly unpredictable consequences of even a moderately-protracted confirmation fight. The fundamental issue for 1972 is the economy. . . . [A]n emotional fight, centering on racial issues, angering Democrats, dividing Republicans and distracting key administration officials from their main substantive efforts would jeopardize this effort. . . . [T]he question is whether the gain from this particular appointment at this particular time justifies the major risks and the certain dangers it carries with it. I personally doubt that it does.[122]

With the ABA now dragging out the review of his qualifications, Poff withdrew his candidacy from formal consideration on October 2.[123] However, Poff's decision lacked the moderating effect that Garment was hoping for. Apparently, Nixon now briefly considered nominating Vice President Spiro Agnew, a Maryland native, to the Supreme Court. Informed by Ehrlichman that the Senate would "clobber" Agnew, Nixon quickly backed off.

The president then told Haldeman he wanted "to get someone worse than Poff and really stick it to the opposition now."[124] According to his chief of staff, Nixon actually toyed with nominating the Senate Majority Whip, Robert Byrd (D-W.Va.), to the Court.[125] After the ambush of Poff, the nomination of Byrd, fifty-three, of West Virginia, would have been a bold counterpunch. Nixon thought Byrd was everything the liberals hated: "a former KKKer," even "more reactionary than [George] Wallace."[126] As a conservative Democrat, Byrd was actually to the right of the White House on a number of social issues.[127] As a Supreme Court justice, Byrd might be even tougher than Poff on capital punishment, law-and-order issues, and school busing. Yet Byrd's legal credentials were notably slim. Having earned a law degree from American University while serving in the U.S. Senate, Byrd had never before practiced law. Even Attorney General Mitchell thought the president went too far in suggesting Byrd as a candidate for the Supreme Court.[128] As a leading Senate Democrat, though, Byrd at least offered the realistic possibility of quick confirmation.[129]

Meanwhile, the Justice Department reduced the original list of candidates for the "female front" to four: Heckler, Kennedy, Lillie, and Peters.[130] Mitchell told Nixon that he personally favored

Mildred Lillie, fifty-six, then serving as a judge on California's Second Appellate District Court since 1958. For the "southern" slot, discussions among Nixon, Mitchell, and Ehrlichman focused on three candidates: Byrd, Senator Howard Baker (R-Tenn.), and Mitchell's close friend from Arkansas, Herschel Friday. Nixon reaffirmed his interest in Byrd, incorrectly telling Mitchell that Justice Frankfurter had never "practiced" law prior to being named to the Supreme Court.[131] Senator Baker was a moderate alternative to Byrd. Meanwhile Mitchell touted Friday as an "Arkansas Harlan."[132] Friday had represented the Little Rock, Arkansas, school board in opposing the integration of Central High School. Nixon ordered Mitchell to have specific recommendations ready for him by October 15.[133] Meanwhile, the Court began its Fall 1971 term that same week with only seven justices presiding.

Mitchell spoke with Friday and Lillie in the days that followed. Dean and Young were also active in the selection process, interviewing candidates referred to them by Mitchell.[134] The Justice Department was especially thorough in its investigation of Friday, who had never before been investigated for a job in public service. Based on his meeting with Friday, Assistant Attorney General William Rehnquist submitted to Mitchell a seven-page memorandum detailing the possible bases for opposition to his candidacy.[135] Rehnquist anticipated three objections to Friday's nomination: (1) his record on civil rights, both as an attorney and as a country club member; (2) his membership with an "establishment" law firm that had represented clients opposed to desegregation; and (3) the total lack of any record of public service in his background.[136] Rehnquist responded as best he could to each objection and then assessed the situation for Mitchell:

There can be no doubt that both civil rights and labor partisans would be disappointed by the nomination of Friday, and would probably make some sort of effort to defeat his confirmation. Our experience with past nominees shows that these two groups together cannot successfully defeat a nominee unless they are able to unfurl some banner other than their own under which they can enlist some of the more middle-of-the-road members of the Senate. In the Haynsworth debates, they used conflict of interest and with Carswell the combination of "mediocrity" [and] some rather thin evidence of hostility to Blacks. . . . From what we can tell now there is no such outside rallying point in the case of Friday.[137]

Without actually endorsing Friday, Rehnquist reminded Mitchell that "the faster the administration moves on these nominations, the better will be its chance of obtaining confirmation."[138] Dean and Young were more pessimistic: they feared Friday was "too much like Carswell" to stand much of a chance in the Senate.[139] Mitchell's support for Friday never wavered.

Eager to make the two nominations quickly, Nixon met with Mitchell and Ehrlichman again on Monday, October 12. The attorney general's tentative recommendation now was for Lillie and Friday, although he added two other names to the mix: (1) Sylvia Bacon, a D.C. trial judge and former Justice Department lawyer who had worked on the district's crime bill; and (2) Charles Clark of Mississippi, a Fifth Circuit judge who had risen to prominence defending Mississippi Governor Ross Barnett against contempt charges.[140] Nixon remained interested in Byrd, hoping to let Senate liberals in the Senate "eat him up for a while . . . they're afraid they'll have to vote on him." But in the end, Nixon resolved to follow Mitchell's lead and name Friday and Lillie as the administration's two Supreme Court nominees later that week.[141]

On October 13 Nixon and Ehrlichman crafted a plan to sell Friday and Lillie to the public. There would be two press announcements: Friday would be announced the first day, Lillie the next. As for Friday's lack of judicial experience, Nixon planned to stress that he had "more years of active practice than any other present member of the Court." Lillie offered the perfect contrast, with "more service as a trial court judge than all the present [justices] combined."[142] Given the administration's previous agreement with the ABA, however, it first needed to submit their names to the organized bar for review. The submitted list included the two prospective nominees, Friday and Lillie; three more controversial figures, Byrd, Bacon, and Clark; and Paul Roney, the Fifth Circuit judge who had replaced Carswell after his abortive run for the Senate in 1970.

Word of the list soon leaked to the press, and its full contents made all the morning papers on October 14. Dismay quickly arose from all sides of the political spectrum. Columnists Rowland Evans and Robert Novak called the six candidates "uniform in both mediocrity and acceptability to the segregationist South."[143] Senator Edward M. Kennedy (D-Mass.), denouncing the list as "one of the great insults to the Supreme Court in its history," claimed that Nixon sought to "undermine one of the basic and vital institutions of our nation . . . the Supreme Court as an equal partner of government."[144] Nixon's top two choices for the Court received harsh attacks as well. Liberals depicted Friday as the "chief architect" of the Arkansas school boards' resistance to desegregation during the 1950s and 1960s. Professor Laurence Tribe of the Harvard Law School discovered that Lillie had been overruled by the Supreme Court unanimously in several key cases.

The president was outraged by the ill-timed disclosures. Meeting with Ehrlichman that morning, he wondered aloud whether Justice Department officials might have leaked the story.[145] Despite the protests, Nixon stubbornly planned to forge ahead, instructing Mitchell to submit Lillie and Friday's names to the FBI, and then prepare to announce their nominations within the next few days.[146] The president also ordered Mitchell to discontinue the short-lived practice of submitting names of prospective nominees to the organized bar.[147] Yet even some close Nixon allies were offended by the list, and they soon made their opinions known within the administration. Prominent among them was Chief Justice Warren Burger. In a "personal and confidential letter" to Mitchell the day before, Burger had argued against appointing a woman "simply because she was a woman."[148] Instead, he urged the administration to consider Lewis Powell and Federal District Judge Frank Johnson of Alabama. Meeting with Mitchell on October 15, the chief justice even threatened to resign from the Court if the president failed to appoint justices "more distinguished" than those on the current list.[149]

On October 18, Nixon learned the ABA had voted 6–6 that it was "not opposed" to Friday, while Lillie had been deemed "unqualified" by an 11–1 vote. Now thoroughly frustrated, Nixon ruled out nominating a female justice altogether. The president was determined not to reward his "enemies," and yet he remained convinced that he could "never find a conservative enough woman for the Supreme Court."[150] Shifting gears, Nixon asked Ehrlichman to have his White House staff canvass the government for a qualified candidate from the South who was readily confirmable. The task of generating new names had now effectively shifted from Mitchell's Justice Department to the White House bureaucracy.

At Ehrlichman's request, Bud Krogh and David Young compiled a list of senators from southern and border states for the first vacancy.[151] They identified six possible candidates from the group:[152]

Howard Baker, Senator (R-Tenn.)
Lloyd Bentsen, Senator (D-Tex.)
Thomas Eagleton, Senator (D-Mo.)
Edward Gurney, Senator (R-Fla.)
David Gambrell, Senator (D-Ga.)
Marlow Cook, Senator (R-Ky.)

Of the six, Howard Baker was viewed as the most attractive option. Ehrlichman reminded Nixon of Burger's suggestion that he once again consider Lewis Powell for a seat on the Court. Powell's age (sixty-four) posed the greatest concern. Additionally, Powell himself had previously rejected interest in a Supreme Court bid. On October 19, Mitchell twice telephoned Powell to see if he would accept the last-minute nomination. Each time Powell refused the attorney general's offer.[153] Finally, the president called Powell personally, telling him it was his duty to accept the nomination.[154] Eventually Powell relented, accepting Mitchell's offer on the afternoon of October 20.[155]

Nixon considered naming one of two individuals to the second seat: either Howard Baker or Judge William H. Mulligan, fifty-three, of the U.S. Court of Appeals for the Second Circuit.[156] At Nixon's request, Mitchell sounded out Baker's interest in the vacancy on the morning of October 20, even before Powell had accepted.[157] But Baker asked for a day to think about the offer; specifically, he wanted to consult with his close friend, Justice Potter Stewart. Meanwhile Richard Moore, the White House Special Counsel, threw a wrench into the process that same day when he recommended that the president nominate William H. Rehnquist, forty-seven, to this second vacancy.[158] Nixon saw in Rehnquist a genuine stalwart conservative with sterling credentials: Rehnquist had finished first in his class at Stanford Law School and had clerked for Robert Jackson, the justice Nixon once referred to as "the only good appointment" Roosevelt ever made.[159] More recently, Rehnquist headed the prestigious Office of Legal Counsel in the Justice Department. Other high-level aides shared a high opinion of him, including Ehrlichman (a law school classmate of Rehnquist's) and Rehnquist's own boss at the Justice Department, John Mitchell. By the time Baker called back the next morning, Nixon had already shifted his focus to Rehnquist.

The president introduced Powell and Rehnquist as his Supreme Court nominees in a nationally televised press conference on the evening of October 21. The Senate easily confirmed Powell by a 98–1 vote on December 6. Rehnquist's confirmation hearings were much more contentious. The assistant attorney general had aroused the ire of senators for his frequent criticism of student demonstrators and his public attacks on the Warren Court. Eventually though, Rehnquist's superlative credentials overcame the opposition. The Senate confirmed Rehnquist by a 68–26 vote on December 10, 1971.

Nixon's criteria-driven selection process caused his administration considerable embarrassment and humiliation. And in the final analysis, a desperate president was forced to compromise on some of his original criteria to avoid further humiliation. The pool of candidates had thus been expanded to include more worthy figures. Had this pool been expanded at the outset—with more loosely defined criteria at work—the administration might have better served the political causes that it was trying to promote. And if the president had replaced Mitchell with a seasoned veteran of Washington politics, rather than encouraging a disorganized free-for-all among aides and outsiders, he might have accomplished those objectives without having to expend so much political capital in the process.

THE STEVENS NOMINATION: THE POLITICS OF CONCILIATION

In 1970 Justice William O. Douglas became the target of impeachment charges in the House of Representatives. House Minority Leader Gerald Ford (R-Mich.) had spearheaded the impeachment drive, formally introducing a resolution urging a full impeachment investigation against the Court's most senior member.[160] Once the charges were dismissed later that fall, Douglas became emboldened, determined to stay on the job "until the last hound dog ha[s] stopped snapping at my heels."[161] But just five years later, poor health finally forced Douglas from the Court. And fate now wielded a cruel touch of irony for Douglas: President Gerald Ford, his former protagonist, would have the opportunity to nominate his successor.

Ford had assumed the presidency in 1974 without the electoral mandate most chief executives normally enjoy. He had become vice president only after Spiro Agnew resigned in disgrace in 1973. A year later he became the unlikely successor to Richard Nixon, forced from office by the Watergate affair. After his controversial pardoning of Nixon in late 1974, Ford struggled with limited success to secure public approval of his presidency. By November 1975, Ford's approval rating stood at 41 percent, a full twenty points below ratings President Nixon had enjoyed during his own nomination battles over Haynsworth and Carswell.[162] With the Democrats holding a twenty-four-seat margin in the Senate, and the presidential election now less than a year away, only a moderate with impeccable credentials would be able to survive confirmation. Even conservatives seemed to appreciate the precariousness of Ford's political position.

Determined to avoid a confrontation with the Senate over Supreme Court nominations, Ford emphasized two strategies for nominee selection. First, he planned to involve the ABA early in the selection process. Second, he would delegate the responsibility for managing the selection process to a well-respected attorney general whose reputation transcended party politics. Ford would eventually employ the first "open" framework for selecting candidates since the Kennedy administration's deliberations over Charles Whittaker's replacement in 1962. Naturally, confirmability would be an important consideration, but Ford did not let that factor unduly restrict his administration's recruitment efforts at the outset.

Most of the critical selection responsibilities would rest with Ford's new attorney general, Edward H. Levi. If the president wanted to politicize the nomination as Nixon had done, Levi would have been as poorly suited to the task as Mitchell. The former professor and dean at the University of Chicago Law School had been only marginally active in Republican politics. Prior to heading the Justice Department, Levi's most substantial public service experience had occurred during a Democratic presidency: between 1940 and 1945, he had served as a special assistant to the attorney general in the Roosevelt administration. In his autobiography, Ford recalled asking Levi what the "Department of Justice needs most."[163] "A nonpolitical head," Levi had reportedly replied.[164]

Neither Ford nor Levi was caught off-guard by Douglas's retirement. Justice Douglas had suffered a stroke on New Year's Eve the year before, hospitalizing him for nearly three months. He returned to the Court at diminished strength in late March 1975. In May the *Wall Street Journal* reported that the justice was no longer writing opinions;[165] Douglas's left side was still partially paralyzed by the stroke, and his left arm was completely immobilized. As the Fall

1975 term began, Douglas seemed barely able to participate in the Court's work.

Aware that the justice might not survive the term, Ford asked Levi that Fall to generate a list of highly qualified potential candidates for the Court that he thought "worthy of consideration."[166] The president's directive was striking for its lack of rigid criteria or other filters. Certainly Levi knew that Ford, a prime mover in the campaign to impeach Douglas, did not want a liberal activist who "made law" from the bench. Otherwise, Levi enjoyed virtually free reign to search for qualified candidates. On November 10, 1975, just two days before Douglas made public his plans to retire, Levi forwarded a tentative list of eighteen candidates to the president:[167]

Arlin Adams, judge (Third Circuit)
Philip Areeda, professor (Harvard)
Robert Bork, solicitor general
Bennett Boskey, private practitioner
Alfred T. Goodwin, judge (Ninth Circuit)
Robert P. Griffin, Senator (Michigan)
Philip Kurland, professor (University of Chicago)
Vincent Lee McKusick, private practitioner
Dallin Oaks, president (Brigham Young University)
Paul H. Roney, judge (Fifth Circuit)
Antonin Scalia, assistant attorney general
John Paul Stevens, judge (Seventh Circuit)
Philip Tone, judge (Seventh Circuit)
J. Clifford Wallace, judge (Ninth Circuit)
William H. Webster, judge (Eighth Circuit)
Charles E. Wiggins, U.S. Representative (Cal.)
Malcolm Wilkey, judge (D.C. Circuit)
James H. Wilson, private practitioner

No person over sixty years of age was included on the list, an indication that youth had also been a significant factor in Levi's calculus.[168] The attorney general then promoted eleven leading names from the larger list and ranked them in three groups, the first of which would receive his "greatest emphasis":

FIRST GROUP
Dallin Oaks
John Paul Stevens
Robert Bork

SECOND GROUP
Arlin Adams
Vincent McKusick

THIRD GROUP
William Webster
J. Clifford Wallace

UNRATED
Paul Roney
Alfred Goodwin
Robert Griffin
Charles Wiggins

Levi included short biographies of the first seven candidates in his memo to Ford. He also attached biographies of Roney and Goodwin, though he offered that neither would be "up to the high standard you have suggested."[169]

In summarizing the merits of each individual candidacy, Levi provided more commentary about Stevens and Adams than the others. The attorney general described Stevens, a fellow Chicagoan whom he had known for years, as a "judge of the first rank, highly intelligent, careful and energetic . . . a moderate conservative."[170] According to Levi, Stevens's opinions "lack the verve and scope of Judge Adams's but are more to the point and reflect more discipline and self restraint." Levi also thought Adams's opinions revealed a "certain weakness . . . in being willing to sometimes by-pass or go beyond the most careful analysis." Levi had much less to say about either Oaks or Bork, the two other candidates in his "first group." He did take note of Bork's conservative credentials, remarking that the solicitor general "would provide strong reinforcement to the Court's more conservative wing."[171]

Ford's private notes provide additional insights into his own thinking about the prospective nominees.[172] The president apparently crossed Oaks's name off the list early on, noting in the margin that a member of the Mormon church might bring a "confirmation fight." Roney was eliminated for reasons that are less clear. Based on his reading of the candidates' biographies and his discussions with Levi, the president firmly ranked nine remaining candidates on Levi's list as follows: (1) Stevens, (2) McKusick, (3) Adams, (4) Bork, (5) Goodwin, (6) Webster, (7) Griffin, (8) Wiggins, and (9) Wallace.

Justice Douglas sent his formal letter of resignation to Ford on November 10. That same day Levi forwarded his list of eleven candidates (including the four unrated ones) to the ABA with a request that all comments be returned to the administration by November 17.[173]

As it turned out, Levi may have submitted his list to the ABA a bit prematurely. The selection process was still in its early stages when the ABA began its formal review; Levi had not yet even tested the political waters. The day after Douglas's retirement, rumblings occurred within and outside the administration about whether Ford might name the first female justice in history. As the press began to openly speculate about the possibility,[174] two separate lists of female candidates were generated by Barbara Greene Kilberg, an associate counsel to the president, and Patricia Lindh, a special assistant to the president for woman's programs in the White House Office of Public Liaison.[175] Various groups and individuals had recommended thirty-three women candidates in all to replace Douglas.[176] First Lady Betty Ford also publicly urged the appointment of a woman to the Supreme Court.[177]

Unfortunately, Levi had already submitted a list of all male candidates to the ABA. The attorney general had also failed to give key Senate Democrats the chance to voice their preferences for the vacancy. On November 14, Ford himself called the chairman of the Senate Judiciary Committee, James Eastland (D-Miss.), to sound out his thoughts on the nomination. Eastland strongly recommended Judge Charles Clark of the Court of Appeals for the Fifth Circuit, a member of the infamous "list of six" that Nixon had submitted to the ABA four years earlier.[178] Once the *New York Times* reported the full contents of the eleven-man list, Levi's omissions seemed even more glaring. Trying to appease the administration's critics, Douglas Bennett, the director of the president's personnel office, urged White House Chief of Staff Richard Cheney to submit a brand new list to the ABA. Bennett hoped that a "president's list" might later be distinguished from the earlier "attorney general's list."[179] But Levi had already taken action to remedy his errors, submitting a revised list to the ABA several days later. The attorney general's new list included two female candidates: Carla Hills, the secretary of housing and urban development, and U.S. District Judge Cornelia Kennedy of Detroit.[180] It also included three additional federal appeals judges: Charles Clark, Malcolm Wilkey, and Philip Tone.[181]

Most of these changes were of course window dressing; little had changed in the minds of either Ford or Levi. Privy to the president's thinking, First Lady Betty Ford declared on November 19 that she was "not as hopeful" as she had been before that her husband would nominate a woman to the high court.[182] Only one candidate dismissed earlier reemerged during the final week of selection: Judge Philip Tone of the U.S. Court of Appeals for the Seventh Circuit.

By November 25, several ABA and FBI reports were still pending on specific candidates. Meanwhile, Philip Buchen, the counselor to the president, finished his own narrow screening of the original eleven candidates. Buchen focused special attention on Stevens.[183] For political reasons, Ford was especially interested in Stevens's positions on environmental questions; but the three environmental cases in which Stevens participated revealed no hostility by the candidate either way to corporations or regulatory agencies.[184] On November 26, Levi informed Buchen that three candidates from the original list were now in the ABA's "first category": Adams, Tone, and Stevens.[185] Levi spent the remainder of his memo touting Stevens. He felt that Stevens's opinions did not substantiate charges that he was "soft on crime," and he praised Stevens's conservative dissent in the infamous "long hair case."[186] What explains the emergence of Adams, Tone, and Stevens in the final threesome? Dallin Oaks was dropped out of fears of confirmation fight. A Bork nomination similarly posed a serious confirmation risk.[187] The situation called instead for a more moderate conservative. Adams, Tone, and Stevens apparently fit the bill, and each had survived the ABA's scrutiny with the highest possible rating.

Levi deserves considerable credit for influencing Ford's final choice of Stevens. The attorney general first became acquainted with Stevens when they had served together on the staff of the House Judiciary Subcommittee in the early 1950s. Stevens had later taught part time at the University of Chicago Law School when Levi was the dean. According to Ford, the final decision eventually came down to two candidates, Adams and Stevens.[188] Ford reviewed opinions written by both jurists and, drawn to Stevens's clear style of writing, he concluded that Stevens was "a more appealing jurist."[189] Thus on November 28, Ford informed the press that he planned to name Stevens as an associate justice of the U.S. Supreme Court.

For the next three weeks Stevens played the role of a "nonpartisan nominee" to perfection. His testimony before the Senate Judiciary Committee was described as "deft, cautious and fairly forthcoming," as Stevens was reasonably careful not to express views on any controversial policy questions.[190] In selecting Stevens, Levi and Ford had focused on the "craftsmanship" in his opinion writing as well as his various analytical skills. Those nonideological qualities now gave Democratic senators little to complain about. On December 17, 1975, the Senate confirmed Stevens by a 98–0 vote.

CONCLUSION

In choosing Supreme Court nominees during their respective presidencies, both Nixon and Ford relied heavily on attorneys general to canvass the field of possible candidates, generate lists of candidates worthy of consideration, and to make specific recommendations. Why then did the two administrations' selection mechanisms seemingly produce such markedly different political results? The battle over Abe Fortas's nomination in 1968 had ushered in a new and more contentious era for Supreme Court appointments. Divided government became a reality in the early 1970s, with senators assuming an increasingly hostile posture against presidential nominees. Enhanced media attention of the process followed. Interest groups, including an increasingly assertive professional bar, jockeyed for position to influence each vacancy. Even more critical was the role President Nixon played in exacerbating these tensions. During the 1968 campaign Nixon declared war on the Warren Court. In doing so, he raised the ideological stakes for each of the appointments that followed.

To maneuver most effectively through this complex political environment, a president would have to rely on a combination of factors: more reasonable expectations from his supporters, decisionmaking flexibility, and highly qualified subordinates. On all three counts, Nixon's failures contrasted markedly with Ford's success: Richard Nixon viewed the selection of justices as a critical component of his administration's overall approach to law enforcement and as a key pillar in its "southern strategy." Hoping to transform the Court's direction, he emphasized the ideological (and political) views of his nominees. Nixon also used his selection process as a means of appealing to certain constituencies. Candidates for the Court were expected to survive a number of carefully delineated filters based on age, experience, demographics, and judicial philosophy. Flexibility was considered a vice, not a virtue in this decisionmaking calculus.

To execute this overtly political selection strategy, Nixon relied heavily on John Mitchell, a close friend and colleague from his former legal practice with limited experience in Washington politics. Mitchell was ill-equipped to carry out the tasks before him. Predictably, the Nixon administration's selection process was soon plagued by poor judgments and mishaps. Success in the 1968 election may have blinded Nixon to the limits of popular tolerance: his campaign rhetoric notwithstanding, Nixon's victory had not afforded him a mandate to name extreme conservative nominees. Confirmation difficulties were inevitable given this context. Following Mitchell's failures over Haynesworth and Carswell, Nixon expanded the selection mechanism to include other aides within his administration. The attorney general now battled with Bud Krogh, John Ehrlichman, Pat Buchanan, and Leonard Garment to influence the process. Eventually he staked his claims with Herschel Friday and Mildred Lillie, each of whom became sources of public embarrassment to an already reeling administration. In the end, Nixon stumbled upon Powell and Rehnquist during a haphazard rush to fill vacancies in 1971.

By contrast, President Ford held few expectations that he could make a dramatic Supreme Court appointment in late 1975. In fact, Ford strove to reduce the level of political conflict in the nomination process. Although he also relied on an attorney general unseasoned in the ways of Washington, Edward Levi's apolitical makeup proved an asset given Ford's priorities. The attorney general restored the role of the organized bar in the process of preselecting nominees. And Levi enjoyed what amounted to an open-ended grant of authority to suggest candidates "worthy of consideration." The attorney general was never limited by a laundry list of demographic and other nominee criteria. Nor did Levi feel compelled to compete with Philip Buchen, Dick Cheney, or any others in the administration for influence. In the final analysis, his lack of experience in partisan politics proved far less debilitating in an open selection environment where quick confirmability represented the president's chief nomination priority.

SIX

REAGAN'S PURSUIT OF CONSERVATIVE IDEOLOGUES

R onald Reagan arrived in Washington in January 1981 sporting an especially ambitious social agenda. Backed by many of his most vocal and articulate followers, the new president strategically targeted a number of Supreme Court decisions from the past two decades.[1] Among the most controversial rulings were those that: banned bible readings in public schools;[2] included some pornography within the First Amendment's protections;[3] approved busing as a means of facilitating racial integration of the schools;[4] required more rigid procedures to protect the rights of the accused;[5] and upheld certain affirmative action programs.[6] During his 1980 presidential campaign, Governor Reagan had directed his fiercest criticism of all at the Court's decision in *Roe v. Wade*,[7] which created a limited right to abortion. With a solidly Democratic House of Representatives in place, even incremental legislation in support of Reagan's social policies was considered unrealistic.[8] Accordingly, administration officials soon directed their attention instead at influencing judicial action directly by fundamentally changing the political makeup of the courts. Early in Reagan's first term the selection of conservative judges at all levels of the federal judiciary assumed its place as a central element in his administration's overall political strategy.

Generally speaking, Reagan took a hands-off approach in most policymaking areas,[9] and judicial appointments would be no exception. As to lower court appointments, the president voiced general goals only, relying on a working group of White House and Justice Department officials to identify persons qualified to serve as district and circuit judges. In this respect Reagan resembled most of his

White House predecessors who had similarly left the politics of staffing lower courts to qualified subordinates.[10] Where Reagan differed from past presidents, however, was in his hands-off approach to Supreme Court nominations. Keeping his distance from most details of the process, Reagan participated actively only in the final stages of Supreme Court nominee selection. Even Dwight Eisenhower, who had granted Herbert Brownell broad authority to manage the selection of high court nominees, played a more active role in the initial stages of the selection process than did Reagan.

At no time was President Reagan tempted to choose nominees whom he knew personally; nor would he override the judgments of others in screening prospective candidates. This was a criteria-driven selection framework to be sure, but the most important criteria were ideological. In short, the Reagan administration wanted to sponsor ardently conservative candidates for the high court. One additional filter entered the process briefly in 1981, when Reagan expressed interest in nominating a female to the Court. Yet even in that instance, the president encouraged his attorney general, William French Smith, to exercise broad discretion in determining the manner by which that promise might be kept. The president's receptiveness to candidates from a broad range of backgrounds opened the door for Sandra Day O'Connor, an Arizona state judge and former state legislator. In 1986 and 1987 Reagan left it to Smith's successor, Edwin Meese III, to identify the most qualified conservatives available for two additional vacancies on the Court. Both Smith and Meese had the freedom to canvass the field for ideological conservatives from any geographic region. Age was a concern, but unlike with Eisenhower and Nixon, the administration did not impose on his subordinates any fixed minimum or maximum at the outset that might preclude the consideration of especially worthy candidates.

Reagan's bureaucratic approach to choosing Supreme Court nominees made possible a considerable degree of advance work by subordinates. Smith and Meese had the latitude to initiate deliberations over Supreme Court selections even before any particular vacancy had arisen. The Reagan administration thus enjoyed the critical advantage of time; top officials did not have to wait for a formal presidential declaration to narrow down the pool of candidates to a select group of finalists. Still, if Truman and Johnson were guilty of not listening to objective counsel on such matters, perhaps Reagan risked going too far in the opposite direction. Reagan's

hands-off management style ultimately encouraged a dispropor-
tionate amount of conflict among advisors within his administration, each clamoring for influence over the final selection outcome.

THE O'CONNOR NOMINATION:
ONE CAMPAIGN PROMISE KEPT

Attorney General William French Smith was by all accounts the
driving force behind the nomination of Justice Sandra Day O'Connor in 1981. The Harvard-educated Smith had been a senior partner with the Los Angeles law firm of Gibson, Dunn & Crutcher
before joining his occasional client, Ronald Reagan, as head of the
Justice Department in 1981. Ironically, Smith was not even the first
official in the administration to learn that a vacancy on the Court
was imminent. In February 1981, Justice Potter Stewart confided
to Vice President Bush that he planned to retire from the Court at
the end of the current term. Bush informed Smith of the upcoming
vacancy on March 4, and Stewart finally met with the attorney general on March 26. While confirming that his decision was final,
Stewart told Smith that he hoped the decision might still be kept
secret, at least until the current term was nearing its conclusion.[11]
    Even though the president was still unaware of a pending va-
cancy,[12] Smith began the formal process of searching for Stewart's
successor. On March 27, he directed Kenneth W. Starr, then counselor to the attorney general, to compile a list of prospective candidates for the Supreme Court.[13] Smith imposed few restrictions on
Starr's search, whether ideological, geographic, or otherwise, although he did suggest that Starr include a number of qualified
women in the pool for political reasons. The previous October
Reagan had hoped to make a dramatic announcement that would
reenergize his presidential campaign.[14] At a news conference in Los
Angeles on October 14, he had promised to name a woman "to
one of the first Supreme Court vacancies in my administration."[15]
Smith knew the president was prepared to stand by his commitment: on at least one occasion after the election Reagan had reminded Smith that he fully intended to live up to that original
promise.[16]
    Starr's research team consisted of F. Henry ("Hank") Habicht,
the special assistant to the attorney general; Emma C. Jordan, a
White House fellow and special assistant to the attorney general;
Rex E. Lee, the solicitor general; Jonathan C. Rose of the Office

of Legal Policy; and Bruce E. Fein, the associate deputy attorney general. Together they analyzed the writings and opinions of numerous prospective candidates.[17] According to press reports, Judge Amalya E. Kearse, a distinguished black female sitting on the U.S. Court of Appeals for the Second Circuit, garnered at least some brief consideration.[18] Three other female candidates received more intensive scrutiny: Judge Cornelia G. Kennedy of the U.S. Court of Appeals for the Sixth Circuit; Judge Sandra Day O'Connor of the Arizona Court of Appeals; and Justice Mary Stallings Coleman of the Michigan Supreme Court.[19]

Warren Burger may have been the first to bring O'Connor's name to Smith's attention; the chief justice had recently become acquainted with the Arizona jurist during a trip he'd taken overseas with a number of state judges. According to Habicht, O'Connor had issued several judicial opinions noteworthy for their "general deference to trial court rulings and findings." The fifty-one-year-old state judge had also demonstrated a "healthy disdain for the exclusionary rule." During her tenure as an Arizona state senator, she had sponsored at least one death penalty bill as well as legislation designed to increase penalties for drug offenders.[20] By contrast, O'Connor's record on abortion rights was still mostly unknown. Kennedy, fifty-eight, was also recognized as having a "generally conservative judicial philosophy," although her opinions were deemed "not always outstanding in conciseness or insight."[21] Coleman's record on the Michigan Supreme Court revealed a particularly hard-line approach to criminal appeals: "she rarely supports a decision which will result in the reversal of conviction."[22] Justice Department officials raised two objections to Coleman: (1) potential criticism that her opinions were "result oriented" and "lacking in consistency";[23] and (2) her age, believed at that time to be over sixty-five.[24]

Starr's group continued to investigate candidates' backgrounds and records throughout April and May 1981. The March 30 assassination attempt on President Reagan's life delayed any opportunity Smith might have had to update the president on the search. In fact, Reagan did not even learn of Justice Stewart's retirement plans until April 21. Reagan finally met with Stewart for the first time on May 18, nearly two months into the selection process.

During the second week of June, Stewart informed the White House that he planned to make public his retirement plans on June 18. Suddenly, the selection process climbed to the top of the White

House agenda. Of course the Justice Department was not alone in its interest in the pending nomination. Around the time of Stewart's announcement, the White House Counsel's Office headed by Fred F. Fielding also began to compile its own list of candidates for the Court. This alternative list, which included five women and thirteen men, purportedly represented "all segments of the public" including some administration officials:[25]

Robert H. Bork, professor (Yale)
William P. Clark, deputy secretary of state
Amalya E. Kearse, judge (Second Circuit)
Cornelia G. Kennedy, judge (Sixth Circuit)
Joan Dempsey Klein, judge (California Superior Court)
Philip B. Kurland, professor (University of Chicago)
Paul A. Laxalt, Senator (R-Nev.)
William H. Mulligan, judge (Second Circuit)
Dallin H. Oaks, president (Brigham Young University)
Sandra Day O'Connor, Judge (Arizona Court of Appeals)
A. Kenneth Pye, professor (Duke)
William P. Rogers, private practitioner
Susie Marshall Sharp, justice (North Carolina Supreme Court)
Joseph S. Tyree, judge (Ninth Circuit)
J. Clifford Wallace, judge (Ninth Circuit)
William H. Webster, FBI Director
Malcolm I. Wilkey, judge (D.C. Circuit)
Ralph K. Winter, professor (Yale)

The two oldest candidates on the White House list, Sharp (seventy-four) and Rogers (sixty-eight), never received any serious consideration.[26] Instead, White House officials marked five names from the list for special consideration: Bork, Kurland, O'Connor, Wallace, and Webster. Additionally, question marks were placed next to the names of Wilkey and Winter.

O'Connor's presence on the White House Counsel's shortlist was hardly an accident: Chief Justice Burger had also spoken to Fielding about O'Connor. Regardless, by most accounts Smith had settled on O'Connor as his choice in early May, and had been internally lobbying on her behalf ever since. Smith was impressed both with O'Connor's record as a judge and as a state legislator. While in the Arizona state senate she had been identified closely with three issues: (1) criminal law reform, (2) state revenue law reform, and

(3) support for women's rights (she backed amendments to state provisions that appeared unduly discriminatory). O'Connor's views on abortion still remained unclear, but her nomination enjoyed the support of Burger and two of her fellow Stanford Law School alumni, Justice William H. Rehnquist and William F. Baxter, assistant attorney general in charge of the Antitrust Division. Her path to Senate confirmation would also be smoothed by three senators who supported her candidacy: Paul A. Laxalt (R-Nev.), Barry M. Goldwater (R-Ariz.), and Dennis DeConcini (D-Ariz.).

At a mid-June meeting attended by Smith, Edwin Meese (then the counselor to the president), and White House Aide Michael A. Deaver, the president remarked that he wanted to find a woman who was qualified for the Court. He encouraged the attorney general to come back and revisit the issue, however, if that somehow wasn't possible.[27] On June 23, Smith met with Reagan alone to discuss various candidates for the Court. Male candidates still under consideration included Oaks, Wallace, and Bork.[28] But Smith focused the discussion on female candidates, and he placed special emphasis on the candidacy of O'Connor. Reagan agreed that O'Connor now merited additional, in-depth investigation.[29] The attorney general then sent Habicht to Arizona for an extended look at O'Connor's background. Habicht reported back that O'Connor had earned "bipartisan respect and affection in Arizona, both as a professional and as a family woman."[30]

Although Reagan was willing to defer to the attorney general's judgment on O'Connor, White House officials sought to influence the process as well. With regard to lower court nominees, the White House Counsel's Office insisted that they all share the president's view that courts should "interpret the law, not enact new law by judicial fiat."[31] Fielding felt that Supreme Court appointments should meet even higher standards of ideological commitment. Accordingly, his deputy, Herbert I. Ellingwood, outlined a formal list of factors to be considered in "judicial appointments to the Supreme Court."[32] Along with detailed considerations of "work capacity," "interpersonal relationships," "character," and "professional background," the outline addressed several questions to be pursued concerning each candidate, including the following:[33]

- "How has this person exercised judicial restraint in the past?"
- "Is there a commitment to being an interpreter, rather than a creator of the law?"

- "What does this person believe are the most important issues before the Court?"
- "Is this person strongly convinced of his/her own philosophy? Will they likely be unduly swayed by liberal, academic, media, peer or other pressures?"

Had Fielding's office participated more actively in the process of gathering information about candidates, O'Connor's selection might have encountered greater resistance. After all, her judicial record provided little indication of her potential views on school prayer, affirmative action, or many other "hot button" conservative issues. Most worrisome was O'Connor's position on abortion rights. In his memoirs, the attorney general would later assert that that there had been no indication of her having taken any public position on abortion."[34] In fact, O'Connor's record as a state senator in Arizona featured some quite troubling ambiguities on the subject. In 1970, she had served as a member of the state senate's judiciary committee when it voted to pass a bill repealing the Arizona criminal statute on abortion. (A decade later there was no record at all of her actual vote on the bill.) In 1973 O'Connor co-sponsored a bill that would have provided "family planning information" to minors. While on the state legislature's judiciary committee in 1974, O'Connor allegedly voted against a "memorialization resolution" calling upon Congress to pass a Human Life Amendment.[35] Finally, O'Connor voted in 1974 against S-1245, a bill that would have permitted the University of Arizona to issue bonds to expand existing sports facilities. The bill included a controversial provision that no abortions could be performed at any educational facility run by the Arizona Board of Regents. O'Connor claimed she opposed the bill on grounds that the Arizona constitution forbade enactment of legislation treating unrelated subjects, but her reasons for so voting were never stated in the record.

Despite these question marks, O'Connor remained Smith's clear preference for the nomination. Consequently, Fielding's decision to rely on Smith's office for research and analysis of O'Connor's ideological record rendered her nomination all but inevitable. On June 27, Smith sent aides Kenneth Starr and Jonathan Rose to interview O'Connor in Phoenix. Two days later O'Connor attended a meeting of the Judicial Fellows Commission in Washington, D.C., dined with the attorney general, and met with other influential

White House officials. She also met with William P. Clark, the deputy secretary of state and Smith's deputy, Edward C. Schmultz. That afternoon O'Connor met with James A. Baker III, Meese, Deaver, and Fielding.

Finally, on July 1, 1981, O'Connor met with the president. Also present at the meeting were Smith, Deaver, Baker, and Meese. According to Deaver, O'Connor's impressive performance during her one-hour session with the president all but clinched her nomination.[36] Notes taken from the meeting indicate that O'Connor assured the president that she was "personally opposed to abortion" and that she found the concept "personally abhorrent."[37] Emphasizing her belief that the regulation of abortions was in fact a legitimate subject for legislative action, O'Connor offered that there had been at least one instance where she had sponsored a pro-life bill in the Arizona state senate.[38] According to Smith, Reagan settled on O'Connor immediately after their session had concluded.[39]

If Reagan and Smith were convinced of O'Connor's resoluteness against abortion, right-to-life groups were not so sure. Just as news of O'Connor's pending candidacy leaked to the press on July 2, pro-life groups began to mobilize. John C. Willke, the president of the National Right to Life Committee, wrote Reagan that O'Connor's nomination "would be seen as a complete repudiation of your pro-life position" and "would produce a firestorm reaction across the nation."[40] A past president of the organization also argued that O'Connor had failed to "measure up" to the Republican Party's position on abortion, as well as to Reagan's own position on "the necessity of bringing men and women of pro-life, pro-family views to the federal bench."[41] Several Republican senators also joined in calls of protest, including Jesse Helms (R-N.C.), Steven D. Symms (R-Idaho), and Don Nickles (R-Okla.).[42]

As a final check against any surprises, Reagan telephoned Smith on July 6, asking him to investigate O'Connor's abortion record one more time. At the attorney general's request, Starr spoke to O'Connor twice that afternoon. In a memo dated July 7, Starr confirmed for Smith that "as a trial and appellate judge [O'Connor] had not had occasion to rule on any issue relating to abortion"; nor had she ever attended or spoken at a women's rights conference on abortion.[43] After briefly running through the all too familiar litany of Arizona legislative initiatives concerning abortion and O'Connor's record of participation in each,[44] Starr reported:

Judge O'Connor further indicated . . . that she had never been a leader or outspoken advocate on behalf of either pro-life or abortion rights organizations. She knows well the Arizona leader of the right-to-life movement, a prominent female physician in Phoenix, and has never had any disputes or controversies with her.[45]

Smith viewed Starr's memo in the most favorable light possible for O'Connor, and predictably stood by her candidacy. Of course with his attorney general undeterred by the opposition, the president would do the same. On July 7, 1981, Reagan announced Sandra Day O'Connor's nomination to the U.S. Supreme Court.

The road to O'Connor's confirmation was a bit bumpy, but its outcome was never in doubt. Reagan found unlikely support for her nomination from liberal senators like Edward M. Kennedy (D-Mass.), who concluded that O'Connor was perhaps the most moderate nominee he could hope for from the administration. Women's groups were generally pleased with the selection. Conservatives, by contrast, were less receptive, fearing that her nomination was a sign of the growing influence of moderates in administration decisionmaking. Despite these rumblings, conservative Senate Republicans fell in line during the final confirmation vote. The Senate confirmed O'Connor by a 99–0 tally on September 21, with the White House expending little political capital in the process.

As a justice, O'Connor has hewed a conservative line on criminal justice, executive powers, and federalism issues. At the same time, she has become an increasingly influential swing justice on issues of importance to Reagan, including church-state relations and abortion. Early in her tenure she rejected the traditional establishment clause test of *Lemon v. Kurtzman* (1971),[46] preferring state neutrality to religion over more strict separation. In *Lynch v. Donnelly* (1984),[47] O'Connor provided the crucial fifth vote to uphold the placement of a crèche in Pawtucket's downtown shopping district; in her concurrence she substituted the question of whether government intends or is perceived to "endorse" religion. Five years later in *Allegheny County v. ACLU* (1989),[48] O'Connor's endorsement test garnered the support of several other justices.

Most significantly, in 1992 she joined a three-justice plurality to uphold the core holding of *Roe v. Wade*.[49] Conservatives could hardly blame Reagan's screening process for failing to anticipate that result. In fact, the Justice Department had a decade before

detected numerous question marks in O'Connor's record on abortion. But Smith's determination to outmaneuver other administration officials and secure her candidacy may have actually blinded
him and his aides to those troubling aspects of her record.

THE REHNQUIST AND SCALIA NOMINATIONS: HARVESTING THE FRUITS OF THE JUSTICE DEPARTMENT'S LABORS

On June 17, 1986, President Reagan set off considerable commo-
tion in Washington with the announcement that he would nominate Justice William Rehnquist to be the nation's sixteenth chief
justice and Judge Antonin Scalia to serve as associate justice in his
place. Members of the press did not even know a vacancy on the
Supreme Court currently existed, let alone a vacancy in the chief
justiceship. Chief Justice Burger was still in excellent physical
health, and many expected him to serve at least through the following court term. The announcement even caught the other justices
off guard. Only the day before Reagan's dramatic press conference,
neither Burger nor Rehnquist had mentioned the pending changes
at a routine conference among the justices. After waiting five years
for a second vacancy on the Court—the longest such wait by a two-
term president since the early nineteenth century[50]—Reagan could
finally cash in on another opportunity to reshape the nation's high
court.

Observers of the administration had already predicted that key
changes in personnel at the Justice Department and the White
House would soon alter the character of the judicial selection process during Reagan's second term. William French Smith's successor as attorney general was the controversial and colorful Edwin
Meese, a close friend and counselor to the president for the past
twenty years. Unlike Smith, Meese brought to the post a definite
ideological bent. Throughout 1985 Meese campaigned publicly for
a "new vision of the Constitution."[51] Arguing that the federal judiciary needed to be restrained, he advocated pure constitutional
originalism: the Constitution should be interpreted to reflect only
the views of those who drafted it. Meese criticized *Roe*, targeted
Miranda as intended to help "guilty defendants," and lashed out
at the Supreme Court's religion decisions as "more policy choices
than articulation of constitutional principle."[52] Meese even called

into question Supreme Court decisions that had incorporated the Bill of Rights into the Fourteenth Amendment, thereby imposing most of its requirements on state and local governments.[53] Once the attorney general launched this more general public debate on constitutional interpretation, Justice Brennan joined the fray to defend his own so-called activism. The senior associate justice countered that it was often necessary to adapt the Constitution's great principles "to cope with current problems and current needs."[54]

Meese's influence was immediately felt in the administration's approach to selecting federal judges. The highly ideological attorney general planned to take a personal hand in staffing the federal judiciary at all levels by recruiting nominees with a compatible constitutional vision, that is, those who understood the limits of their own judicial power. In all likelihood, Meese would have the opportunity to put his stamp on the Supreme Court as well. At the start of Reagan's second term, five justices had reached the age of seventy-five: Brennan (seventy-eight), Burger (seventy-seven), Powell (seventy-seven), Marshall (seventy-six), and Blackmun (seventy-six). Even Byron White was now sixty-seven years old, a full year older than Potter Stewart had been when he announced his own retirement in 1981.

Anticipating a vacancy in the not-so-distant future, Meese and other Justice Department officials began considering possible nominees in early 1985. Beginning that February, an informal group led by high-level officials in the Justice Department was formed. Charles J. Cooper, head of the Office of Legal Counsel, and William Bradford Reynolds, the head of the civil rights division, oversaw this intensive review of Supreme Court prospects. An internal task force led by Roger A. Clegg, a special assistant to the attorney general, had crafted a paper defining the attributes of a so-called ideal Supreme Court candidate.[55] Clegg's report emphasized the importance of the candidate's commitment to interpretivism[56] generally and to a more limited judicial role, as indicated by twelve (often overlapping) factors:

(1) "awareness of the importance of strict justiciability and procedural requirements"
(2) "refusal to create new constitutional rights for the individual"
(3) "deference to states in their spheres"
(4) "appropriate deference to agencies"
(5) "commitment to strict principles of 'nondiscrimination' "[57]

(6) "disposition towards criminal law as a system for determining guilt or innocence"

(7) "disposition towards 'less government rather than more' "

(8) "recognition that the federal government is one of enumerated powers"

(9) "appreciation for the role of the free market in our society"

(10) "respect for traditional values"

(11) "recognition of the importance of separation of powers principles of presidential authority"

(11) "legal competence"

(12) "strong leadership on the court/young and vigorous"

Using the task force criteria as a guide, the evaluation committee combed the federal circuit courts for candidates who showed a propensity to fulfill these requirements. For each candidate, a member of the group generated a lengthy report detailing his or her adherence to these criteria in actual judicial opinions. Never before in history had there been such an excruciatingly detailed examination of judicial rulings by the Justice Department in anticipation of a Supreme Court nomination.

Eventually six jurists became the focus of especially intense Justice Department scrutiny:[58]

Robert Bork, judge (D.C. Circuit)

Patrick E. Higginbotham, judge (Fifth Circuit)

Anthony M. Kennedy, judge (Ninth Circuit)

Antonin Scalia, judge (D.C. Circuit)

J. Clifford Wallace, judge (Ninth Circuit)

Ralph K. Winter Jr., judge (Second Circuit)

All six were strong proponents of conservative principles. Nevertheless, significant reservations were raised about four of the six: Higginbotham, Winter, Wallace, and Kennedy. Higginbotham, forty-eight years old, allegedly had failed to chart a "clear jurisprudential course" during his time on the Fifth Circuit. His record of judicial restraint seemed grounded in the "practical limits" of the judiciary rather than in its "inherent institutional limitations."[59] Officials also noted Higginbotham's tendency to unnecessarily expand the "equality of results" analysis in employment discrimination cases beyond Supreme Court precedent.[60]

Winter, fifty, also evoked a "minor, but not significant, note of caution."[61] In several opinions the former Yale Law School professor had failed to appreciate fully the importance of "redressability in Article I standing."[62] In another instance Winter had disagreed with Judge Henry Friendly's decision to immunize the state regulation of alcoholic beverages from federal antitrust laws.[63] Even more distressing was Judge Winter's lack of deference to administrative decisionmaking: in two "significant" cases he refused to respect the reasoned judgment of an administrative agency.[64]

Summaries of Kennedy and Wallace, the two most conservative jurists then sitting on the Ninth Circuit, brought a mix of praise and harsh criticism. Kennedy, forty-nine, was considered a devotee of judicial restraint as classically defined.[65] As Justice Department aide Steven Matthews observed:

> Judge Kennedy usually will narrow the scope of the issues involved, will narrow the announced rule, will avoid constitutional issues, will circumscribe the scope of review of lower court or administrative decisions, will follow precedent, and will be careful to avoid intruding on other centers of authority such as administrative bodies or states.[66]

A thorough search of Kennedy's judicial record revealed some striking inconsistencies, however. Despite arriving at what many conservatives viewed as the "right" result in *Chadha v. INS* (1980),[67] Kennedy's record on separation of powers as a whole struck conservatives as a mixed blessing, because he generally favored the judiciary "in any contest between the judiciary and another branch."[68] In criminal rights cases Kennedy usually favored the prosecution, although he seemed to take extra care to ensure that all law enforcement activities were "reasonable" as a matter of constitutional law.[69]

Even more disturbing were Judge Kennedy's opinions approving new and creative claims of constitutional protection. In 1979, Judge Kennedy applied the "one-man, one-vote" rule to a novel set of circumstances, arguing that such rights of participation might "ebb and flow" with changed material conditions.[70] Three years later Kennedy recognized a due process right based on a probationary employee school teacher's "property interest" in a job from which he had been dismissed for sexual misconduct.[71] And in what may have been the most disheartening example of all, in 1980 Judge Kennedy had "only grudgingly" upheld the validity of naval regulations prohibiting homosexual conduct, citing *Roe v. Wade* and other "privacy right" cases very favorably in the process.[72] Matthews concluded, "This easy acceptance of privacy rights as something guaranteed by the constitution is really very distressing."

Wallace, fifty-seven, was a "consistent advocate and practitioner of judicial restraint."[73] Yet officials criticized his commitment to judicial restraint as "undertheorized."[74] After fourteen years on the court of appeals he had failed to articulate a powerful underlying theory as to why courts should be so limited,[75] and he had still not authored any landmark opinions taking important steps in that direction. Moreover, Wallace's Achilles heel for conservatives was his position on affirmative action. In numerous cases he had tolerated, if not supported, certain "quota-type" systems of affirmative action.[76] One Justice Department official described his opinions as demonstrating a "marked, and inexcusable tolerance for racial and gender quotas."[77]

To most members of the working group the two remaining candidates under consideration, Judges Robert Bork and Antonin Scalia of the Court of Appeals for the D.C. Circuit, enjoyed unparalleled records as ideologically conservative jurists. The lesser known of the two was Scalia. The fifty-year-old former law professor had served as an assistant attorney general in the Office of Legal Counsel during the Ford administration. On the issue of judicial restraint, the report described Scalia as "especially creative and successful in transforming the common intuition that 'courts are running the country' into a set of coherent principles about what courts should not do."[78] His opinions on separation of powers and jurisdictional questions in particular were deemed "brilliant" and "ground-breaking." Indeed, Justice Department officials marveled at Scalia's ability to perceive jurisdictional issues even when they were not briefed.[79] Even more remarkably, a thorough search of Scalia's judicial record uncovered *not a single opinion* in which either the result or the ground of decision seemed problematic from a conservative point of view.[80]

Robert Bork was a more controversial figure. As acting attorney general during the infamous "Saturday Night Massacre," the well-known former Yale law professor and solicitor general had agreed to fire the Watergate special prosecutor, Archibald Cox.[81] Even so, Bork was heralded in legal circles as the model of a conservative, originalist jurist. He was perhaps the leading spokesman for an interpretivist theory of constitutional law and judicial restraint over the previous twenty years. One Justice Department report summarized Bork's guiding philosophy as follows:

the judicial branch should interfere with the policy choices made by elected representatives at the federal or state level only when the majority seeks to infringe on those freedoms expressly enshrined in the Constitution. If the judiciary overrules democratically sanctioned choices by creating rights not found in the constitutional text, it has engaged in an illegitimate—indeed, tyrannical—suppression of self-government through an assumption of powers the judiciary clearly does not possess in our tripartite system of government.[82]

First as a law professor and then as a jurist, Bork had criticized liberal positions on the First Amendment, separation of powers, agency deference, and rights of privacy. Reynolds, Cooper, and the others barely addressed the issue of Bork's confirmability during this early stage of the selection process. To them, the task force's "ideal justice" amounted to a description of "Judge Bork in action."[83]

Because Scalia and Bork received the working group's highest ratings, comparisons between the two jurists were perhaps inevitable. Both men had been law professors and each had served as officials in the Justice Department. Both were now respected judges on the U.S. Court of Appeals for the D.C. Circuit. Each was considered an articulate and devoted adherent to the "interpretivist theory." Indeed, the working group thought that Scalia's judicial philosophy mirrored Bork's philosophy almost precisely, with one important exception:

> In seeking to determine the breadth of rights contained in the constitutional text, Scalia would probably be more inclined than Bork to look at the language of the constitutional provision itself, as well as its history, to determine if it grants an affirmative mandate for the judiciary to inject itself into the legislative process. . . . [W]hile Bork certainly shares these precepts of judicial restraint, he will be somewhat more inclined in certain circumstances to give broader effect to a "core" constitutional value.[84]

In other words, Scalia focused less than Bork on the so-called big picture of jurisprudential questions.[85]

Ultimately, age provided the clearest way to differentiate between their two candidacies. While Bork was fifty-nine years old, Scalia had only recently turned fifty. This factor alone gave Scalia an advantage over Bork, although officials reasoned that, unlike Bork, he would have to "undergo a relatively brief get-acquainted period" on the Supreme Court (perhaps because he lacked Bork's experience as solicitor general).[86]

Recognizing that Chief Justice Burger might also retire, Justice Department officials separately considered criteria for a new chief justice. Here again, they sought ideological compatibility with the administration. Specifically, they wanted a candidate who had "evinced a consistent and strong commitment to the president's view of the inherently limited role of the judiciary in our system of government."[87] Officials also wanted someone with "a clear philosophic vision of where he wants to take the law," so that Burger's successor might provide intellectual as well as social leadership.[88]

Finally, the group deemed interpersonal skills and familiarity with the other justices to be especially relevant considerations in choosing a new chief justice. According to one report:

> the most important prerogative of the chief justice is determining which justice will be assigned to write an opinion. . . . [T]hus, the chief justice must be familiar with the predelictions of his colleagues, as well as being savvy and subtle enough to choose that justice who will produce the best product, without offending other justices. . . . [T]he chief justice must also have the energy, and political, personal and intellectual talent to form majorities and build a consensus among the justice on difficult legal issues.[89]

Even if Bork and Scalia were the most qualified on strictly intellectual grounds, some doubts existed about their interpersonal skills. Scalia in particular was considered "prone to an occasional outburst of temper," causing fears that as a justice "he might rub one of his colleagues the wrong way."[90]

The working group's emphasis on "familiarity with other justices" seemed inevitably to point toward a promotion from within. Of the eight associate justices, only three were considered realistic possibilities for the chief justiceship: Rehnquist, O'Connor, and White.[91] White was clearly the long shot of the bunch. Once a Kennedy Democrat, the justice had endeared himself to conservatives by parting company with his liberal colleagues on abortion. His most consistently conservative rulings came in criminal rights cases, as White dissented from the Court's more liberal rulings in *Escobedo v. Illinois* (1964)[92] and *Miranda v. Arizona* (1966).[93] Finally, White and Rehnquist were the lone dissenters in *Roe*. But now in his late sixties, White was clearly too old for the position. O'Connor and Rehnquist represented more attractive possibilities.

The administration could again make history if it nominated O'Connor, now fifty-six years old, to be the first female chief justice. But Justice Department officials were not at all enthusiastic about her candidacy. In their view, a number of O'Connor's decisions created "serious concerns about the depth and consistency of her commitment to judicial restraint and fundamental constitutional values."[94] Her record in criminal and civil rights included a "troublesome propensity" to file concurring opinions that diluted the force of more conservative rulings of the Court.[95] During the past term she had written a 5–4 opinion that substantially expanded the reach of *New York Times v. Sullivan* (1964).[96]

In the minds of Justice Department officials, O'Connor's biggest sin came in religion cases where she had often provided a critical fifth vote for Brennan's liberal coalition. By daring to offer a novel theory of "endorsement," she had forged a majority on a badly divided tribunal. One official complained:

> she has consistently taken the indefensible position that legitimate efforts to accommodate religion or to enact purely secular programs that incidentally benefit religious organizations violate the establishment clause of the First Amendment. She has thus voted to strike down educational programs that benefit private religious and nonreligious schools, state enactments requiring a moment of silence in public schools, laws requiring employers to excuse employees from working on their Sabbath and a municipal ordinance allowing churches to prevent the granting of a liquor license to nearby establishments.[97]

At least in this one issue area, O'Connor had actively resisted Reagan's social agenda.

By contrast, Rehnquist's prospective candidacy drew unabashed praise. In all areas of constitutional law important to the administration—criminal procedure, due process, civil rights, freedom of press, and religion—Rehnquist's jurisprudence had been "scrupulously premised" on the principles of federalism and separation of powers.[98] Rehnquist had attempted to pioneer the rehabilitation of dual federalism principles in the short-lived precedent of *National League of Cities v. Usery* (1976).[99] He continued to oppose *Roe v. Wade.* Even more important, Justice Department officials believed that Rehnquist possessed the necessary interpersonal skills to build conservative coalitions on a diverse Court. One official praised him in terms of his *realpolitik:*

by dint of his personal qualities, intellect and sheer cleverness in reshaping erroneous precedent, Rehnquist has formed a consensus on a generally rudderless Court behind fundamental principles which might well have been otherwise rejected. . . . [H]e enjoys a warm collegial relationship with, and is genuinely respected by all of his fellow justices, even those with whom he often disagrees. His fourteen-year tenure on the Court has given him valuable insights into the predilections of these justices and the politics and machinations on the court.[100]

Although the working group was at first divided over whether Scalia or Bork would be preferable as associate justice, it reached a quick consensus in favor of promoting the sixty-one-year-old Rehnquist to be chief justice in the event of Burger's retirement. That conclusion was based largely on research conducted during 1985 and early 1986, even before the administration knew for certain that a vacancy would arise.[101]

Of course once a vacancy did arise, others in the administration were prepared to stake their own claims in the selection process.[102] On May 27, 1986, Burger informed President Reagan of his intention to retire from the Court, effective at the end of the current term. Until that point there had been widespread speculation that Burger would remain on the job at least until September 17, 1987, when he would celebrate his eightieth birthday and preside as chairman of the Constitution's bicentennial commission.[103] But the chief justice told Reagan that his obligations to the commission, combined with his court duties, created excessive burdens on him physically.[104] Apparently Burger was also concerned that Republicans would lose their Senate majority that fall, making confirmation of a conservative chief justice considerably more difficult. In closing, he provided the president with a brief memorandum recommending six candidates as possible replacements: Rehnquist, White, Bork, Scalia, Wallace, and Judge Edward Re of the International Court of Trade in New York.

Two days later Meese, Donald Regan (the White House chief of staff) and Peter Wallison (the White House Counsel) met to discuss the forthcoming selection process. As Fielding had done five years earlier, Wallison decided to prepare his own list of candidates, which he planned to present to the president on June 9. Although William Bradford Reynolds forwarded the working group's summaries to Wallison, the White House Counsel asked his staff to conduct its own separate research and analysis of the candidates recommended by the Justice Department. Thus Wallison refused to be beholden to the Justice Department's research efforts. In the White House Counsel's view, his Office occupied a "different institutional position in the administration," with different concerns and priorities. While the Justice Department had worked for over a year sifting through opinions and analyzing candidates, lawyers in the White House Counsel's Office worked at a feverish pace to research and prepare its own recommendations for the president.

Two lawyers working for Wallison, Alan C. Raul and C. Christopher Cox, met with the rest of the staff to allocate responsibilities for the search process. A full report of each candidate would include: (1) a biographical summary; (2) a description of the candidate's ideological leanings, including his or her record on at least four critical issues: criminal justice, federalism, separation of powers, and economic issues; (3) reversal rates and ABA ratings where available; (4) a description of the candidate's age and health; and (5) analysis of confirmability, including any statements by senators about the candidate in question. Only this last aspect of analysis covered entirely new substantive ground. The Justice Department's working group had paid only scant attention to confirmability during the course of its own review.

White House lawyers also added a female candidate to the Justice Department's list of six candidates: Judge Cynthia Holcomb Hall of the U.S. Court of Appeals for the Ninth Circuit.[105] The White House then generated its own separate reports for each of seven candidates under consideration for the position of associate justice. Although officials considered Rehnquist's promotion closely as well, no report was generated concerning Rehnquist's chief rival for the position, Sandra Day O'Connor. Eventually the White House Counsel's Office concurred with most of the Justice Department's findings. Bork and Scalia were the frontrunners for the associate justice seat. Lawyers in the White House Counsel's Office believed that neither candidate would have any difficulty achieving Senate confirmation. Of Scalia's prospects, one White House lawyer felt that confirmation should be "relatively easy" because even liberal Democrats conceded he was a first-rate legal scholar. [106] Enhancing Scalia's confirmation prospects would be his status as the first person of Italian lineage appointed to the Court. Also, "he did not seem to have antagonized any particular groups or powerful individuals in his rise to prominence."[107]

Given his generally high stature in the legal community, White

House officials believed Bork's involvement in the Saturday Night Massacre was "not likely to diminish his confirmation prospects significantly."[108] Their report noted:

> Bork is also described as more likely to be confirmed by even a Democratic Senate because he is "much older and less radical then some of the other alternatives." He is thought to be about as liberal a nominee as the Democrats believe they will get from President Reagan and perhaps not as vigorous in his disdain for precedents. The media will also be kind to Bork because of his strong support for the First Amendment.[109]

Of the five other candidates, Cynthia Hall received glowing praise for her judicial philosophy and opinions.[110] The White House Counsel considered Hall "an excellent prospect for the court. . . . [S]he stands shoulder-to-shoulder with the small group of male Supreme Court candidates, based solely on her individual merits."[111] Meanwhile, those same officials detected a worrisome "independent streak" in Higginbotham.[112] They also viewed Judge Kennedy's conservatism as "intellectual rather than practical," leading him to an occasionally anomalous result.[113]

The group praised Wallace for his "conservative streak," but his public statements concerning the relationship of his religion to many of his decisions raised some concern.[114] According to the White House report, a profile in 1981 quoted Wallace as saying that the Bible gives "great scriptural support for the death penalty." And Wallace's biography in *Who's Who in America* reportedly contained an unusual italicized personal statement declaring that the teachings of Jesus Christ provided the basis for his life and his work. Officials feared that those statements could, "if used unfairly against him, present confirmation problems."[115]

Judge Winter received the most negative comments of all from within the White House. Despite his impressive reputation as an advocate before the Supreme Court, he suffered from a "somewhat checkered reputation" at the Yale Law School. He was "not known for intensive preparation for class or rigorous commitment to scholarship."[116] His judicial record was also a mixed bag of "loose conservatism" sprinkled with notable exceptions. The report concluded, "Winter is frequently mentioned as a potential Supreme Court nominee, but very little detail supports any of these references."[117]

Finally, the White House Counsel's report on William Rehnquist was glowing, although more cautious about the justice's confirmation prospects. Rehnquist was described as an "intellectual giant . . . universally considered to be the Supreme Court's most consistently conservative and ideological judge."[118] White House lawyers believed that his "legal acuity and personal amiability" had enhanced his ability to work with the other justices. Still, they predicted a fight over Rehnquist's nomination:

> the confirmation process will undoubtedly cause Rehnquist's old memorandum to his former boss, Justice Jackson to reemerge. In that memorandum, Rehnquist had argued against the principles adopted in *Brown v. Board of Education*. An allegation of racial prejudice is absolutely one of the last things the president's judicial nominees need at this time.[119]

On Thursday June 5, Wallison and Reynolds met for two hours at the Justice Department to discuss the ongoing selection process.[120] They agreed that Bork and Scalia were the leading candidates for associate justice and that Rehnquist, O'Connor, and Bork would receive consideration for chief justice. Reynolds thought that potential objections to Rehnquist were moot; he believed Rehnquist had grown tired of the Court and would reject the chief justiceship in any event.[121] The president then met with Wallison, Donald Regan, and Attorney General Meese for forty-five minutes on June 9. According to Wallison, everyone in the room was "of the view that sitting judges or justices who had a clearly articulated philosophy were the most likely to remain steadfast in their views."[122] Despite questions raised about Rehnquist's confirmability and his interest in the position, all three advisors supported Rehnquist for the Court's top post. The discussion then turned to a consideration of Bork and Scalia for Rehnquist's associate justice seat. Donald Regan argued that nominating Rehnquist together with Bork might be too difficult a battle to win.[123] The president then focused on the advantages of a Scalia nomination. Scalia had rated equally with Bork among Justice Department officials. He was nine years younger than Bork. Finally, the president seemed intrigued that Scalia would be the Court's first Italian-American appointee. Reagan met with both Rehnquist and Scalia the following week.

Just as O'Connor had charmed President Reagan in 1981, Rehnquist had the same effect during his own thirty-minute meeting with the president on June 12. The main topic of conversation was the justice's health. The Justice Department had turned up some evidence of a back problem, but no other health concerns. Assured that he was fit, the president told Rehnquist that he was "the unanimous choice of all of us" and offered him the chief justiceship on the spot, an offer he accepted immediately.[124] Four days later on June 16, the president met with Judge Scalia and after a short discussion, he offered Rehnquist's vacant seat to Scalia. The next day President Reagan introduced Rehnquist and Scalia to the press as his two nominees for chief justice and associate justice, respectively.

President Reagan, meeting with Rehnquist and Scalia for less than an hour each, had moved quickly to offer them nominations. But in truth, the most critical selection decisions had been rendered months earlier by officials in the Justice Department. Unlike with the selection of O'Connor, the president refused to rely on the Justice Department's recommendations alone. This time Reagan divided authority among a three-member search committee composed of his chief of staff, the attorney general, and the White House Counsel. Although each official was determined to influence the selection process, Attorney General Meese was able to exert considerable leverage over his colleagues by virtue of his still formidable command over resources and information. The Justice Department had been preparing for this moment for over a year, sifting through hundreds of opinions by conservative jurists around the country. Still, Wallison and Regan did provide their own significant input into the process. Their concerns about Rehnquist's confirmability—a point all but ignored by Reynolds's working group—led inevitably to the decision to push Scalia as part of a more confirmable package of nominations.

The assumptions propelling the choice of Scalia over Bork appeared prophetic in the short term. As White House officials had predicted, Justice Rehnquist's promotion was tied up for months in divisive, often acrimonious debate. Senator Edward M. Kennedy (D-Mass.) and other liberal senators criticized Rehnquist for being too extreme on issues of race, women's rights, freedom of speech, and the separation of church and state. Yet few of Rehnquist's harshest critics would dispute the nominee's powerful intellect or his understanding of the law.[125] The Senate finally confirmed Rehnquist's nomination on September 17, 1986, by a 65–33 vote. Still, Rehnquist's thirty-three negative votes were the most ever cast against a successful nominee for chief justice.

Meanwhile, Scalia received the same kid-glove treatment that

Lewis Powell had enjoyed fifteen years earlier when he had been similarly paired with Rehnquist. Italian-American politicians responded warmly to Scalia's nomination, and the hard-fought battle to stop Rehnquist drained senators of the energy required for a second battle. Scalia's confirmation hearings seemed at times farcical, as the nominee avoided committing himself on a variety of issues large and small.[126] At one point he refused even to comment on the validity of *Marbury v. Madison* (1803), which had established the Supreme Court's power of judicial review over acts of Congress. Ultimately, even Scalia's well-articulated conservative ideology caused him no problems. The Senate confirmed him handily by a 98–0 vote on the same day it confirmed Rehnquist.

Bork's record as a Nixon administration official and outspoken leader of judicial conservatives might have been too much for the Senate to accept had he been coupled with Rehnquist in 1986. By comparison, Scalia appeared almost as a "peace offering" from the administration. In fact, Rehnquist and Scalia have both provided generally reliable conservative votes during the past decade. Scalia has even espoused a more formalistic approach than Rehnquist on important separation of powers issues.[127] On the whole though, the Court's ideological configuration did not change dramatically with Scalia's nomination. Rehnquist had anchored the Court's conservative wing for the previous fifteen years, and Scalia was replacing Burger, himself a conservative jurist. The real battle lines would be drawn once a liberal or moderate justice finally retired from the bench. That scenario would demand even more open and cautious deliberations by White House and Justice Department officials.

THE NOMINATIONS OF BORK, GINSBURG, AND KENNEDY: IDEOLOGY, VENGEANCE, AND A NOTE OF CAUTION

Robert Bork just missed being nominated to the Supreme Court in 1986. If another vacancy arose during Reagan's second term, he was certain to be the odds-on favorite of the Justice Department for that open seat. Most court-watchers believed that Justices Brennan and Marshall, then eighty-one and seventy-nine years old respectively, would wait at least until after the next presidential election before retiring. Rumors of Justice Powell's resignation had been circulating for years, only to prove false on each occasion. Pressing for a vacancy, senior executive officials in March 1987

tried without success to convince Justice Byron White to serve as
the administration's new FBI director.[128]

Justice Powell finally succumbed to a combination of old age, ill
health, and his own personal desire to see a Republican president
name his successor. On June 26, 1987, Chief Justice Rehnquist
alerted the White House that Powell planned to announce his retirement at the close of that morning's court session. For Meese,
Reynolds, and Cooper, a thorough canvassing of the field of candidates at this late date seemed unnecessary. During the past year
they had maintained an open and updated file of future Supreme
Court justices. Robert Bork had been one of the Justice Department's two leading candidates a year earlier. Learning of Powell's
retirement, the attorney general hoped the president would move
quickly and forcefully to nominate Bork.

White House support for a Bork nomination seemed less certain,
however. During the previous year President Reagan had appointed
a new White House Counsel, Arthur B. Culvahouse, and a new
chief of staff, Howard Baker. A former Senate majority leader,
Baker had been brought into the administration to smooth the waters with Congress in the wake of the Iran-Contra affair and its
widening negative publicity. More so than Meese, both Baker and
Culvahouse feared that a Bork nomination would spur a costly and
unnecessary confirmation fight in the Senate, which was now controlled by the Democrats. On June 26, Culvahouse held a staff
meeting at the White House Counsel's Office to discuss the search
for Powell's replacement. Those present at the meeting included
C. Christopher Cox, Alan Charles Raul, Patricia M. Bryan, Peter
Keisler, and Benedict Cohen.[129] No doubt aware of the Justice Department's strong preference for Bork, members of the group
weighed the costs and benefits of a Bork nomination, including
concerns about Bork's participation in the "Saturday Night Massacre." The group also agreed to conduct research and analysis regarding ten candidates in all for the Court:

> Robert Bork, judge (D.C. Circuit)
> Cynthia Hall, judge (Ninth Circuit)
> Patrick Higginbotham, judge (Fifth Circuit)
> Anthony Kennedy, judge (Ninth Circuit)
> J. Clifford Wallace, judge (Ninth Circuit)
> Ralph Winter, judge (Second Circuit)
> Orrin Hatch, Senator (R-Utah)

Howell Heflin, Senator (D-Ala.)
Amalya Kearse, judge (Second Circuit)
William Wilkins judge (Fourth Circuit)

In effect, the group had decided to add four new names to Wallison's list from the previous year. Senators Heflin (sixty-six) and Hatch (fifty-three) were strategic additions to the list. As members of the Senate Judiciary Committee, either one could expect considerable bipartisan support if nominated. Heflin, a conservative Democrat, had served as chief justice of the Alabama Supreme Court from 1971 through 1977. Hatch had been a reliable advocate for the administration on a variety of criminal justice initiatives. He had also authored critical sections of the Omnibus Crime Control Act of 1984, which featured the abolition of parole in the federal criminal justice system. Either senator would have to overcome potential constitutional obstacles to their candidacies: during the previous year Congress had raised the pay levels of Supreme Court justices, seemingly barring any member of Congress from a Supreme Court appointment under the Constitution's ineligibility clause.[130]

The final two candidates on the list were more curious additions. Judge Amalya Kearse, fifty, was a respected black judge who had received some brief consideration for Potter Stewart's seat back in 1981. One might have thought her past membership on the NAACP's board of directors and her moderate-to-liberal record on the court of appeals would have precluded her from receiving any serious consideration for this critical vacancy. Judge William Wilkins, forty-five, benefited from the critical backing of Senator Strom Thurmond (R-S.C.), the ranking Republican on the Senate Judiciary Committee. Twice before Thurmond had backed Wilkins for judicial appointments, first for a federal district judgeship in 1981, and later for a seat on the Court of Appeals for the Fourth Circuit in 1986. Thurmond's support for Wilkins did not stop at judicial appointments. At the senator's urging in 1985, President Reagan had appointed Wilkins to chair the U.S. Sentencing Commission. Two years later, Thurmond strongly recommended his friend as FBI director, an effort that proved unsuccessful.[131]

Not surprisingly, Thurmond was now enthusiastically pushing Wilkins as the logical successor to Lewis Powell's "southern seat." The White House entertained Thurmond's pleas for the time being, including Wilkins among the dozen or so finalists for the Supreme Court. In subsequent days the White House list was supplemented with at least one additional candidate: Judge Pasco Bowman, fifty-three, of the U.S. Court of Appeals for the Eighth Circuit.

Each member of the White House Counsel's Office was assigned the responsibility of researching and analyzing one or more of the candidates then under consideration. Many of their reports borrowed heavily from those generated in the previous year, though White House lawyers updated them with comprehensive LEXIS and NEXIS searches.[132] Given the obstacles posed by a Democratic-controlled Senate, White House officials paid particular attention to recent developments that might have shifted various candidates' confirmation prospects. Reporting on Bork's candidacy, for example, one lawyer offered new data on Bork's potential confirmability.[133] That report included Senator Biden's statement during the past year that he would vote to confirm Bork if nominated to the Supreme Court, but added a cautionary note:

> In the wake of Justice Powell's resignation . . . Biden himself has at least implicitly pulled back from endorsing Bork, stating that because of his concern about altering "the balance of the Court" he would not necessarily support an individual with views extremely similar to those of Justice Scalia. Nonetheless, his earlier high praise for Bork will make it difficult for him effectively to challenge Bork's qualifications. The media will also be kind to Bork because of his strong support.[134]

Based on this assessment, the White House Counsel's Office remained cautiously optimistic about Bork's chances.

Meanwhile, reports on other candidates were generally positive. Judge Wallace's prospects seemed to have risen during the past year as a result of his growing recent friendship with Senator Hatch. According to one White House report, Hatch had recently named Wallace—after Bork and Rex Lee, a former solicitor general—as his favorite candidate for the next Supreme Court vacancy.[135] Judge Bowman, who had spent the preponderance of his career as a professor and dean at several law schools in the South and Midwest, was described as "highly intelligent and conservative."[136] The report on Hatch, though glowing, included a note of caution concerning Hatch's various disagreements with the New Right on social issues.[137] For example, Hatch had recently proposed a constitutional amendment to restore the status quo before *Roe v. Wade* with the so-called Human Life Federalism Amendment, which would have restored decisionmaking to the states. Activists of the New Right bitterly opposed Hatch's effort for not going far enough: they preferred Senator Jesse Helms's proposed amendment requiring states to criminalize abortions according to a broad national definition of "personhood."[138]

On June 29, the president met with Baker, Culvahouse, Meese, and Reynolds to discuss the pending vacancy. Although Bork's nomination garnered considerable enthusiasm from the Justice Department, Baker and Culvahouse cautioned about the tough (although they believed winnable) confirmation battle that would follow. Baker convinced the president that it was in the administration's best interests to canvass the views of key senators before formally submitting any nomination to the Senate. Thus he and Meese visited numerous senators' offices the following day, each sporting a list of several names thought to be under serious consideration by the administration, including Bork and Anthony Kennedy. Meanwhile, organized opposition to Bork was already forming. Leaders of more than forty interest groups met in Washington over the next few days to organize a coalition opposing Bork.[139]

Speaking to the press on the afternoon of June 30, Baker emphasized the administration's efforts to seek the Senate's counsel in filling the latest Supreme Court vacancy. According to Baker, the president viewed the selection process as a "partnership between the executive branch and the Senate"; Bork was merely one of several candidates still under consideration. But the administration's decisive actions in the hours that followed left the distinct impression that this had really been a single-candidate show from the outset.

Biden and Senator Robert Byrd (D-W.Va.), the Democratic majority leader, made clear to both Baker and Meese that a Bork nomination would incite a heated confirmation battle. Despite their warnings, Culvahouse met with Bork at a Washington hotel early the morning of July 1. Discovering no evidence of skeletons or other personal problems in Bork's background, Culvahouse reported favorably to the president. Later that same morning Reagan called Bork into the Oval Office and formally offered him the nomination. Baker's interest in gauging the senators' reactions the previous day was no doubt sincere, but for Meese and the president, that visit to the Hill had been a gesture devoid of any real significance. In truth, the White House had barely enough time to digest the reactions of individual senators before announcing Bork's nomination on July 1, 1987.

For all their fears of a costly confirmation battle over Bork, neither Culvahouse nor Baker ever entertained the possibility that a jurist with such sterling qualifications could actually be defeated. Even they had badly miscalculated the degree of opposition that would be raised against Bork. Senator Kennedy initiated the onslaught of public attacks on Bork hours after his nomination became public when he famously declared:

> Robert Bork's America is a land in which women would be forced into back alley abortions, blacks would sit at segregated lunch counters, rogue policemen could break down citizens' doors in midnight raids, school children could not be taught about evolution, writers and artists could be censured at the whim of government.[140]

As Henry Abraham later recalled, "once Kennedy had unleashed the politics of the swing seat, there was no turning back."[141]

The Bork nomination became a watershed in terms of interest group involvement in the appointment process. According to John Maltese, more than three hundred groups opposed Bork, employing "a wide variety of tactics including advertising, grass roots events, focus groups and polling."[142] White House officials were simply unprepared for the intensity of this lobbying effort. Making matters worse, Senator Biden delayed Bork's confirmation hearings until mid-September, giving opposition groups the additional advantage of time. Bork's abundant scholarly writings (sometimes featuring harsh criticisms of Warren Court precedents) provided a paper trail that left him particularly vulnerable to their efforts.

The Reagan administration did wage a major public relations offensive in support of its nominee. President Reagan made over thirty public statements on Bork's behalf, far and away the most ever by a president for one Supreme Court nomination.[143] The administration was also counting—as it turns out quite mistakenly—on Bork's ability to sell himself to the public. Bork took the unusual step of actively courting the press, beginning with an hour-long interview with the *New York Times* on July 7. Two months later he provided the Senate Judiciary Committee with "the longest and most detailed public testimony" of any Supreme Court nominee in history.[144] Yet instead of allaying fears about his own candidacy, Bork engaged senators in sweeping constitutional discussions. His exchange with Senator Arlen Specter (R-Pa.) evolved into a "great debate" over constitutional interpretation and the role of the Supreme Court in our constitutional system. White House and Justice Department vetters never considered Bork's suitability to perform in a forum that rewarded candidates for their terseness and ability to practice subtle evasion. Bork's lecture-like answers to senators' questions actually harmed his own cause.

Prior to the selection of Bork, lawyers in the White House Counsel's Office had considered the possibility that Biden might eventually oppose Bork. In fact, Biden publicly declared his opposition to Bork's nomination long before the confirmation hearings even began. After the hearings the nominee lost the support of key Democrats on the Judiciary Committee such as Senators Dennis DeConcini (D-Ariz.) and Howell Heflin (D-Ala.). They were soon joined by Specter, whose negative vote crushed Bork's already slim hopes.

The Reagan administration had not missed a "smoking gun" that buried Bork's nomination. Rather, administration officials simply underestimated the degree to which Bork's nomination would galvanize massive resistance. Much of the problem lay in the president's misplaced reliance on the Justice Department, which had never focused on these confirmation difficulties in its own analysis. The attorney general was busy lobbying for Bork's selection without really taking note of the increasingly hostile environment surrounding the lame-duck administration. Moreover, the short period of time (four days) between Powell's resignation and Bork's nomination afforded neither the White House nor the Justice Department sufficient time to reflect upon the implications of nominating Bork to a seat formerly held by Powell, the "swing" justice who had epitomized moderate consideration of court issues.

The Senate formally rejected Bork's nomination by a 58–42 vote on October 23, 1987. In reality, that outcome had been preordained weeks earlier. By the first week of October, fifty-three senators had already gone on record against Bork's nomination. Although publicly the president remained committed to Bork until the bitter end, privately administration officials were already preparing a list of new nominees in anticipation of his pending defeat.

During the first week of October, the White House Counsel's Office team met again to consider a new list of candidates for Powell's seat. They revived interest in five candidates from previous lists:[145] Pasco Bowman, Cynthia Hall, Patrick Higginbotham, Anthony Kennedy, and J. Clifford Wallace. Meanwhile, Justice Department officials, refusing to yield to calls for a "safe" moderate, prepared materials on an entirely new set of candidates. They focused on eleven persons, all but one a federal judge:

James L. Buckley, judge (D.C. Circuit)
Peter Thorp Faye, judge (Eleventh Circuit)
Douglas H. Ginsburg, judge (D.C. Circuit)
Edith H. Jones, judge (Fifth Circuit)
Roger J. Miner, judge (Second Circuit)
Sam Pointer, judge (N.D. Ala.)
Pamela A. Rymer, judge (C.D. Cal)
Lawrence H. Silberman, judge (D.C. Circuit)
Gerald B. Tjoflat, judge (Eleventh Circuit)
William H. Webster, FBI Director
Ralph K. Winter, judge (Second Circuit)

Reynolds forwarded the Justice Department's list of eleven names to Culvahouse. Once again, lawyers in the White House Counsel's Office then conducted their own separate investigation of each candidate. Eventually, the staff prepared a notebook of twelve candidates for Culvahouse's review. Four names from the Justice Department's list were deleted from this final notebook: Silberman, Rymer, Miner, and Faye.

Still, it remained unclear how the president and his top advisors planned to approach this particular vacancy. To some White House officials, a quick and smooth confirmation process was now the administration's top priority. Culvahouse's office had already generated a three-step plan of attack calling for: (1) "rapid submission of the nominee to the Senate," (2) "a short wait" for the Senate hearings, and (3) "quick hearings" with little controversy.[146] Of course the latter two steps required the administration to steer clear of naming a conservative ideologue. Thus White House officials urged a "conciliatory" approach to the second nomination. To protect the president's immediate political interests, they were willing to risk the ire of conservatives by selecting a candidate more acceptable to Senate moderates—Anthony Kennedy or Patrick Higginbotham, for example.

Conservative elements within the Republican Party favored the opposite approach. Unwilling to cave in to liberals, they urged Reagan to stand strong by nominating an equally conservative nominee in place of Bork. Reagan himself seemed to favor this approach as well. He vowed at a meeting of Republican contributors to pick a nominee that would upset Democrats "just as much" as Bork did.[147] Just as Nixon had declared war in the wake of Haynsworth's defeat, Reagan prepared to do battle with the Senate on much the same terms as before.

Meese, Reynolds, and other Justice Department officials favored the more aggressive strategy. Thus Judge Douglas Ginsburg of the D.C. Circuit emerged as their leading candidate for the post. Only forty-one years old, Ginsburg had been a Harvard law professor until 1984, when he became deputy assistant attorney general of the Antitrust Division at the Justice Department. The attorney general was certainly aware that Ginsburg's nomination to the Court would generate some controversy. When he had been appointed to the circuit a year earlier, the ABA's Standing Committee had rated him only "qualified" for the post, largely because his experience up to that point had been almost entirely academic—Ginsburg had argued only one case in court during his entire legal career. But in one official's words, Ginsburg's nomination would constitute a "continuation of the program by Attorney General Meese and President Reagan to fill the courts of appeals with very conservative judges who have developed their ideological positions and who will not vary much from them."[148] Issues of confirmability, even in the wake of Bork's defeat, continued to take a backseat among the Justice Department's priorities.

By the end of October the working list had apparently been winnowed down to three candidates: Ginsburg, Kennedy, and Winter.[149] Baker and Culvahouse reportedly leaned towards Kennedy, whose moderate record held the promise of a certain and quick confirmation. Meese and Reynolds supported Ginsburg. William Wilkins's name continued to appear in the press, and Justice Department lawyers even flew Wilkins in to Washington for an interview during the last week of October, along with Kennedy and Ginsburg. But in truth, the latter two candidates garnered much more serious consideration for the post. And the two sides made few attempts to compromise on their preferred outcomes.

White House officials confirmed to the president that Ginsburg would indeed face confirmation problems, particularly if the ABA gave him another lukewarm recommendation.[150] Thus in some ways Ginsburg's nomination fit the definition of a "spite nomination" better than Carswell's sixteen years earlier, if only because the administration was on notice that its nominee's credentials made him an especially problematic choice. Nonetheless, the president cast his lot once again with the Justice Department. On October 29 he nominated Douglas Ginsburg for the seat vacated by Lewis Powell.

In less than a week Ginsburg's nomination was derailed for reasons that even White House officials had not foreseen. Ginsburg confirmed to the press on November 4 that he had once smoked marijuana as a law professor at Harvard. Meese and Reynolds had quizzed Ginsburg prior to his nomination about whether anything in his background might jeopardize the nomination. On those and other occasions Ginsburg had never mentioned his use of marijuana. This sudden, public revelation now doomed his support among those in the Justice Department who had been pressing for his nomination just days earlier. A solemn Ginsburg asked the president to withdraw his nomination on November 7.

No frantic search for a nominee followed Ginsburg's withdrawal. In the White House, the feelings of anger and vindictiveness over Bork's defeat had turned into feelings of outright embarrassment. The next presidential election was less than a year away, and the exasperated mood on the Hill left the White House with limited options. Senator Patrick Leahy (D-Vt.), a member of the Senate Judiciary Committee, warned that if the White House failed to produce a "readily acceptable" nominee on the third try, there would not be another Supreme Court nominee from this administration.[151] Even administration allies had grown fearful. Senate Robert Dole (R-Kan.), the Senate minority leader, urged the president to "proceed with caution."[152]

For Reagan, the exercise of caution would not require undue delay. Judge Anthony Kennedy had long been considered one of the least controversial names on the administration's lists. His quick confirmation thus appeared a certainty. On November 11, 1987, the president struck a conciliatory note by nominating Kennedy. Though most senators warned that the nominee could still expect intense scrutiny, no real confrontation on the Hill ever materialized. Kennedy's confirmation hearings lasted only three days, compared to Bork's twelve. During those hearings Kennedy showed himself to be a master of soothing rhetoric, distancing himself quite specifically from Bork in the areas of First Amendment law and privacy. On February 3, 1988, the Senate confirmed Kennedy unanimously.

In his written responses to a standard Judiciary Committee questionnaire, Judge Kennedy offered that "life tenure is in part a constitutional mandate to the federal judiciary to proceed with caution."[153] That cautious note, so evident in the work of the justice he replaced, soon reappeared in Justice Kennedy's performance as a Supreme Court justice.[154] To be sure, Kennedy's votes have more often than not tipped the balance of the Court in favor of conservatives. In particular, Kennedy has been solidly in the conservative camp on affirmative action and voting rights issues[155] and with regard to criminal defendants' rights.

An unpredictable streak of libertarianism has often marked Kennedy's work, garnering him considerable criticism from conservatives. In *Lee v. Weisman* (1992),[156] for example, Kennedy reaffirmed the unconstitutionality of graduation prayers in public schools. His concurrence in *Texas v. Johnson* (1989)[157] expressed unqualified support for the majority decision striking down flag desecration statutes, although the justice was careful to note the "personal toll" exacted by his agonizing decision.[158] In *Casey*, Kennedy joined O'Connor and Souter in upholding the core abortion rights decision of *Roe v. Wade*. More recently, in *Romer v. Evans* (1996),[159] Justice Kennedy served as the Court's primary spokesmen against a Colorado constitutional provision preventing localities from offering special protections to homosexuals. Writing for a 7–2 majority, Kennedy wrote: "Central both to the idea of the rule of law and to our own guarantee of equal protection is the principle that government and each of its parts remain open on impartial terms to all who seek its assistance."

Certainly when viewed as a group, the Reagan appointees have more than lived up to the former president's expectations. In the areas of criminal justice and race-based remedial programs, the four justices (joined by Byron White and/or Clarence Thomas) have often formed a decisive conservative majority. A justice situated somewhere on the ideological spectrum between Bork and Kennedy might well have led to even greater ideological change. But the administration's all-or-nothing, ideological approach to selecting Supreme Court justices eventually cost it that extra influence.

CONCLUSION

The Reagan administration enjoyed a number of advantages over previous presidencies when considering and selecting nominees to the U.S. Supreme Court. A well-defined set of ideological criteria facilitated the effective delegation of sifting and winnowing responsibilities to Justice Department and White House bureaucracies. Unlike in the Nixon or Eisenhower administrations, however, these criteria were not so restrictive as to unduly narrow the pool of qualified candidates. Advances in research technology allowed the administration to perform quick computer searches of candidates' backgrounds and to review the complete body of judicial opinions for each jurist under consideration. The administration also enjoyed some advance notice from two of the three outgoing justices.

Why then did the administration enjoy only mixed success in the appointment process? Ronald Reagan's criteria-driven mechanism for selecting justices actually borrowed from various of his predecessors' practices. From Presidents Kennedy and Johnson he borrowed the tactic of surprise: the Reagan administration tried to get a jump on its critics by moving quickly to announce Supreme Court nominations. From Eisenhower in particular, Reagan borrowed the practice of relying heavily on his subordinates, trusting advisors to oversee most of details of the selection process. But Reagan also fell into traps that bedeviled some of his predecessors. Like Johnson, Reagan stubbornly held firm to one candidate in 1987 (Robert Bork) whose nomination drained the administration of precious political capital. And Reagan essentially institutionalized the multiple advisor approach to Supreme Court selections to which Nixon had resorted out of desperation in late 1971. Because bureaucracies in the Justice Department and the White House had been active in vetting nominees, a large number of officials sporting their own agendas enjoyed unprecedented influence over the selection process. The president's interests were not always served by such a haphazard arrangement.

In reality, changes in the political environment surrounding Supreme Court appointments have rendered the expansion and socialization of the appointment conflict a systemic problem. Reagan's approach to selecting nominees only exacerbated this condition. The increasingly public confirmation process now featured televised hearings, forcing nominees to defend (or avoid) conservative positions before an attentive (and generally less conservative) public. Advances in legal research provided a boon not only to administration lawyers doing their homework, but also to opposition groups in search of a "smoking gun" that might defeat the president's nominee. Abortion's central position in the public conscience during the 1980s raised the stakes further, drawing even more outsiders into the nomination process.

Reagan was counting on intensive preparation by the Justice Department and the White House to uncover any and all possible objections. Yet even with all this advance planning, Reagan's selection process ultimately foundered in 1987. Reagan delegated perhaps too much of the selection process to others, and he was unable to effectively mediate among competing factions with his own administration. Instead of insisting on a compromise, Reagan yielded to the pleas of his attorney general, then backed by two years of intense research and analysis. The increasingly public nature of the conflict—combined with Reagan's unassertive political leadership—thus led to unexpected difficulties in the confirmation process. Ironically, an administration accused of "overpoliticizing" the selection process was, in the final analysis, not always political enough for its own good.

SEVEN

A CLOSER LOOK

Patterns and Problems in

Nominee Selection

During the last half-century Supreme Court appointments have become high-stakes political events. As a result, many social scientists have been drawn to study heated confirmation battles as a means of gaining broad new insights into the nature of Supreme Court recruitment. By contrast, this study offers a quite different perspective from which to analyze Supreme Court recruitment: it focuses instead on the building of consensus and the resolution of conflicts during the initial nominating stage of the appointment process. Such an alternative way of viewing the process in no way discounts the influence that a looming confirmation battle may have on initial deliberations over prospective candidates. Successful confirmation politics often depends on whether the president has made astute selection decisions during those earlier stages of the appointment process.

Consider the political tightrope modern presidents must walk as they attempt to choose nominees in this highly charged political atmosphere. Organized interests on all sides of the political spectrum may try to influence their choice of a candidate at the outset. Senators, attuned to these changes in the political environment, may assume more aggressive postures against a rumored nominee even before the president has formally designated him or her for a Supreme Court seat. Increased media attention may scare some potential nominees away, further constraining presidential discretion. Fortunately, modern presidents do possess the means to respond to heightened expectations in this context. The steady growth and expansion of executive branch resources has afforded chief executives the ability to invest considerable manpower into the selection of candidates. Officials now enjoy access to sophisticated computer research technology for finding information about prospective nominees. Additionally, the growth in size and influence of the federal judiciary has expanded the pool of qualified candidates available to the president when filling any one vacancy.

I have attempted to document the nominee selection process as it unfolded during seven separate administrations between 1945 and 1987. Characteristics of the process may vary depending on the individual goals of the current occupant of the White House, his management style, and the nature of the vacancy at hand. Still, upon closer examination a number of significant patterns in nominee selection can be readily identified. First, in formulating his administration's approach to filling Supreme Court vacancies, a president often feels compelled to improve upon the practices of his predecessor and, in particular, to avoid any previous mistakes. Sometimes the current office-holder is responding to criticisms that a past president selected nominees of a generally low quality. Perhaps the previous president was forced to compromise his ideological priorities prematurely; the sitting president thus may want to persist more firmly in his goal of finding a like-minded Supreme Court candidate. At the opposite extreme, a previous president may have sent a highly controversial nominee to the Senate, only to see his nomination go down to ignominious defeat. In the process, that president may have weakened both his own standing with the public and his relations with Congress. Those negative experiences may provide an ominous backdrop for subsequent presidents forced to choose among conflicting priorities.

Unfortunately, presidents "try to fight the last war"—more often than not they "overreact" when seeking to duck the criticisms that were leveled at their predecessors. Perhaps the new president contributed much of this criticism himself as part of his election campaign; if so, his eagerness to avoid hypocrisy would be understandable. President Eisenhower reacted to Truman's deference for "cronies" by demanding that each high court nominee (at least after Earl Warren) possess some judicial experience in his background. President Kennedy responded to Eisenhower's "stilted" method of picking nominees by conducting a more comprehensive search, less fettered by such restrictive criteria. In 1968, candidate Nixon watched the Fortas affair closely; once in office he made sure to choose candidates he barely knew. Distancing himself from Nixon's public rejection of the ABA review process, the Ford administration relied heavily on the ABA to vet candidates for Justice Douglas's old seat in 1975. Reagan's aides in the Justice Department knew well the history of past Republican presidents growing disillusioned with nominees who unexpectedly turned liberal on the Court. Accordingly, they focused their recruitment efforts on judges with proven records as conservatives.

Reagan administration officials thus fell into line with a second modern trend in Supreme Court recruitment: federal circuit court judges have become the "darlings" of the selection process in modern times. Eisenhower was arguably the first president to aggressively pursue such a strategy. His public commitment to choose justices with prior judicial experience led him to name federal circuit judges to three of the five vacancies that arose during his administration. Almost a decade later Nixon picked up where Eisenhower left off: four of Nixon's six high court nominees were federal appeals judges, including his choice for chief justice, Warren Burger. Gerald Ford chose John Paul Stevens of the U.S. Court of Appeals for the Seventh Circuit to fill a vacancy on the Court in 1975. A decade later President Reagan confirmed his preference for federal circuit court judges by nominating four consecutive federal appeals judges to associate justice vacancies beginning in 1986. While only a third of the fifteen individuals nominated between 1945 and 1968 were federal appeals judges, sixteen of nineteen nominees since then have emerged from this elite pool of candidates.

Moreover, federal circuit court judges have often figured prominently on shortlists even when none are ultimately selected. Nonjudges Lewis Powell and William Rehnquist emerged as frontrunners in 1971 only after the administration's formal list of six candidates—which included Fifth Circuit Judges Charles Clark and Paul Roney—was leaked to the press. In 1981, Sandra Day O'Connor of the Arizona Court of Appeals edged out Cornelia Kennedy of the U.S. Court of Appeals for the Sixth Circuit for a Supreme Court bid. J. Clifford Wallace of the Ninth Circuit also received serious consideration for Potter Stewart's seat that same year. And as was noted above, the Reagan administration considered federal circuit judges almost exclusively during its second term in office.

Several factors have contributed to this heightened interest in federal appeals judges. Although hardly dispositive, federal appellate opinions offer perhaps the best gauge available for predicting an individual's future voting behavior on the Supreme Court. Thus an administration committed to a particular ideological blueprint may gravitate towards federal circuit judges who have addressed many of these same issues before. During the Reagan administration, several academics with Supreme Court aspirations (Bork, Scalia, Ralph Winter, and Richard Posner, to name just a few) accepted prestigious judgeships on the circuit courts, allowing administration officials to watch as their judicial philosophies matured.[1] Federal appeals judges also make for less controversial nominees before the U.S. Senate. Most escape the public's attention during their tenures on the courts of appeals. Opposition groups may be forced to expend considerable resources trying to turn a federal appeals judge into a political lightning rod during the confirmation process.[2] Admittedly, candidates for circuit court judgeships undergo a far less rigorous path to Senate confirmation than candidates for the Supreme Court, but they may benefit from having already survived the scrutiny of a complete FBI investigation and ABA review. Nearly all have already testified at least once before the Senate Judiciary Committee. Even more crucial are the ties many federal appeals judges enjoy to political patrons in the Senate. A senator from that judge's home state was probably responsible for his or her being offered that federal judgeship in the first place. Such connections with senators may later prove critically important when that judge is named to the U.S. Supreme Court.[3]

Finally, most circuit court judges chart a course of moderation on policy issues, carefully avoiding the polarizing viewpoints that later make for a troublesome paper trail. By contrast, law professors, congressmen, executive branch officials and others often achieve success in those positions precisely because they are willing to confront society's most heated public controversies. The active recruitment of federal circuit judges for the Supreme Court may thus represent a de facto move by presidential administrations to steer away from candidates whose legal philosophies fit into simple "black" or "white" categories, and towards more moderate candidates whose positions are difficult to categorize. Obviously, most circuit court opinions are readily available to the public, providing ready targets for determined members of the opposition. Yet more often than not, a circuit judge's opinions tend to betray outsiders' perceptions of that judge as a sharp ideological extremist. Even Robert Bork, noted for his controversial views on abortion, free speech, and other constitutional issues as a law professor, exercised uncharacteristic restraint and caution during his five years on the bench. Opponents of Bork's nomination were eventually forced to seek most of their ammunition from his earlier writings as a law professor. Even the ABA—which later split on the issue of Bork's fitness for the high court—regarded Bork's circuit court opinions as both "balanced in judgment" and "fair in treatment of the arguments of losing parties and dissenters."[4]

The patterns depicted above are indeed striking. Yet perhaps the most significant development of all has been the overall shift in the locus of candidate winnowing and vetting from the president himself to subordinates in the White House, the Justice Department, and elsewhere. In effect, the president has yielded what was traditionally a quite "personal" decision to various executive branch officials under his command. Criteria-driven frameworks for decisionmaking have facilitated this development: presidents may feel more comfortable transferring discretion to subordinates when that discretion is cabined within clearly defined guidelines. As was the case during the Eisenhower administration, those criteria may later prove so restrictive as to hinder a comprehensive search for candidates. The criteria may also prove too broad to effectively assist subordinates charged with weeding through lists of prospective candidates. In the latter case, a fierce battle among presidential advisors with competing viewpoints is likely to ensue. In either event, the president's overall goals and interests may not be maximized.

Before assessing the ways in which institutional and structural changes in government have influenced contemporary selection practices, we may benefit from a more informed comparison between the three decisional frameworks first outlined in chapter 1: "open," "single-candidate," and "criteria-driven." Once we understand the role that executive branch officials and their accompanying bureaucracies play in different selection frameworks, it becomes possible to assess the implications these developing roles may have on presidential success. Are the president's goals undermined by less flexible, more rigid selection frameworks? Or have presidents been forced to alter their goals in light of these institutional changes?

FRAMEWORKS FOR DECISIONMAKING: THE SHIFT TO A CRITERIA-DRIVEN SELECTION PROCESS

This book's empirical discussion of how modern presidents choose Supreme Court nominees lays the foundation for constructing a

more detailed model of how the president, the White House bureaucracy, the Justice Department, and other political actors influence the decisionmaking process. In *Courts and Politics: The Federal
Judicial System*,[5] Howard Ball attempts to chart "relevant patterns
of behavior" in this selection process for Supreme Court nominees.
While recognizing that "each nomination process is different," Ball
asserts that there is still some regularity to the selection process:
once it is known that there is a vacancy, the president, attorney
general, Justice Department officials, senators, pressure groups,
judges and potential candidates jockey for position to participate
in what he calls "judicial transactions."[6] Ball's depiction of the
initial phase of the selection process, extending from the moment
a vacancy first arises up to and including the formal submission of
a candidate's name to the Senate, is recreated in part in figure 1.
The diagram's strict emphasis on decisionmaking influences that
converge only *after* a vacancy arises must now be reassessed in light
of new evidence concerning the actual nature of the selection process. By drawing on presidential papers and interviews with former
high-level officials in the White House and Justice Department, we
can more precisely portray the range and timing of influences that
affect presidential decisionmaking in this nomination context.

An "open" decisionmaking framework for Supreme Court recruitment adheres most closely to the model of the process contemplated by Ball. This framework posits that few of the essential selection decisions (the identification of priorities, establishment of

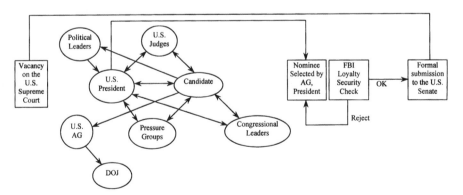

FIGURE 1 Ball's depiction of the Supreme Court nominee selection process (from vacancy through formal submission to the U.S. Senate). Drawn
from Howard Ball, *Courts and Politics: The Federal Judicial System* (Englewood Cliffs, N.J.: Prentice-Hall, 1980), 174.

criteria, the actual choice of candidates, etc.) will be settled upon until an actual vacancy arises. Surprisingly, between 1945 and 1987 only five nominations (including just one in the past thirty-five years) fell squarely within this category: Burton (Truman), Vinson (Truman), Clark (Truman), White (Kennedy), and Stevens (Ford). By utilizing an open decisionmaking framework (see fig. 2), the president may enjoy optimal flexibility. Prior commitments can be altered or adapted according to the vagaries of the immediate context. For example, the president may need to appease political leaders or interest groups based on sudden changes in the political environment.

Harry Truman's initial flexibility in addressing Supreme Court vacancies was in part a product of his own apathy on judicial matters, as little of the Supreme Court's docket held much interest for him. Thus Truman treated the first three high court vacancies of his presidency as he did most other vacancies within his own administration: he assessed the current political climate, weighed his options carefully, and then tried to reward friends and loyalists of his administration if at all possible.

Truman's experience illustrates both the benefits and the risks of the open selection framework. On one hand, he was able to react quickly to shifting political winds, both favorable and unfavorable. As a brand-new president in 1945, the highly partisan Truman succumbed to political pressures that compelled him to cross party lines and name a Republican to the Court. When Truman per-

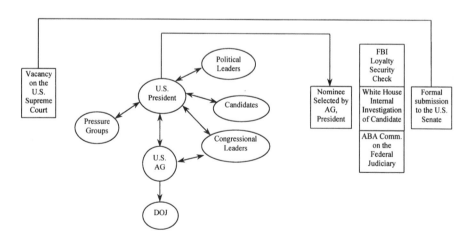

FIGURE 2 Open selection framework

ceived the need for a "peacemaker" as chief justice, he chose Fred Vinson over countless others with more judicial experience, including then-sitting Justice Robert Jackson. And when the political winds shifted back to Truman after his surprise election victory in 1948, Truman confidently turned to his own attorney general, Tom Clark, for the next Supreme Court seat.

In Truman's case, the flexibility and discretion allowed by an open selection mechanism proved a liability as well. Because he zealously kept most critical decisions to himself, there was no forceful attorney general or White House Counsel available to challenge Truman's political instincts when they were wrong or misguided. In the long run, Burton, Vinson, and Clark all proved to be relatively noninfluential jurists. By contrast, Presidents Kennedy and Ford relied heavily on their attorneys general to manage an open selection framework and advise them on candidates. All those considered for Charles Whittaker's vacant seat in 1962—a distinguished group that featured Arthur Goldberg, Byron White, Paul Freund, and William H. Hastie, among others—possessed sterling legal credentials. When President Ford initiated an open-ended search for William Douglas's successor in 1975, Attorney General Edward Levi invited the American Bar Association to screen all potential candidates under consideration. Needing a candidate who would be easily confirmable in a hostile climate, Ford ultimately settled on John Paul Stevens, a moderate noncontroversial jurist of unquestioned credentials.

At the opposite extreme from an open decisionmaking framework would be a selection process that targets just one candidate from the outset. In what amounts to an essentially "closed" selection mechanism, the nomination process becomes a pro forma political exercise. Remarkably, of the twenty-eight formal nominations considered in this book, nine such nominations emerged out of a single-candidate-focused framework: Minton (Truman), Warren (Eisenhower), Harlan (Eisenhower), Goldberg (Kennedy), Fortas I (Johnson), Marshall (Johnson), Fortas II (Johnson), Thornberry (Johnson), and Bork (Reagan).

In each of these nine cases, presidents or their duly authorized subordinates effectively settled on their respective nominees even before an actual vacancy had come into existence. (When Eisenhower considered candidates other than Earl Warren for chief justice in 1953, he was exercising wishful thinking: once Warren confirmed his interest in the Court's top spot, Eisenhower deferred to the original promise he made to the California governor, effectively terminating the more open search process.) Between 1945 and 1987, the average time elapsed from the administration's actual notice of a vacancy to the formal submission of a nomination to the Senate was just thirty-eight days. Yet in the nine cases above that time was cut by nearly 40 percent, to approximately twenty-three days. Presidents were thus able to preempt much of the political jockeying that normally occurs in the wake of a vacancy (see fig. 3).

Figure 3 modifies Ball's initial model of the process in several important ways. In the nomination process portrayed above, more formal selection practices that normally follow news of a vacancy (consultation with pressure groups, congressional leaders, etc.) are all but eliminated. Warren, Harlan, and Goldberg had each received promises of a Supreme Court seat from the administration in power. In 1949, President Truman was determined to reward Sherman Minton for his loyalty, and he never considered other candidates for Justice Rutledge's former seat. President Johnson employed a similarly closed approach when filling each high court vacancy that arose during his presidency. Robert Bork became the Justice Department's presumptive candidate in 1987 after finishing second to Antonin Scalia for a Supreme Court post the previous year. In each case there was no selection process analogous to that which Ball described: no formal process of gathering names of prospective candidates and no shortlists of alternative candidates.

By informally settling on one candidate in advance of a high-court vacancy, the White House effectively prevented interest groups and other outsiders from unduly influencing the nominee selection process. Few groups can effectively mobilize their members over a "hypothetical" Supreme Court vacancy that may arise

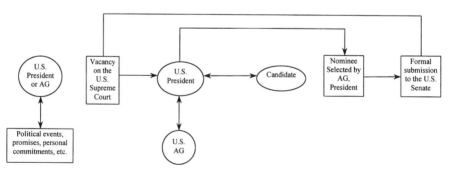

FIGURE 3 Single candidate–focused selection framework

some time in the future. Even senators sitting on the Senate Judiciary Committee rarely focus their energies on Supreme Court personnel matters when there is no current vacancy pending. Such an extreme containment of selection conflict may exact some political costs, however. Political circumstances may change dramatically. What may have seemed like a politically wise commitment a year ago can become a self-inflicted political wound at a later point in time. Sometimes a president is willing to jettison the single-candidate mechanism under such circumstances, as President Kennedy did in deferring his promise to Arthur Goldberg in March 1962. Others are not so politically nimble. Eisenhower was privately frustrated that, by fulfilling his promise to Earl Warren, he was denied the opportunity to name a renowned jurist as the next chief justice. President Johnson refused to heed his aides' warnings that a Fortas-Thornberry ticket was no longer politically viable in 1968; his decision to remain steadfast in favor of Fortas's promotion may have cost the Democrats their final chance this century to name a chief justice of the United States. Robert Bork's nomination might have survived Senate scrutiny in 1986 when the Republicans were in control by a 53–47 margin; but it stood far less chance in 1987 with a Democratic majority back at the helm.

At least three presidents discussed in this study (Eisenhower after 1955, Nixon, and Reagan) managed to avoid either of the two "open" or "closed" selection extremes, opting instead for a "criteria-driven" framework for decisionmaking. Fully half of the twenty-eight nominees addressed in this book emerged out of this type of selection framework, including eleven of thirteen nominations since 1969. In each case final candidates successfully survived multiple filters and guidelines established by the administration to assist the identification of prospective justices. Those nominations included the following: Brennan (Eisenhower), Whittaker (Eisenhower), Stewart (Eisenhower), Burger (Nixon), Haynsworth (Nixon), Carswell (Nixon), Blackmun (Nixon), Powell (Nixon), Rehnquist I (Nixon), O'Connor (Reagan), Scalia (Reagan), Rehnquist II (Reagan), Ginsburg (Reagan), and Kennedy (Reagan).

A president may prefer the criteria-driven selection framework for several reasons. He may perceive the need to strategize in advance about future vacancies. Perhaps the president wants to reassure vital constituencies of his commitment to their particular causes or interests. He may also view the appointment of Supreme Court justices as a high policy priority of his administration, worthy of advance consideration. Still, by settling only on criteria (and not actual individuals) for future vacancies, the administration theoretically enjoys some flexibility to maneuver even after a vacancy arises. Consistent with his original mandate, the president remains free to choose any nominee able to meet all of the prescribed criteria. The level of discretion he can exercise thus depends primarily on the size of the candidate pool remaining after all relevant filters have been applied.

A criteria-driven framework also allows the president to on one hand delegate extensive authority to subordinates, while at the same time maintaining ultimate authority and control over the process. The president may have been actively involved both in formulating the most appropriate criteria for future candidates (directly or indirectly) and then, once a vacancy arises, the president may act to enforce the guidelines. Of course he and his advisor(s) may also be forced to mediate among the various groups still seeking to influence the process (see fig. 4).

Figure 4 expands on Ball's model by incorporating into the diagram deliberations that occur both before and after a particular vacancy arises. Unlike in Ball's model, political leaders and pressure groups may directly influence the president in the advance formulation of criteria. And unlike in the "single-candidate" framework depicted in figure 3, political leaders and prospective candidates

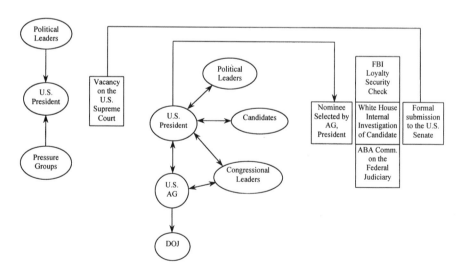

FIGURE 4 Criteria-driven selection framework

themselves may influence the president's choice within these restrictions. Presidents Eisenhower, Nixon, and Reagan each relied heavily on top advisors to manage the selection process once a vacancy occurred, canvassing the available pool of candidates for likely nominees who might satisfy the administration's prescribed criteria. Eisenhower directed Attorney General Brownell in 1956 to find a state judge who was Catholic, a Democrat, and below the age of sixty. William Brennan was one of few judges in the country able to satisfy each of those stringent conditions. For his final two nominations, Eisenhower insisted on Republican judges from the U.S. Court of Appeals between the ages of fifty and sixty; he gave in on the minimum age requirement in 1958 only after Attorney General William Rogers persuaded him of forty-three-year-old Potter Stewart's merits. Within those boundaries there was room to maneuver. Roy Roberts successfully lobbied for Charles Whittaker's appointment, but his efforts might have fallen on deaf ears had Whittaker not met each of the administration's filters to perfection. Richard Nixon was determined to name as associate justice a southerner with a conservative record, preferably under the age of sixty. He viewed experience as a federal judge preferable, though not a hard and fast requirement. Clement Haynsworth and G. Harrold Carswell fit the president's criteria precisely, although each of their two candidacies met with disastrous consequences in the Senate. Harry Blackmun received a nomination only after a reluctant President Nixon introduced a new filter in the final hour: Blackmun was a Minnesota native, and thus fit the president's sudden need for a federal appeals judge from the North. In late 1971 Nixon nominated Lewis Powell, a sixty-four-year-old Democrat from Virginia with no previous judicial experience: with the appointment of a confirmable southerner now the president's top priority, Nixon was forced to abandon other criteria (Powell violated his age criterion) that had limited the pool substantially up to that point.

As Ronald Reagan's priorities for the Court shifted during his two terms in office, so did his administration's criteria for selecting Supreme Court nominees. In 1981 Reagan sought to fulfill an earlier campaign promise to name the first woman to the Supreme Court. During the second term his administration placed considerably greater weight on ideological criteria, sifting through opinions written by prospective justices for evidence of conservative leanings. By the time Warren Burger announced his retirement as chief justice in May 1986, the Justice Department had already effectively

narrowed the list of potential Supreme Court candidates to six federal appeals judges. By doing its homework well in advance, the
administration was able to streamline the selection process once an
actual vacancy arose. The Justice Department's list stayed virtually
intact even after Burger made his retirement plans known. President Reagan did not unduly limit the subsequent selection process,
however: the pool of young, conservative, federal appeals judges
considered by his administration was still large enough to allow the
flexible pursuit of administration interests. Accordingly, his administration was able to choose between more controversial conservative candidates (Ginsburg, Bork, and Scalia) favored by Meese's
Justice Department, or those who were considered more readily
confirmable (i.e., Anthony Kennedy).

UNDERMINING PRESIDENTIAL INTERESTS?
MULTIPLE ADVISORS, OVERLAPPING
RESPONSIBILITIES

One of the defining characteristics of the modern presidency has
been its heavy reliance on White House and executive branch bureaucracies for assistance in decisionmaking. In this spirit, recent
presidents have increasingly turned to trusted advisors and subordinates to aid them in their Supreme Court recruitment efforts. Frustrated by an increasingly hostile atmosphere for appointments,
President Nixon enlisted multiple officials both inside and outside
the White House to aid him in the process of screening potential nominees. Similarly, during his two terms in office President
Reagan unabashedly relied on a troika of high-level advisors (the
attorney general, the White House chief of staff, and the White
House Counsel) to help him identify and select Supreme Court
candidates. In turn, each of those officials aggressively deployed
their own departmental resources to size up the field of potential candidates. Yet despite such an impressive show of executive
branch manpower, both of those two administrations suffered em-
barrassing nomination mishaps and squandered precious political
capital in the process. Did the delegation of decisionmaking authority to so many different offices and advisors actually undermine
presidential interests in this context?

  Noted scholar Sheldon Goldman has identified three types of
goals a president may wish to pursue in selecting judicial nominees.[7]
Personal goals include the desire to favor a personal friend or associ-

ate with a nomination. *Policy goals* include any substantive or ideological goals the president holds for the Court itself (most achieved only in the long term, if at all). Finally, a president may pursue short-term *partisan goals* in hopes of preserving or even increasing political support for himself and his party. Although numerous motives and rationales may often come into play in the course of filling any one Supreme Court vacancy, presidential success can be measured fairly only by examining the degree to which the president achieves the goals he sets out for himself when filling a particular vacancy.

Neither Nixon nor Reagan ever expressed any interest in fulfilling personal goals through the appointment process. Rather, their administrations' recruitment efforts were geared towards meeting specific partisan goals in the case of each vacancy, and towards the accomplishment of broader policy goals, including a more conservative Supreme Court. Given those priorities, some delegation of selection responsibilities was perhaps inevitable. For Nixon, the strategy of relying on overlapping staff structures arose in response to a growing perception inside the White House that his attorney general had been overwhelmed by the magnitude of the selection process. By contrast, Reagan adopted such an approach hoping that the involvement of multiple officials early on would both broaden the field of candidates under consideration, as well as bring numerous and varied perspectives to the deliberation process. Unfortunately, these decisionmaking schemes were also fraught with potential hazards.

At least one school of organizational theory posits that if one part of an organization simply duplicates a function being performed by another, negative consequences will be caused to the organization as a whole.[8] From an economic perspective this makes perfect sense: duplicative functions cause an unnecessary drain on the organization's resources. Even more troubling, however, is the negative impact such overlapping responsibilities may have on the quality of information produced by the separate departments. Specifically, the quality of information and advice received by the organization's head (in this case the president) from department heads suffers when the latter are thrust into a competition of sorts, with each trying to inject their own interests into the political equation.

An astute president may earnestly try to reduce the likelihood of competition among his immediate brain trust. Even so, competition among advisors is all but inevitable in a narrow decisionmaking context such as this, where only one outcome (the final selection of a nominee) carries any significance. Conflicts may spring initially from differences in advisors' modes of perceiving reality—given even the slightest degree of ambiguity, members inevitably disagree about what the organization as a whole ought to be doing.[9] Drawing on their own distinct suborganizations for research and analysis, each official brings to the table different information about the same subject, encouraging the coexistence of a variety of views about the likely outcome of given action.[10] Respectful disagreements may escalate into broader conflicts, as dedicated officials take on additional roles as advocates for their subgroup's own special interests.

These officials may sincerely believe their own department's information is more reliable than that produced by others. Because each official's success as an advocate determines his subgroup's general prestige and status within the administration, subgroup members' respect and willingness to work for that official "will be greatly affected by the degree to which he is able to influence his own superiors through vigorous advocacy." Officials at all levels understand that "a bureau headed by a 'tiger' who 'fights for his men'—that is, who advocates their specialized functions against others—tends to have a higher esprit de corps than a bureau headed by an impartial official who sympathizes equally with other bureaus." These cultural expectations in turn only encourage department heads to further behave like advocates; after all, others may interpret an attitude of compromise by him or her as a sign of weakness or apathy.[11]

The negative effects that such behavior may have on actual nomination decisions should not be underestimated. When a bureau (whether it is the Justice Department, the White House Counsel's Office, or the Office of the White House Chief of Staff) reaches its own conclusions on the merits of any given issue, it normally prepares some type of communication or memorandum in support of its findings. However, in a competitive environment, that message "necessarily leaves out or drastically simplifies many of the inputs that went into the actual choice process. . . . [O]fficials in other parts of the bureau thus see only the rather simplified final result."[12] "Outcome optimism" also pervades this process. As one leading organizational theorist explained:

> Forming a winning coalition almost always leads coalition members to
> overestimate the positive consequences to be expected. . . . Structurally,

since programs are rarely adopted when expectations are erroneously pessimistic, the sample of programs actually adopted is more likely to exhibit errors of overoptimism than of overpessimism. . . . Policies will, on average, be oversold. . . .[13]

Clearly a president may not be acting on the best information available to him under these conditions; rather, he is forced to choose among competing versions of the alleged truth, each crafted to counter the others. Presidential decisionmaking surely suffers as a consequence.

Consider the role played by a White House chief of staff whose job responsibilities lead him to favor the president's *partisan* interests (high standing with the public, preservation of political capital for his party, etc.). When faced with competition from competing advisors, he may try to oversell a candidate best equipped to achieve only those limited objectives. By contrast, the attorney general in that same instance may be focused on achieving the president's *policy* goals (overturning *Roe v. Wade*, etc.), and in order to outmaneuver the competition he may choose to ignore relevant partisan minefields while backing a more "ideologically correct" candidate along the way. Certainly it would have been useful for the president to rank order his priorities and goals, as few candidates are able to maximize every goal at once. Still, what about a candidate who would advance both partisan *and* policy goals, although to a lesser degree on each count than the original two candidates? A president surely benefits from also considering candidates who—without maximizing any one objective—manage to strike a favorable balance among numerous interests.

Unfortunately, the scenario described above may encourage only the most extreme options to come to the fore. By contrast, if the attorney general was the *only* advisor in the process, he might be more willing to sacrifice some of his own personal agenda to maximize the president's overall interests. After all, his position of influence would never be threatened; he will not only live to fight another day, he will still be in charge on that later day as well! Additionally, the pressures from within the attorney general's subgroup (the Justice Department) would be far less pronounced in a single-advisor scenario. The attorney general cannot lose face so easily; the only defeat he may suffer will be at the hands of the president himself. Finally, the Justice Department's relative prestige vis-à-vis another department is never called into question. In their efforts to improve access to information, Presidents Nixon and Reagan involved multiple advisors in the nominee selection process. By transforming the decisionmaking process into a competitive environment, they inadvertently introduced a countervailing force into the deliberations, one that placed a higher cost on that same information.

Before 1969, most presidents were able to minimize internal conflict within their administrations in this context of Supreme Court recruitment. Presidents Truman and Johnson pursued deeply personal goals in recruiting Supreme Court nominees, and their so-called advisors on this matter played little (if any) role in the selection process. Presidents Eisenhower and Kennedy shared little in common except for their strict attention to partisan goals and their respective commitments to grant broad and exclusive selection authority to their attorneys general. Indeed, Eisenhower insisted that all other officials in his administration (including Special Counsel Bernard Shanley) go through the attorney general with any suggestions or recommendations for Supreme Court vacancies. Because Brownell was the only authoritative figure in the process aside from the president himself, the risk of corrupt information was reduced considerably. In fact, in early 1957 Brownell dutifully recommended Charles Whittaker, the candidate who best fit the president carefully defined criteria (a Midwestern federal appeals court judge, Republican, under sixty) even though he personally lacked enthusiasm for Whittaker's candidacy. President Kennedy also enjoyed some measure of success relying primarily on the expertise and political instincts of Justice Department officials. For example, even Robert Kennedy's vehement opposition to Paul Freund did not prevent him from engaging in a free and open discussion of the merits of Freund's candidacy.

By contrast, examples abound of internal competition interfering with, and in some cases corrupting, recruitment efforts during the Nixon and Reagan administrations. Declining to consider any personal goals in selecting his Supreme Court nominees, Nixon relied on the expertise of subordinates to help him fulfill policy goals (the creation of a more conservative court) and partisan goals (shoring up southern support for his administration). Those objectives were quickly undermined, however, by two critical handicaps the administration was laboring under: his attorney general's lack of political effectiveness and the unduly restrictive filters Nixon insisted on applying to each Supreme Court vacancy. Following back-to-back

Senate rejections of Haynsworth and Carswell, Nixon refused to replace Mitchell with a more qualified selection authority; instead the president invited numerous other officials into the decisionmaking process to possibly spar with Mitchell—Pat Buchanan, John D. Ehrlichman, Bud Krogh, David Young, and Richard Moore. Even with this bevy of advisors, the administration continued to suffer under the weight of its own distorted information channels. In 1971, Richard Poff's expected nomination came undone publicly because Pat Buchanan (Poff's chief supporter in the White House) conveniently overlooked the negative effects of his favorite candidate's support for the Southern Manifesto. In advocating close friend Herschel Friday for one vacancy, Mitchell was pursuing his own personal agenda rather than the administration's: he too ignored the relative weaknesses in Friday's credentials.

The Reagan administration breathed life once again into Nixon's multiple-advisor scheme, instituting it as formal administration policy. Attorney General William French Smith may have masterminded the selection of Sandra Day O'Connor in 1981, but her nomination also required the approval of White House Counsel Fred Fielding, whose office generated its own list of candidates to recommend to the president. Fielding, looking out for the president's policy interests, might have had misgivings about any candidate whose position on abortion rights was open to question. But the more moderate attorney general was more concerned with the president's partisan goals (appointment of a female, smooth confirmation), and so he redoubled his efforts on O'Connor's behalf. During his second term, Reagan relied on aides from three different offices to provide critical input concerning Supreme Court candidates. When political circumstances were favorable for the administration—as they were in 1986—Attorney General Edwin Meese was able to pursue the administration's policy goals without regard to partisan concerns: Antonin Scalia's nomination was a victory for partisan and policy goals; indeed it was a home run on both counts.

By contrast, Meese's insistence the following year on the pursuit of policy goals at all costs ultimately dealt a serious blow to the administration's partisan interests. Despite warnings of a possible confirmation fight, Meese and his assistants argued forcefully on behalf of Bork, pressing for an announcement mere days after Powell's retirement. The quick rush to judgment benefited Meese's aggressive pursuit of policy goals, as potentially competing points of view in the White House Counsel's Office were denied the necessary time to mobilize. This competition among advisors may have exaggerated Meese's perceived costs of losing; after all, Bork's replacement might now be some other official's first choice, rather than Meese's own second choice. The competition thus indirectly encouraged this rush to judgment and discouraged more reasoned contemplation about Bork's candidacy. In fact, the multiple advisors' scheme may have actually generated a "winners' curse" during the later Reagan years: an advisor's preferences would only be satisfied if his probable return was somehow unduly exaggerated.

In the final analysis, this scheme of overlapping staff responsibilities often failed to reap the benefits Presidents Nixon and Reagan were hoping for. Assuming the president remained unwilling to digest every piece of paper generated in the wake of a vacancy, the task of filtering information would inevitably assume a place of primary importance in any decisionmaking scheme. Overlapping staff structures risk distorting information flow, and therefore corrupting the advice a president must necessarily rely upon. The adage "too many cooks spoil the broth" has never proved more apt.

SOME FINAL THOUGHTS

Drawing on evidence derived from presidential papers and interviews, this book attempted to systematically compare Supreme Court nominee selection practices from the Truman administration through the Reagan administration. From a strictly scientific perspective, twenty-eight case studies is probably too small a number from which to draw generalizations about relevant do's and don't's in Supreme Court recruitment. So many conclusions one might draw may be circumstantially biased or fact-dependent: the president's standing with the public, the type of justice being replaced, or even unrelated political events occurring at the time of a vacancy, may all represent significant variables in this equation. Even with those qualifications so noted, various insights about the strategic exercise of presidential power stand out in this context.

Rather than ignoring modern developments in the selection process, presidents must learn to embrace them. Advisors and department heads with access to sophisticated technological resources and legal talent may access a broader pool of candidates than was ever before possible. The primary challenge for presidents in the modern era has been to determine how to harness those resources effectively and direct them towards the pursuit of presidential goals.

To that end, one eminently qualified presidential advisor (either the attorney general or the White House Counsel) must be entrusted with the bulk of recruitment responsibilities; ideally, that individual should combine political savvy with formidable legal expertise. Although it may be preferable to establish some guidelines for judicial recruitment, overly restrictive criteria may unduly hamper the selection process, undercutting even the most diligent advisor's best efforts to choose a qualified Supreme Court nominee. It may also force the quality of selection outcomes down to its lowest common denominator. A president should rarely involve more than one executive branch office or agency in this decisionmaking process early on—by encouraging numerous officials to assume overlapping responsibilities, the president risks reducing the quality of the information he receives. The lesson is clear: modern presidents have *too much* information about prospective candidates at their disposal. Judicial selection mechanisms should thus be designed with an eye towards filtering information for the president in as unbiased a fashion as possible.

Since the beginning of the Republic, the appointment of Supreme Court nominees has been divided into two parts: the initial *nomination phase* of the appointment process, dominated by the president, and the *confirmation phase* of the appointment process, dominated by the Senate. The former decisionmaking phase, traditionally ignored by journalists and scholars, is finally starting to get its due. Frankly, what we discover about this process upon closer examination is not always a pretty sight. Rather than complaining about their lack of input in the initial stages of a nomination, senators would be well advised to leave the current system alone. For a president, the choices are virtually unlimited, and at the same time, unduly narrow. And to more and more Americans, the stakes have never been higher.

EPILOGUE
THE SELECTION PRACTICES
OF BUSH AND CLINTON
Some Initial Observations

The preceding study documented the methods used by presidents to identify and select Supreme Court nominees during the period from 1945 through 1987. These time boundaries were chosen for practical reasons. This book attempts to provide a *comparative* analysis of different administrations' selection mechanisms. Accordingly, it was necessary to draw on reasonably similar types of data and materials when analyzing relevant case studies. Certainly there are more officials still available to be interviewed from the Reagan and Ford administrations than from the Truman or Eisenhower administrations; yet ample oral histories available from those earlier administrations managed to level out the evidentiary landscape considerably. Even more critical to this comparative analysis was the availability of papers from all seven administrations located in presidential libraries and other archival facilities around the country. In most cases I was able to verify facts and information gleaned from interviews and oral histories by corroborating them with information found in primary source materials and documents. Although no method of qualitative research is infallible, this system of cross-referencing documents with oral accounts proved more than adequate to the task at hand.

What about the selection practices of more recent administrations? During the early 1990s we witnessed four additional nominations to the Supreme Court. President Bush appointed David Souter to the Court in 1990, and followed with the appointment of Clarence Thomas a year later. President Clinton tapped Ruth Bader Ginsburg for a high court vacancy in 1993, and then appointed Stephen Breyer to the Court in 1994. At the time this book

went to press, papers from the Bush administration were only starting to be made available to scholars, and even then they have been
released only on a limited basis. By statute, papers from the Clinton
administration will not be made available to scholars until January
2006 at the earliest. Despite these practical obstacles, I attempt in
this final section to venture some initial observations about these
four most recent appointments to the high court. I base my findings
primarily on the limited data that is available—mostly newspaper
reports and secondary accounts of the process. Any conclusions
drawn must therefore be considered tentative at best.

   While Abe Fortas, Clement Haynsworth, and G. Harrold Carswell all saw their nomination hopes disappointed in previous years,
Robert Bork's ill-fated Supreme Court bid in 1987 fundamentally
changed the nature of public discourse that would surround all
future Supreme Court appointments. By their persistent attacks
on Bork's academic writings, Democratic senators established a
precedent for challenging future nominees on strictly ideological
grounds. Through the advent of live, nationally televised hearings,
the greater public was able to gain access to this process as well.
Sophisticated advertising campaigns and successful lobbying efforts
by interest groups helped to shift public opinion on the merits of
Bork's candidacy. Encouraged by their success, these and other
special interests naturally would vie for influence over future Supreme Court appointments as well. Nor would these developments
be strictly limited to judicial appointments: presidential nominees
for a variety of offices risked becoming scapegoats or casualties in
the increasingly hostile political environment of the late 1980s and
early 1990s. John Tower, Zoë Baird, Lani Guinier, and even Henry
Foster could all trace some aspect of their unfortunate confirmation
experiences to the events surrounding Bork's failed nomination in
1987.

   Officials in both the Bush and Clinton administrations astutely
recognized that in such a contentious political atmosphere even the
most sophisticated public relations tactics might not rescue an ill-
advised nomination. Both presidencies thus placed considerable
emphasis on selection practices that preceded the formal submission of an individual nominee to the Senate. How well did the two
presidents fare in this regard? All four nominees were eventually
confirmed, three of them by especially wide margins. Although all
of the nominees were peppered with questions about their policy
views, none of the four sets of confirmation hearings inspired the

furious ideological debate reminiscent of the Bork affair. In fact, the only truly controversial nominee of the group, Clarence Thomas, eventually drew most of his most ardent criticism from allegations that he had sexually harassed a subordinate, Anita Hill, in a previous capacity as a federal official.

To be sure, both presidents pursued objectives beyond merely the guarantee of a successful confirmation outcome; otherwise, neither Clarence Thomas nor Mario Cuomo would have been considered for Supreme Court seats in the first place. (Thomas accepted Bush's offer; Cuomo declined interest in a similar offer from Clinton.) Certainly they aspired to choose nominees who (at least in general terms) would not assume positions antithetical to their party's ideological views. But political capital was also at a premium for both presidents in the early 1990s. A long, drawn-out confirmation fight might significantly endanger their respective legislative and policy agendas. Debts incurred to senators casting critical votes on confirmation might come back to haunt the president at inopportune moments later on. The Bush administration was willing to take some calculated risks in this regard, especially after weathering charges of having caved in to the Democrats with the nomination of Souter. To Clinton, however, this interest in a quick and painless confirmation process quickly turned into an obsession, infiltrating nearly every stage of his decisionmaking process. Although we lack primary source data from which to draw any definitive conclusions in this regard, we may still be able to construct a vivid enough picture of their respective recruitment practices to judge (at least in more qualified terms) the relative effectiveness of their administrations' organizational and decisionmaking tactics.

While campaigning for president in 1988, George Bush assured voters that he planned to "continue the Reagan legacy" in most respects. In the context of his Supreme Court nominations, however, Bush did not completely live up to that promise. In truth, Bush was never the committed ideologue Reagan had been on most social issues. But social conservatives helped elect Bush as president, and his administration's commitment to name conservatives justices to the Supreme Court seemed to them a political entitlement. Like Reagan, President Bush asked his aides to draw up a list of possible Supreme Court candidates long before the first vacancy of his administration arose during the summer of 1990. Bush also borrowed Reagan's tactic of utilizing a three-person committee to advise him on prospective nominations. Attorney General Dick

Thornburgh, White House Chief of Staff John Sununu, and White House Counsel C. Boyden Gray all enjoyed their share of influence and input into the recruitment process. Where Bush parted ways with his former boss, however, was in the way he set priorities for each vacancy. During the Reagan administration, ideological conservatism had been a primary consideration in most deliberations. For Bush, other factors—in particular, confirmability—came to the fore early and often as he considered prospects for the Supreme Court.

In 1990, George Bush's obsession with finding a "Trojan horse" or "stealth" candidate who might avoid Bork's fate produced the nomination of David Souter, a U.S. Court of Appeals judge from Boston. Immediately after Bush administration officials learned of Associate Justice William Brennan's decision to retire on July 20, they had already narrowed a previously compiled list of candidates to four frontrunners: Souter, Judge Edith Jones of the U.S. Court of Appeals for the Fifth Circuit, and Judges Lawrence Silberman and Clarence Thomas of the U.S. Court of Appeals for the D.C. Circuit. C. Boyden Gray and Richard Thornburgh agreed that Thomas, still just three months into his tenure on the D.C. Circuit, should serve additional time on the circuit before being promoted. Thomas might also serve as a potential political lightning rod were he to be promoted with so little judicial experience behind him; Bush wanted a candidate with a lower national profile who could emerge from the confirmation process unscathed. Eventually the group of officials considering the nomination—Bush, Thornburgh, Gray, and Sununu—focused their attention on the candidacies of Jones and Souter exclusively.

Jones, forty-one, was the more ideologically conservative of the two candidates. She attracted Bush's interest at this late stage for one main reason: according to officials, during her five-year stint as a federal appeals judge she had never written directly on the abortion issue or on any other matter that might now cause confirmation difficulties. Still, Jones could be a polarizing figure. Liberal advocates labeled her temperamental and doctrinaire, citing her somewhat questionable habit of chastising defense lawyers in death penalty cases.[1] Meanwhile, Republican and conservative advocates viewed her as one of the brightest young exponents of judicial restraint. With the 1990 budget battle looming and critical midterm elections just a few months away, a battle to confirm Jones might drain the administration of vital political resources.

Souter, at age fifty, was considered even less vulnerable to attack. Most of his judicial experience had been amassed on the New Hampshire Supreme Court, where controversial questions of federal constitutional law were far and few between. In fact, despite serving in a number of different public capacities, Souter's paper trail was generally sparse. In the twenty-two years since he had left private law practice, Souter had altogether avoided the subject of abortion rights, having never given a speech, written a law review article, or taken a public position of any kind on the correctness of *Roe v. Wade.* Thus by the administration's way of thinking, Souter was the "anti-Bork." Souter's credentials also seemed beyond reproach: two Harvard degrees, a Rhodes Scholarship at Oxford, and experience as a judge at both the state and federal levels. His candidacy further benefited from the presence of several strategically situated supporters. The well-respected Senator Warren Rudman (R-N.H.) had first brought Souter's name to the attention of Reagan administration officials in late 1987 just as support for Bork was collapsing. Souter also enjoyed the enthusiastic support of John Sununu, who as governor of New Hampshire had appointed Souter to the New Hampshire Supreme Court years earlier.

Souter and Jones flew to Washington on July 22 and each met the following day with C. Boyden Gray and the president. After these meetings, Bush reportedly leaned towards Souter; his stance was encouraged in no small part by Sununu's continued praise for his candidacy. The president was now counting on Sununu's backing to help shore up conservative support for this lesser-known candidate. Although social conservatives had been suspicious about Bush to begin with, Sununu enjoyed a particularly strong reputation among conservatives and—unlike Souter—his stance against abortion rights was a matter of public record. Thus if Souter's conservative credentials were ever challenged, he would enjoy the support of at least one official in the administration whose credentials in that regard were unquestioned. On the afternoon of July 23, Bush announced his plans to nominate Judge David Souter to the U.S. Supreme Court to replace William Brennan. The Senate easily confirmed Souter's nomination as an associate justice two months later on October 2, 1990, by a 90–9 vote.

Although it may seem surprising in retrospect, those same interests in confirmability dominated selection deliberations in 1991, when Bush faced the challenge of replacing Thurgood Marshall on the Supreme Court. The former civil rights advocate and jurist announced his intention to retire from the Court after twenty-four years of service on June 27, 1991. Once again the president hoped to find a candidate who would be difficult for the Democratic-controlled Senate to attack. Indeed, the stakes seemed even higher this time around, as any prolonged delay in confirmation might well produce a Democratic stonewall until after the 1992 election. Conflicting pressures came from conservatives within the party who required assurance of the administration's continued commitment to their social agenda. Their fears had gained some substance in the past year: During his initial term on the Court, Justice Souter had revealed himself to be a moderate ally of Justice Sandra Day O'Connor, voting with her in all twenty-four split decisions of the Court. A second "moderate" nominee might gut conservative enthusiasm for Bush reelection campaign the following fall.

To the administration's way of thinking, Clarence Thomas seemed in most respects an ideal candidate for striding the line between confirmability and allegiance to conservatives. To be certain, Thomas had created his own set of political enemies. A graduate of Yale Law School, he had compiled an elaborate resume working in the federal government under two Republican presidents: first as assistant secretary of education, and later as chairman of the Equal Employment Opportunity Commission. While at the EEOC Thomas had honed his conservative credentials, taking positions at odds with most civil rights groups. His carefully nurtured reputation as a political conservative was sure to attract unwelcome attention from liberals on the Senate Judiciary Committee.

On the other hand, Thomas's Yale pedigree and fifteen months' service on the most prestigious federal appeals court would probably land him a positive ABA rating. And several administration officials including Gray were certain that Thomas's nomination would at a minimum pose a tricky dilemma for civil rights groups. As an African American, Thomas's selection would in effect continue the so-called black seat on the Court vacated by Marshall; his defeat might endanger the seat's existence for the time being, just as Fortas's rejection had eventually led to the suspension of the "Jewish seat." Thomas's selection would also free Bush from the inevitable criticism that would follow the appointment of any white nominee to replace Marshall. Indeed, it appeared to Bush's aides that the *only* way the administration could nominate a verifiable conservative would be to in effect wrap him or her up in the tradition of the "black seat."

   In the wake of Marshall's June 27 announcement, press speculation focused immediately on Jones, Silberman, and Thomas, all finalists for the Court from the previous year. If there were still any
lingering doubts in the administration about Thomas at this point,
C. Boyden Gray moved quickly to stifle them. The president's chief
legal advisor had gotten to know Thomas socially in Washington's
conservative circles, and was struck by his adamant rejection of the
principles of affirmative action. Apparently Gray and Thomas had
discussed the issue while running a ten-kilometer road race together; Thomas had suggested that the recently proposed civil
rights legislation would only hurt fellow African Americans by
encouraging them to look to the government for help.[2] Gray
and Thornburgh initiated contact with Thomas and interviewed
him immediately following Marshall's announcement. Although
Thornburgh was duly impressed with the judge, he raised concerns
again about Thomas's confirmability; the attorney general warned
the president at a June 28 meeting that Thomas's politics had inspired the enmity of civil rights groups. As an alternative, Thornburgh reportedly lobbied the president to also consider a Hispanic
for Marshall's seat. Sununu signed onto Thornburgh's premise,
suggesting that the president was more likely to reap political re-
wards from Hispanics than blacks in the following year's presidential election. Thornburgh even compiled a new shortlist featuring
four Hispanic candidates: U.S. District Judge Ricardo H. Hinojosa
of southern Texas; Judge Emilio Garza of the U.S. Court of
Appeals for the Fifth Circuit; Judge Ferdinand F. Fernandez of the
U.S. Court of Appeals for the Ninth Circuit; and Judge Jose
Cabranes, a former Yale law professor then sitting on the U.S. district court in Connecticut.
   The appointment of a Hispanic might well have given the administration the political cover it needed in replacing Marshall. But
Gray was committed to Thomas and he continued to campaign on
the candidate's behalf. The White House Counsel soon found two
key allies in his effort: Vice President Dan Quayle and Senator John
Danforth (R-Mo.). Danforth in particular offered steadfast support
for Thomas, who had once served as a legislative assistant in his
office. To strengthen his case, Gray put out feelers in the civil rights
community concerning Thomas, ostensibly as a means of testing
his confirmability in advance. Would civil rights leaders openly and
actively oppose the appointment of a black conservative to Marshall's seat? Through intermediaries Gray learned that Benjamin

Hooks of the NAACP would agree to steer his organization away from actively opposing Thomas.[3] From the White House's admittedly biased perspective, confirmability appeared to be an asset rather than a weakness of Thomas's candidacy. As a final concession to Thornburgh and Sununu on the issue, the president agreed to interview at least one of the Hispanic candidates on their list. Thus Judge Emilio Garza flew up to the president's retreat in Kennebunkport to meet with the President. Like Thomas, Garza was only forty-three years old. But Garza had sat on the appeals court for a mere two months, a full year less than Thomas. Even Thomas's mostly political credentials seemed to outshine those of Garza. On Monday July 1, the president—still vacationing in Maine—introduced Thomas to a crowd of reporters as his newest nominee to serve on the U.S. Supreme Court.

Confirmability had been a key factor in Thomas's selection, just as it had been a year earlier in the selection of Souter. This time, however, the administration also tried to capture the imagination of conservatives with the appointment; the so-called African American seat provided the critical linchpin in the administration's efforts to join two seemingly conflicting interests (confirmability and ideological conservatism) together into one nomination. Unfortunately for Bush, Gray badly underestimated the level of opposition Thomas would attract, the assurances of others notwithstanding. Despite Hooks's earnest efforts to repress opposition from the NAACP's national organization, the group eventually opposed his nomination by a decisive 49–1 vote. The National Bar Association (a conference of prominent black attorneys from across the country) and the National Council of Black Lawyers also opposed Thomas. The appointment of an ardently black conservative was obviously causing less of a dilemma for these groups than Bush and Gray had hoped. In fact, of all the major civil rights groups whose approval the administration was seeking, only the Southern Christian Leadership Conference came out in support of Thomas's nomination.[4]

Thomas's showing at his initial confirmation hearings was uneventful overall, as he steered away from providing any lethal ammunition to his opponents. Specifically, the candidate skillfully avoided any statement on how he might vote as a justice, and soon appeared headed for confirmation by a decisive (if not overwhelming) margin. Even Senate Democrats opposed to Thomas confessed that the hearings probably had not raised enough warning flags to swing the necessary number of votes against him. Only last-minute allegations of sexual harassment brought by a former aide of Thomas's, Anita Hill, helped prevent a relatively quick close to these confirmation proceedings. After Hill detailed her charges during a second set of Senate Judiciary Committee hearings, Thomas denied the allegations forthrightly in hearings that were televised and reported widely in the media. Despite the new charges, the Senate Judiciary Committee chose to make no formal recommendation to the full Senate. Finally, on October 15, 1991, the Senate voted to confirm Thomas's nomination by a narrow 52–48 margin.

In contrast to his two Republican predecessors in office, ideology played little or no role at all in the selection of Supreme Court nominees during Bill Clinton's first term as president. Certainly his administration planned to draw from a pool of mostly liberal and Democratic candidates. Yet as early as fall of 1992, then-Governor Clinton was already giving public hints about his preferences for future Supreme Court nominees, and his declared emphasis was on backgrounds and political experience rather than beliefs and ideological viewpoints. For example, Clinton talked of putting a seasoned politician on the Court, someone who might be able to build judicial coalitions just as Earl Warren had done. In fact, on two separate occasions during his presidential campaign Bill Clinton the candidate glowingly spoke of New York Governor Mario Cuomo as a possible Supreme Court nominee.[5] Of course those comments came before Bill Clinton the president was forced to weigh the effect a controversial nominee might have on his ambitious legislative agenda.

After Byron White announced his intention to retire from the Court on March 19, 1993, the Clinton administration initiated a long, drawn-out selection process that seemed to jut back and forth between satisfying the president's desire for an "ex-pol," on one hand, and bending to political reality on the other hand. Still quite early in his first term, Clinton had already found himself embroiled in a number of confirmation battles, first over the nomination of Zoë Baird to serve as attorney general, and then over the prospective nomination of Judge Kimba Wood to the same position.[6] Lani Guinier's ill-fated bid to become civil rights head at the Justice Department soon followed.

On March 20, Clinton's first formal conference to discuss the nomination included an especially large contingent of advisors:

White House Chief of Staff Thomas "Mack" McLarty, Policy Advisor Bruce Lindsey, Deputy White House Counsel Vince Foster, and Vice President Albert Gore. Foster's boss, White House Chief Counsel Bernard Nussbaum, had been invited but apparently was unable to attend. The president's requirements for the vacancy seemed apparent enough: Clinton hoped for a big-name politician for the position, who could assume a position of leadership with the Court right away. Clinton's advisors took a more realistic approach.[7] Nussbaum had apparently provided the president with a list of forty-two candidates, including many state and federal judges; the list came replete with eight-to-ten-page legal and personal profiles.[8]

Even in the wake of his problems filling the top post at Justice, Clinton remained keenly interested in Mario Cuomo and thus urged his aides to thoroughly investigate the governor's written record. Newspapers soon joined in the speculation, openly considering the impact a "Justice Cuomo" might have on the Supreme Court.[9] The looming threat of a confirmation fight stopped Clinton from extending the nomination to Cuomo this early, however. Eventually, after a number of failed telephone connections between Cuomo and the president in late March, the frustrated New York governor put an end to the issue by publicly withdrawing his name from consideration. But the president still resisted drawing from the lists of federal and state judges compiled by his aides. One reporter claimed that Clinton asked his friend Richard Riley, the secretary of education and former governor of South Carolina, if he would be interested in the Supreme Court seat. According to the report, Riley politely declined. Any hope of an April announcement on the Supreme Court selection now dissipated in the wake of Cuomo and Riley's rejection of interest. On May 9 the *New York Times* reported that fully seven weeks into the selection process, the president and his aides had yet to even settle on a shortlist of candidates for the Court.[10]

Finally in mid-May Clinton turned his attention once again to the longer list of judges his aides had compiled two months earlier. From a now-growing list of candidates, two jurists seemed to emerge as frontrunners capable of coasting through the confirmation process: Judge Jon O. Newman of the U.S. Court of Appeals for the Second Circuit and Chief Judge Stephen G. Breyer of the U.S. Court of Appeals for the First Circuit in Boston. Other names on the list included U.S. District Judge Jose Cabranes of Connecticut, Judge Amalya Kearse of the U.S. Court of Appeals for the Second Circuit, Judge Patricia Wald of the D.C. Circuit, and Gilbert Merritt, the chief judge of the U.S. Court of Appeals for the Sixth Circuit.[11] Each of these names was leaked to the press during the final week of May and the first week of June. If Clinton was to be denied the big-name politician he had been looking for, he at least wanted to avoid the confirmation battles that had plagued him in the cases of Baird, Wood, and Guinier. Hence the administration's engagement in a "politics by trial balloon," with candidates effectively devoured by the media before the president had even committed to them as nominees.

From a shortlist of candidates that posed few political risks to the administration, Breyer's ties with key Senate Judiciary Committee members seemed to make him the most confirmable of all. A former law professor at Harvard, Breyer had served as chief counsel to the committee in the late 1970s and would now receive crucial support from both sides of the aisle. Senators Ted Kennedy (D-Mass.) and Orrin Hatch (R-Utah) had both been instrumental in pushing Breyer's nomination to the U.S. Court of Appeals in 1980, even as the approaching presidential election threatened to halt a number of President Carter's other appointments in their tracks. Hatch in particular knew and liked Breyer. As ranking Republican on the committee, Hatch alone possessed the power to guarantee the Democratic administration a smooth and uneventful confirmation process.

Yet just as the process seemed to be reaching a sense of closure in Breyer's favor, Clinton decided to reopen the process once again during the first week in June. No official had enough at stake in the process or in its results to resist Clinton's surprising decision. Certainly not Attorney General Janet Reno, who had up to that point played no role whatsoever in the recruitment process. Apparently, President Clinton was mounting one last effort to entice an experienced politician to join the Court. Cuomo's rejection seemed definitive, and further entreaties might cause embarrassment to both sides. The president then briefly considered naming Senate Majority Leader George Mitchell (D-Me.), but reasoned that he could not afford to lose another key Democrat from the Senate. For much the same reason, Senator Joseph Lieberman (D-Conn) was quickly eliminated from consideration. A second offer to Riley was again declined. Finally, Clinton became enamored with the idea of nominating Interior Secretary Bruce Babbitt to the Supreme

Court. Like Riley, Babbitt was a former governor who had defied any real ideological labels. The president met with Babbitt to discuss the nomination for the first time on June 7.[12] Clinton's sudden interest in Babbitt was not really surprising: He fit nearly every criteria Clinton had set forth when the search first began. Unfortunately for Babbitt, Clinton still remained "indecisive, too easily swayed by the last person with whom he'd spoken, too eager to please."[13] The president thus opted to prolong the process with yet another trial balloon: His aides leaked Babbitt's name to the press on June 8 so they could gauge how the public might react to his candidacy.

Clinton's hesitation in naming Babbitt had two immediate consequences. First, it invited Babbitt's enemies to openly criticize him even before he enjoyed any official stamp of presidential approval. Senate minority leader Robert Dole publicly challenged Babbitt's merits, charging that his lack of judicial experience rendered him unqualified for the position.[14] Hatch similarly joined the opposition. But the invitation to comment on Babbitt swept even more broadly: those who actually supported the interior secretary's favorable western land policies (including many environmental groups) declared their preference that Babbitt remain at the Department of the Interior. Second, by introducing Babbitt's name into the pool of candidates Clinton had inadvertently sent a signal to outsiders that the administration's shortlist was still in flux almost three months after White's announcement. At this late date there was apparently room for yet another candidate to emerge.

Wednesday, June 9 proved to be a pivotal day in Clinton's search for a successor to Justice White. The president, fresh off his "escape" on the Lani Guinier matter a few days earlier,[15] opted to set aside Babbitt's candidacy for fear of engaging in another messy confirmation struggle with Republicans. On the president's orders, Vince Foster, his associates Ron Klain and Ricki Seidman, and private attorney James Hamilton went up to Boston to interview Breyer. That same day Bernard Nussbaum put the name of D.C. Circuit Judge Ruth Bader Ginsburg back on the list of candidates to be reviewed more carefully.[16] Ginsburg had been on the longer list of candidates for some time, but until the first week of June she had never been considered seriously, ostensibly because of fears that her candidacy might cause a stir among key Democratic constituencies. A former ACLU litigator, Ginsburg had recently been targeted by some of the very groups she had once championed.

Representatives from women's rights groups and pro-choice orga-
nizations had spoken out against her publicly, primarily because of
Ginsburg's surprising criticism of the legal opinion issued in *Roe v.
Wade*.[17]

   Nussbaum's renewed interest in Ginsburg so late in the selection
process was no accident. When the president had prompted Senator Daniel Patrick Moynihan (D-N.Y.) for his opinion on the vacancy in May, Moynihan had offered Ginsburg as his "first and
only recommendation for the Court."[18] Immediately thereafter,
Ginsburg's husband, Georgetown Law Professor Martin Ginsburg,
had engineered a letter-writing campaign on his wife's behalf. According to Richard Davis, letters rushed in to the White House from
two groups: (1) women's rights attorneys and (2) academics, including Columbia University President Michael Sovern, a former
dean of the law school at Columbia where Ginsburg had once been
a professor. At least one of the letters referred to a remark from
Harvard Law School Dean Erwin Griswold, that Ginsburg was the
"Thurgood Marshall of gender equality law."[19] In a fortuitous
move, Martin Ginsburg had encouraged the letter-writers to direct
their efforts at Bernard Nussbaum in particular.

   Although Nussbaum generally supported Breyer, he was realistic. Breyer's meeting with Foster and his aides had not gone well.
The administration learned that Breyer and his wife had not paid
Social Security taxes on a household worker. Once Zoë Baird's own
"nanny problems" became public, Breyer had gone back and paid
taxes for 1992. But other actions taken by the candidate seemed
much less sincere. Breyer did not pay any back taxes from earlier
years until after Justice White announced his retirement. Foster also
discovered that penalties and interest due on those additional back
taxes had not been paid until immediately after Cuomo withdrew
his name from consideration. Despite some misgivings, Breyer was
invited to join the president at a lunch scheduled for Friday June
11. This meeting also went poorly. Clinton told his aides that he
felt "Breyer was selling himself too hard, that his interests in the law
were too narrow, that he didn't have a big heart."[20] The president
gathered his advisors in the Oval Office at 11:15 that same evening
for one last conference on the Supreme Court nomination. At this
point the team advising Clinton had expanded drastically from
three months earlier: along with Gore, McLarty, Lindsey, and Foster, Clinton was now joined by Nussbaum, Foster assistants Klain
and Seidman, recently appointed Counselor to the President David

Gergen, Policy Advisor George Stephanopoulos, White House Political Director Rahm Emmanuel, and Clinton's chief congressional liaison, Howard Paster. According to reporter Elizabeth Drew, the president asked each advisor to choose between Babbitt and Breyer. The lack of consensus that existed in the room soon became apparent:

> Klain said that Breyer presented too many problems and that the President should be given another option, and he argued for taking a closer look at [Ruth Bader] Ginsburg. Nussbaum and Gergen were for Breyer. Stephanopoulos and Lindsey were for going back to Babbitt. . . . Foster was against Breyer. Gore was at first for Breyer but then moved away from that position.[21]

After three months of looking, little had been resolved. Clinton then accepted Klain's advice and agreed to meet Ginsburg. Upon a second look, the president was now attracted to her record as a pioneer in woman's rights. Ginsburg met with the president on Sunday June 13. Aides said later that Clinton "fell in love" with Ginsburg and her story: a law review student unable to get a top flight job out of Columbia Law School, Ginsburg had gone on to litigate landmark cases in women's rights before the U.S. Supreme Court. Ginsburg's age—she was sixty years old—was never voiced as a concern. The fact that Ginsburg was Jewish—she would be the first Jewish justice since Abe Fortas resigned in 1969—was barely a factor in the decisionmaking calculus.

Clinton probably wanted to mull over Ginsburg's candidacy, and even float a trial balloon of her candidacy to the press if possible, just as he had done with Cuomo and Babbitt. Yet increasingly hostile media coverage of the nomination process had effectively eliminated that option. In recent weeks reporters had begun to mock the White House's earlier promises of a quick conclusion to the process; by the second week in June much of the press had bought into the storyline of an administration incapable of making a decision. In response, Clinton administration officials now promised a decision that same week. So Ruth Bader Ginsburg became the beneficiary of these increased pressures: the president would not have the opportunity to fluctuate again. On June 14, Clinton formally introduced Ginsburg to the press as his first nomination to the U.S. Supreme Court. Ginsburg certainly defied a number of criteria Clinton had outlined from the beginning. She was not a big-name politician. Unlike Cuomo, most Americans had never even heard of Ruth Bader Ginsburg before she was nominated for the Supreme Court. But Ginsburg had been a pioneer in woman's rights litigation, and her court of appeals record was decidedly moderate, a factor that would ease her confirmation considerably. The Senate Judiciary Committee approved Ginsburg's nomination by an 18–0 vote in August, and the Senate followed suit by a 96–3 margin. Ginsburg was eventually sworn in as an associate justice on August 10, 1993.

The Clinton administration forthrightly rejected the media's characterization of Ruth Bader Ginsburg's nomination as a "haphazard" and disorganized "scramble" for a nominee. Still, the perception persisted that Clinton had publicly vacillated for months about candidates before settling on Ginsburg at the eleventh hour. Justice Harry Blackmun's decision to retire on April 6, 1994, gave the Democrats another opportunity to reshape a court dominated by the more conservative appointments of Reagan and Bush. More important for the president, it afforded his administration the chance to erase some of those negative perceptions from the year before.

To some of Clinton's aides, a more orderly and efficient selection process would only be possible if management of the process fell to one official capable of resisting the president's troubling propensity to shift from one priority to another. The logical source of such stability was Lloyd Cutler, the recently appointed special White House Counsel. Cutler enjoyed the respect of Washington insiders, including those who were among President Clinton's sharpest critics. Even more important, Cutler's sterling reputation afforded him the instant respect of most officials in the administration, including the president himself. Cutler had accepted the job only on an interim basis, but he would be there at least for the duration of the Supreme Court selection process, and could see the nomination through to its conclusion. Cutler represented the administration's best hope of bringing order to what had seemed an especially chaotic selection process just a year earlier.

On April 5, 1994, with rumors of Blackmun's impending retirement already circulating around Washington, White House spokesmen identified Cutler as the "manager" of the upcoming search process, aided principally by Deputy Counsel Joel Klein, associate counsel Victoria Radd, presidential advisor Bruce Lindsey, and Deputy Chief of Staff Philip Lader.[22] Cutler indicated on April

6 that he was preparing a list of "about a dozen potential candidates," including several names that been on Lindsey and McLarty's list the previous year. In discussions with Cutler, Clinton again expressed hope that he might nominate a big-name politician to the Court. The president offered interest in Senator Mitchell, who had recently announced his plans to retire from the Senate at the end of the current session. According to press reports, the tentative list of contenders at that time also included Cabranes; Solicitor General Drew Days III and appeals judge Amalya Kearse (either of whom would become the third black justice ever if selected); Judge Richard Arnold, a jurist from the U.S. Court of Appeals for the Eighth Circuit and a long-time friend of Clinton's; and Breyer.

Clinton was most enamored with Mitchell's candidacy. The Senate majority leader had once before served as a U.S. district judge in Maine and thus possessed the requisite judging experience many senators preferred. Moreover, his candidacy would enjoy a degree of additional deference during the subsequent Senate confirmation process. Mitchell's prospective candidacy even had the blessing of Senate Minority Leader Robert Dole (R-Kan.) and most other Republicans.[23] White House officials believed (perhaps accurately) that the confirmation hearings for Mitchell would be penetrating, but not unduly invasive. Clinton met with Mitchell on Monday April 11 to discuss the Supreme Court seat. Mitchell feared his nomination would make it more difficult to steer the president's health care and initiatives through Congress during the current legislative session, and he was also concerned that the time-consuming nature of the confirmation proceedings, combined with "unforeseen complications that might arise," would make juggling the two roles (Supreme Court nominee and Senate majority leader) nearly impossible. Mitchell publicly withdrew his name from consideration the following day.

With his leading candidate gone, the president turned back to the longer list of experienced jurists that Cutler and his associates had generated. Dissatisfied with his options, Clinton directed his political advisors (Lindsey and Lader) and his legal advisors (Cutler, Klein, and Radd) to broaden the search for a candidate.[24] The president still wanted a nominee who could combine elements of political experience and sensibility. But with health care high atop the administration's list of priorities, he also hoped to find a candidate who could be easily confirmed without upsetting the administration's delicate relations with Congress. Teams of lawyers at five different Washington law firms were asked to assemble summaries and biographical material on at least a dozen or so candidates then under consideration.[25] In previous days, when Mitchell's nomination had seemed a foregone conclusion, interested parties favoring alternative candidates had conserved their efforts. But with Mitchell out of the picture, various individuals and groups began lobbying in favor of one candidate or in opposition to another. In particular, several Hispanic groups began pressing for Judge Jose Cabranes's candidacy. Although support for his candidacy was by no means universal, members of the Congressional Hispanic Caucus and the Hispanic National Bar Association put aside traditional differences on a host of issues and together endorsed Cabranes, a federal district judge of Puerto Rican descent who would have become the first Hispanic justice. Women's advocacy groups opposed Richard Arnold because of two disturbing rulings: his 1983 decision upholding the right of the Jaycees to exclude women[26] and his decision in 1988 to join six other judges in upholding a Minnesota law requiring underage women to notify their parents prior to obtaining an abortion.[27]

By early May the administration had narrowed its search down to four or five leading candidates, each representing a distinct political interest. Naturally, Cabranes was the Hispanic candidate under serious consideration. Richard Arnold and Stephen Breyer were the two white male jurists still in the running, although conflicting reports about Arnold's health rendered him an increasingly unlikely prospect.[28] Amalya Kearse was the only African American or woman still under active consideration by the administration. Finally, Clinton reintroduced the possibility of promoting Babbitt. Cutler's influence aside, the president had once again reopened the process just as it was starting to reach closure. But Clinton was adamant about his interest in Babbitt: for the second consecutive year the interior secretary represented the president's final opportunity to nominate a candidate with considerable political experience to the Court. Unfortunately, Babbitt was still attracting fire from Orrin Hatch; this time he and other western senators were feuding with the interior secretary about a number of environmental issues. As a political lightning rod, Babbitt's candidacy offered troubling confirmation prospects.

White House aides would later portray the president as spending the second week in May agonizing over three candidates: Babbitt, Arnold, and Breyer. Babbitt was the empathetic politician Clinton had longed to place on the Supreme Court, and Arnold was a child-hood friend from Arkansas with impeccable credentials. But both nominees threatened to bog the administration down in a pro-longed confirmation battle: Arnold, because of his controversial rulings and especially close ties to Clinton, and Babbitt, because of the hostility he would inevitably draw from certain Republican senators. Meanwhile Breyer, who had long ago paid all taxes he owed for domestic help, seemed like the most readily confirm-able of the three. Senators Hatch and Kennedy remained firm supporters of the fifty-three-year-old jurist. And by appointing Breyer, Clinton would avoid spending precious political capital that might be better applied to the upcoming fight over health reform.

Clinton formally nominated Breyer to the Court on May 14, 1994, nearly a year after Breyer's first interview with the president had gone so badly. By this time Breyer's "nanny problems" seemed far in his past. And despite some questions raised at his confirmation hearings about the nature of his personal financial investments, Breyer sailed to confirmation in the Senate by an 87–9 vote.

From the time Blackmun first announced his retirement, the process of recruiting his successor had devolved into a series of meetings held by the president with assorted advisors, aides, and political operatives. Each of these various officials had attempted to influence the president in his selection. Lloyd Cutler was sup-posed to play a critical role in managing the nomination process, but in the end he was reduced to being just one of numerous "spokes" on Clinton's organizational wheel. Criteria came and went depending on the president's mood and his sense of optimism at any given moment. And the selection process had lasted thirty-seven days, drawing on the time, energy, and resources of nu-merous administration officials. Clinton possessed definitive ideas about prospective Supreme Court nominees, just as Presidents Truman and Johnson had before him, but unlike in the past, the political environment surrounding Supreme Court nominations would not allow the president to simply submit his preferences to the Senate without warning. During these first two years of his pres-idency, there was far too much at stake for Clinton and the Demo-crats to take such a bold and daring approach to the selection pro-cess. The end result was the appointment of two lesser known, but eminently confirmable, Supreme Court nominees.

CONCLUSION

Our two most recent presidents each enjoyed the opportunity to fill multiple Supreme Court vacancies during their respective terms in office. Bush's criteria-driven selection framework placed confirmability on a higher level of priorities than the pursuit of ideological conservatism. In 1990 the Bush administration sought a justice who would be the "anti-Bork," a conservative with little or no paper trail that might threaten his or her confirmation. When John Sununu enthusiastically championed David Souter for the post, there was little disagreement among Bush's aides. A year later the criteria proved a bit more limiting: the president now sought a conservative minority, perhaps a black or a Hispanic, in place of the retired Thurgood Marshall. C. Boyden Gray promoted Clarence Thomas's candidacy from an exceedingly small pool of candidates. In the case of both of Bush's appointments, the president rested his final decision on the personal assurances of one or more advisors. Bill Clinton's more open, free-wheeling selection framework amounted to a form of personal soul searching, with advisors playing a far more limited role in the final outcome. It also produced two nominees of the highest caliber, although only after weeks of public contemplation about prospective candidates that were either not politically viable or were simply not interested in the position. Rather than trusting in his administration's own research and analysis, Clinton's constant vacillating meant he could gauge the public's reaction to a nominee before any formal offer had been made. If Clinton could not get the "ex-pol" he so desired for the post, at least the practice of "politics by trial balloon" would eliminate surprises and ensure a smooth confirmation process for the nominees. Clinton's own aversions to inviting a prolonged confirmation battle came to dominate his administration's deliberations over prospective nominees, just as it had during the Bush administration.

In the final analysis, neither of these two presidents took the lessons of past chief executives enough to heart. Bush's selection process was a creature of rigid and unyielding criteria: only federal appeals judges ever garnered serious consideration from his administration, with state judges, trial judges, and others all but ignored. Additionally, Bush seized upon the same "three-person committee" format that had led to internal strife and factionalism during the latter part of the Reagan administration. While Souter and Thomas were the favorite candidates of Sununu and Gray, respectively, it is unclear whether their appointments actually helped maximize Bush's overall best interests. Regardless, only a limited set of alternatives was ever presented to him. At the opposite extreme, Clinton was barely willing to delegate any significant decisionmaking power to subordinates, like Truman and Johnson before him. Without a manager entrusted with sufficient authority over the selection process, a myriad of candidacies fell in and out of favor in accordance with the president's shifting sense of moods. Both presidents clearly suffered from a case of "confirmability myopia": Bush and Clinton desperately wanted to avoid the embarrassment and humiliation of an ugly confirmation defeat. For better or worse, the ill-fated 1987 nomination of Robert Bork had continued to cast its long and influential shadow over all high court nominations in its wake.

Notes

The following abbreviations are used in the notes:

HSTL	Harry S. Truman Library
DDEL	Dwight D. Eisenhower Library
JFKL	John F. Kennedy Library
LBJL	Lyndon B. Johnson Library
NPMP	Nixon Presidential Materials Project, National Archives, College Park, Maryland
GRFL	Gerald R. Ford Library
RRPL	Ronald Reagan Presidential Library
LOC	Manuscript Division, Library of Congress, Washington, D.C.

PREFACE

1. The Senate has only formally rejected four nominees during this century: John J. Parker, Clement Haynsworth Jr., G. Harrold Carswell, and Robert Bork. (The nominations of Abe Fortas (to be chief justice), Homer Thornberry, and Douglas Ginsburg were each withdrawn prior to a formal Senate vote.) Other than in those seven instances, nominees have enjoyed relatively smooth sailing in the Senate. Of the fifty-five successful nominees this century, only one (Clarence Thomas in 1991) failed to receive at least 65 percent of the Senate votes cast, and thirty-four nominees were confirmed without a single dissenting vote registered.

2. Technically, the Constitution also specifies a third phase of the appointment process beyond nomination and Senate advice and consent, by which the president must "appoint . . . Judges of the Supreme Court." See Article II, § 2, cl. 2. No president this century has failed to formally appoint his own confirmed nominee to the Court.

3. See, e.g., John Massaro, *Supremely Political: The Role of Ideology and Presidential Management in Unsuccessful Supreme Court Nominations* (Albany: State University of New York Press, 1990); John Maltese, *The Selling of Su-*

preme Court Nominees (Baltimore: Johns Hopkins Press, 1994); Mark Silverstein, *Judicious Choices* (New York: Norton, 1993).

Works that focus on one particular failed or controversial nomination include Robert Shogan, *A Question of Judgment: The Fortas Case and the Struggle for the Supreme Court* (Indianapolis: Bobbs-Merrill, 1971); John P. Frank, *Clement Haynsworth, The Senate, and the Supreme Court* (Charlottesville: University Press of Virginia, 1979); Richard Harris, *Decision* (New York: E. P. Dutton, 1971) (chronicling the unsuccessful nomination of G. Harrold Carswell); Ethan Bronner, *The Battle for Justice: How the Bork Nomination Shook America* (New York: Norton, 1989); Michael Pertschuk and Wendy Schaetzel, *The People Rising: The Campaign against the Bork Nomination* (Washington, D.C.: Thunder's Mouth Press, 1989); Patrick McGuigan and Dawn Weyrich, *Ninth Justice: The Fight for Bork* (Washington D.C.: Free Congress Foundation, 1990); Timothy Phelps and Helen Winternitz, *Capitol Games: Clarence Thomas, Anita Hill and the Story of a Supreme Court Nomination* (New York: Hyperion Books, 1992); Christopher Smith, *Critical Judicial Nominations and Political Change: The Impact of Clarence Thomas* (Chicago: Praeger, 1993); Jane Mayer and Jill Abramson, *Strange Justice: The Selling of Clarence Thomas* (Boston: Houghton Mifflin, 1994).

CHAPTER ONE

1. 505 U.S. 833 (1992).

2. 410 U.S. 113 (1973).

3. In *Casey* the Court indicated that "the essential holding of *Roe* should be retained and once again reaffirmed," while eliminating *Roe*'s trimester approach, which it viewed as "unnecessary" to accomplish the objective of promoting a woman's right to choose abortion.

4. In 1981 a confidential memorandum from Kenneth Starr, then counselor to Attorney General William French Smith, recounted O'Connor's record as an Arizona legislator dealing with the abortion issue. Starr specifically discussed her activities in 1973 as cosponsor of a bill that would have permitted Arizona state agencies to participate in "family planning" activities and to disseminate information with respect to family planning. Memo, Kenneth Starr to William French Smith, 7 July 1981, Appointments–Supreme Court–O'Connor [1] file, OA 2408, Edwin Meese Files, RRPL. Starr's findings were based on a phone interview he conducted with the candidate on July 6, 1981, the day before her nomination was announced. His memo was in part a response to the growing concerns of right-to-life organizations that had already begun to detail O'Connor's alleged "pro-abortion position" publicly and in letters to the White House. See, e.g., Letter, John Willke to Ronald Reagan, 3 July 1981, Supreme Court Nomination 1981 [5] file, OA 3489, Fred Fielding Files, RRPL.

Anthony Kennedy's potential views on abortion and privacy rights were more readily ascertainable. In 1986, Deputy Attorney General Steven Matthews, conducting research on potential candidates for the U.S. Supreme Court, drafted an eight-page memorandum in which he reviewed the complete body of Kennedy's work on the Ninth Circuit. Memo, Steven Matthews to Special Projects Committee, 23 May 1986, Supreme Court Rehnquist/ Scalia Notebook I (3 of 4) file, OA 14287, Peter Wallison Files, RRPL. According to Matthews, Kennedy had "cited *Roe v. Wade* and other 'privacy right' cases very favorably and indicated fairly strongly that he could not uphold the validity of laws prohibiting homosexual conduct outside of the context of the military. *This easy acceptance of privacy rights as something guaranteed by the Constitution is really very distressing.*" Ibid. (emphasis added). Despite these clear warnings, Kennedy appeared on short lists for the Supreme Court generated by both the Justice Department and the White House Counsel's Office that same summer, and then again in 1987. Kennedy's consistent reemergence on these short lists made possible his appointment as a compromise candidate in November 1987, as Democratic senators identified Kennedy as one of few candidates on the administration's short list that could be confirmed prior to the 1988 presidential election. See also chapter 6.

5. Gerald Gunther, *Learned Hand: The Man and The Judge* (Cambridge: Harvard University Press, 1994), 553–70.

6. Henry Abraham, *Justices and Presidents*, 3d ed. (New York: Oxford University Press, 1991), 124.

7. Richard Watson and Rondal Downing, *The Politics of the Bench and Bar* (New York: Wiley & Sons, 1969), 341.

8. Ibid. According to Watson and Downing, "The recruitment phase of the process eliminates many of these attorneys for a number of reasons: legal requirements of eligibility; desire to stay in private practice; and informal availability factors related to age, practice background, and political experience and involvement. Those who overcome the obstacles created by the recruitment mechanism are . . . required to 'pass muster' with the nominating commissioners and the Governor . . . , the judiciary, the 'attentive publics' of the court and the state political system."

9. J. Woodford Howard, *Courts of Appeals in the Federal Judicial System* (Princeton: Princeton University Press, 1981), 101.

10. Most of the relevant constitutional history that informs this discussion was drawn from David M. O'Brien, "Background Paper," in Twentieth Century Fund, *Judicial Roulette: Report of the Twentieth Century Task Force on Judicial Selection* (New York: Priority Press, 1988), 30–32.

11. Ibid., 31.

12. Ibid., 33.

13. 1 U.S. Stat. 73, §35 (1789).

14. Cornell Clayton, *The Politics of Justice: The Attorney General and the Making of Legal Policy* (New York: M. E. Sharpe, 1992), 16.

15. Because Supreme Court justices performed circuit riding duties during much of the calendar year, Supreme Court terms until 1873 usually began in December or January and lasted for less than three months. Of the first twenty-two attorneys general, only Richard Rush (1814–1817) maintained his primary residence in the capital.

16. Leonard White, *The Federalists* (New York: Macmillan Co., 1948), 166.

17. Clayton, *Politics of Justice*, 16–17; Nancy Baker, *Conflicting Loyalties:*

Law and Politics in the Attorney General's Office, 1789–1990 (Lawrence: University Press of Kansas, 1992), 51–52.

18. Attorneys general commonly received consideration themselves as prospective candidates for the Supreme Court. During the nineteenth century, three attorneys general were later named to the Court: Roger Taney, Nathan Clifford, and Joseph McKenna.

19. Between 1870 and 1900, Congress responded to increases in the government's legal work (spurred by an increase in federal legislation) by creating temporary positions rather than increasing the Justice Department's full-time staff. Still, by the turn of the century Congress had established nine assistant and special assistant attorneys general, including one each assigned to the Court of Claims, Post Office Department, and Interior Department, and three others assigned to perform more general duties.

20. Alpheus T. Mason, *Brandeis: A Free Man's Life* (New York: Viking Press, 1946), 467.

21. Ibid.

22. James Pfiffner, *The Modern Presidency* (New York: St. Martin's Press, 1994), 51.

23. Maltese, *Selling of Supreme Court Nominees*, 24.

24. Michael J. Brodhead, *David J. Brewer: The Life of a Supreme Court Justice, 1837–1910* (Carbondale: Southern Illinois Press, 1994), 73.

25. Ibid., 73–74.

26. Donald G. Morgan, *Justice William Johnson: The First Dissenter* (Columbia: University of South Carolina Press, 1954), 49.

27. Sheldon Novick, *Honorable Justice: The Life of Oliver Wendell Holmes* (Boston: Little, Brown and Co., 1989), 234.

28. Ibid., 236. See also John A. Garraty, "Holmes' Appointment to the Supreme Court," *New England Quarterly* 22 (1949): 291, 297.

29. Grant's first choice for the seat, Roscoe Conkling of New York, declined Grant's offer of the nomination. Grant then offered the chief justiceship in turn to two senators, Timothy Howe of Wisconsin and Oliver Morton of Indiana, each of whom declined the president's entreaties. Grant's secretary of state, Hamilton Fish, also declined the position; he pleaded incompetency to assume such a high judicial office after having spent twenty years away from the bar. Finding a willing applicant, Grant nominated his attorney general, George Williams for the post. Soon thereafter he witnessed Williams's nomination come apart amid damaging charges of corruption. Grant asked Williams to withdraw his name, and followed with the (now permanent) offer of a Supreme Court seat to Caleb Cushing. But Cushing's hopes for confirmation ended with the discovery of a letter he wrote to Confederate president Jefferson Davis in 1861; the communication left an implication of treasonous contact. Nearly eight months after Chase's death Grant finally named Morrison Waite of Ohio to serve as the new chief justice. Waite was confirmed unanimously for the post.

30. C. Peter McGrath, *Morrison R. Waite: The Triumph of Character* (New York: Macmillan, 1963), 9–10. At the Cabinet meeting Fish "expressed a very high estimate of Cushing's ability . . . but felt the force of the objection

to Cushing's age and the question of the propriety of dispensing an office of that character on a conditional tenure." Ibid.

31. Ibid., 13, 15.

32. Hoyt Warner, *The Life of Mr. Justice Clarke: A Testament to the Power of Liberal Dissent in America* (Cleveland: Western Reserve University Press, 1959), 63.

33. Ibid.

34. Tinsley E. Yarbrough, *Judicial Enigma: The First Justice Harlan* (New York: Oxford University Press, 1995), 105.

35. William H. Taft, "Mr. Wilson and the Campaign," *Yale Review* 10 (October 1920): 19–20. Taft wrote, "There is no greater domestic issue in this election than the maintenance of the Supreme Court as the bulwark to enforce the guaranty that no man shall be deprived of his property without due process of law. . . ."

36. See generally David J. Danelski, *A Justice Is Appointed* (New York: Random House, 1964). Although Taft claimed also to have secured Stone's appointment by Calvin Coolidge in 1925, declaring, "I rather forced the president into his appointment," Stone dubbed the claim nonsense. According to Stone, Coolidge actually had "little regard" for the chief justice's opinions on these matters. Alpheus Mason, *Harlan Fiske Stone: Pillar of the Law* (New York: Viking Press, 1956), 184.

37. Clayton, *Politics of Justice*, 34.

38. Stephen Hess, *Organizing the Presidency* (Washington, D.C.: Brookings Institution, 1988), 5.

39. Baker, *Conflicting Loyalties*, 14.

40. O'Brien, "Background Paper," 18–19.

41. During its final two years the Democratic Wilson administration faced a Republican House and Senate (1919–1920), although no vacancies on the Court arose during that period.

42. Maltese, *Selling of Supreme Court Nominees*, 88.

43. Ibid., 87.

44. The lone exception of course was Douglas Ginsburg (nominated by President Reagan in 1987), who withdrew his nomination before any formal hearings were conducted.

45. Nina Totenberg, "The Confirmation Process and the Public: To Know or Not to Know," *Harvard Law Review* 101 (1988): 1213.

46. O'Brien, "Background Paper," 83.

47. The ABA first acquired a measure of legitimacy in reviewing lower court nominees during the Eisenhower administration, when President Eisenhower and Attorney General Herbert Brownell formalized a relationship between the ABA and the Justice Department. Since then the group's role in passing on such nominations has fluctuated markedly. For example, the Kennedy administration granted a virtual "veto power" over lower court appointments to the ABA committee. See Joel B. Grossman, *Lawyers and Judges: The ABA and the Politics of Judicial Selection* (New York: Wiley & Sons, 1965), 212–13. By contrast, the Johnson administration sometimes refused the ABA any role whatsoever in passing on controversial lower court nominations. At-

torney General Nicholas Katzenbach continually asserted the administration's right to make exceptions to the practice of submitting names to the ABA "if circumstances should in [the president's] judgment require a contrary action." Letter, Nicholas deB. Katzenbach to Robert W. Meserve, 2 July 1965, "ABA: Standing Committee on Judiciary" folder, Papers of Nicholas Katzenbach, JFKL.

48. Since 1955 the committee's rating system for Supreme Court nominees has varied in terminology. Generally the ABA rankings have fallen into three different tiers. Candidates ranked in the top tier have been labeled in five different ways: (1) "eminently qualified" (Harlan, Brennan, and Whittaker); (2) "exceptionally well-qualified" (Stewart and White); (3) "Highly acceptable from the viewpoint of professional qualifications" (Goldberg, Fortas [twice], Marshall, Thornberry, Burger, and Haynsworth); (4) "Meeting high standards of professional competence, temperament and integrity" (Blackmun and Stevens); and (5) "Well qualified" (Rehnquist [twice], Scalia, Bork, Kennedy, Souter, Ginsburg, and Breyer). Beginning in 1970, the ABA created a middle tier in the ranking system, represented initially by the ranking of "Not opposed" and later, by the ranking of "Qualified" (Carswell and Thomas). To date, no candidate to the Supreme Court has ever received the ABA's third-tier ranking of "not qualified" (although four members of the committee rated Bork "not qualified" in 1987 and two committee members rated Thomas "not qualified" in 1991).

Two candidates for the Court—Lewis Powell and Sandra Day O'Connor—each merited more candidate-specific appraisals by the ABA. The committee indicated in 1971 that Powell "in an exceptional degree meets high standards of professional competence, judicial temperament and integrity, and is one of the best qualified lawyers available for appointment to the Supreme Court." As for O'Connor, the committee endorsed her candidacy in 1981 as follows:

> Judge O'Connor meets the highest standards of judicial temperament and integrity. Her professional experience to date has not been as extensive or challenging as that of some other persons who might be available for appointment to the Supreme Court of the United States. Nevertheless after considering her outstanding academic record, her demonstrated intelligence and her service as a legislator, a lawyer and a trial and appellate judge, the committee is of the opinion that she is qualified from the standpoint of professional competence for appointment to the Supreme Court of the United States.

49. This arguably occurred when Clarence Thomas received the lower rating of "qualified," the first such rating given to a candidate since G. Harrold Carswell's nomination twenty years earlier. One of the committee's fifteen members also rated Bork as "qualified" in 1987, although a clear majority of the committee (ten out of fifteen) rated Bork as "well-qualified."

50. Maltese, *Selling of Supreme Court Nominees*, 127.

51. See ibid., 36–44.

52. Ibid., 59–69.

53. Thus Benjamin Harrison waited nine months to name a replacement to Justice Stanley Matthews's seat in 1889 (he ultimately named David Brewer to the Court); Franklin Roosevelt similarly took his time replacing the late Benjamin Cardozo. Six months after Cardozo's death he finally submitted Felix Frankfurter's name to the Senate.

54. 60 U.S. 393 (1857).

CHAPTER TWO

1. Roberts reached the age of seventy on May 2, 1945, qualifying him for full retirement benefits under the Federal Judicial Retirement Act.

2. Memorandum on "Supreme Court Judgeships," 23 July 1945, Supreme Court folder, Clark papers, HSTL. The memorandum was initially entitled "Applicants for Supreme Court Judgeship," although the first two words were later crossed out by hand. Listed by name were the following: Florence Allen, Thurman Arnold, Warren R. Austin, Jesse W. Barrett, Francis Biddle, John Biggs Jr., Sam G. Bratton, Henry A. Bundshu, John H. Cantrell, Richard Duncan, Evan A. Evans, Walter F. George, Abe Gitlin, William W. Grant, Pierson M. Hall, Maurice E. Harrison, Lindsay D. Hawkins, Arthur Garfield Hays, Lister Hill, Joseph C. Hutcheson Jr., Marvin Jones, Dorothy Kenyon, Frank L. Kloeb, Paul J. McCormick, Edward F. McFadden, Clarence E. Manion, Justin Miller, Sherman Minton, Roland S. Morris, John J. Parker, Robert P. Patterson, Claude Pepper, Orie L. Phillips, Charles S. Reid, Samuel Irving Rosenman, John B. Sanborn, Lewis B. Schwellenbach, David Andrew Simmons, Harold Stephens, Horace Stern, Roger J. Traynor, H. Jerry Voorhis, Earl Warren, John D. Wickhem, Robert N. Wilkin, Ignatius M. Wilkinson, and Charles B. Zimmerman.

3. Memorandum on "Applicants for Supreme Court Judgeship," 31 July 1945, Supreme Court folder, Clark papers, HSTL.

4. Memorandum on "Supreme Court Possibilities," Supreme Court folder, Clark papers, HSTL.

5. While Clark was not formally sworn in as attorney general until June 30, 1945, he had been acting as a de facto attorney general virtually from the moment Truman nominated him for the post on May 24.

6. Francis Heller, ed., *The Truman White House: The Administration of the Presidency 1945–1953* (Lawrence: Regents Press of Kansas, 1980), 29.

7. Oral history interview, Tom C. Clark, 17 October 1972, HSTL, 44.

8. Daniel McHargue, "One of Nine—Mr. Justice Burton's Appointment to the Supreme Court," *Western Reserve Law Review* (winter 1953): 129.

9. Robert H. Ferrell, *Harry S. Truman: A Life* (Columbia: University of Missouri Press, 1994), 150.

10. Long after Truman had abandoned the notion of appointing Schwellenbach, Irving Brant (a liberal columnist and Truman confidant) continued to urge the president to consider him, often referring to Schwellenbach as the "man whom you want there" after all. Irving Brant to Harry S. Truman, 25 August 1945, Supreme Court file, PSF, Truman papers, HSTL.

11. "Party Chiefs Urge Republican Be Named Roberts' Successor," *Washington Post*, 31 July 1945, 9.

12. Ibid.

13. According to Secretary of the Interior Harold Ickes, Truman had told him as early as July 6 that he "had it in his mind to name a Republican to succeed Roberts." Harold L. Ickes to Harry S. Truman, 16 July 1945, Endorsements "A–D" folder, WHCF: OF 41-A, Truman papers, HSTL.

14. One other Democrat that Truman might have briefly considered for the appointment was Sherman Minton, a former Senate colleague now sitting on the U.S. Court of Appeals for the Seventh Circuit. Minton was considered one of Truman's closest friends in Washington, and a few notable Democratic legislators pressed his candidacy, including Senator Claude Pepper of Florida. William D. Hassett to Claude Pepper, 17 August 1945, Endorsements "L–O" (Recommendations resulting from specific vacancies) folder, WHCF: OF 41-A, Truman papers, HSTL. Minton approached Truman about the vacancy while he was in Washington on August 10, only to learn that Truman was planning to appoint a Republican. Entry of 10 August 1945, President's Diary, PSF, Truman papers, HSTL. Minton was thus considered for all three associate justice vacancies that arose during the Truman administration.

15. Mary Spargo, "Gov. Dewey Suggested for Roberts' Seat," *Washington Post*, 18 July 1945, 1.

16. Desk calendars–August 1945 file, Presidential Appointments File, PSF, Truman papers, HSTL.

17. Daily Sheets–August 1945 file and Desk Calendars–September 1945 file, The President's Appointments File, PSF, Truman papers, HSTL.

18. On September 12, President Truman announced he would appoint Parker to serve as an alternate to Francis Biddle on the war crimes tribunal at Nuremberg. This was a meager scrap for Parker, but Truman hoped it would appease Parker's supporters and convince them that the judge had been seriously considered for the Supreme Court post.

19. At a White House meeting on August 14 the president had asked his aides if Parker was the man rejected by the Senate two decades earlier. So informed, Truman reportedly asked: "Is he not getting old?" According to Eben Ayers, it seemed plain that Parker would receive no further consideration after that point. Entry of 14 August 1945, Eben Ayers Diary, Ayers papers, HSTL.

20. President Hoover, a Republican, had appointed Patterson to a federal judgeship in the Southern District of New York in 1930. President Roosevelt then promoted him to the U.S. Court of Appeals for the Second Circuit in March 1939. In July 1940, Roosevelt appointed Patterson to serve as assistant secretary of war, and then undersecretary of war, a post he held until 1945.

21. Truman told Burton that he had first offered the position to Patterson, but had withdrawn the offer soon after. Entry of 17 September 1945, Harold Burton Diaries, Harold Burton Papers, LOC. 22.

22. Oral history interview, Tom C. Clark, 17 October 1972, HSTL, 44. Apprised of Truman's desire to appoint a Republican, Clark included three Republicans from his original list of ten on the final list he submitted to the president. Clark's only original contribution to this process was with his sug-

gestion of McCormick; several years earlier Clark had practiced before the California judge and admired his work.

23. Oral history interview, Tom C. Clark, 17 October 1972, HSTL, 45–46.

24. Entry of 17 September 1945, Harold Burton Diaries, Harold Burton Papers, LOC.

25. Apparently Truman was aware that shifting these divisions to Schwellenbach's control would cause consternation among his immediate staff.

26. An eyewitness account of the press conference is provided by Eben Ayers in his diary. See 1945 File, Eben Ayers's Diary, Ayers papers, HSTL.

27. Entry of 1 May 1946, Charles Ross Diary, Charles G. Ross File, Elsey Papers, HSTL.

28. Edwin Yoder, *The Unmaking of a Whig and Other Essays in Self-Definition* (Washington, D.C.: Georgetown University Press, 1990), 38.

29. Irving Brant to Harry S. Truman, 29 April 1946, Supreme Court 1945–1947 folder, PSF, Truman papers, HSTL.

30. See Joseph Alsop and Stewart Alsop, "Truman in Dilemma Choosing Chief Justice," *New York Herald Tribune*, 18 May 1946 (cited in Yoder, *The Unmaking of a Whig*, 23–24).

31. Donald R. McCoy, *The Presidency of Harry S. Truman* (Lawrence: University Press of Kansas, 1984), 63. By November 1945, Schwellenbach had all but ceased participating in labor-management conferences, attending them but saying little. Secretary of Commerce Henry A. Wallace got the impression that "Schwellenbach's blood pressure is so low that it is very difficult for him to act." Oral history interview, Henry A. Wallace, Columbia University Oral History Collection, 4248.

32. William E. Pemberton, *Harry S. Truman: Fair Dealer and Cold Warrior* (New York: Twayne Publishers, 1989), 57.

33. Later, after Truman had decided to select Vinson as chief justice, Schwellenbach confessed to Truman: "I am a complete failure as secretary of labor, and I have let you down." Entry of 29 May 1946, Harold D. Smith Diary, Harold Smith papers, HSTL. Truman showed his loyalty to Schwellenbach by keeping him on as secretary of labor for another two years until his death in 1948.

34. Alpheus Mason, *The Supreme Court from Taft to Burger* (Baton Rouge: Louisiana State University Press, 1979), 153.

35. 319 U.S. 624 (1943).

36. In *Minersville School District v. Gobitis*, 310 U.S. 586 (1940), the Court had upheld a law mandating a flag salute and recitation of the Pledge of Allegiance in public schools, rejecting a free exercise challenge brought by a member of the Jehovah's Witnesses. Only one dissent, that of Chief Justice Stone, was registered in the *Gobitis* case.

37. 319 U.S. at 646 (Frankfurter, J., dissenting).

38. J. Woodford Howard Jr., *Mr. Justice Murphy: A Political Biography* (Princeton: Princeton University Press, 1968), 394.

39. Yoder, *The Unmaking of a Whig*, 36.

40. Mason, *Supreme Court,* 170.

41. Yoder, *The Unmaking of a Whig,* 36.

42. 325 U.S. 161 (1945). The Court held that coal miners were due "portal-to-portal" pay—i.e., compensation from the instant they entered the mine to the instant they left it. The rule would hold no matter how much of that time was consumed by the often lengthy travel to the coal faces where work actually began, a boon to John L. Lewis's United Mine Workers union.

43. Tony Freyer, "Jackson-Black Feud," in Kermit Hall, ed., *The Oxford Companion to the Supreme Court of the United States* (New York: Oxford University Press, 1992), 445.

44. Howard, *Mr. Justice Murphy,* 392. According to Howard, Justice Roberts's resignation during the summer of 1945 brought much of this bitterness into public view. During his final term Roberts was so embittered over the Court's decisions that he "refused to lunch with the others in their customary 30-minute break . . . and the Court, unable to agree even about the language of a customary letter of farewell [to Roberts], let his resignation pass in ungrateful, and ungraceful, silence until autumn." Ibid.

45. See, e.g., Arthur Krock, "Supreme Court Choice to Show Truman Policy," *New York Times,* 8 July 1945, 4:3 ("The Supreme Court as presently constituted is more or less a battleground. . . ."); Arthur Krock, "New Truman Nominees Classed as 'Sound' Men," *New York Times,* 9 June 1946, 4:3 (remarking on "the philosophical and personal controversy that has divided the Court and made it at times a field of *bitter, open dispute.*").

46. Yoder, *The Unmaking of a Whig,* 32.

47. Ibid., 29.

48. Irving Brant to Harry S. Truman, 29 April 1946, Supreme Court [1945–1947] folder, PSF, Truman Papers, HSTL.

49. Justice Frankfurter, a supporter of Jackson's, privately intimated that Black tried to block Jackson's nomination in order to attain the office himself. See Freyer, "Jackson-Black Feud," 445. Hearing rumors to that effect while in Nuremberg, Jackson lashed out at his critics by telegram once Vinson's nomination was announced.

50. Clark Clifford, *Counsel to the President* (New York: Random House, 1991), 70.

51. Arthur Krock, "A Game That Nothing Can Discourage," *New York Times,* 25 April 1946, 20.

52. Yoder, *The Unmaking of a Whig,* 30.

53. There would be speculation later that Hannegan and Snyder had actually lobbied for Vinson's candidacy as a way of eliminating him from a position of competing influence in the White House. Snyder's later ascension to Vinson's post at the Treasury Department only seemed to add credence to that theory. Such a notion seems unlikely, however. A savvy politician, Hannegan must have known that Vinson's elevation to chief justice would not eliminate his influence as an advisor to Truman. Indeed, long after his appointment to the Court Truman would maintain a direct line to Vinson, consulting with him on various domestic policy matters. Once Jackson's prospects dimmed, it was Truman that focused on Vinson as a possibility for chief justice. Han-

negan and Snyder merely painted a picture of intra-Court factionalism that would have boosted any outsider's prospects for the vacancy.

54. Notes from November 15, 1951, press conference, Supreme Court–general folder, Ayers papers, HSTL.

55. Daily Sheet for 29 April 1946, President's Appointments Files, PSF, Truman papers, HSTL.

56. The controversy was stirred up by inquiries from biographers Eugene C. Gerhart and Merlo J. Pusey to the White House beginning in 1951. Gerhart was at the time working on a forthcoming biography of Justice Jackson. See Eugene C. Gerhart, *America's Advocate: Robert H. Jackson* (Indianapolis: Bobbs-Merrill, 1958). Pusey, who had just completed a biography of Hughes based in part on recorded conversations with the former chief justice, see Merlo J. Pusey, *Charles Evans Hughes* (New York: Macmillan, 1951), now sought to do some "additional checking on this interesting historical point." Merlo J. Pusey to Harry S. Truman, 24 April 1952, Supreme Court of United States folder, OF 41-Misc., Truman papers, HSTL.

57. Merlo J. Pusey to Harry S. Truman, 24 April 1952, Supreme Court of United States folder, OF 41-Misc., Truman papers, HSTL. When Vinson's nomination was announced, Hughes recalled expressing his disbelief to one sitting justice: "I am not sure that I ever met him. I may have seen him once." Ibid. Hughes's daughter, Chauncey L. Waddell, also told Pusey that some time after Vinson's appointment she was riding in Virginia with her father when he pointed out a house and said: "This is Justice Jackson's place. You know, I recommended him to the president for the chief justiceship." Ibid.

58. Joseph H. Short to Merlo J. Pusey, 29 April 1952, Supreme Court of United States folder, OF 41-Misc., Truman papers, HSTL.

59. At least one other part of Truman's recollection was clearly inaccurate. Specifically, the president recalled that at the time he was considering Vinson, Jackson had already disqualified himself for the chief justiceship by a controversial statement from Nuremberg in which he criticized Justice Black for his actions in *Jewell Ridge* and other matters. In fact, Jackson did not issue that statement until June 9, 1946, three days after the announcement of Vinson's nomination and a full month after the president's conference with Hughes.

60. Appointment sheet for 21 May 1946, President's Appointments Files, PSF, Truman papers, HSTL. The president's secretary noted on the appointment sheet that Roberts had "asked for this some time ago, by letter."

61. See Memorandum, Supreme Court folder #1, Supreme Court folder, PSF, Truman papers, HSTL.

62. See, e.g., Sherman Minton to Harry S. Truman, 22 May 1946, Sherman Minton folder, PSF Personal Files, Truman papers, HSTL. The future justice began his letter to Truman expressing that he was "sorry if Chief Justice Hughes unsettled your determination to promote someone on the Court."

63. Truman had wanted to first consult with Bob Hannegan, who was leaving for Cincinnati the following day. Hannegan conferred with the presi-

dent about Vinson's nomination, and suggested John W. Snyder as Vinson's successor at Treasury.

64. This version of their conversation is based on William O. Douglas's own attempt to piece together a number of accounts. See Oral history interview, William O. Douglas, 27 December 1961, Mudd Manuscripts Library, Princeton University, 209.

65. Edward T. Folliard, "President's Choice Leaves Burton as Only Republican on High Court," *Washington Post,* 7 June 1946, 1.

66. Felix Belair Jr., "Vinson Named Chief Justice; Snyder to Head Treasury; Truman to Let OWMR Lapse," *New York Times,* 7 June 1946, 1.

67. Charles Ross, "Supreme Court Vacancy: Murphy Seen Unavailable If He Feels Election Is Dictated by Religion," *Washington Star,* 29 November 1939, 2.

68. Peyton Ford to William M. Boyle Jr., 2 August 1949, OF 41, Truman papers, HSTL.

69. McGrath, though just forty-five years old, desperately sought the Supreme Court nomination. See Ferrell, *Harry Truman: A Life,* 366.

70. Draft, "Tom C. Clark," Box G267 (3 of 3), Papers of Drew Pearson, LBJ Library. Three months later, on October 15, 1949, Truman appointed Fahy to the U.S. Court of Appeals for the D.C. Circuit.

71. Ibid.; Ruth Montgomery, "Truman Picks Clark for Supreme Court; Atty. General Post Offered Sen. McGrath," *Washington Times Herald,* 29 July 1949, 1.

72. Oral history interview, Henry A. Wallace, Columbia University Oral History Collection, 1337.

73. According to one scholar, Vinson himself suggested to the president that Clark be placed on the Court as a way of shoring up the chief justice's center bloc so that he could dominate the Frankfurter-Jackson and Black-Douglas combines. Bert Cochran, *Harry Truman and the Crisis Presidency* (New York: Harper and Row, 1973), 123. An unidentified newspaperman also suggested that Vinson wanted at least one man on the bench "who knew even less law than he did." Ibid.

74. Memorandum on "Inherent Executive Power to Deal with Emergencies . . . ," Justice Department Folder, Baldridge papers, HSTL.

75. Maeva Marcus, *Truman and the Steel Seizure Case: The Limits of Presidential Power* (New York: Columbia University, 1977), 190.

76. In Merle Miller's controversial oral biography of Truman, *Plain Speaking* (New York: Berkeley, 1974), Truman is reported to have called Clark a "damn fool from Texas" who was "no damn good as attorney general." Miller, *Plain Speaking,* 225. Miller's account, which he held for publication until after the president's death, has been heavily criticized for including large portions of so-called presidential conversations that may simply have been invented. See Robert Ferrell and Francis Heller, "Plain Faking," *American Heritage,* May/June 1995, 14–16. Truman was certainly frustrated with some of Clark's subsequent decisions on the Supreme Court. For example, he termed the decision of the Court in the Steel Seizure case as "in line with the *Dred Scott* decision." Harry S. Truman to Tom C. Clark, 10 November

1961, Tom Clark folder, PPF Name files, Truman papers, HSTL. Yet there is no evidence that Truman appointed Clark to the Supreme Court as a means of ridding himself of his attorney general.

77. McCoy, *The Presidency of Harry S. Truman,* 148, 308.

78. Draft, "Tom C. Clark," Box G267 (3 of 3), Papers of Drew Pearson, LBJL.

79. Tom Connally to Harry S. Truman, 19 April 1945, Attorney General–Tom Clark folder, Subject File (Cabinet), Truman papers, HSTL; Sam Rayburn to Harry S. Truman, 18 April 1945, Attorney General–Tom Clark folder, Subject File (Cabinet), Truman papers, HSTL; Oral history interview, Henry A. Wallace, Columbia University Oral History Collection, 3942, 3943, 3963, 3968.

80. Oral history interview, Tom C. Clark, 8 February 1973, HSTL, 77.

81. A year earlier Truman had appointed Maurice J. Tobin, an Irish Catholic New Englander, to replace the recently deceased Lewis Schwellenbach as secretary of labor.

82. Oral history interview, Matthew Connelly, 30 November 1967, HSTL, 445.

83. Daily sheet for 26 July 1949, President's Appointments Files, PSF, Truman papers, HSTL.

84. Entry of 27 July 1949, Eben Ayers Diary file, Ayers papers, HSTL.

85. Oral history interview, William O. Douglas, 18 December 1962, Mudd Manuscripts Library, Princeton University, 257–58.

86. Oral history interview, Tom C. Clark, 8 February 1973, HSTL, 207.

87. Ferrell, *Harry S. Truman: A Life,* 366. McGrath lacked Clark's drive as attorney general, and his "do-nothing" approach made it hard to deflect criticism about the "mess in Washington" towards the end of Truman's second term.

88. Entry of 28 July 1949, Eben Ayers Diary file, Ayers papers, HSTL.

89. Truman, *Public Papers of the Presidents of the United States, 1949* (Washington, D.C.: U.S. Government Printing Office, 1964), 404.

90. Oral history interview, Donald S. Dawson, 8 August 1977, HSTL, 91.

91. William O. Douglas, *The Court Years, 1939–1975* (New York: Random House, 1980), 247.

92. See Sherman Minton to Harry S. Truman, 26 November 1948, Endorsements "A–F" folder, OF 209-G, Truman papers, HSTL; Harry S. Truman to Sherman Minton, 23 August 1949, Sherman Minton folder, Chron. file, PSF, Truman papers, HSTL; Harry S. Truman to Harold Ickes, 19 September 1949, Harold Ickes folder, Chron. file, PSF, Truman papers, HSTL.

93. Harry S. Truman to Harold Ickes, 19 September 1949, Harold Ickes folder, Chron. file, PSF, Truman papers, HSTL.

94. In fact, two days after the announcement of Minton's nomination, Truman read aloud with pride Ickes's letter of praise for Minton at his weekly staff meeting. Entry of 17 September 1949, Eben Ayers diary file, Ayers papers, HSTL.

95. Abraham, *Justices and Presidents,* 245.

96. These ratings come from a 1970 study of the court conducted by law school deans and professors of law, history, and political science. The results of that study were published in *The First One Hundred Justices: Statistical Studies on the Supreme Court of the United States* (New York: Shoe String Press, 1978). This study was partially updated in 1990 and published three years later in *Great Justices of the U.S. Supreme Court* (New York: Peter Lang, 1993). There were, however, no changes in the original assessment of Truman's four appointees.

97. To many, Minton only confirmed his reputation as a "Truman crony" when he authored a dissenting opinion in the Steel Seizure Case.

98. *Dennis v. United States*, 341 U.S. 494 (1951).

99. See *Brandenburg v. Ohio*, 395 U.S. 444 (1969).

CHAPTER THREE

1. For example, Defense Secretary Charles Wilson's authority was severely limited during the Eisenhower administration. Fred Greenstein, *The Hidden-Hand Presidency: Eisenhower as Leader* (New York: Basic Books, 1982), 83.

2. Stephen E. Ambrose, *Eisenhower*, vol. 2, *The President* (New York: Simon and Schuster, 1984), 22.

3. Ibid., 124.

4. Dwight D. Eisenhower to Edgar N. Eisenhower, 8 November 1954, Ann C. Whitman Files, DDEL.

5. In later years Eisenhower openly recalled his frustrations with the highly partisan judicial appointment process of his predecessors. See, e.g., Dwight D. Eisenhower to Lord, Day and Lord, 30 September 1965, "Bra—" file, Post-Presidential Papers of Dwight D. Eisenhower, DDEL.

6. Dwight D. Eisenhower to Edward E. Hazlett, 23 October 1954, October 1954(1) file, Ann C. Whitman Files, DDEL. Writing to brother Milton, the president singled out "Murphy, Rutledge, and a few others" as having harmed the prestige of the Court. Dwight D. Eisenhower to Milton S. Eisenhower, 11 September 1953, August–September 1953(2) file, DDE Diary Series, Ann C. Whitman Files, DDEL.

7. Eisenhower praised Earl Warren for his "middle-of-the-road views." Dwight D. Eisenhower to Edgar N. Eisenhower, 1 October 1953, Edgar Eisenhower 1958(1) file, Ann C. Whitman Files, DDEL.

8. Ibid.

9. During the previous year the Truman administration had inaugurated a system of consultation with the ABA on lower court nominees before final nomination decisions were made. Yet by the time the system was in place, the adjournment of Congress had become imminent and no further appointments were made. Grossman, *Lawyers and Judges*, 69.

10. Diary entry of 17 January 1955, DDE Diary (1955–56)(2) file, DDE Diary Series, Ann C. Whitman Files, DDEL.

11. Ibid.

12. Dwight D. Eisenhower to William D. Pawley (Cross-reference sheet), 26 January 1955, Official File 100-A, Supreme Court 1953–56 file, White House Central Files, DDEL.

13. Dwight D. Eisenhower to Edward E. Hazlett, 23 October 1954–October 1954(1) file, Ann C. Whitman Files, DDEL.

14. Ibid.

15. Justice Frankfurter later became a fierce critic of the administration's policy favoring candidates with judicial experience. See Felix Frankfurter, "The Supreme Court in the Mirror of Justices," *University of Pennsylvania Law Review* 105 (1958): 781.

16. Gunther Bischof and Stephen E. Ambrose, *Eisenhower: A Centenary Assessment* (Baton Rouge: Louisiana State University Press, 1995), 92.

17. Herbert Brownell, interview by author, 15 August 1995, New York City; Dwight D. Eisenhower to Lord, Day and Lord, 30 September 1965, "Bra—" file, Post-Presidential Papers of Dwight D. Eisenhower, DDEL. Notably, the president added this requirement only after Earl Warren, with no previous judicial experience, was named chief justice. John Marshall Harlan's decision to accept a Second Circuit appointment in January 1954 was predicated in part on Herbert Brownell's argument that some judicial experience would be necessary to earn him consideration for a Supreme Court vacancy.

18. According to one commentator, "Eisenhower frequently said in private conversations reliably attributed to him that he could not understand why Supreme Court justices were not selected largely from the ranks of court-of-appeals judges and state supreme court justices. . . . [H]e was aware that in England this was the firmly established practice." "What Lawyer for the Supreme Court," *U.S. News and World Report,* 13 January 1969, 51.

19. See William P. Rogers to Felix Frankfurter, 19 May 1959, "Fra–Freed" file, William P. Rogers Papers, DDEL. Frankfurter himself was appointed to the Supreme Court by Franklin Roosevelt in 1939, despite having never before served in any judicial capacity. In his Roberts Memorial Lecture of 1958, Justice Frankfurter argued that judicial service was an "irrelevance" for the Supreme Court and that the "correlation of prior judicial experience and fitness for the Supreme Court is zero."

20. Oral history interview, Bernard M. Shanley, 16 May 1975, DDEL.

21. Rogers played a considerably more active role in the case of lower court vacancies.

22. Warren had been considered a rising star in the Republican ranks, having been nominated to be the party's vice-presidential candidate four years earlier. Some evidence suggests that Lucius Clay actually tested Warren's interest in becoming secretary of the interior, though no formal offer was ever tendered. See William Ewald, *Eisenhower the President: Crucial Days, 1951–1960* (Englewood Cliffs, N.J.: Prentice-Hall, 1981), 79. Realistically, Warren would have more seriously considered an offer to be attorney general or secretary of state. But by late November 1952, Eisenhower had already settled on Herbert Brownell and John Foster Dulles, respectively, for those two positions.

23. Herbert Brownell, interview by author, 21 February 1996, New York City.

24. Brownell devised this proposed change in convention rules from a reading of the Republican convention of 1912.

25. Two such accounts may be found in Piers Brendon, *Ike: His Life and Times* (New York: Harper and Row, 1986), 215 ("Warren himself was given some type of commitment about being promoted to the Supreme Court"); Ewald, *Eisenhower The President*, 78 ("Warren got a commitment . . . that Eisenhower would offer him a position of his own choice in the new administration").

26. Warren had come out in favor of the Fair Play Amendment at the Republican Governors' conference in early July before he or anyone else could have foreseen that it would be used to secure Eisenhower's nomination.

27. Drew Pearson claims that Warren was not overly enthusiastic about the 1952 ticket because of some remarks General Eisenhower had made in 1950 while traveling in California. Governor Warren had taken a firm public stand against the demands of the Board of Regents of the University of California for a faculty loyalty oath. Visiting the San Francisco press club at that time, Eisenhower noted off-the-record that he "didn't know of any loyalty oath [he] wouldn't be willing to stand up and swear to." Warren questioned Eisenhower's motives in making such a statement, noting to one friend, "it is interesting that the general made his remarks off the record so it would not be quoted in the East. . . . [I]t happens that the university which Ike heads has more communists and reds than any other in the country." Drew Pearson, "Merry-Go-Round release," 9 October 1952, Chief Justice Earl Warren File, Drew Pearson Papers, LBJL.

28. Herbert Brownell, interview by author, 21 February 1996, New York City.

29. Ewald, *Eisenhower the President*, 79.

30. Herbert Brownell, interview by author, 15 August 1995, New York City.

31. Indeed, few close associates of Roosevelt would take such a "promise" from him at face value, as Roosevelt casually promised everything to everyone with a "shameless promiscuity of commitment." Edwin Yoder, *The Unmaking of a Whig*, 10.

32. See Dwight D. Eisenhower to Herbert Brownell, 5 August 1953, Herbert Brownell 1952–54(6) File, Administrative Series, Papers of Dwight D. Eisenhower as President, 1953–61, DDEL.

33. Holding his younger brother Milton in the highest esteem, the president wrote to him often for advice during the course of his presidency. Indeed, Milton Eisenhower was an advisor to various presidents beginning with Franklin Delano Roosevelt. As the years passed, President Eisenhower in particular came to believe that communications between the two were so easy because they thought "so much alike." Dwight D. Eisenhower to Milton S. Eisenhower, Milton Eisenhower 1958(2) file, Ann C. Whitman Files, DDEL.

34. Dwight D. Eisenhower to Milton S. Eisenhower, 11 September 1953, August–September 1953 file, DDE Diary series, Ann C. Whitman Files, DDEL.

35. Dwight D. Eisenhower to Young B. Smith, 14 September 1953, Supreme Court–Chief Justice File, Administrative Series, Papers of Dwight D. Eisenhower as President, 1953–61, DDEL.

36. Herbert Brownell, interview by author, 15 August 1995, New York City.

37. "Phillips Says He's 'In Dark' on Supreme Court Chances," *Washington Evening Star*, 18 September 1953, A3.

38. Eisenhower recalled having privately asked Dulles whether he might be interested in the job, to which Dulles, then sixty-five, reportedly responded to the president: "Well in the first place, I'm too old to start that work and secondly my entire interest is in the job I have and as long as I am satisfying you there, I don't want any other governmental job." Oral history interview, Dwight D. Eisenhower, 28 July 1964, Dulles Oral History Project, DDEL. See also Dwight D. Eisenhower, *Mandate for Change* (New York: Harper and Bros., 1963), 227. Brownell could not recall Dulles's name ever coming up in any of his discussions with the president about the chief justiceship, although he admitted Eisenhower might have spoken to Dulles without his personal knowledge. Herbert Brownell, interview by author, 15 August 1995, New York City.

39. Brownell had been Dewey's national campaign manager in 1948 when the New York governor narrowly lost the general election to President Truman.

40. Joseph Paull, "Govs. Dewey, Warren Lead for Court Job," *Washington Post-Times Herald*, 9 September 1953, 1; Lawrence E. Davies, "Warren Advances for Chief Justice," *New York Times*, 9 September 1953, 25 ("Speculation in Washington counted Dewey among several possibilities for the Court vacancy."); *Wall Street Journal*, 9 September 1953, 1 ("other possible appointees mentioned: New York's Governor Dewey."); "Warren Leads in Speculation on Justice Vinson's Successor," *Washington Evening Star*, 8 September 1953, A1 ("Another Republican whose name has figured in court speculation is Governor Thomas E. Dewey of New York.").

41. Diary entry of 8 October 1953, DDE Diary Series, Ann C. Whitman Files, DDEL.

42. See Eisenhower, *Mandate for Change*, 227. Picking up on this reference in Eisenhower's memoirs, Davis's candidacy is also referenced in Bichof and Ambrose, *Eisenhower: A Centenary Assessment*, 88; and in Brendon, *Ike: His Life and Times*, 128–29. Although Bischof and Ambrose deem Davis's candidacy "incredibl[e] enough," they seem more shocked that Eisenhower would consider South Carolina's lead attorney in the pending school desegregation case, while making no mention of Davis's advanced age.

43. Davis had twice before declined a Supreme Court bid. As he told a friend: "I have taken the vows of chastity and obedience but not of poverty." William Harbaugh, *Lawyer's Lawyer: The Life of John W. Davis* (New York: Oxford University Press, 1973), 192.

44. Phone call summaries, 11 September 1953, DDE Diary Series, Ann C. Whitman Files, DDEL.

45. 341 U.S. 494 (1951).

46. 339 U.S. 382 (1950).

47. Herbert Brownell, interview by author, 21 February 1996, New York City.

48. Robert Jackson, *The Struggle for Judicial Supremacy* (New York: Vintage, 1941).

49. See chapter 2.

50. Herbert Brownell, interview by author, 15 August 1995, New York City.

51. Dwight D. Eisenhower to Edgar N. Eisenhower, 1 October 1953, Edgar Eisenhower–1953(1) file, Name Series, Ann C. Whitman Files, DDEL.

52. Dwight D. Eisenhower to Milton S. Eisenhower, 9 October 1953, DDE Diary Oct. 1953(4) file, DDE Diary Series, Ann C. Whitman Files, DDEL.

53. Dwight D. Eisenhower to Edward E. Hazlett, 23 October 1954, DDE Diary–10/54(1) file, DDE Diary Series, Ann C. Whitman Files, DDEL.

54. Oral history interview, Bernard M. Shanley, 16 May 1975, DDEL. In Shanley's account, Eisenhower claimed that he had learned of Marshall's impressive background in public service from having read Albert Beveridge's four-volume biography of the nineteenth-century justice.

55. Diary entry of 8 October 1953, DDE Diary Series, Ann C. Whitman Files, DDEL.

56. Ibid.

57. In his letter to boyhood friend Edward Hazlett one year later, Eisenhower said he came to Warren because he "refused to appoint anyone to the Supreme Court who was over 62 years of age." Dwight D. Eisenhower to Edward E. Hazlett, 23 October 1954, DDE Diary–10/54(1) file, DDE Diary Series, Ann C. Whitman Files, DDEL.

58. The previous two chief justices—Charles Evan Hughes and Harlan Fiske Stone—both were sixty-eight years old at the time of their respective appointments as chief justice. Indeed, prior to Warren, no chief justice this century had served below the age of sixty-four.

59. In a lengthy Chicago trial, Harlan successfully defended the DuPont brothers and a number of their corporate interests from antitrust charges growing out of the defendants' grip on General Motors and the United Rubber Company.

60. Herbert Brownell, interview by author, 15 August 1995, New York City.

61. Tinsley E. Yarbrough, *John Marshall Harlan: Great Dissenter of the Warren Court* (New York: Oxford University Press, 1992), 74.

62. John Marshall Harlan to Herbert Brownell, 6 November 1933, H(2) file, Herbert Brownell Papers, DDEL. (Harlan offered Brownell his regrets "that we were not successful in keeping you on the Fusion ticket.")

63. According to Yarbrough, "Harlan's correspondence and personal contacts with the governor went back to 1931." Yarbrough, *John Marshall Harlan*, 74.

64. Herbert Brownell, interview by author, 21 February 1996, New York City.

65. Yarbrough, *John Marshall Harlan*, 80.

66. Herbert Brownell, interview by author, 15 August 1995, New York City.

67. Herbert Brownell to John Marshall Harlan, 8 August 1953, Herbert Brownell file, John Marshall Harlan Papers, Mudd Manuscripts Library, Princeton University.

68. Theodore R. Kupferman to John Marshall Harlan, 2 October 1953, Appointment to Second Circuit file, John Marshall Harlan Papers, Mudd Manuscripts Library, Princeton University.

69. John Marshall Harlan to Theodore R. Kupferman, 6 October 1953, Appointment to Second Circuit file, John Marshall Harlan Papers, Mudd Manuscripts Library, Princeton University.

70. Herbert Brownell, interview by author, 15 August 1995, New York City.

71. Edward M. Howrey, then an FTC Commissioner, recalled being told how Harlan's appointment was part of a top-secret agreement reached between Dewey, Harlan, and Brownell. By this account of events, Dewey would take Harlan's place in the law firm, and in return Brownell and Dewey would support Harlan's bid to fill the next vacancy on the Supreme Court. Edward Howrey, *Washington Lawyer* (Des Moines: Iowa College of Law, 1983), 242. Such an agreement seems unlikely, however, given Brownell's dominant influence over the Supreme Court selection process; Dewey's endorsement of Harlan—while helpful—would not have carried much weight. Meanwhile, as a former governor of New York, Dewey's presence as a partner would probably have been welcome at Root, Clark with or without the support of Brownell and Harlan.

72. Herbert Brownell to John Marshall Harlan, 22 January 1954, Appointment to Second Circuit file, John Marshall Harlan Papers, Mudd Manuscripts Library, Princeton University.

73. Diary entry of 26 October 1954, White House Years File, Bernard M. Shanley Diary, Bernard M. Shanley Papers, DDEL.

74. Phone call summaries, 12 October 1954, June–December 1954 file, DDE Diary Series, Ann C. Whitman Files, DDEL.

75. Phone call summaries, 26 October 1954, June–December 1954 file, DDE Diary Series, Ann C. Whitman Files, DDEL.

76. Presidential Secretary Ann Whitman's phone call summaries indicate that while Eisenhower committed to Harlan's nomination early in the process, he never fully shared the degree of Brownell's enthusiasm for Harlan. As late as October 26 the president asked for Brownell's continued assurances that he had not changed his mind "as to the desirability of the man chosen." Ibid.

77. Ibid.

78. "Harlan to the Court," *Washington Post*, 10 November 1954, 16.

79. Although Eisenhower did not formally declare his intention to run for reelection until the spring of 1956, select administration aides spent much of 1955 smoothing the waters for a possible run, registering the president for key primaries and caucuses and scheduling Eisenhower to meet with key constituencies whenever possible.

80. At a White House meeting held in late September 1956 to discuss the progress of the presidential campaign, "Catholic vote" was listed as the second of seven major items on the political agenda. Agenda of 28 September 1956, September 1956 file, Gerald Morgan Papers, DDEL.

81. Dwight D. Eisenhower to Herbert Brownell, 8 March 1955, Herbert Brownell 1955-56 file, Ann C. Whitman Files, DDEL.

82. Kim Isaac Eisler, *A Justice for All* (New York: Simon and Schuster, 1993), 89. President Hoover appointed Benjamin Cardozo, the chief judge of the New York Court of Appeals, to the Supreme Court in 1932. Cardozo died six years later, leaving the Court without a sitting justice from the state courts between 1938 and 1956.

83. Herbert Brownell, interview by author, 15 August 1995, New York City; Herbert Brownell, interview by author, 21 February 1996, New York City.

84. Dwight D. Eisenhower to Herbert Brownell, 4 December 1954, December 1954 file, Ann C. Whitman Files, DDEL.

85. Robert Fredrick Burk, *The Eisenhower Administration and Black Civil Rights* (Knoxville: University of Tennessee Press, 1984), 148.

86. Herbert Brownell, *Advising Ike: The Memoirs of Herbert Brownell* (Lawrence: University Press of Kansas, 1993), 99.

87. Sherman Minton to Dwight D. Eisenhower, 7 September 1956, Supreme Court of United States file, White House Central Files, DDEL.

88. According to Eisenhower biographer William Ewald, Eisenhower's secretary often took notes of the President's conversations from an extension phone in the other room. See Ewald, *Eisenhower the President*, 87.

89. Phone call summaries, 7 September 1956, September 1956 phone calls file, Ann C. Whitman Files, DDEL.

90. Ibid.

91. Herbert Brownell, interview by author, 15 August 1995, New York City.

92. Ibid.; William P. Rogers, interview by author, 22 January 1996, phone conversation from Washington, D.C.

93. Stephen J. Wermiel, "The Nomination of Justice Brennan: Eisenhower's Mistake? A Look at the Historical Record," *Constitutional Commentary* 11 (1994-95): 515, 518-21.

94. Ibid., 519. Wermiel also discovered in Brennan's own office files a copy of a speech marked, "Address by Honorable William J. Brennan Jr., Prepared for Delivery before the National Conference on Congestion in the Courts." Still, Wermiel allows for the possibility that Brennan at least drew on Vanderbilt's notes in part "because he did not have time to prepare his own material."

95. Perhaps Brownell still had a bad taste left in his mouth from his initial experience in appointing Danaher to a federal judgeship in 1953. Danaher's ultimate appointment to the U.S. Court of Appeals for the D.C. Circuit was actually a consolation prize; Brownell had briefly considered the former senator from Connecticut for a seat on the prestigious Second Circuit until members of the Yale Law School faculty vigorously opposed his appointment.

Many years later Brownell recalled: "I didn't want to get into a row with them, and have a lot of publicity which would hurt everybody, so I arranged to have him go on the court of appeals in D.C." Herbert Brownell, interview by author, 15 August 1995, New York City.

96. If the president had required only that the nominee be Catholic, a host of qualified Republicans and practicing lawyers would have been available for the President's consideration, most notably Albert E. Jenner Jr., the distinguished forty-eight-year-old former president of the Illinois Bar Association, then practicing law in Chicago. But Jenner was a Republican and possessed no previous judicial experience.

97. Herbert Brownell, interview by author, 15 August 1995, New York City.

98. Eisenhower had twice suggested that his attorney general find an "anti–New Deal" Democrat, but he did not aggressively reassert this position during the selection process. Brennan by all accounts had publicly supported the New Deal even when he was representing corporate interests in private practice.

99. Wermiel, "The Nomination of Justice Brennan," 525.

100. Diary entry of 29 September 1956, White House Years File, Bernard M. Shanley Diary, Bernard M. Shanley Papers, DDEL.

101. Apparently Spellman was especially irritated with Shanley, the official who he believed had engineered the appointment without consulting him.

102. Diary entry of 29 September 1956, White House Years File, Bernard M. Shanley Diary, Bernard M. Shanley Papers, DDEL. According to Shanley, as late as 1976, Brennan remarked to him: "Why don't you stop denying that you were instrumental in my appointment?"

103. Eisenhower, *Mandate for Change*, 230 ("Justice Brennan . . . was suggested by New Jersey Chief Justice Vanderbilt").

104. See Wermiel, "The Nomination of Justice Brennan," 529; Herbert Brownell, interview by author, 15 August 1995, New York City; William P. Rogers, interview by author, 22 January 1996, phone conversation from Washington, D.C.

105. Eisenhower, *Mandate for Change*, 230.

106. Appointment sheet of 29 September 1956, President's Appointments Files, Papers of Dwight D. Eisenhower as President, 1953–61, DDEL.

107. Eisler, *A Justice for All*, 86–106.

108. See *Washington Evening Star*, 2 May 1956, 1 ("Brownell Says Court Slows Fight on Reds"); *New York Times*, 2 October 1956, 1 ("Brownell Names Two Red Fronts").

109. Judith Cole's fine survey of Charles Whittaker's nomination details Eisenhower's frustrations with Warren as early as 1956, as evidenced in personal letters he wrote to Senator Henry Bellmon of Oklahoma and other national political leaders. See Judith Cole, "Mr. Justice Charles Evans Whittaker: A Case Study in Judicial Recruitment and Behavior" (master's thesis, University of Missouri, Kansas City, 1972). According to Eisenhower biographer Elmo Richardson, when Eisenhower was asked later if he had made any mistakes when he had been president, he replied: "yes, two, and they are

both sitting on the Supreme Court." Elmo Richardson, *The Presidency of Dwight D. Eisenhower*, 108. "Both," of course, referred to Warren and Brennan.

110. Herbert Brownell, interview by author, 15 August 1995, New York City.

111. Those fourteen court of appeals judges were: John A. Danaher (fifty-eight years old) and Warren E. Burger (forty-nine) of the D.C. Circuit; J. Edward Lumbard (fifty-six) of the Second Circuit; Elbert P. Tuttle (fifty-nine), Warren L. Jones (sixty-two), and John R. Brown (forty-four) of the Fifth Circuit; Potter Stewart (forty-two) of the Sixth Circuit; Charles J. Vogel (fifty-nine), Martin Van Oosterhuit (fifty-seven), and Charles E. Whittaker (fifty-six) of the Eighth Circuit; Richard H. Chambers (fifty), Stanley N. Barnes (fifty-seven), and Frederick G. Hamley (fifty-four) of the Ninth Circuit; and David T. Lewis (forty-four) of the Tenth Circuit.

112. Herbert Brownell, interview by author, 15 August 1995, New York City.

113. Phone call summaries, 31 January 1957, January 1957 file, Ann C. Whitman Files, DDEL.

114. See, e.g. Roy A. Roberts to Dwight D. Eisenhower, 3 May 1955, Roy A. Roberts File, Ann C. Whitman Files, DDEL; Dwight D. Eisenhower to Roy A. Roberts, 10 May 1955, Roy A. Roberts File, Ann C. Whitman Files, DDEL.

115. Leonard W. Hall to Dwight D. Eisenhower, 6 October 1954, Leonard W. Hall File, Ann C. Whitman Files, DDEL.

116. Cole, "Mr. Justice Charles Evans Whittaker," 36 (quoting Douglas Stripp, a member of Whittaker's law firm).

117. A full description of the various factors and interests involved in Whittaker's two lower court appointments can be found in Cole, "Mr. Charles Justice Whittaker," 36. Cole cites the comments of William Orr, active in local Kansas City Republican politics for many years and a personal friend of Whittaker's, who discounted proportionately the influence on Whittaker's career of Harry Darby and other Republican party officials. According to Orr those men were "for him and that was all fine, but he needed somebody with a direct line to the White House and that was Roy Roberts." Ibid., 35.

118. Ibid., 38.

119. Herbert Brownell, interview by author, 21 February 1996, New York City.

120. Duke Shoop to William P. Rogers, 30 January 1956, "S's" Name File, DDEL; Herbert Brownell, interview by author, 21 February 1996, New York City.

121. Daniel M. Berman reached this conclusion in his own analysis of Whittaker's published opinions up through his Supreme Court nomination. Daniel M. Berman, "Mr. Justice Whittaker: A Preliminary Appraisal," *Missouri Law Review* 24 (1959): 1.

122. Herbert Brownell, interview by author, 21 February 1996, New York City.

123. When Brownell finally departed from the Justice Department in late 1957, Eisenhower quickly tapped Rogers to be his successor.

124. William P. Rogers, interview by author, 22 January 1996, Phone conversation, Washington, D.C. Citing health concerns, Whittaker finally resigned from the Court four years later.

125. Diary entries of 13 June 1958, 1 July 1958, and 14 July 1958; Harold H. Burton Diaries, Papers of Harold H. Burton, LOC.

126. Rogers later mentioned both district court judges to Eisenhower during their July 17 meeting. Diary entry of 17 July 1958, Harold H. Burton Diaries, Papers of Harold H. Burton, LOC.

127. Ibid.

128. In *Watkins v. United States*, 354 U.S. 178 (1957), decided a month earlier, the Supreme Court (per Chief Justice Warren) set aside a labor union officer's conviction for contempt of Congress; the witness had refused to answer questions from Congress about persons who may in the past have been, but were no longer, members of the Communist Party. Although the ruling itself was narrow, Warren's rhetoric was broad. Specifically, the Court held that while the public was entitled to be informed as to the workings of government, "this does not mean that Congress has the power to invade the lives of private individuals."

129. Diary entry of 17 July 1958, Harold H. Burton Diaries, Papers of Harold H. Burton, LOC.

130. In fact, a closer look at Stewart's record would have produced ample evidence of a judge eminently qualified to serve on the Court. Stewart, a former New York lawyer and later a partner with a Cincinnati firm, had served on the Sixth Circuit for almost four years. He possessed more experience as an appellate judge than three of Eisenhower's four other appointees and had logged more time as a federal judge than any of the four. Stewart also had worked in local government, serving as member of the Cincinnati City Council as well as one term as vice mayor.

131. See *Cooper v. Aaron*, 358 U.S. 1 (1958). Two sets of arguments were heard in *Cooper* on August 28 and September 11, 1958; the decision in the case was handed down on September 12, 1958.

132. According to Burton, "He [Rogers] said the president had delayed considering it so as to avoid conflict with the Court news as to desegregation." Diary entry of 19 September 1958, Harold H. Burton Diaries, Papers of Harold H. Burton, LOC.

133. Dwight D. Eisenhower to William P. Rogers, 17 September 1958, William P. Rogers File, Ann C. Whitman Files, DDEL.

134. Ibid.

135. The president had long desired to appoint Brownell to the Supreme Court, but the attorney general had consistently resisted the president's entreaties in favor of returning to more lucrative private practice. Near the end of his first term, the president had even tried to get Brownell to accept a seat on the Second Circuit, so that he might fulfill the requisite of appellate judicial experience that Eisenhower viewed as necessary for Supreme Court candi-

dates. Herbert Brownell, interview by author, 21 February 1996, New York City.

136. Diary entry of 19 September 1958, Harold H. Burton Diaries, Papers of Harold H. Burton, LOC.

137. Anthony Lewis, "Ohioan Is Chosen for Burton's Post on Supreme Court," *New York Times*, 7 October 1958, 1.

138. See chapter 5.

139. William Pederson and Norman Proviser, eds., *Great Justices of the U.S. Supreme Court* (Peter Lang, 1993). The results were based on a survey sent to 493 scholars, lawyers, and judges across the country.

CHAPTER FOUR

1. Roger Hilsman, *To Move a Nation* (New York: Doubleday, 1967), 19–20.

2. Hess, *Organizing the Presidency*, 83.

3. Whittaker's letter to the president included both the justice's certification that he had "become permanently disabled from performing my duties as an associate justice of the Supreme Court" and an additional certificate of disability signed by Chief Justice Warren, in accordance with the federal retirement provisions under 28 U.S.C. §372(1).

4. Nicholas deB. Katzenbach, interview by author, 6 June 1996, Princeton, N.J.; oral history interview of Nicholas deB. Katzenbach by Anthony Lewis, 16 November 1964, JFKL.

5. Victor Lasky, *Arthur Goldberg: The Old and the New* 23 (New Rochelle: Arlington House, 1970). As the union's chief attorney, Goldberg conferred with Senator Kennedy and his brother Robert (the subcommittee's chief counsel) about ways to address racketeering, corruption, and loose financial practices in unions. Goldberg proved instrumental in helping redraft the Landrum-Griffin bill in a form amenable both to Senator Kennedy and George Meany of the AFL-CIO. Judie Mills, *John F. Kennedy*, 143–44 (New York: Franklin Watts, 1988).

6. For example, with Goldberg's assistance Kennedy sponsored an early version of the Landrum-Griffin labor bill in 1958 that union officials, including AFL-CIO head George Meany, bitterly opposed. Goldberg later worked assiduously to calm labor suspicions about Kennedy arising from those legislative efforts. His willingness to oppose labor interests was not surprising to close friends and associates. Although he had formally represented unions in the past, Arthur Goldberg had never been a "house counsel" or direct employee of a union itself; throughout the 1950s Goldberg remained merely a member of a private law firm looking after union business. The only union card Goldberg ever carried was that of the Hod Carriers' Union dating back to jobs he took as a laborer on construction projects while working his way through law school. Alan Adams, "Knight of the Bargaining Table—Arthur Goldberg," in *The Kennedy Circle*, ed. Lester Tanzer (Washington, D.C.: Luce, 1961). Eva Rubin explained, "union leadership does not always trust this professional class and attempts to keep it out of policy formation as much

as possible." Eva Redfield Rubin, "The Judicial Apprenticeship of Arthur J. Goldberg, 1962–1965," (Ph.D. diss., Johns Hopkins University, 1967), 10.

7. Lasky, *Arthur Goldberg,* 24.

8. Ibid., 24–25.

9. Ibid. Of the sixteen justices nominated by the previous three Democratic presidents, four (Justices McReynolds, Murphy, Jackson, and Clark) had served as attorney general and two (Reed and Jackson) had served as solicitor general.

10. According to Theodore Sorenson, Goldberg, who had advised Kennedy in many fields outside of the field of labor, "might have been attorney general had Bob Kennedy's initial 'no' been accepted." Theodore Sorenson, *Kennedy* (New York: Harper and Row, 1965).

11. Adams, "Knight of the Bargaining Table," 269.

12. By early 1961, Goldberg's relationship with Meany had soured considerably. Goldberg was no longer regarded as pro-union and labor officials blew up at the suggestion that Goldberg (who had worked against their interests in drafting the Landrum-Griffin legislation and supporting Johnson) would now head the Labor Department. Ignoring Goldberg, Meany proposed five other individuals for the post, all union officials: Joseph Beirne of the Communications Workers; George Harrison of the Railway Clerks; James Suffridge of the Retail Clerks; Al J. Hayes of the Machinists; and Joseph Keenan, the secretary-treasurer of the Electrical Workers. Meany later grudgingly approved Goldberg's appointment, and he persuaded his fellow labor officials to follow suit.

13. Oral history interview of Nicholas deB. Katzenbach by Anthony Lewis, 16 November 1964, JFKL.

14. Nicholas deB. Katzenbach, interview by author, 6 June 1996, Princeton, N.J.

15. Industry officials had not raised the price of steel since 1958. According to Hugh Sidey, Kennedy firmly believed an increase in the price of steel would not only bring new wage demands from the steel workers, but would "send its ripples throughout industry, causing price increases in virtually all other fields because steel was such a basic commodity." Hugh Sidey, *John F. Kennedy, President* (New York: Atheneum, 1964), 292.

16. Ibid.

17. Goldberg's crucial role in these negotiations was evident throughout March 1962. As late as March 28, just two days before the announcement of Whittaker's successor, the secretary of labor informed the president that while "steel negotiations are progressing towards an agreement," he believed the president should refrain from further comment "until final settlement has been concluded . . . and the terms announced by the parties." Memorandum, Arthur J. Goldberg to John F. Kennedy, 28 March 1962–29 March 1962 folder, Press Conference Series, President's Official Files, JFKL.

18. Nicholas deB. Katzenbach, interview by author, 6 June 1996, Princeton, N.J.

19. For a closer examination of the lower court appointment process dur-

ing the Kennedy administration, see Harold W. Chase, *Federal Judges* (Minneapolis: University of Minnesota Press, 1972); Joel B. Grossman, *Lawyers and Judges* (New York: Wiley and Sons, 1965). White and Assistant Attorney General Joseph Dolan worked together during 1961 and early 1962 to fill the large number of vacancies that had arisen in the federal courts. The Omnibus Judgeship Bill passed in May 1961 established ten new seats on the circuit courts of appeals and sixty-three new district court judgeships. In addition, nearly sixty-eight vacancies caused by death or retirement were left to the Kennedy administration to fill. In all, Kennedy was asked to fill 141 vacancies during the first sixteen months of his presidency, more than the Hoover, Coolidge, or Harding administrations filled in all. White and Dolan amassed an extensive system of appointment files at the Justice Department during this period.

20. Joseph F. Dolan, interview by author, 12 June 1996, phone conversation from Denver, Colorado; Nicholas deB. Katzenbach, interview by author, 6 June 1996, Princeton, N.J.

21. Joseph F. Dolan, interview by author, 12 June 1996, phone conversation from Denver, Colorado.

22. Theodore C. Sorenson, interview by author, 11 September 1996, phone conversation from New York City.

23. Memorandum, Theodore C. Sorenson to John F. Kennedy, 21 March 1962, Supreme Court Folder, President's Official Files, JFKL.

24. Ibid.

25. Ibid.

26. Ibid.

27. Nicholas deB. Katzenbach, interview by author, 6 June 1996, Princeton, N.J.; Oral history interview of Nicholas deB. Katzenbach by Anthony Lewis, 16 November 1964, JFKL.

28. For example, when presidential advisor Clark Clifford first saw White's name on Sorenson's list, he opposed his candidacy, arguing that the "bar would regard Byron as primarily political" because his tenure in his present job had been "too brief." Memorandum, Theodore C. Sorenson to John F. Kennedy, 21 March 1962, Supreme Court Folder, President's Official Files, JFKL.

29. Indeed, Dolan had urged Senator Kennedy in 1959 to name White to head up his presidential campaign in Colorado. Letter, Joseph F. Dolan to Theodore C. Sorenson, 30 April 1959, Colorado-Dolan 22 January 1959–29 June 1959 folder, Pre-Presidential Papers, Box 928, JFKL; Joseph F. Dolan, interview by author, 12 June 1996, phone conversation from Denver, Colorado.

30. Hess, *Organizing the Presidency*, 82.

31. Joseph F. Dolan, interview by author, 12 June 1996, phone conversation from Denver, Colorado. According to Dolan, Robert Kennedy was fairly interpreting White's comments to him during a phone conversation they had immediately after learning of Whittaker's retirement.

32. Theodore C. Sorenson, interview by author, 11 September 1996, phone conversation from New York City.

33. Oral history interview of Nicholas deB. Katzenbach by Anthony Lewis, 16 November 1964, JFKL. According to Katzenbach, White spoke to him by phone from Denver and said, "Well, I wouldn't be unhappy if you scratched me off entirely. Go ahead."

34. Katzenbach's memorandum remains sealed from the public, but the eight-page memo, dated March 18, 1962, is referenced in a library withdrawal sheet located in the "Justice 1/62-3/62 file," President's Official Files, Box 80, JFKL ("N. deB. Katzenbach memo to R.F. Kennedy re background information on William Hastie"). Katzenbach later described the contents of this memo in an interview with Anthony Lewis. See Oral history interview of Nicholas deB. Katzenbach by Anthony Lewis, 16 November 1964. He had concluded that Hastie's alleged connections with the Lawyers' Guild did not amount to any credible evidence of left-wing political connections.

35. Ibid. Katzenbach believed that Hastie was "not really very intellectual. . . . I think he's rather pedestrian."

36. Robert Kennedy later admitted that he did not know when another vacancy might come up and he thought it would make an important statement across the country and abroad to have a "Negro" on the Supreme Court. Oral history interview of Robert F. Kennedy by John B. Martin, 14 May 1964, JFKL.

37. Sorenson, *Kennedy,* 50. One of the first civil rights bills since Reconstruction had proposed to institute proceedings against local voting officials who had defied court orders concerning the registration of blacks. The so-called jury trial amendment would have required a jury to hear charges of criminal or civil contempt. Civil rights leaders argued that southern juries would acquit local officials of these crimes. Freund, along with Harvard colleague Mark DeWolfe Howe, argued to Kennedy that acceptance of the amendment would not betray his principles. Ultimately, Kennedy supported a bill which incorporated the amendment intact.

38. Oral history interview of Abram Chayes by Eugene Gordon, 18 May 1964, JFKL.

39. Apparently, the president himself called Freund several times to urge him to accept the position. Abram Chayes recalled: "He was in the midst of the Holmes bequest . . . of which he was senior editor . . . he was very reluctant to leave that. He had been in the solicitor general's office as the chief assistant to the solicitor general and felt somewhat that this would be more of the same." Ibid.

40. Ibid.

41. Oral history interview of Robert F. Kennedy and Burke Marshall by Anthony Lewis, 4 December 1964, JFKL.

42. Judge Hastie had been serving as a federal appeals judge in Philadelphia since 1949.

43. Marshall had been sitting on the circuit court by virtue of a recess appointment he received on October 6, 1961. On September 7, 1962, almost eleven months later, the Senate Judiciary Committee finally approved his confirmation by a vote of 11-4. Less than a week later the Senate confirmed Marshall by a 54-16 vote.

44. As a circuit judge in Philadelphia, Hastie had established a reputation as a moderate jurist. When Robert Kennedy called Earl Warren to solicit suggestions for potential Supreme Court candidates, the chief justice reportedly objected to Hastie as being "not liberal enough." Entry of March 19, 1962, Robert F. Kennedy Desk Diary, 1962 folder, Papers of Robert F. Kennedy, JFKL; oral history interview of Robert F. Kennedy by John B. Martin, 13 April 1964, JFKL. According to Kennedy's account of their conversation, Warren "was very much against having him on—rather interesting—but he said he wasn't liberal enough and so he didn't want him on." Ibid. Justice William O. Douglas also dismissed Hastie as "a pedestrian type of person, very conservative." Oral history interview of William O. Douglas, 31 March 1962, Mudd Manuscripts Library, Princeton University.

45. Joseph F. Dolan, interview by author, 12 June 1996, phone conversation from Denver, Colorado.

46. Oral history interview of Nicholas deB. Katzenbach by Anthony Lewis, 16 November 1964, JFKL. According to Arthur Schlesinger Jr., the president remarked to him later that "I didn't want to start off with a Harvard man and a professor . . . we've taken so many Harvard men that it's damn hard to appoint another." Arthur Schlesinger Jr., *A Thousand Days: John F. Kennedy in the White House* (Boston: Houghton Mifflin Co., 1965), 698.

47. Oral history interview of Nicholas deB. Katzenbach by Anthony Lewis, 16 November 1964, JFKL.

48. Memorandum, McGeorge Bundy to John F. Kennedy, 30 March 1962, Supreme Court folder, Departments and Agencies file, President's Official Files, JFKL. Addressing Kennedy's possible concerns that Freund would merely echo Frankfurter's brand of judicial restraint, Bundy referred to the Supreme Court's recent decision in *Baker v. Carr,* arguing that "the best and most confidential advice from Cambridge is that Paul Freund would have voted with the majority in the Tennessee re-apportionment case, and might even have carried Frankfurter with him."

49. Bundy maintained a close relationship with Justice Frankfurter even after he went to work for the Kennedy administration, fueling speculation that Frankfurter himself influenced Bundy's decision to press Freund's candidacy. See, e.g., Memorandum, McGeorge Bundy to John F. Kennedy, 26 July 1962, Supreme Court folder, Departments and Agencies Files, President's Official Files, JFKL. ("Justice Frankfurter is a man I love").

50. 369 U.S. 186 (1962).

51. Nicholas deB. Katzenbach, interview by author, 6 June 1996, Princeton, N.J.

52. According to William Douglas, who ran into Arthur Goldberg around the time rumors of Frankfurter's retirement were circulating, the two men talked about the vacancy and Goldberg "expressed, at that time, a great eagerness for it." Oral history interview of William O. Douglas, 9 June 1962, Mudd Transcripts Library, Princeton University.

53. Lasky, *Arthur J. Goldberg,* 39.

54. Ibid.

55. Bruce Allen Murphy, *Fortas: The Rise and Ruin of a Supreme Court Justice* (New York: William Morrow, 1988), 162.

56. According to Bruce Allen Murphy, Johnson frequently told aide Walter Jenkins that "Abe Fortas would make a great Supreme Court justice and I would put him there if I could." Ibid., 163.

57. While on the Supreme Court, Goldberg had maintained close communications with the administration, personally seeking Johnson's assistance for a number of his off-the-court activities, including sponsorship of the 1965 World Law Day Conference. Many of these communications date from before July 14, 1965, when U.S. Ambassador Adlai Stevenson died. See Memo, Jack Valenti to Lyndon Johnson, 23 June 1965, Supreme Court of United States 25 March 1965–19 March 1966 file, WHCF-FG 535, LBJL; Memo, Jack Valenti to Lyndon Johnson, 11 June 1965, Supreme Court of United States 25 March 1965–19 March 1966 file, WHCF-FG 535, LBJL.

58. Transcript, Arthur Goldberg Oral History interview, 23 March 1983, by Ted Gittinger, Tape 1, LBJL.

59. Memo, Mildred Stegall to Cartha D. DeLoach, 10 May 1965, Arthur Goldberg file, Office Files of John Macy, LBJL; Memo, Mildred Stegall to Cartha D. DeLoach, 10 May 1965, Arthur Goldberg file, Office Files of John Macy, LBJL.

60. Transcript, Arthur Goldberg Oral History interview, 23 March 1983, by Ted Gittinger, Tape 1, LBJL; Murphy, *Fortas*, 171–72.

61. Murphy, *Fortas*, 170.

62. See Laura Kalman, *Abe Fortas: A Biography* (New Haven: Yale University, 1990), 240–41; Murphy, *Fortas*, 163–65. Galbraith was a former ambassador to India and like Stevenson, a hero to liberals. Johnson might well have viewed him as ideally suited for the United Nations job. Ibid., 163–64.

63. In his memoirs, Lyndon Johnson recalled that Galbraith referred to Goldberg as "restless" at the Supreme Court. Lyndon B. Johnson, *Vantage Point: Perspectives of the Presidency, 1963–1969* (New York: Holt, Rinehart and Winston, 1970), 543–44. Apparently, Galbraith had spoken to the justice a few weeks earlier in Cambridge and conveniently recalled that the justice was unhappy with the "more deliberative pace" of the work on the Court. Murphy, *Fortas*, 164. Goldberg later rejected Galbraith's interpretation of their conversation, denying that he was "bored" with the Court. Transcript, Arthur Goldberg Oral History interview, 23 March 1983, by Ted Gittinger, Tape 1, LBJL.

64. President's Daily Diary, July 1965, LBJL; Murphy, *Fortas*, 169–72.

65. Lady Bird Johnson, *A White House Diary* (New York: Holt, Rinehart and Winston, 1970), 299.

66. Fortas and his wife had recently committed to the purchase of a $250,000 house in Washington, D.C. If he became an associate justice, Fortas's current salary of approximately $200,000 per annum would be reduced to $39,500, the amount that members of the Supreme Court received at that time.

67. One of the founding partners at Fortas's firm, Thurman Arnold, was reportedly in poor health in mid-1965. Additionally, the firm recently had

enjoyed an upsurge in business since the Johnson administration's rise to power, and so Fortas's role as a managing partner charged with overseeing the firm's growth would carry added importance.

68. Fortas's wife, Carolyn Agger, would later lament that the financial sacrifice caused by her husband's nomination might force them to give up their home and other undertakings. Agger reportedly was so upset by Fortas's appointment that she initially refused to take the president's phone calls. See Murphy, *Fortas*, 183–84.

69. Transcript, Paul Porter Oral History interview, 2 October 1970, LBJL; Kalman, *Abe Fortas*, 241.

70. Letter, Abe Fortas to Lyndon Johnson, 19 July 1965, Supreme Court of United States file, WHCF-FG 535, LBJL.

71. Nicholas deB. Katzenbach, interview by author, 6 June 1996, Princeton, N.J.

72. Ibid.

73. Memo, Nicholas deB. Katzenbach, 22 July 1965, WHCF EX FG 535/ A, LBJL; Memo, "Mary Jo" to "Vicki," 23 July 1965, Diary Backup, President's appointments file, LBJL.

74. Memo, Nicholas deB. Katzenbach, 22 July 1965, WHCF EX FG 535/ A, LBJL.

75. Ibid.

76. Ibid.

77. Robert Shogan, *A Question of Judgment: The Fortas Case and the Struggle for the Supreme Court* (Indianapolis: Bobbs-Merrill, 1972), 111 (emphasis added).

78. When Fortas ultimately accepted the nomination, Johnson thanked Douglas for his efforts, referring to Fortas's decision as the one "we wanted him to make." Letter, Lyndon Johnson to William O. Douglas, 28 July 1965, WHCF EX FG 535/A, LBJL.

79. William O. Douglas, *The Court Years 1939–1975: The Autobiography of William O. Douglas* (New York: Random House, 1980), 318.

80. Transcript, Paul Porter Oral History interview, 2 October 1970, LBJL.

81. Notes of 27 July 1965, May 1965 file, Papers of Nicholas deB. Katzenbach, JFKL.

82. See Murphy, *Fortas*, 176.

83. Joseph A. Califano Jr., *The Tragedy and Triumph of Lyndon Johnson* (New York: Simon and Schuster, 1991), 47–48.

84. 347 U.S. 483 (1954).

85. 358 U.S. 1 (1958).

86. James J. Kilpatrick, "Term's End," *National Review*, 25 July 1967, 805.

87. Randall Bland, *Private Pressure on Public Law: The Legal Career of Justice Thurgood Marshall* (Port Washington, N.Y.: Kenikat Press, 1973), 129.

88. Mark Tushnet, *Making Constitutional Law: Thurgood Marshall and the Supreme Court, 1961–1991* (New York, Oxford University Press, 1997), 18.

89. Memo, Nicholas deB. Katzenbach to Lyndon Johnson, 8 July 1965,

Folder 2, White House Correspondence/President 1965 file, Papers of Nicholas deB. Katzenbach, JFKL.

90. Ibid.

91. Transcript, Thurgood Marshall Oral History interview, 10 July 1969, by T. H. Baker, Tape 1, LBJL.

92. Bland, *Private Pressure*, 129. Moreover, even if there never was such an elaborate plan for the solicitor general's future promotion, Katzenbach apparently assumed Marshall was being groomed for a future Supreme Court seat when he drafted the aforementioned memorandum of July 22, 1965, in which he had first suggested candidates to succeed Goldberg. The president had nominated Marshall to be solicitor general only nine days earlier. In discussing possible replacements for Goldberg, the attorney general had argued against choosing a nominee from New York at that time since the president "might wish to go to New York for your next appointment I think, other things being equal." Addressing the candidates' religious affiliations, Katzenbach also pointed out to Johnson that "your next appointment is not likely to be a Jew." Finally, Katzenbach's list failed to include even one black candidate, a surprising omission from Johnson's relatively liberal attorney general. The looming candidacy of Thurgood Marshall would explain most of Katzenbach's assumptions, as well as his carefully chosen words. Memo, Nicholas deB. Katzenbach to Lyndon Johnson, 22 July 1965, WHCF EX FG 535/A, LBJL.

93. Three former solicitors general—William Howard Taft, Stanley F. Reed, and Robert Jackson—had each risen to become a Supreme Court Justice. According to Carl Rowan, knowledge of this fact had a significant influence on Thurgood and Cissy Marshall's deliberations over whether he should take on the new position in 1965. See Carl Rowan, *Dream Makers, Dream Breakers: The World of Justice Thurgood Marshall* (Boston: Little, Brown and Co., 1993), 289.

94. Ibid.

95. Bland, *Private Pressure*, 150–51.

96. Phone conversation between Ramsey Clark and Lyndon Johnson, Tape No. K67.01, 1/25/67, 8:22 P.M., PNO:6, LBJL.

97. Ibid.

98. Ironically, the president considered his own positions on judicial issues most closely identified with those of Justice Clark. Johnson accused the justice's son of being "too damn radical, liberal. . . . I think you got a dash of that University of Chicago in you." Ibid.

99. Between 1964 and 1967, Justice Black began to side with the government in a number of well-publicized "sit-in" cases, see, e.g., *Bell v. Maryland*, 38 U.S. 226 (1964), and privacy cases, e.g., *Griswold v. Connecticut*, 381 U.S. 479 (1965).

100. Phone conversation between Ramsey Clark and Lyndon Johnson, Tape No. K67.01, 25 January 1967, 8:22 P.M., PNO:6, LBJL. Johnson seemed to delight in the liberal bloc's support for defendant's rights, remarking that "they wouldn't send a man to the penitentiary by God for raping a woman if you had a photograph of him."

101. John MacKenzie, "Ramsey Clark Named Attorney General," *Washington Post,* 1 March 1967, A8; Fred Graham, "Ramsey Clark Nominated to Be Attorney General; Father to Quit High Court," *New York Times,* 1 March 1967, 1. With Ramsey Clark's appointment imminent, Justice Clark had solicited the advice of Supreme Court expert and lawyer John P. Frank as to the propriety of his serving for the remainder of the term. After surveying relevant case law, Frank concluded that in the current situation, "the justice was perfectly proper to sit in the overwhelming number of cases (very nearly all of them, if not all) in which the relationship of the attorney general to the case is, as Chief Justice Stone put it, 'pro forma,' or as Justice Jackson said, 'nominal.' " Letter, John P. Frank to Tom C. Clark (undated), John P. Frank 1967–1977 folder, Box B47, Papers of Tom Clark, University of Texas Law School Library. Despite those assurances, Clark declared his intention to retire once his son's formal appointment was announced.

102. Nicholas deB. Katzenbach, interview by author, 6 June 1996, Princeton, N.J.

103. Ibid.

104. Michael D. Davis and Hunter R. Clark, *Thurgood Marshall: Warrior at the Bar, Rebel on the Bench* (New York: Birch Lane Press, 1992), 263–66.

105. Memo, James R. Jones to Lyndon Johnson, 11 June 1968, ExFG 535, LBJL.

106. Memo, James R. Jones for the record, 13 June 1968, 17 June 1969–30 June 1968 file, FG 535/A, LBJL; Murphy, *Fortas,* 270.

107. Transcript, Earl Warren Oral History interview, LBJL.

108. See Murphy, *Fortas,* 234–68; Kalman, *Abe Fortas,* 293–318.

109. Shogan, *A Question of Judgment,* 110. The propriety of Fortas's continued consultations with Johnson while he was an associate justice became a controversial subject of inquiry at Fortas's confirmation hearings later that summer.

110. Califano, *Triumph and Tragedy,* 307.

111. Shogan, *A Question of Judgment,* 148.

112. As Johnson pointed out to one aide, Fortas was already on the Court so "what is the difference if he sits here or there?" Ibid., 148–49.

113. The Senate confirmed Fortas to serve as associate justice by acclamation on August 11, 1965.

114. Transcript, Everett Dirksen Oral History interview, 21 March 1969, LBJL.

115. President's Daily Diary, 21 June 1968, Box 16, LBJL.

116. Transcript, Homer Thornberry Oral History interview, 21 December 1970, LBJL.

117. Although senatorial courtesy usually predominated in lower federal court selections, Johnson maintained an understanding with President Kennedy that as vice president he would have influence on all patronage appointments in Texas. According to Leon Jaworski, Johnson practically had veto power over judicial selections in the state, much to the chagrin of Democratic Senator Ralph Yarbrough (D-Tex.), who complained to Kennedy of the prac-

tice on numerous occasions. Transcript, Leon Jaworski Oral History interview, 23 December 1968, LBJL. Johnson should have expected little resistance from Kennedy regarding a Thornberry nomination. While a congressman on the House Rules Committee Thornberry had supported President Kennedy 95 percent of the time. Murphy, *Fortas*, 285.

118. ABA Committee Chairman Robert Meserve took the Johnson administration to task for violating what he believed was a firm understanding between the ABA and the Justice Department—that no such appointments would be submitted to the Senate without first being screened by the ABA's Committee. Letter, Robert Meserve to Nicholas deB. Katzenbach, 18 June 1965, ABA Standing Committee on Federal Judiciary file, Papers of Nicholas deB. Katzenbach, JFKL. Attorney General Katzenbach responded by supporting the president's right to exercise his constitutional powers alone "in circumstances in which he considers it to be in the best interests of the country that he act otherwise," although he assured Meserve that such circumstances would be "unlikely." Letter, Nicholas deB. Katzenbach to Robert Meserve, 2 July 1965, ABA Standing Committee on Federal Judiciary file, Papers of Nicholas deB. Katzenbach, JFKL.

119. Murphy, *Fortas*, 285.

120. Shogan, *A Question of Judgment*, 150.

121. President's Daily Diary, 22 June 1968, LBJL.

122. Clifford, *Counselor to the President*, 555–56.

123. Clifford's account of this conversation is confirmed in Kalman, *Abe Fortas*, 327–28; Douglas Frantz and David McKean, *Friend in High Places: The Rise and Fall of Clark Clifford* (Boston: Little, Brown and Co., 1995), 243–45.

124. Kalman, *Abe Fortas*, 328; Frantz and McKean, *Friends in High Places*, 244.

125. Clifford, *Counselor to the President*, 556.

126. Transcript, Warren Christopher Oral History interview, 31 October 1968, LBJL.

127. In a memorandum to the president dated June 24, 1968, Clark concluded that there was "nothing in our history suggesting that a president should refrain from filling a Court vacancy that will otherwise last an appreciable time." Memo, Ramsey Clark to Lyndon Johnson, 24 June 1968, Supreme Court of United States file, WHCF-FG 535, LBJL. Clark's reliance on the Brennan appointment as precedent (President Eisenhower gave Brennan a recess appointment less than a month before the 1956 presidential election) was misplaced: Eisenhower was running for reelection at that time; Johnson, by contrast, was a lame-duck president at the time of Fortas's proposed nomination to chief justice.

128. Vaughn Davis Bornet, *The Presidency of Lyndon Johnson* (Lawrence: University Press of Kansas, 1983), 314; Murphy, *Fortas*, 284.

129. Califano, *Triumph and Tragedy*, 308.

130. Shogan, *A Question of Judgment*, 150.

131. Ibid., 154–55.

132. Memo, Mike Manatos to Lyndon Johnson, 25 June 1968, Homer Thornberry file, WHCF–Name Files, LBJL.

133. 381 U.S. 479 (1965).

CHAPTER FIVE

1. Thus after Nixon informed Carswell of his nomination in January 1971, he told the nominee: "I'll never talk to you except socially." Diary entry of 19 January 1970 in H. R. Haldeman, *The Haldeman Diaries: Inside the Nixon White House* (New York: G. P. Putnam, 1994), 122.

2. Nixon first became close to Mitchell in 1967 when his law firm merged with Mitchell's firm (Caldwell, Trimble and Mitchell). Nixon instantly struck up a friendship with his fellow partner and increasingly relied on him for advice and counsel on political matters.

3. By contrast, Herbert Brownell was a corporate lawyer seasoned in political battles; he had served in the New York State Assembly for five years and had been chairman of the Republican National Committee before taking over the Justice Department in 1953.

4. According to journalist Tom Wicker, Mitchell was an especially forceful man and early in Nixon's first term he became the "strongman of the administration." Tom Wicker, *One of Us: Richard Nixon and the American Dream* (New York: Random House, 1991), 414.

5. The exceptions were two Maryland Court of Appeals Judges: Frederick Singley Jr., fifty-six, and Marvin Smith, fifty-two.

6. See Memo, John D. Ehrlichman to Richard M. Nixon, 23 May 1969, Supreme Court of United States file, EX FG 51, NPMP; John P. Frank, *Clement Haynsworth, the Senate and the Supreme Court* (Charlottesville: University Press of Virginia, 1991), 27. One of Nixon's top White House officials, John D. Ehrlichman, argued that "the unique nature of Supreme Court Justice appointments precludes the involvement of attorneys at the local level in investigations and canvasses of this kind."

7. Letter, Earl Warren to Lyndon B. Johnson, 13 June 1968, Chronological File: Duplicates, Box 4, Special Files Pertaining to Fortas/Thornberry, LBJL.

8. Anthony Lewis, "Warren Firm on Retiring; Leaves Date Up to Nixon," *New York Times,* 15 November 1968, 6.

9. John Robert Greene, *The Limits of Power: the Nixon and Ford Administrations* (Bloomington: Indiana University Press, 1992), 37.

10. Herbert Brownell, interview by author, 21 February 1996, New York City. Brownell's role in the Little Rock schools crisis was a visible one; his most lasting contribution to integration efforts, however, came with his decision to fill federal judicial posts in the South with judges who were strong-willed, independent and sensitive to civil rights issues.

11. After Nixon selected Burger in May he described Brownell as one of a number of candidates who had declined interest in the position. See Robert Semple, "Nixon Influenced by Fortas Affair in Court Choices," *New York Times* 23 May 1969, 1.

12. John D. Ehrlichman, *Witness to Power* (New York: Simon and Schuster, 1982), 113.

13. John L. Steele, "Haynsworth v. U.S. Senate (1969)," *Fortune,* March 1970, 91.

14. Frank, *Clement Haynsworth,* 24.

15. Warren E. Burger to Herbert Brownell, undated, Warren Burger 1968-70(2) file, Herbert Brownell Papers, DDEL.

16. See various contents of Warren Burger 1957-67 file, Herbert Brownell Papers, DDEL.

17. Herbert Brownell to Dwight D. Eisenhower, 16 September 1965, Warren Burger 1957-67(1) file, Herbert Brownell Papers, DDEL. In his letter to Eisenhower, Brownell quoted from Burger's opinion in *Pauling v. McNamara,* 331 F.2d 796 (D.C. Cir. 1963), a case in which Linus Pauling and others brought a class action suit to enjoin nuclear testing activities. Burger wrote for the majority: "We are unwilling to suggest, even so indirectly, any erosion of the fundamental principle that the executive action challenged by the pleadings plainly falls in that area where the Executive and Legislative Branches are supreme and final, reviewable only by the electorate, not by the Courts."

Brownell also quoted extensively from a recent article in which Burger classified his approach to judging as follows:

I cherish the independence of the American judiciary as indispensable to our purpose, but I try not to confuse independence with omnipotence—and especially with omniscience. . . . The judicial function is inherently one of conservation and I do not regard my commission as a mandate to correct all the mistakes of the legislative and executive branches or to bring about a perfect society. If we ever achieve that it will be the people through *elected* representatives, not life tenure judges, who will get it done.

Finally, Brownell cited favorably Burger's dissenting opinion in *Killough v. United States,* 315 F.2d 241 (D.C. Cir. 1962), in which he advocated granting additional authority to police to examine criminal suspects. The *Killough* majority excluded a voluntary confession made nearly twenty-four hours after judicial warnings in a preliminary hearing where the defendant had rejected offers of counsel. Burger wrote: "What Congress clearly intended as a protection will have become a weapon of special advantage exclusively for the guilty." 315 F.2d at 260 (Burger, J., dissenting).

18. Warren E. Burger to Herbert Brownell, undated, Warren Burger 1968-70(2) file, Herbert Brownell Papers, DDEL. Although the letter itself does not indicate it was written in October 1968, Burger makes specific reference to the ongoing presidential election contest between "HHH" and "RN," and to rumors that "Fortas is out" as a nominee for chief justice.

19. Burger's statement was factually incorrect. In late 1968 the Court's membership included two justices who met Burger's broad definition of a "Midwesterner": Potter Stewart of Ohio and Byron White of Colorado.

20. Warren E. Burger to Herbert Brownell, undated, Warren Burger 1968–70(2) file, Herbert Brownell Papers, DDEL.

21. In *Witherspoon v. Illinois*, 391 U.S. 510 (1968), the Supreme Court, per Justice Stewart, held that a sentence of death could not be carried out if the jury that imposed or recommended it was chosen by excluding veniremen for cause simply because they voiced "general objections to the death penalty or expressed conscientious or religious scruples against its infliction."

22. Warren E. Burger to Herbert Brownell, undated, Warren Burger 1968–70(2) file, Herbert Brownell Papers, DDEL.

23. Warren E. Burger to Herbert Brownell, 5 January 1969, Warren Burger 1968–70(2) file, Herbert Brownell Papers, DDEL.

24. Inventory of File No. 277 (Judge Warren Burger), 1 July 1969–31 December 1969 file, EX FG 51, White House Central Files: Subject files, NPMP.

25. Frank, *Clement Haynsworth*, 24.

26. Herbert Brownell, interview by author, 21 February 1996, New York City.

27. Memo, Pat Buchanan to Richard M. Nixon, 6 May 1969, Supreme Court of United States (Beginning–30 June 1969) file, EX FG51, White House Central Files: Subject files, NPMP. Buchanan added that Nixon could then name a "constitutionalist" from the federal courts of appeals as associate justice to replace Harlan. To Buchanan this represented "the best of all worlds": Harlan's appointment would earn universal praise from the legal community, and Harlan's demise would then give Nixon the opportunity to name two chief justices in his first term.

28. Memo, Leonard Garment to H. R. Haldeman, 15 May 1969, January–June 1969 file, Leonard Garment White House Memos, White House Central Files: SMOF, NPMP.

29. After announcing that he would nominate Burger as chief justice, Nixon told reporters that several candidates had voluntarily taken themselves out of the running for chief justice, including Justice Stewart, John Mitchell, and Thomas E. Dewey. Given Nixon's desire to nominate a younger justice and to avoid charges of cronyism, his comments regarding Dewey (then sixty-seven years old) and Mitchell were most likely self-serving attempts to lavish praise on two political acquaintances.

30. Fred Graham, "Stewart Tells of Barring His Elevation," *New York Times*, 28 May 1969, 36.

31. Rumors that Abe Fortas might resign from the Court had been circulating around Washington since May 5, when members of Congress learned that the justice had received a $20,000 fee from Louis Wolfson while the financier was being investigated for criminal charges. Fortas reportedly kept the fee for eleven months before returning it. Meanwhile Wolfson was convicted of illegally manipulating stocks in April 1969.

32. Diary entry of 19 May 1969, Haldeman, *Haldeman Diaries*, 59.

33. Unaware that Nixon had decided to move ahead with the nomination of Burger on May 19, William Safire argued in a memo to H. R. Haldeman on May 20 that the two appointments should be announced between ten and

twenty days apart, with the associate justice announcement first to avoid an "anticlimax." Memo, William Safire to H. R. Haldeman, 20 May 1969, Supreme Court Confirmation file, Alphabetical subject files, Papers of H. R. Haldeman, White House Special Files: SMOF, NPMP. As it turned out, Nixon waited nearly three months, until August 18, 1969, to reveal that he would nominate Clement Haynsworth to fill Fortas's vacant seat.

34. Diary entry of 20 May 1969, Haldeman, *Haldeman Diaries*, 60.

35. Robert Semple, "Warren Burger Named Chief Justice by Nixon; Now on Appeals Bench," *New York Times*, 22 May 1969, 1. Hugh Scott, the Republican minority whip in the Senate, had prepared his statement days before hailing Justice Stewart's appointment.

36. The Committee later found Judge Burger "well-qualified" for the post of chief justice.

37. Press announcement of 21 May 1969, *Public Papers of the Presidents of the United States: Richard Nixon (1969)* (Washington, D.C.: U.S. Government Printing Office, 1971), 389.

38. *New York Times*, 22 May 1969, 36.

39. Nixon intentionally deferred the consideration of Northern candidates that he found appealing, at least until a later date. In response to public speculation that Judge Charles Breitel of the New York Court of Appeals was a front-runner for the vacancy, Nixon informed the attorney general: "John— Not now. If he's okay give him the Harlan vacancy." Memo, Alexander Butterfield to John Mitchell, 23 June 1969, Supreme Court of United States (1969–1970) file, FG 51, White House Special Files: WHCF, NPMP.

40. Memo, Harry Dent to John Mitchell, 20 June 1969, Clement Haynsworth [3 of 3] file, Papers of Harry Dent, White House Central Files: SMOF, NPMP.

41. In 1916 Louis Brandeis became the first Jewish justice. Since then the Court had not been without a Jewish justice. Their ranks included (with some overlap) Benjamin Cardozo, Felix Frankfurter, Arthur Goldberg, and Abe Fortas.

42. Ironically, one of the few White House aides to even raise the issue of the Jewish seat was Pat Buchanan, who advised Nixon to appoint an Italian-American to "offset criticism of ending the Jewish seat on the Court." Memo, Pat Buchanan to Richard M. Nixon, 26 May 1969, President's Official Files; White House Special Files, NPMP.

43. Hoff, *Nixon Reconsidered*, 47.

44. Letter, James J. Kilpatrick to Richard M. Nixon, Beginning to 30 June 1969 file, Supreme Court of United States folder, EX FG 51, NPMP.

45. Frank, *Clement Haynsworth*, 24.

46. Powell declined Johnson's request to chair the committee, but he did agree to serve as one of its members.

47. Knowing of the president's penchant to find a young candidate, Dent wrote Mitchell on June 20 to make sure he knew that Haynsworth was fifty-six and not fifty-seven as Mitchell had previously suggested. Harry Dent memo to John Mitchell, 20 June 1969, Haynsworth [3 of 3] file, Papers of Harry Dent, White House Central Files: SMOF, NPMP.

48. Ibid., 23.

49. Memo, Pat Buchanan to Richard M. Nixon, 15 October 1969, Doc No. 69-10-12-A04, *Part 2—Papers of the Nixon White House: The President's Meeting File, 1969–1974* (Frederick, Md.: University Publications of America, 1987).

50. Frank, *Clement Haynsworth*, 25.

51. Ibid., 24.

52. Haynsworth had voted with the majority in rejecting an NLRB ruling that the Darlington Manufacturing Company of South Carolina was guilty of unfair labor practices in 1956 when it closed its plant rather than allow its workers to unionize. See *Darlington Manufacturing Co. v. NLRB*, 325 F.2d 682 (4th Cir. 1963). At the time, Haynsworth had been serving as first vice president of the Carolina Vend-A-Matic Corporation, a vending machine firm which held $50,000 worth of contracts with Darlington Manufacturing's parent company, Deering Milliken and Co. The unions claimed that Haynsworth had ruled despite a conflict of interest, but the court's highly respected chief judge, Simon Sobeloff, cleared Haynsworth of wrongdoing when he discovered that the judge had resigned as vice president while the case was in litigation, but before the decision had been rendered.

53. Nixon later criticized Mitchell for coasting on these two senators' assurances. Diary entry of 21 November 1969, Haldeman, *Haldeman Diaries*, 110.

54. Ibid.

55. Steele, "Haynsworth v. U.S. Senate," 92.

56. Frank, *Clement Haynsworth*, 26.

57. Haynsworth was accused of purchasing shares in the Brunswick corporation after he had voted on a case involving the company but before the decision had been announced.

58. Abraham, *Justices and Presidents*, 15.

59. Diary entry of 12 November 1969, Haldeman, *Haldeman Diaries*, 107.

60. Diary entry of 21 November 1969, Haldeman, *Haldeman Diaries*, 110.

61. See Massaro, *Supremely Political*, 93–104.

62. Ibid., 80.

63. Wicker, *One of Us*, 497.

64. On January 15, 1894, President Grover Cleveland—then serving his second, nonconsecutive term in office—saw the Senate defeat two of his nominees in a row: William Hornblower (rejected 30–24 on January 15, 1894) and Wheeler Peckham (rejected 41–32 on February 16, 1894). Three days later he nominated Edward D. White, who was confirmed by acclamation later that day.

65. In 1958, Rogers had been instrumental in making Carswell, then thirty-eight, the youngest federal judge in the country.

66. Frank, *Clement Haynsworth*, 101.

67. Robert Semple, "Southerner Named to Supreme Court; Carswell, 50, Viewed as Conservative," *New York Times*, 20 January 1970, 20.

68. Notes, G. Harrold Carswell file, Papers of John D. Ehrlichman, White House Special Files: SMOF, NPMP. Some groups had even described Cars-

well as more hostile to black litigants than any other federal jurist in Florida. "Carswell Supports Legal Precedents," *Washington Post*, 20 January 1970, A6.

69. See Attachment to Memo, Egil "Bud" Krogh to Bryce Harlow, 20 January 1970, G. Harrold Carswell file, Papers of John Ehrlichman, White House Special Files: SMOF, NPMP.

70. Although Carswell had served as a district judge in northern Florida for eleven years, Rehnquist could cite only a handful of his decisions favoring the rights of the accused, civil rights claimants, or unions. He included one case from 1965 in which Carswell held that a barber shop was subject to the Civil Rights Act, an unremarkable finding given the Supreme Court's decisions the previous year in *Heart of Atlanta Hotel v. United States* and *Katzenbach v. McClung*. Indeed, the best Rehnquist could offer was that Carswell had not openly defied the Supreme Court: "he made a conscientious effort to decide the case under the established law." Ibid.

71. "Carswell Supports Legal Precedents," *Washington Post*, 20 January 1970, A6.

72. William Safire, *Before the Fall: An Inside View of the Pre-Watergate White House* (New York: Doubleday, 1975), 267.

73. Abraham, *Justice and Presidents*, 16.

74. Massaro, *Supremely Political*, 125.

75. At his confirmation hearings, the nominee assured the Senate Judiciary Committee that he had not looked at documents concerning the golf club episode. When after the hearings it was discovered that in fact Carswell had reviewed some other documents with Justice Department officials prior to testifying, many senators jumped to the conclusion that Carswell had deceived the Senate. In fact, two different sets of documents may have been in question.

76. Massaro, *Supremely Political*, 107.

77. In a particularly clumsy attempt at defending Carswell, Senator Hruska of Alaska, the ranking Republican on the Senate Judiciary Committee, uttered the devastating comment that even the "mediocre deserve representation on the Supreme Court."

78. Peter Fish, "Spite Nominations to the United States Supreme Court: Herbert C. Hoover, Owen J. Roberts, and the Politics of Presidential Vengeance in Retrospect," *Kentucky Law Journal* 77 (1988–89): 545.

79. Ibid., 552.

80. Haldeman reported that the president's immediate reaction to the Carswell's rejection was "to decide not to submit another nomination until after the election, and then go for Bob Byrd of West Virginia." Diary entry of 8 April 1970, Haldeman, *Haldeman Diaries*, 147. Senator Robert Dole (R-Kan.) argued in favor of Nixon holding off naming a new candidate so that he might make his appointment power a campaign issue that fall. Dole told the president he might be able to use the supposed "impairment of his nominating powers" as an argument for Republican control of the Senate.

81. Robert Semple, "Nixon Condemns Senators Who Barred Two Judges; Will Pick Non-Southerner," *New York Times*, 10 April 1970, 1; Spen-

cer Rich, "Southern Nominees Ruled Out by Nixon," *Washington Post-Times Herald*, 10 April 1970, A1.

82. Frank, *Clement Haynsworth*, 118.

83. 379 F.2d 33 (8th Cir. 1965), rev'd sub nom. *Jones v. Alfred Mayer Co.*, 392 U.S. 409 (1968).

84. See *Holdridge v. United States*, 282 F.2d 302 (8th Cir. 1960) (upholding a conviction for illegal reentry onto a military reservation despite the prosecution's inability to produce evidence at trial of the defendant's criminal intent).

85. See *Bass v. United States*, 324 F.2d 168 (8th Cir. 1963).

86. 379 F.2d at 45. Blackmun was probably relieved when the Supreme Court overturned his ruling in a landmark decision that breathed new life into the 1866 statute. See *Jones v. Alfred H. Mayer Co.*, 392 U.S. 409 (1968).

87. See *Jackson v. Bishop*, 404 F.2d 571 (8th Cir. 1968).

88. Diary entry of 10 April 1970, Haldeman, *Haldeman Diaries*, 149. Even before committing to Blackmun, Nixon expressed concern that he might be charged with caving in to liberals. The president wrote Haldeman: "it is vitally important that somebody like Hruska praise the nomination as being that of a man who has the same philosophy on the Constitution as Haynsworth or Carswell. . . . Blackmun is to the right of both on law and order . . . slightly to the left only in the field of civil rights." Memo, Richard M. Nixon to H. R. Haldeman, 13 April 1970, Papers of H. R. Haldeman, NPMP.

89. Massaro, *Supremely Political*, 154.

90. Maltese, *The Selling of Supreme Court Nominees*, 90.

91. After the 1970 midterm elections, the Senate's membership consisted of fifty-four Democrats, forty-four Republicans, one Independent (Harry Byrd of Virginia), and one Conservative (James Buckley of New York).

92. Memo, Pat Buchanan to Richard M. Nixon, 20 September 1971, presidential memos–1971 file, Papers of Patrick Buchanan, White House Central Files: SMOF, NPMP.

93. Diary entry of 20 September 1971, Haldeman, *Haldeman Diaries*, 357. Harlan's doctors told the press on September 23 that Harlan was suffering from bone cancer. According to Hugo Black's biographer, Roger K. Newman, Harlan delayed his announcement for a week to avoid detracting from the "accolades and attention Black would receive and Harlan wanted him to receive." Roger K. Newman, *Hugo Black: A Biography* (New York: Pantheon, 1994), 623.

94. Ibid.

95. Memo, Egil "Bud" Krogh to Richard M. Nixon, September 24, 1971, Supreme Court nominations file, Papers of David Young, White House Special Files: SMOF, NPMP.

96. This exchange was sparked by a Law Day Address delivered by Lawrence Walsh, chairman of the ABA's Standing Committee on Federal Judiciary, on May 1, 1970. Commenting on the committee's examination of Carswell, Walsh complained that the committee had not been given enough time to do a good job of investigating the nominees. He concluded that the ABA's

role in Supreme Court nominations operated "less satisfactorily" than its role in rating nominees for other federal judgeships. See Memo, Bryce Harlow to Richard M. Nixon, 19 May 1970, 1 January 1970–31 May 1970 file, EX FG 51, White House Central Files: Subject files, NPMP.

97. As part of this agreement, the ABA reserved the right to appear before the Senate Judiciary Committee at the nominee's confirmation hearings.

98. Egil "Bud" Krogh memo to Nixon, 24 September 1971, Supreme Court nominations file, Papers of David Young, White House Special Files: SMOF, NPMP.

99. Joan Hoff, *Nixon Reconsidered* (New York: Basic Books, 1994), 294. The term "Plumbers" referred to the White House unit charged with spying on administration officials in order to identify and plug unauthorized information leaks.

100. In the spring of 1956, Poff joined one hundred other congressmen in signing the first such manifesto, a written declaration of hostility to desegregation. The Court's "unwarranted" decision in *Brown*, said the manifesto, was "a clear abuse of judicial power" and substituted the justices' "personal political and social ideas for the established law of the land." The congressmen thus swore "to use all lawful means to bring about a reversal of this decision which is contrary to the Constitution." See Richard Kluger, *Simple Justice* (New York: Vintage Books, 1977), 753. Southern members seeking reelection were under significant pressure to sign the document—only Senators Lyndon Johnson (D-Tex.), Estes Kefauver (D-Tenn.), and Albert Gore (D-Tenn.) refused.

101. House Minority Leader Gerald Ford (R-Mich.) lauded Poff's "unassailable reputation for fairness and character," noting that he had "never known anyone" with a higher moral standard. See Letter, Gerald R. Ford to Richard M. Nixon, 22 September 1971, folder Honorable Richard Poff–U.S. Supreme Court, Robert Hartmann Papers, GRFL.

102. Poff had expressed interest in a judicial career in large part because the 1970 census had caused his House district to be merged with that of a fellow GOP incumbent, Rep. William Wampler (R-Va.).

103. Memo, Pat Buchanan to Richard M. Nixon, 20 September 1971, presidential memos–1971 file, Papers of Patrick Buchanan, White House Central Files: SMOF, NPMP.

104. Memo, Pat Buchanan to Richard M. Nixon, 29 September 1971, Supreme Court file 11 January 1971–18 December 1972 file, EX FG 51, White House Central Files: Subject file, NPMP.

105. Ibid. Apparently Poff did enjoy the support of some respected liberal senators, including Margaret Chase Smith (R-Me.), an ardent opponent of both the Haynsworth and Carswell nominations. Smith wrote Poff after his withdrawal, offering that she had in fact planned to vote for his confirmation. Letter, Margaret Chase Smith to Richard Poff, 4 October 1971, Presidential handwriting file 1 October 1971–15 October 1971, President's Official Files, NPMP.

106. John P. MacKenzie, "Rights Leaders Set to Oppose Poff for Court," *Washington Post*, 22 September 1971, A4.

107. John P. MacKenzie, "Court Fitness of Poff Is Attacked," *Washington Post,* 27 September 1971, A2.

108. Memo, Pat Buchanan to Richard M. Nixon, 29 September 1971, Supreme Court file, 11 January 1971–8 December 1972 file, EX FG 51, White House Central Files: Subject file, NPMP.

109. White House aides Patrick Moynihan and Peter G. Peterson each lent their support to Levi's candidacy in early October. Ibid.; Memo, Pete Peterson to John D. Ehrlichman, 7 October 1971, Supreme Court of United States, 11 January 1971–8 December 1972 file, EX FG 51, White House Central Files: Subject file, NPMP; Memo, Pete Peterson to John D. Ehrlichman, 6 October 1971, Supreme Court of United States 11 January 1971–18 December 1972 file, EX FG 51, White House Central Files: Subject file, NPMP. Ehrlichman was impressed enough with Levi that he forwarded Peterson's letters of support to Mitchell on 8 October. Tod R. Hullin memo to John Mitchell, 8 October 1971, Supreme Court of United States 11 January 1971–18 December 1972 file, EX FG 51, White House Central Files: Subject files, NPMP.

110. There is some evidence that Nixon briefly considered looking for a Jewish nominee when he first learned of Justice Black's intention to resign. On September 17, 1971, Haldeman wrote in his diary that Nixon instructed Mitchell to consider [Philadelphia District Attorney] Arlen Specter for a "Jewish seat." Diary entry of 17 September 1971, Haldeman, *Haldeman Diaries,* 355. Nixon had actually raised this possibility for the first time in April 1970, when he had spoken well of Specter as a "possible future appointee" to Senator Bob Dole (R-Kan.). Later, when it became apparent that Nixon was not considering any Jewish candidates for either of the two vacancies, Clayton Fritchey of the *New Republic* charged that the "administration is touched with anti-Semitism." According to Stephen Ambrose, Nixon angrily told his aides: "with Kissinger, Garment, Safire, and Burns? Someone should really crack him for this inexcusable innuendo." Stephen E. Ambrose, *Nixon,* vol. 2, *The Triumph of a Politician, 1962–1972* (New York: Simon and Schuster, 1989), 470.

111. Memo, Pat Buchanan to Richard M. Nixon, 29 September 1971, Supreme Court of United States 11 January 1971–18 December 1972 file, EX FG 51, White House Central Files: Subject file, NPMP.

112. Ambrose, *Nixon,* 2:469. Apparently Pat Nixon felt so strongly about her husband naming a female justice that she made uncharacteristic public statements on the subject, telling the press at one point "Don't you worry . . . I'm talking it up." Ibid.

113. Diary entry of 25 September 1971, Haldeman, *Haldeman Diaries,* 358.

114. Diary entry of 26 September 1971, Haldeman, *Haldeman Diaries,* 358.

115. This initial list of thirteen names was regenerated a week later along with the identification of each candidate's current position, state of origin, party, age, and estimated political leanings. Chart, Supreme Court appointments file, Papers of John Dean, White House Special Files: SMOF, NPMP.

116. Ibid. Mentschikoff had merited some consideration on Nicholas Kat-

zenbach's list of suggested candidates to fill the seat vacated by Justice Gold-berg in 1965. See chapter 5.

117. Notes from 28 September 1971, Papers of John Ehrlichman, White House Special Files: SMOF, NPMP.

118. Ibid. Nixon may have been referring to Justice Douglas's reputation for propositioning women, a reputation that has never been substantially confirmed.

119. Letter, Richard A. Kleindienst to Lawrence Walsh, 28 September 1971, Supreme Court of United States, 11 January 1971–18 December 1972 file, EX FG 51, White House Central Files: Subject file, NPMP.

120. Memo, Egil "Bud" Krogh to David Young, Richard Poff/Supreme Court file, Papers of David Young, White House Central Files: SMOF, NPMP.

121. Memo, Leonard Garment to Richard M. Nixon, 30 September 1971, Supreme Court of United States 11 January 1971–18 December 1972 file, EX FG 51, White House Central Files: Subject file, NPMP. Garment also mentioned two other objections to Poff that might draw opposition, albeit on a lesser scale: (1) his sponsorship of legislation requiring Supreme Court appointees to be native born; and (2) his support of the so-called Wiggins Limitations on the Equal Rights Amendment.

122. Ibid.

123. Statement of 2 October 1971, Supreme Court of United States, 11 January 1971–18 December 1972 file, EX FG 51, White House Central Files: Subject file, NPMP. In his statement to the press Poff said he wanted to avoid a "long and divisive confirmation battle" and the impact it would have on the nation, and on his family.

124. Diary entry of 2 October 1971, Haldeman, *Haldeman Diaries*, 361.

125. Ibid.

126. Ibid.

127. Byrd had complained to Harry Dent in 1970 about the administration's "shift to the left" regarding "the tax-exempt status for private schools, the marshals going South and other matters." Memo, Harry Dent to Bryce Harlow et al., 27 July 1970, Doc No. 70-8-2(1)-E04, *Papers of the Nixon White House, Part II*, National Archives Publications.

128. Jeffries, *Justice Lewis F. Powell, Jr.*, 3.

129. Senate support for Byrd was not universal, however. Senator George McGovern (D-S.D.), one of the most liberal members of the Senate and a candidate for the 1972 Democratic presidential nomination, was notably uncomfortable with the prospect of Byrd's candidacy. Initially McGovern said he would support his Democratic colleague, but later issued a public statement: "I cannot accept a man who is mediocre, who is racist and who is unethical, for membership on the U.S. Supreme Court." "Nixon Considers Byrd, Two Women for Court," *Washington Evening Star*, 12 October 1971, A7.

130. The most experienced conservative judge from the original list, Susie Marshall Sharp of the North Carolina Supreme Court, was apparently dropped from serious consideration at this time. Justice Department officials

may have been discouraged by her age (she was sixty-four years old) as well as by a general reluctance to nominate a ticket composed entirely of southerners.

131. Notes from 8 October 1971, Notes of meetings with president, 3 August 1971–31 December 1971 [3 of 5] file, Papers of John D. Ehrlichman, White House Special Files: SMOF, NPMP. Of course, Nixon was not correct in his depiction of Frankfurter's pre-Court career. While a Harvard Law School professor in the 1920s and 1930s Frankfurter took on a number of legal causes. Frankfurter worked tirelessly on the legal defense for Sidney Hillman's Amalgamated Clothing Workers' Union, under siege in Rochester, New York for several strikes. In Boston, Frankfurter and Zechariah Chafee had participated amici curiae, filing writs of habeas corpus on behalf of William Coyler and nineteen other aliens who had been arrested during the "Palmer raids." Frankfurter performed his most famous legal work on behalf of two Italian immigrants, Nicola Sacco and Bartolomeo Vanzetti, whose robbery and homicide convictions in the summer of 1920 became a cause celebre. He entered the case five years later, working on day-to-day defense strategy as the defendants' appeals were being heard in the state's Supreme Judicial Court. See generally Michael E. Parrish, *Felix Frankfurter and His Times* (New York: Free Press, 1982). By contrast, Senator Byrd had never participated as counsel in any trial or other form of litigation.

132. Notes from 8 October 1971, Notes of meetings with president, 3 August 1971–31 December 1971 [3 of 5] file, Papers of John D. Ehrlichman, White House Special Files: SMOF, NPMP.

133. Memo, John D. Ehrlichman to President's file, 8 October 1971, "Beginning 10/3/71" file, Memoranda for President folder, President's Official Files, NPMP.

134. During the week of 10 October Dean and Young met with Lillie and Friday, among others. Although the bulk of their discussions concerned constitutional issues and how they would handle confirmation hearings, their questions covered a wide range of subjects including: (1) each candidate's financial net worth; (2) possible conflicts of interest; (3) psychiatric background; (4) family relationships; (5) associations; (6) "life style" (extramarital affairs, abortions, religion, drinking, gambling); (7) military or educational background; (8) legal positions; (9) law practice; (10) health; (11) interest in serving on the Supreme Court; and (12) dealings with special interest groups. See Outline, Supreme Court appointments file, Papers of John Dean, White House Special Files: SMOF, NPMP.

135. Memo, William H. Rehnquist to John Mitchell, 12 October 1971, Supreme Court Appointments file, Papers of John Dean, White House Special Files: SMOF, NPMP.

136. Ibid.

137. Ibid.

138. Ibid.

139. Ambrose, *Nixon*, 2:469.

140. Notes from 12 October 1971, Notes of Meetings with President, 3 August 1971–31 December 1971 [3 of 5] file, Papers of John D. Ehrlichman, White House Special Files: SMOF, NPMP. Governor Barnett had tried to

block James Meredith and other blacks from enrolling at the University of Mississippi in direct violation of a federal district court order.

141. Ibid.

142. Ibid.

143. Rowland Evans and Robert Novak, "Nixon and Material for the Court," *Washington Post*, 18 October 1971, A23.

144. "Kennedy and Bayh Assail Nixon's Way of Filling Court Vacancies," *New York Times*, 16 October 1971, 28; Jonathan Schell, *The Time of Illusion* 186–87 (New York: Knopf, 1976).

145. Apparently the president wanted Ehrlichman's plumbers to pursue the leak, yelling: "Tell your boys to get going—kick their ass!" Notes from 14 October 1971, Notes of Meetings with President, 3 August 1971–31 December 1971 file, Papers of John D. Ehrlichman, White House Special Files: SMOF, NPMP.

146. Ibid.

147. Ibid.

148. Bob Woodward and Scott Armstrong, *The Brethren* (New York: Simon and Schuster, 1979), 159–60.

149. Diary entry of 15 October 1971, Haldeman, *Haldeman Diaries*, 365. According to Haldeman, Nixon was furious about Burger's threats. On 15 October Haldeman wrote: "The P[resident]'s view is, if that's his feeling, let him resign. . . . [The president] feels quite strongly about it on the grounds that Burger would never have even been considered for the Court, let alone chief justice, except by Nixon." Ibid.

150. Ibid.

151. Young also searched the list of ambassadors appointed by the president and identified two possible candidates: Kenneth Rush, U.S. Ambassador to Germany and Joseph Farland, the ambassador to Pakistan. Memo, David Young to John D. Ehrlichman, 19 October 1971, Supreme Court Nomination file, Papers of David Young, White House Special Files: SMOF, NPMP.

152. Memo, Egil "Bud" Krogh and David Young to John D. Ehrlichman, undated, Supreme Court Nomination file, Papers of David Young, White House Special Files: SMOF, NPMP.

153. Jeffries, *Justice Lewis F. Powell, Jr.*, 5. After Mitchell's second offer, Powell suggested a wide range of alternative candidates that Nixon might want to consider. Among the candidates Powell suggested were Mitchell himself; William Rogers; John Connally, the secretary of the treasury; Elliot Richardson, the secretary of health, education, and welfare; and a handful of private practitioners, law professors, and judges.

154. Apparently it was Solicitor General Erwin Griswold who first suggested that the president play hardball by telling Powell it was his "duty" to accept the appointment. Erwin Griswold, *Ould Fields, New Corne* (St. Paul: West, 1992), 283–84.

155. Jeffries, *Justice Lewis F. Powell, Jr.*, 6–7.

156. Diary entry of 20 October 1971, Haldeman, *Haldeman Diaries*, 366. David Young had scouted Mulligan, a former dean at the Fordham University Law School who was especially active in the New York bar. See Notes, Su-

preme Court nomination file, Papers of David Young, White House Special Files: SMOF, NPMP.

157. Diary entry of 21 October 1971, Haldeman, *Haldeman Diaries*, 367. Richard Moore, the White House special counsel, told Haldeman of Nixon's offer to Baker.

158. Richard Moore, oral history interview in Gerald Strober and Deborah Strober, eds., *Nixon: An Oral History of His Presidency* (New York: HarperCollins, 1994), 66. Richard Nixon's memoirs essentially backed up Moore's claim that he was responsible for first suggesting Rehnquist. Richard M. Nixon, *RN: The Memoirs of Richard Nixon* (New York: Grosset and Dunlap, 1978), 424.

159. Ibid.

160. Douglas's liberal views as a jurist had inspired much of this opposition. Critics also accused Douglas of improperly associating with the Parvin Foundation (which had been accused of maintaining gambling and underworld connections) and of having written an article in *Avant Garde*, a low-grade publication edited by the controversial Ralph Ginzburg. When asked to define "impeachable offense," Ford replied: "The only honest answer is that an impeachable offense is whatever a majority of the House of Representatives considers it to be at a given moment in history."

161. William O. Douglas, *The Court Years* (New York: Random House, 1980), 377.

162. In August 1969, Nixon's approval rating stood at 62 percent; in January 1970 his rating had risen to near 66 percent, among the highest of his presidency.

163. Gerald Ford, *A Time to Heal* (New York: Harper and Row, 1979), 237.

164. Ibid.

165. *Wall Street Journal*, 23 May 1975, 1.

166. Memo, Edward H. Levi to Gerald R. Ford, 10 November 1975, Supreme Court Nominations–Letters to the President, 10 November 1975–12 November 1975 file, Richard Cheney Files, GRFL.

167. Ibid.

168. The oldest candidate on the list was Bennett Boskey, born in 1916. Levi wrote Ford that in his original conversation with the president he had two other federal judges in mind: Judge Edward Gignoux, a U.S. district judge in Portland, Maine, and Judge Carl McGowan of the Court of Appeals for the D.C. Circuit. Now Levi eliminated the two judges from consideration because of their ages. Like Boskey, Gignoux was born in 1916. McGowan was born in 1911.

169. Memo, Edward H. Levi to Gerald R. Ford, 10 November 1975, Supreme Court Nominations–Letters to the President, 10 November 1975–12 November 1975 file, Richard Cheney Files, GRFL.

170. Ibid.

171. Ibid.

172. Memo, Richard Cheney to James E. Connor, 9 December 1975, President's handwriting file, FG 51, GRFL.

173. Memo, 13 November 1975, Supreme Court vacancy file, Philip

Buchen Files, GRFL. Levi was dutifully following the advice of Warren Christopher, then head of the ABA's Standing Committee on Federal Judiciary, who had urged him to submit names to his committee before a final decision was reached. Victor Kramer, "The Case of Justice Stevens: How to Select, Nominate and Confirm a Justice of the United States Supreme Court," *Constitutional Commentary* 7 (1990): 325, 330.

174. See, e.g., Lyle Denniston, "Will Ford Name a Woman to Douglas Post?" *Washington Star*, 13 November 1975, A1.

175. Memo, Patricia Lindh to Douglas P. Bennett, 13 November 1975, Supreme Court Nomination–General file, Bobbie Greene Kilberg Files, GRFL; Memo, Bobbie Greene Kilberg to Philip Buchen, Richard Cheney, and Douglas P. Bennett, 13 November 1975, Shirley Hufstedler file, White House Central Files: Name Files, GRFL. Kilberg's memo mentioned five women who she believed would be "qualified to sit on the U.S. Supreme Court": Soia Mentschikoff, Ellen Peters, Shirley Hufstedler, Carla Hills, and Barbara Jordan. Lindh's more comprehensive memo listed eighteen possible nominees: Sylvia Bacon, Mary Coleman, Julia Cooper, Martha Griffiths, Cynthia Holcomb Hall, Rita Hauser, Margaret Haywood, Carla Hills, Shirley Hufstedler, Norma Holloway Johnson, Florence Kelly, Cornelia Kennedy, Elizabeth Kovachevich, Soia Mentschikoff, Betty S. Murphy, Dorothy Nelson, Harriet Robb, and Susie M. Sharp. One day later, on November 14, 1975, Lindh followed up her earlier memo with another note to Douglas Bennett in the President's Personnel Office: "Another name has come to my attention and I felt it important to pass it on to you. The person is Sandra O'Connor, Judge, Superior Court, Court of Maricopa, Arizona."

176. Memo, Douglas P. Bennett to Richard Cheney, undated, Supreme Court Nomination–Backgrounds on recommended candidates file, Richard Cheney Files, GRFL. The continuously changing list was presented to White House Counsel Philip Buchen in its final form on November 26, 1975 with seventy-nine names divided into three categories: Judges, legal scholars, and "attorneys in other activities." See Memo, Douglas P. Bennett to Philip Buchen, 26 November 1975, Supreme Court–compilation of nomination recommendations received file, Philip Buchen Files, GRFL. The final list included Lindh's recommendation of Sandra Day O'Connor, as well as forty-two-year-old Ruth Bader Ginsburg of the Columbia Law School, one of several candidates recommended by the National Women's Political Caucus.

177. John Goshko and John MacKenzie, "Douglas' Successor's Nomination Expected in Two Weeks," *Washington Post*, 14 November 1975 ("Mrs. Ford has brought up the possibility of naming a woman to the Court"), A2.

178. Memo, John O. Marsh to Philip Buchen, 14 November 1975, President's Handwriting File, FG 51, GRFL.

179. Memo, Douglas P. Bennett to Richard Cheney, 17 November 1975, Supreme Court vacancy–General file, Philip Buchen Files, GRFL.

180. Ford, *A Time to Heal*, 335.

181. Lesley Oelsmer, "Woman Reported on New Court List," *New York Times*, 20 November 1975, 16. Eastland later shifted his support to another Fifth Circuit judge, J. P. Coleman. Even at this late date, Cheney urged submission of Coleman's name to the ABA. Memo, Richard Cheney to Philip

Buchen, 21 November 1975, Supreme Court–Letters Recommending Potential Nominees, Philip Buchen Files, GRFL.

182. "Mrs. Ford's Comments," *New York Times,* 20 November 1975, 16.

183. Memo, E. C. Schmults, 21 November 1975, Supreme Court–Stevens Nomination (1) file, Edward Schmults Files, GRFL.

184. Memo, Philip Buchen to Richard Cheney, 25 November 1975, Supreme Court Nominations–opinions of J. P. Stevens on environmental questions, Richard Cheney Files, GRFL. Ford was especially sensitive to the possibility that his nominee might be criticized for his anti-environment bias. Over the past year Ford had been subjected to intense criticism by environmental groups for his administration's handling of anti-pollution policies. The president may have expected that his record on the environment might be a target of Democrats in the following year's election.

185. Memo, Edward H. Levi to Philip Buchen, 26 November 1975, Supreme Court–Stevens, John Paul file, Philip Buchen Files, GRFL.

186. See *Arnold v. Carpenter,* 459 F.2d 939 (7th Cir. 1972). In *Arnold,* Stevens dissented from the majority's ruling that a high school dress code provision regulating the length of hair for male students violated the students' constitutional rights. Stevens wrote: "Society does have a legitimate interest in both the continuity and the mutability of its mores. . . . I find nothing offensive in a dress code which merely requires conformity unless excused by a child's parents." 459 F.2d at 944–45 (Stevens, J., dissenting).

187. Apparently, the solicitor general was still tainted by the "Saturday Night Massacre" of two years earlier in which he had fired Archibald Cox as the Watergate special prosecutor. Bork's "most conservative" views were also sure to stir up a confirmation fight.

188. Gerald R. Ford, interview by author, 11 March 1996, Rancho Mirage, California.

189. Ibid.

190. Kramer, "The Case of Justice Stevens," 336.

CHAPTER SIX

1. Richard Hodder Williams, "Ronald Reagan and the Supreme Court," in Joseph Hogan, ed., *The Reagan Years: The Record in Presidential Leadership* (Manchester: Manchester University Press, 1990), 143.

2. *Engel v. Vitale,* 370 U.S. 421 (1962).

3. *Miller v. California,* 413 U.S. 15 (1973).

4. *Swann v. Charlotte-Mecklenburg Board of Education,* 402 U.S. 1 (1971); *North Carolina State Board of Education v. Swann,* 402 U.S. 43 (1971).

5. *Miranda v. Arizona,* 384 U.S. 436 (1966); *Mapp v. Ohio,* 367 U.S. 634 (1961); *Gideon v. Wainwright,* 372 U.S. 335 (1963); *Massiah v. United States,* 377 U.S. 201 (1964).

6. *Regents of the University of California v. Bakke,* 438 U.S. 265 (1978); *Fullilove v. Klutznick,* 448 U.S. 448 (1980); *United Steelworkers of America v. Weber,* 443 U.S. 193 (1979).

7. 410 U.S. 113 (1973).

8. Initially, the Reagan administration was not content to leave its conser-

vative agenda to the courts. On economic issues Reagan achieved some early legislative success, passing a program of decreased taxes and social security reform. Yet with a Democratic House of Representatives and a politically moderate Senate, the administration generally fell short of its legislative goals. Anti-abortion proposals were stifled, and Congress actually strengthened the Voting Rights Act in 1982 in the face of intense administration opposition.

9. For a discussion of Reagan's presidential management style in general, see Stephen Hess, *Organizing the Presidency* (Washington, D.C.: Brookings Institution, 1988).

10. Williams, "Reagan and the Supreme Court," 155–61. See also Sheldon Goldman, *Picking Federal Judges: Lower Court Selection from Roosevelt through Reagan* (New Haven: Yale University Press, 1997).

11. William French Smith, *Law and Justice in the Reagan Administration: The Memoirs of an Attorney General* (Palo Alto, Cal.: Hoover Institution Press, 1991), 63.

12. Under normal circumstances, the president might have learned of Stewart's retirement plans within days of Smith's initiation of the selection process. But the March 30 assassination attempt on Reagan put off such notice for at least three weeks. Although Vice President Bush knew of the impending vacancy, he would have been reluctant to interfere with the chain of command on appointments in any event.

13. Smith, *Law and Justice,* 64.

14. On 14 October 1980, Richard Wirthlin, a Republican pollster, tracked President Carter as maintaining a marginal lead in the national polls, the first such lead held by the incumbent during that year's general election campaign.

15. News release, 14 October 1980, OA 3489, Supreme Court Nominations 1981 file, Fred Fielding Files, RRPL.

16. Smith, *Law and Justice,* 64.

17. Ibid.

18. "Brethren Gets First Sister," *Time,* 20 July 1981, 11.

19. Report on Honorable Cornelia Kennedy, OA 3489, Supreme Court Nomination 1981 file, Fred Fielding Files, RRPL; Report on Honorable Sandra Day O'Connor, State Government–Arizona File, WHORM: Subject file, RRPL; Report on Honorable Mary Stallings Coleman, OA 3489; Supreme Court Nomination 1981 file, Fred Fielding Files, RRPL.

20. Habicht recounted the highlights of this research in a later memo to Herbert Ellingwood, the deputy counsel to the president. See Memo, Hank Habicht to Herbert Ellingwood, 7 July 1981, State Government–Arizona file, WHORM: Subject file, RRPL.

21. Report on Honorable Cornelia Kennedy, OA 3489, Supreme Court Nomination 1981[3] file, Fred Fielding Files, RRPL.

22. Report on Honorable Mary Stallings Coleman, OA 3489; Supreme Court Nomination 1981[2] file, Fred Fielding Files, RRPL.

23. The report cited Coleman's opinion in *People v. Plantefaber,* 410 Mich. 594 (1981), in which she dissented from the majority opinion reversing a conviction on the ground that a warrantless search for marijuana conducted in the luggage of a suspect preparing to depart from an airport was unreasonable.

24. Justice Department officials could not discern Coleman's age from biographies or any other source, although they inferred she was over sixty-five on the basis of the year she received her undergraduate degree (1935).

25. Attachment to Report on judicial selection criteria, Supreme Court Nomination 1981[1] file, OA 3489, Fred Fielding Files, RRPL.

26. Ibid.

27. Lou Cannon, *President Reagan: The Role of a Lifetime* (New York: Simon and Schuster, 1991), 804.

28. Stephen Weisman, "Reagan Selects Woman, an Arizona Judge, for Supreme Court," *New York Times*, 8 July 1981, A12.

29. Smith, *Law and Justice*, 65.

30. Ibid., 66.

31. Memo on judicial selection criteria, 18 June 1981, Supreme Court Nomination 1981[1] file, OA 3489, Fred Fielding Files, RRPL.

32. Memo, Herbert Ellingwood to Fred Fielding, 23 June 1981, Supreme Court Nomination 1981[1] file, OA 3489, Fred Fielding Files, RRPL.

33. Ibid.

34. Smith, *Law and Justice*, 66.

35. O'Connor told administration officials that she had forgotten how she voted on the memorialization resolution. Because Arizona state legislative records do not include minutes of the senate judiciary committee hearings, there is no official record of how she voted.

36. Lisa Myers, "Politics Played Major Role in Selecting Justice," *Washington Star*, 8 July 1981, A6.

37. Notes, Sandra Day O'Connor 1981 file, OA 10588, Margaret Tutwiler Files, RRPL.

38. Ibid. In 1973 Senator O'Connor prepared and introduced Senate Bill 1333, which would have permitted hospital employees to refuse to perform abortions. O'Connor was a leading proponent of the bill. Yet she could not recall how she voted either on the 1970 senate bill to legalize abortion or on the memorialization resolution. O'Connor did recall voting to provide "family planning information" to minors in 1973 because she saw it as a way to provide contraceptive information. "It never got out of committee. . . . [It was] never described as a pro-abortion measure."

39. Smith, *Law and Justice*, 68.

40. Letter, John Willke to Ronald Reagan, 3 July 1981, Supreme Court Nomination 1981[5] file, OA 3489, Fred Fielding Files, RRPL.

41. Letter, Carolyn Gerster to Ronald Reagan, 6 July 1981, Supreme Court Nomination 1981[5] file, OA 3489, Fred Fielding Files, RRPL.

42. Memo, Max Friedersdorf to James Baker et al., 6 July 1981, Appointments–Supreme Court–O'Connor(2) file, OA 2408, Edwin Meese Files, RRPL.

43. Memo, Kenneth Starr to William French Smith, 7 July 1981, Appointments–Supreme Court–O'Connor[1] file, OA 2408, Edwin Meese Files, RRPL.

44. O'Connor's responses, as described in Starr's memo to Smith, were consistent with the responses she gave to the president a week earlier. See

White House Notes, Sandra Day O'Connor 1981 file, OA 10588, Margaret Tutwiler Files, RRPL.

45. That "prominent female physician" was Carolyn Gerster, a former National Right-to-Life Committee chairperson, who told reporters days after O'Connor's nomination that she still harbored an eleven-year grievance with O'Connor for breaking her word and burying anti-abortion legislation in an Arizona state legislative caucus. Gerster called O'Connor "one of the most powerful pro-abortionists in the [Arizona state] senate." Rowland Evans and Robert Novak, "Why Did He Choose Her?" *Washington Post*, 10 July 1981, A23.

46. 403 U.S. 602 (1971). Under the *Lemon* test, a statute is invalid if it has a primary purpose or effect of advancing or inhibiting religion, or if it causes excessive government entanglement with religion.

47. 465 U.S. 668 (1984).

48. 492 U.S. 573 (1989).

49. See *Planned Parenthood of Pennsylvania v. Casey*, 505 U.S. 833 (1992).

50. Despite assuming office in March 1817, President James Monroe waited 2,269 days for his first and only opportunity to fill a Supreme Court vacancy. Justice Henry Brockholst Livingston died on March 18, 1823, more than halfway into Monroe's second term. Monroe deliberated over five months before appointing Smith Thompson, his fifty-five-year-old secretary of the navy, to Livingston's vacant seat on the Court. Thompson's appointment was confirmed by the Senate on December 19, 1823.

51. Philip Shenon, "Meese and His New Vision of the Constitution," *New York Times*, 17 October 1985, B10.

52. Ibid.

53. Speaking before a gathering of the American Bar Association in Washington, D.C., on July 9, 1985, Meese reviewed a litany of recent Supreme Court decisions in the areas of federalism, criminal procedure, and religious freedom. He urged that the Supreme Court be guided instead by a clear "jurisprudence of original intent." See "Meese Hits High Court Rulings," *Chicago Tribune*, 10 July 1985, 3; Federalist Society, *The Great Debate: Interpreting Our Written Constitution* (Washington, D.C.: Federalist Society, 1986).

54. Justice Brennan formally entered the debate during a "Text and Teaching Symposium" held at Georgetown University on October 12, 1985. Noting the difficulties of applying constitutional originalism, Brennan advocated instead a jurisprudence based on a principle of "human dignity" with the Court free to move beyond the views of that earlier age where values have evolved. Ibid.

55. Although Clegg's original seven-page paper has not yet been made available to the public, its contents may be reconstructed by examining judicial profiles tailored to adhere to the terms of the criteria "defining the ideal candidate for the Court." Withdrawal sheet, 6 August 1996, Supreme Court/Rehnquist/Scalia General Selection Scenario [1 of 3] file, Box 14287, Peter Wallison Files, RRPL; Report on Patrick Higginbotham paper, Supreme Court/Rehnquist/Scalia—Notebook (2 of 4) file, Peter Wallison Files, RRPL.

56. "Interpretivism" is usually defined as constitutional interpretation limited to the text and the intention behind that text, as compared to "noninterpretivism," defined as constitutional interpretation that goes beyond the "four corners" of the text to interpret its meaning.

57. To Meese and Reynolds, this principle implied a vigorous adherence to a so-called colorblind view of the constitution and civil rights laws, including hostility to all affirmative action or "reverse discrimination" programs.

58. See Supreme Court Rehnquist/Scalia Notebooks (4 volumes), OA 14287, Peter Wallison Files, RRPL. The contents of these notebooks are referred to in Memo, Peter Wallison to file, 29 August 1986, Supreme Court Rehnquist/Scalia General Selection Scenario file, Box 14287, Peter Wallison Files, RRPL.

59. Report on Patrick Higginbotham, Supreme Court–Rehnquist/Scalia Notebook (2 of 4) file, Peter Wallison Files, RRPL; Report on Patrick Higginbotham, Supreme Court (1 of 2) file, OA 15671, Jay Stephens Files, RRPL.

60. Ibid.

61. Report on Ralph Winter, Supreme Court–Rehnquist/Scalia Notebook (4 of 4) file, Peter Wallison Files, RRPL.

62. See, e.g., *NAACP v. Town of Huntington*, 689 F.2d 391 (2d Cir. 1982). In *Huntington*, the court granted standing to a group that was precluded by an allegedly discriminatory zoning ordinance from building a low-income housing project. Judge Winter found standing despite the absence of federal funding without which, the parties and the court conceded, the project could not begin.

63. See *Battipaglia v. New York Liquor Authority*, 745 F.2d 166 (2d Cir. 1984) (Winter, J., dissenting).

64. See *Stevic v. Sava*, 678 F.2d 401 (2d Cir. 1982) (rejecting the INS's interpretation of section 243(h) of the Immigration and Naturalization Act); *Franklin Mint Corp. v. TWA*, 690 F.2d 303 (2d Cir. 1982) (refusing to accord deference to an agency decision to use the price of gold as a standard of conversion in valuing lost foreign cargo under an international convention).

65. Memo, Steven Matthews to Special Project Committee, 23 May 1986, Supreme Court Rehnquist/Scalia–Notebook (3 of 4) file, OA 14287, Peter Wallison Files, RRPL.

66. Ibid.

67. 634 F.2d 408 (9th Cir. 1980). In *Chadha*, Judge Kennedy held that the House was without constitutional authority to order Chadha's deportation. The court invalidated section 244(c)(2) of the Immigration and Naturalization Act on the grounds that it violated the constitutional doctrine of separation of powers. Kennedy's opinion was later affirmed by the Supreme Court. See *INS v. Chadha*, 463 U.S. 919 (1983).

68. Ibid. See, e.g., *Agana Bay v. Supreme Court of Guam*, 529 F.2d 952, 958 (9th Cir. 1976) (suggesting the existence of substantial limits on congressional authority to alter the appellate jurisdiction of the Supreme Court).

69. See, e.g., *United States v. Hillyard*, 677 F.2d 1336, 1340 (9th Cir. 1982) (upholding a search warrant because it "reasonably" guided the officers in avoiding seizure of protected property); *United States v. Sledge*, 650 F.2d

1075, 1082 (9th Cir. 1981) (upholding the warrantless search of a defendant's apartment because the landlord and the officers acted "reasonably" in relying on the appearance of abandonment).

70. *James v. Ball*, 613 F.2d 180 (9th Cir. 1979).

71. *Vanelli v. Reynolds*, 667 F.2d 773 (9th Cir. 1982).

72. *Beller v. Middendorf*, 632 F.2d 788 (9th Cir. 1980). In *Beller* Judge Kennedy also indicated that he would not uphold the validity of laws prohibiting homosexual conduct outside of the military context.

73. Report on J. Clifford Wallace, Supreme Court–Rehnquist/Scalia–Notebook (4 of 4) file, Peter Wallison files, RRPL.

74. Ibid.

75. As the Justice Department's report on Wallace noted, his failure to theorize principles of judicial restraint was not entirely for want of trying. Judge Wallace wrote several articles in which he argued that interpretivism is superior to non-interpretivism because it better protects democracy. The report concluded that none of these articles were "very interesting or persuasive."

76. See *Johnson v. Armored Transport of California*, 813 F.2d 1041 (9th Cir. 1987).

77. Report on J. Clifford Wallace, Supreme Court (2 of 2) file, Jay Stephens Files, RRPL.

78. Report on Antonin Scalia, Supreme Court–Scalia (3 of 5) file, Peter Wallison Files, RRPL.

79. Ironically, under the classic definition of "judicial restraint" such an approach might be viewed as a form of judicial activism.

80. Report on Antonin Scalia, Supreme Court–Scalia (3 of 5) file, Peter Wallison Files, RRPL.

81. Bork had served as solicitor general for four months when Nixon, in the heat of the Watergate crisis, demanded that Attorney General Elliot Richardson fire Special Prosecutor Archibald Cox on October 20, 1973. Richardson resigned rather than do so. William D. Ruckelshaus, the deputy attorney general, also refused to carry out the order and quit as well. Bork, who then became acting attorney general, obeyed the order and fired Cox. During the 1982 hearings on his nomination to the federal court of appeals, Bork argued that he too had toyed with the idea of quitting after the Cox firing, but Richardson had urged him to stay on as the Justice Department was at that time under "great pressure" and needed his leadership. Congress, Senate, Committee on the Judiciary, *The Selection and Confirmation of Federal Judges*, 97th Cong., 2d Sess., 27 January 1982, 9–10. Both Richardson and Ruckelshaus have substantially confirmed Bork's version of events.

82. Report on Robert Bork, Supreme Court–Rehnquist/Scalia–Notebook (1 of 2) file, Arthur Culvahouse Files, RRPL.

83. Report on Robert Bork, Supreme Court–Rehnquist/Scalia–Notebook (1 of 4) file, Peter Wallison Files, RRPL.

84. Report on Antonin Scalia, Supreme Court [2 of 2] file, Jay Stephens Files, RRPL.

85. Ibid.

86. Ibid.

87. Chief Justice Profile, Supreme Court [1 of 2] file, Jay Stephens Files, RRPL.

88. Ibid. Although Justice Department records avoided any direct reference to Chief Justice Burger, several officials believed Burger lacked this intellectual capacity.

89. Ibid.

90. Report on Antonin Scalia, Supreme Court [2 of 2] file, Jay Stephens Files, RRPL.

91. Justice Powell, then seventy-eight years old, was plainly too old to be considered. Meanwhile, the remaining four justices on the court—Justices Brennan, Marshall, Stevens, and Blackmun—could all be eliminated from consideration because of their advanced ages or less conservative ideologies.

92. 378 U.S. 478 (1964).

93. 384 U.S. 436 (1966).

94. Report on Justice Sandra Day O'Connor, Supreme Court Rehnquist/Scalia–Notebook (1 of 4) file, Peter Wallison Files, RRPL.

95. Ibid. For example, in *Wygant v. Jackson Board of Education*, 476 U.S. 267 (1986), O'Connor's concurring opinion undercut the plurality's condemnation of racial quotas by accepting claims of racial discrimination even absent any findings of past discrimination in the record. According to the working group, her concurrence demonstrated "an error in strategic judgment as well because it attempts to create a consensus among the various justices where there clearly was not one. Such 'diplomatic efforts' are inevitably doomed to failure and simply provide the dissenters with further ammunition in future cases." Report on Justice Sandra Day O'Connor, Supreme Court Rehnquist/Scalia–Notebook (1 of 4) file, Peter Wallison Files, RRPL.

96. 376 U.S. 254 (1964). In *Philadelphia Newspapers, Inc. v. Hepps*, 475 U.S. 767 (1986), O'Connor voted to invalidate on First Amendment grounds a state law requiring defendants in libel suits to prove that defamatory allegations were true. Report on Justice Sandra Day O'Connor, Supreme Court Rehnquist/Scalia–Notebook (1 of 4) file, Peter Wallison Files, RRPL.

97. Ibid. See *Grand Rapids School District v. Ball*, 473 U.S. 373 (1985) ; *Wallace v. Jaffree*, 472 U.S. 38 (1985); *Thornton v. Caldor, Inc.*, 472 U.S. 703 (1985); *Larkin v. Grendel's Den*, 459 U.S. 116 (1982).

98. Report on Justice William Rehnquist, Supreme Court (1 of 2) file, Jay Stephens Files, RRPL.

99. 426 U.S. 833 (1976).

100. Report on Justice William Rehnquist, Supreme Court (1 of 2) file, Jay Stephens Files, RRPL.

101. There is some indication that research and analysis of the two candidates for chief justice was continually updated, even after word had reached Edwin Meese that Warren Burger was planning to announce his retirement. The Justice Department's analysis of O'Connor's record on the Supreme Court cited her decision to join the liberal majority in *Batson v. Kentucky*, 476 U.S. 79 (1986), handed down on April 30, 1986, and her concurrence in *Wygant*, handed down on May 19, 1986.

102. Peter Wallison detailed the sequence of events between Burger's dis-

closure of his retirement on May 27, 1986, and the president's announcement of his two new appointments on June 17, 1986, in a confidential memorandum to the file. See Memo, Peter Wallison to file, 29 August 1986, Supreme Court Rehnquist/Scalia General Selection Scenario (1 of 3) file, Peter Wallison Files, RRPL.

103. President Reagan had appointed Burger to the commission's top post the previous summer. As head of the Bicentennial Commission of the United States, Burger was actively planning the celebration of the 200th anniversary of the Constitution, slated to begin during the summer of 1987.

104. Stephen Wermiel, "Changes on High Court Are Likely to Increase Conservatives' Clout," *Wall Street Journal*, 18 June 1986, 1.

105. Notes from meeting, Judicial Candidates: Notes file, Christopher Cox Files, RRPL.

106. Report on Antonin Scalia, Supreme Court (2 of 2) file, Jay Stephens Files, RRPL.

107. Ibid.

108. Report on Robert Bork, Supreme Court Rehnquist/Scalia–Notebook [1 of 2] file, Arthur Culvahouse Files, RRPL.

109. Ibid.

110. Report on Cynthia Hall, Supreme Court (1 of 2) file, Jay Stephens Files, RRPL.

111. Ibid.

112. Report on Patrick Higginbotham, Supreme Court (1 of 2) file, Jay Stephens Files, RRPL.

113. Report on Anthony Kennedy, Supreme Court (1 of 2) file, Jay Stephens Files, RRPL.

114. Report on J. Clifford Wallace, Supreme Court (2 of 2) file, Jay Stephens Files, RRPL.

115. Ibid.

116. Report on Ralph Winter, Supreme Court (2 of 2) file, Jay Stephens Files, RRPL.

117. Ibid.

118. Report on William Rehnquist, Supreme Court (1 of 2) file, Jay Stephens Files, RRPL.

119. Ibid.

120. Memo, Peter Wallison to file, 29 August 1986, Supreme Court Rehnquist/Scalia General Selection Scenario file, Box 14287, Files of Peter Wallison, RRPL.

121. Ibid.

122. Ibid.

123. Donald T. Regan, *For the Record: From Wall Street to Washington* (San Diego: Harcourt Brace, 1988), 332.

124. Memo, Peter Wallison to file, 29 August 1986, Supreme Court Rehnquist/Scalia General Selection Scenario file, Box 14287, Peter Wallison Files, RRPL.

125. Abraham, *Justices and Presidents*, 350.

126. Ibid., 354.

127. For example, in *Morrison v. Olsen*, 487 U.S. 654 (1988), the other justices on the Court (including Chief Justice Rehnquist, who authored the opinion) seemed inclined to move toward a flexible, pragmatic conception of separation of powers that permitted the use of some innovations to deal with intractable problems. Scalia was the lone dissenter, arguing forcefully for a more rigid conception of separation of powers. Scalia appeared to view any deviation, no matter how minor or apparently inconsequential, as causing a threat to liberty. 487 U.S. 654, 710–11 (Scalia, J., dissenting).

128. David Hoffman, "Justice White Discussed as Possible FBI Director," *Washington Post*, 19 March 1987, A1.

129. Notes, Supreme Court–Powell Replacement folder, Alan Raul Files, RRPL.

130. Article I, section 6 of the Constitution states: "No Senator or Representative shall, during the Time for which he was elected, be appointed to any civil office under the United States . . . the Emoluments whereof shall have been increased during such time." On its face, the provision appears to bar the appointment of members of Congress to executive or judicial positions if they served during terms in which pay levels for those positions had been increased. In the case of some nonjudicial posts, Congress previously had attempted to cure the problem by passage of a special statute lowering the salary for the particular office for which the senator or representative in question had been proposed. There were at least two objections raised to passing such a statute in the immediate context: (1) a disputed legal question still existed as to whether such a statute was even constitutional; and (2) practical questions had arisen as to whether the constitutionality of the method could even be tested until *after* the appointment, at which point it would then be too late for the administration to fill the seat if the appointment was eventually nullified. In any case, Senator Joseph Biden (D-Del.), chairman of the Senate Judiciary Committee, had already declared that appointment of a current senator would be invalid, and he pointedly told administration officials that the matter was "non-negotiable." Report on Howell Heflin, Profiles: Possible Supreme Court Nominees (ca. 1987) file, C. Christopher Cox Files, RRPL.

131. Letter, Strom Thurmond to Howard Baker, 4 March 1987, FG 017-04, WHORM: Subject File, RRPL.

132. The computer-generated results of these LEXIS and NEXIS searches were found in the files of Alan Charles Raul, Peter Keisler, and C. Christopher Cox at the Ronald Reagan Presidential Library.

133. Report on Robert H. Bork, Profiles: Possible Supreme Court Nominees (ca. 1987) file, Christopher Cox Files, RRPL.

134. Ibid.

135. Report on J. Clifford Wallace, Profiles: Possible Supreme Court Nominations (ca. 1986–87)(3) file, Christopher Cox Files, RRPL.

136. Report on Pasco Bowman, Profiles: Possible Supreme Court Nominations (ca. 1986–87)(3) file, Christopher Cox Files, RRPL.

137. Report on Orrin Hatch, Supreme Court Notebook on Candidates [2] file, Arthur Culvahouse Files, RRPL.

138. Ibid. Meanwhile, Senator Heflin, described as having a "moderate

to conservative temperament," held views largely unknown on various current legal issues. Report on Howell Heflin, Profiles: Possible Supreme Court Nominees (ca. 1987) file, Christopher Cox Files, RRPL.

139. Michael Pertschuk and Wendy Schaetzel, *People Rising: The Campaign Against the Bork Nomination* (New York: Thunder's Mouth Press, 1989), 41. See also Ethan Bronner, *Battle for Justice* (New York: Norton, 1989).

140. Press Release, Office of Senator Edward M. Kennedy, 1 July 1987.

141. Abraham, *Justices and Presidents,* 357.

142. Maltese, *Selling of Supreme Court Nominees,* 137–38.

143. Ibid., 88.

144. Ibid., 130.

145. Table of Contents, Judicial Nominees: Supreme Court file, Dean McGrath Files, RRPL.

146. Notes, Bork: WHO Post Mortem(1) file, David M. McIntosh Files, RRPL.

147. Steven V. Roberts, "Reagan Vows New Appointment as Upsetting to His Foes as Bork's," *New York Times,* 14 October 1987, A1.

148. Report on Douglas Ginsburg, Candidates for Supreme Court (Notebook One)(1) file, Kenneth Duberstein Files, RRPL.

149. Table of Contents, Candidates for Supreme Court (notebook three)(1) file, Kenneth Duberstein Files, RRPL.

150. Steven V. Roberts, "Ginsburg Choice Renews Tension between Factions in White House," *New York Times,* 31 October 1987, A1.

151. Al Kamen and Ruth Marcus, "Ginsburg Withdraws as Nominee to the Supreme Court," *Washington Post,* 8 November 1987, A1.

152. Ibid.

153. Abraham, *Justices and Presidents,* 360.

154. See Jeffrey Rosen, "Annals of Law: The Agonizer," *New Yorker,* 11 November 1996, 83–90.

155. See, e.g., *Adarand Constructors, Inc. v. Pena,* 115 S. Ct. 2097 (1995).

156. 505 U.S. 577 (1992).

157. 491 U.S. 397 (1989).

158. Justice Kennedy reaffirmed his commitment to protecting extremely provocative expression in *United States v. Eichmann,* 496 U.S. 310 (1990), when he joined another 5–4 majority invalidating the 1989 Flag Protection Act on grounds similar to those in *Johnson.*

159. 116 S. Ct. 1620 (1996).

CHAPTER SEVEN

1. Not surprisingly, Reagan's appointees to the circuit courts have decided cases in a more conservative fashion than either President Carter's appointees or President Nixon's appointees. See Sheldon Goldman, *Picking Federal Judges: Lower Court Selection from Roosevelt through Reagan* (New Haven: Yale University Press, 1997); Deborah J. Barrow, Gary Zuk, and Gerald S. Gryski, *The Federal Judiciary and Institutional Change* (Ann Arbor: University of Michigan Press, 1996); C. K. Rowland, Donald R. Songer, and Robert A. Carp,

"Presidential Effects on Criminal Justice in the Lower Federal Courts: the Reagan Judges," *Law and Social Review* 22 (1988): 191–200.

2. Judge Robert Bork was a notable exception. Despite five years' service on the circuit court, Bork was still well known for his controversial academic writings as well as for his role as Nixon's solicitor general in the Saturday Night Massacre.

3. In recent years the role of Senate "benefactors" has expanded to include two new duties: shepherding prospective justices around the Hill to meet individual senators and introducing the nominee at their initial hearing before the Senate Judiciary Committee.

4. See Letter, Harold R. Tyler to Joseph Biden, 21 September 1987, reprinted in Congress, Senate, Committee on the Judiciary, *The Nomination of Robert H. Bork to Be Associate Justice of the Supreme Court of the United States*, 100th Cong., 1st sess., 21 September 1987, 1232.

5. Howard Ball, *Courts and Politics: The Federal Judicial System* (Englewood Cliffs, N.J.: Prentice-Hall, 1980).

6. Ibid., 175.

7. In his authoritative work, *Picking Federal Judges: Lower Court Selection from Roosevelt to Reagan* (New Haven: Yale University Press, 1997), Goldman utilized this tripartite categorization in analyzing presidential success in the selection of lower court judges.

8. See Daniel Katz and Robert L. Kahn, *The Social Psychology of Organizations* (New York: Wiley and Sons, 1966), 72.

9. Anthony Downs, *Inside Bureaucracy* (Boston: Little, Brown and Co., 1967), 50; David Silverman, *The Theory of Organizations* (New York: Basic Books, 1971), 62.

10. Downs, *Inside Bureaucracy*, 50

11. Ibid., 105.

12. Ibid., 106.

13. James G. March, *A Primer on Decisionmaking: How Decisions Happen* (New York: Free Press, 1994), 171.

EPILOGUE

1. According to one report, in 1988 Jones had chastised a lawyer in a death penalty case for what she considered to be a "spurious" last-minute appeal for a stay of execution. In another case she complained to a lawyer defending a capital client that a last-minute appeal had forced her to miss the birthday party of one of her sons.

2. Phelps and Winternitz, *Capitol Games*, 3.

3. Ibid. Bush and his advisors discovered later that they had grossly overestimated Hooks's influence over the current NAACP. In late July the NAACP's Board of Directors voted 49–1 to oppose Thomas. Even Hooks, who had managed to delay the vote for weeks in hopes of building momentum for a neutral stand on the appointment, had the political acumen to stick with the majority in opposing Thomas.

4. See Lee Sigelman and James S. Todd, "Clarence Thomas, Black Pluralism and Civil Rights Policy," *Political Science Quarterly* 107 (1992): 231.

5. Kevin Sack, "Clinton and 'Justice Cuomo': The Real Thing or Just Talk?" *New York Times*, 20 March 1993, 9.

6. Zoë Baird's nomination to become the first female Attorney General was doomed by revelations that she had hired illegal aliens for domestic help and had not paid social security taxes on them. Wood's own arrangements with domestic help seemed far less egregious: Wood had employed an illegal immigrant as a babysitter at a time when it was technically legal to do so. Nevertheless, Wood was accused of not being forthcoming with presidential aides about her own "Zoë Baird problem" and she withdrew her name from consideration as well.

7. Elizabeth Drew, *On the Edge: The Clinton Presidency* (New York: Simon and Schuster, 1994), 213.

8. Barbara A. Perry and Henry J. Abraham, "A 'Representative' Supreme Court? The Thomas, Ginsburg and Breyer Appointments," *Judicature* 81 (1998): 162.

9. *New York Times*, 4 April 1993, 4:14.

10. Stephen Labaton, "Shifting List of Prospects to Be Justice," *New York Times*, 9 May 1993, 22.

11. David M. O'Brien, "Clinton's Legal Policy and the Courts: Rising from Disarray or Turning Around and Around?" in Colin Campbell and Bert A. Rockman, eds., *The Clinton Presidency: First Appraisals* (Chatham, N.J.: Chatham House, 1996), 147. New York State Court of Appeals Judge Judith Kaye, chief judge of that state's court, had also been high on the administration's list before she withdrew her name from consideration in late April.

12. See, e.g., Thomas Friedman, "Latest Version of Supreme Court List: Babbitt in Lead, 2 Judges Close Behind," *New York Times*, 8 June 1993, A20.

13. John Brummett, *High Wire: The Education of Bill Clinton* (New York: Hyperion, 1994), 17.

14. Richard Berke, "Hatch Assails Idea of a Justice Babbitt," *New York Times*, 9 June 1993, A17.

15. Guinier's name was withdrawn from consideration on 3 June 1993, less than a week before his meeting with Babbitt.

16. Drew, *On the Edge*, 215.

17. 410 U.S. 113 (1973). On 9 March 1993, Ginsburg had delivered a speech at New York University Law School in which she criticized the scope of the *Roe* decision. While not disagreeing with the results, she argued that the decision should have been limited only to the case at hand.

18. Richard Davis, "The Ginsburg Nomination: The Role of the Press, Interest Groups, and the Public in the Selection of a Supreme Court Nominee," Paper presented at the annual meeting of the American Political Association, New York, 31 August 1994–3 September 1994, 15.

19. Ibid., 16.

20. Drew, *On the Edge*, 215.

21. Ibid., 216.

22. Ruth Marcus, "Blackmun Set to Leave Court," *Washington Post*, 6 April 1994, A1.

23. Helen Dewar and Ruth Marcus, "Mitchell Turns Down Supreme Court Offer," *Washington Post*, 13 April 1994, A1.

24. Gwen Ifill, "Choosing a Court Nominee: Quick and Easy? Forget it," *New York Times*, 16 April 1994, 1.

25. Ibid.

26. See *United States Jaycees v. McClure*, 709 F.2d 1560 (8th Cir. 1983).

27. See *Hodgson v. Minnesota*, 853 F.2d 1452 (8th Cir. 1988).

28. Arnold had been diagnosed with Lymphoma and would be forced to undergo intensive therapy over the next few years.

Bibliography

MANUSCRIPT COLLECTIONS

Ayers, Eben. Papers, Harry S. Truman Library, Independence, Missouri.
Baldridge, Homer. Papers, Harry S. Truman Library, Independence, Missouri.
Brownell, Herbert. Papers, Dwight D. Eisenhower Library, Abilene, Kansas.
Buchanan, Pat. Papers, Nixon Presidential Materials Project, National Archives II, College Park, Maryland.
Buchen, Philip. Files, Gerald R. Ford Library, Ann Arbor, Michigan.
Burton, Harold H. Papers, Manuscript Division, Library of Congress.
Cheney, Richard. Files, Gerald R. Ford Library, Ann Arbor, Michigan.
Clark, Tom C. Papers, Harry S. Truman Library, Independence, Missouri.
———. Papers, University of Texas Law School, Austin, Texas.
Cox, Christopher. Files, Ronald Reagan Library, Simi Valley, California.
Culvahouse, Arthur B. Files, Ronald Reagan Library, Simi Valley, California.
Dean, John. Papers, Nixon Presidential Materials Project, National Archives II, College Park, Maryland.
Duberstein, Kenneth. Files, Ronald Reagan Library, Simi Valley, California.
Ehrlichman, John D. Papers, Nixon Presidential Materials Project, National Archives II, College Park, Maryland.
Eisenhower, Dwight D. Name Files, Dwight D. Eisenhower Library, Abilene, Kansas.
———. Papers of Dwight D. Eisenhower as President, 1953–1961, Dwight D. Eisenhower Library, Abilene, Kansas.
———. Post-Presidential Papers, Dwight D. Eisenhower Library, Abilene, Kansas.
———. White House Central Files, Dwight D. Eisenhower Library, Abilene, Kansas.
Elsey, George M. Papers, Harry S. Truman Library, Independence, Missouri.
Fielding, Fred. Files, Ronald Reagan Library, Simi Valley, California.

[Ford, Gerald R.]. White House Central Files, Gerald R. Ford Library, Ann Arbor, Michigan.

Frankfurter, Felix. Papers, Manuscript Division, Library of Congress.

Harlan, John Marshall. Papers, Mudd Manuscripts Library, Princeton University, Princeton, New Jersey.

Hartmann, Robert. Papers, Gerald R. Ford Library, Ann Arbor, Michigan.

Johnson, Lyndon B. President's Appointments File, Lyndon Baines Johnson Library, Austin, Texas.

———. President's Daily Diary, Lyndon Baines Johnson Library, Austin, Texas.

———. Special Files Pertaining to Fortas/Thornberry, Lyndon Baines Johnson Library, Austin, Texas.

———. White House Central Files, Lyndon Baines Johnson Library, Austin, Texas.

Katzenbach, Nicholas. Papers, John F. Kennedy Library, Boston, Massachusetts.

Kennedy, John F. Pre-presidential Files, John F. Kennedy Library, Boston, Massachusetts.

———. President's Official Files, John F. Kennedy Library, Boston, Massachusetts.

Kilberg, Bobbie Greene. Files, Gerald R. Ford Library, Ann Arbor, Michigan.

McGrath, Dean. Files, Ronald Reagan Library, Simi Valley, California.

McIntosh, David. Files, Ronald Reagan Library, Simi Valley, California.

Macy, John. Office Files, Lyndon Baines Johnson Library, Austin, Texas.

Meese, Edwin. Files, Ronald Reagan Library, Simi Valley, California.

Morgan, Gerald. Papers, Dwight D. Eisenhower Library, Abilene, Kansas.

Nixon, Richard M. President's Official Files, Nixon Presidential Materials Project, National Archives II, College Park, Maryland.

———. White House Central Files, Nixon Presidential Materials Project, National Archives II, College Park, Maryland.

———. White House Special Files, Nixon Presidential Materials Project, National Archives II, College Park, Maryland.

Pearson, Drew. Papers, Lyndon B. Johnson Library, Austin, Texas.

Rogers, William P. Papers, Dwight D. Eisenhower Library, Abilene, Kansas.

Shanley, Bernard M. Papers, Dwight D. Eisenhower Library, Abilene, Kansas.

———. Papers, Seton Hall University Library, South Orange, New Jersey.

Smith, Harold D. Papers, Harry S. Truman Library, Independence, Missouri.

Stephens, Jay. Files, Ronald Reagan Library, Simi Valley, California.

Truman, Harry S. Official Files, Harry S. Truman Library, Independence, Missouri.

———. President's Personal Files, Harry S. Truman Library, Independence, Missouri.

———. President's Special Files, Harry S. Truman Library, Independence, Missouri.

———. Subject Files, Harry S. Truman Library, Independence, Missouri.

———. White House Central Files, Harry S. Truman Library, Independence, Missouri.

Tutwiler, Margaret. Files, Ronald Reagan Library, Simi Valley, California.

Wallison, Peter. Files, Ronald Reagan Library, Simi Valley, California.

Whitman, Ann C. Files, Dwight D. Eisenhower Library, Abilene, Kansas.

Young, David. Papers, Nixon Presidential Materials Project, National Archives II, College Park, Maryland.

BOOKS

Abraham, Henry J. *The Judicial Process: An Introductory Analysis of the Courts of the United States, England and France.* 5th ed. New York: Oxford University Press, 1986.

———. *Justices and Presidents.* 3d ed. New York: Oxford University Press, 1991.

Ambrose, Stephen E. *Eisenhower.* Vol. 2, *The President.* New York: Simon and Schuster, 1984.

———. *Nixon.* Vol. 2, *The Triumph of a Politician, 1962–1972.* New York: Simon and Schuster, 1989.

Baker, Nancy. *Conflicting Loyalties: Law and Politics in the Attorney General's Office, 1789–1990.* Lawrence: University Press of Kansas, 1992.

Barrow, Deborah J., Gary Zuk, and Gerald S. Gryski. *The Federal Judiciary and Institutional Change.* Ann Arbor: University of Michigan Press, 1996.

Bischof, Gunther, and Stephen E. Ambrose. *Eisenhower: A Centenary Assessment.* Baton Rouge: Louisiana State University Press, 1995.

Bland, Randall. *Private Pressure on Public Law: The Legal Career of Justice Thurgood Marshall.* Port Washington, N.Y.: Kenikat Press, 1973.

Bornet, Vaughn Davis. *The Presidency of Lyndon Johnson.* Lawrence: University Press of Kansas, 1983.

Brendon, Piers. *Ike: His Life and Times.* New York: Harper and Row, 1986.

Brodhead, Michael J., and David J. Brewer. *The Life of a Supreme Court Justice, 1837–1910.* Carbondale: Southern Illinois Press, 1994.

Bronner, Ethan P. *The Battle for Justice: How the Bork Nomination Shook America.* New York: E. P. Dutton, 1971.

Brownell, Herbert. *Advising Ike: The Memoirs of Herbert Brownell.* Lawrence: University Press of Kansas, 1993.

Brummett, John. *High Wire: The Education of Bill Clinton.* New York: Hyperion, 1994.

Burk, Robert Frederick. *The Eisenhower Administration and Black Civil Rights.* Knoxville: University of Tennessee Press, 1984.

Califano, Joseph A., Jr. *The Tragedy and Triumph of Lyndon Johnson.* New York: Simon and Schuster, 1991.

Campbell, Colin and Bert A. Rockman, eds. *The Clinton Presidency: First Appraisals.* Chatham, N.J.: Chatham House, 1996.

Cannon, Lou. *President Reagan: The Role of a Lifetime.* New York: Simon and Schuster, 1991.

Cashman, Sean Dennis. *African-Americans and the Quest for Civil Rights.* New York: NYU Press, 1991.

Chase, Harold W. *Federal Judges*. Minneapolis: University of Minnesota Press, 1972.

Clayton, Cornell. *The Politics of Justice: The Attorney General and the Making of Legal Policy*. New York: M. E. Sharpe, 1992.

Clayton, James E. *The Making of Justice: The Supreme Court in Action*. New York: E. P. Dutton, 1964.

Clifford, Clark. *Counsel to the President*. New York: Random House, 1991.

Cochran, Bert. *Harry Truman and the Crisis Presidency*. New York: Harper and Row, 1973.

Danelski, David J. *A Justice is Appointed*. New York: Random House, 1964.

Davis, Michael D., and Hunter R. Clark. *Thurgood Marshall: Warrior at the Bar, Rebel on the Bench*. New York: Birch Lane Press, 1992.

Douglas, William O. *The Court Years 1939–1975: The Autobiography of William O. Douglas*. New York: Random House, 1980.

Downs, Anthony. *Inside Bureaucracy*. Boston: Little, Brown and Co., 1967.

Drew, Elizabeth. *On the Edge: The Clinton Presidency*. New York: Simon and Schuster, 1994.

Ehrlichman, John D. *Witness to Power*. New York: Simon and Schuster, 1982.

Eisenhower, Dwight D. *Mandate for Change*. New York: Harper and Bros., 1963.

Eisler, Kim. *A Justice for All: William Brennan Jr. and the Decisions That Transformed America*. New York: Simon and Schuster, 1993.

Ewald, William. *Eisenhower the President: Crucial Days, 1951–1960*. Englewood Cliffs, N.J.: Prentice-Hall, 1981.

Fenno, Richard. *The President's Cabinet*. Cambridge: Harvard University Press, 1959.

Ferrell, Robert H. *Harry S. Truman: A Life*. Columbia: University of Missouri Press, 1994.

Ford, Gerald R. *A Time to Heal*. New York: Harper and Row, 1979.

Frank, John P. *Clement Haynesworth, the Senate, and the Supreme Court*. Charlottesville: University Press of Virginia, 1991.

Friedman, Lawrence, and F. L. Israel, eds. *The Justices of the Supreme Court*. New York: Chelsea House, 1980.

Gerhart, Eugene C. *America's Advocate: Robert H. Jackson*. Indianapolis: Bobbs-Merrill, 1958.

Goldman, Robert L. *Thurgood Marshall: Justice for All*. New York: Carroll and Graf, 1992.

Goldman, Sheldon. *Picking Federal Judges: Lower Court Selection from Roosevelt to Reagan*. New Haven: Yale University Press, 1997.

Greene, John Robert. *The Limits of Power: The Nixon and Ford Administrations*. Bloomington: Indiana University Press, 1992.

Greenstein, Fred. *The Hidden-Hand Presidency: Eisenhower as Leader*. New York: Basic Books, 1982.

Griswold, Erwin. *Ould Fields, New Corne*. St. Paul: West, 1992.

Grossman, Joel B. *Lawyers and Judges: The ABA and the Politics of Judicial Selection*. New York: Wiley and Sons, 1965.

Gunther, Gerald. *Learned Hand: The Man and the Judge.* New York: Knopf, 1994.

Haldeman, H. R. *The Haldeman Diaries: Inside the Nixon White House.* New York: G. P. Putnam, 1994).

Hall, Kermit, ed., *The Oxford Companion to the Supreme Court of the United States.* New York: Oxford University Press, 1992.

Hamby, Alonzo L. *Man of the People: A Life of Harry S. Truman.* New York: Oxford University Press, 1995.

Harbaugh, William. *Lawyer's Lawyer: The Life of John W. Davis.* New York: Oxford University Press, 1973.

Harris, Richard P. *Decision.* New York: E. P. Dutton, 1971.

Heller, Francis, ed. *The Truman White House: The Administration of the Presidency 1945–1953.* Lawrence: Regents Press of Kansas, 1980.

Hess, Stephen. *Organizing the Presidency.* Washington, D.C.: Brookings Institution, 1988.

Hilsman, Roger. *To Move a Nation.* New York: Doubleday, 1967.

Hoff, Joan. *Nixon Reconsidered.* New York: Basic Books, 1994.

Hogan, Joseph, ed., *The Reagan Years.* Manchester: Manchester University Press, 1990.

Howard, J. Woodford., Jr. *Courts of Appeals in the Federal Judicial System.* Princeton: Princeton University Press, 1981.

———. *Mr. Justice Murphy: A Political Biography.* Princeton: Princeton University Press, 1968.

Jackson, Robert H. *The Struggle for Judicial Supremacy.* New York: Vintage, 1941.

Jeffries, John C., Jr., *Justice Lewis F. Powell, Jr..* New York: Scribner's, 1994.

Johnson, Lyndon B. *Vantage Point: Perspectives of the Presidency, 1963–1969.* New York: Holt, Rinehart and Winston, 1970.

Johnson, Mrs. Lyndon B. *A White House Diary.* New York: Holt, Rinehart and Winston, 1970.

Kalman, Laura. *Abe Fortas: A Biography.* New Haven: Yale University Press, 1990.

Katz, Daniel and Robert L. Kahn. *The Social Psychology of Organizations.* New York: Wiley and Sons, 1966.

Lasky, Victor. *Arthur J. Goldberg, the Old and the New.* New Rochelle: Arlington House, 1970.

March, James G. *A Primer on Decisionmaking: How Decisions Happen.* New York: Free Press, 1994.

March, James G. and Herbert A. Simon. *Organizations.* Cambridge: Blackwell Publishers, 1993.

McCoy, Donald R. *The Presidency of Harry S. Truman.* Lawrence: University Press of Kansas, 1984.

McFeeley, Neil G. *Appointment of Judges: The Johnson Presidency.* Austin: University of Texas Press, 1987.

McGrath, C. Peter. *Morrison R. Waite: The Triumph of Character.* New York: Macmillan Co., 1963.

MacKenzie, G. Calvin. *The In-and-Outers: Presidential Appointees and Tran-*

sient Government in Washington. Baltimore: Johns Hopkins University Press, 1987.

Maltese, John A. *The Selling of Supreme Court Nominees.* Baltimore: Johns Hopkins University Press, 1994.

Marcus, Maeva. *Truman and the Steel Seizure Case: The Limits of Presidential Power.* New York: Columbia University Press, 1977.

Mason, Alpheus T. *Brandeis: A Free Man's Life.* New York: Viking Press, 1946.

———. *Harlan Fiske Stone: Pillar of the Law.* New York: Viking Press, 1956.

———. *The Supreme Court from Taft to Burger.* Baton Rouge: Louisiana State University Press, 1979.

Massaro, John. *Supremely Political: The Role of Ideology and Presidential Management in Unsuccessful Supreme Court Nominations.* Albany: State University of New York Press, 1990.

Meyer, Marshall. *Theory of Organizational Structure.* Indianapolis: Bobbs-Merrill, 1977.

Mills, Judy. *John F. Kennedy.* New York: Franklin Watts, 1988.

Morgan, Donald G. *Justice William Johnson: The First Dissenter.* Columbia: University of South Carolina Press, 1954.

Murphy, Bruce Allen. *Fortas: The Rise and Ruin of a Supreme Court Justice.* New York: William Morrow and Co., 1988.

Novick, Sheldon. *Honorable Justice: The Life of Oliver Wendell Holmes.* Boston: Little, Brown and Co., 1989.

Pederson, William, and Norman Proviser, eds. *Great Justices of the U.S. Supreme Court.* New York: Peter Lang, 1993.

Pemberton, William E. *Harry S. Truman: Fair Dealer and Cold Warrior.* New York: Twayne Publishers, 1989.

Perry, Barbara A. *A "Representative" Supreme Court? The Impact of Race, Religion and Gender on Appointments.* New York: Greenwood Press, 1991.

Pertschuk, Michael and Wendy Schaetzel. *The People Rising: The Campaign against the Bork Nomination.* Washington, D.C.: Thunder's Mouth Press, 1989.

Pfiffner, F. James. *The Modern Presidency.* New York: St. Martin's Press, 1994.

Phelps, Timothy and Helen Winternitz. *Capitol Games: Clarence Thomas, Anita Hill and the Story of a Supreme Court Nomination.* New York: Hyperion Books, 1992.

Pollack, Jack Harrison. *Earl Warren: The Judge Who Changed America.* Englewood Cliffs, N.J.: Prentice-Hall, 1979.

Prewitt, Kenneth. *The Recruitment of Political Leaders: A Study of Citizen Politicians.* Indianapolis: Bobbs-Merrill Co., 1970.

Pusey, Merlo J. *Charles Evans Hughes.* New York: Macmillan, 1951.

Regan, Donald T. *For the Record: From Wall Street to Washington.* San Diego: Harcourt Brace, 1988.

Rohde, David, and Harold Spaeth. *Supreme Court Decisionmaking.* San Francisco: W. H. Freeman, 1976.

Richardson, Elmo. *The Presidency of Dwight D. Eisenhower.* Lawrence: Regents Press of Kansas, 1979.

Rowan, Carl. *Dream Makers, Dream Breakers: The World of Justice Thurgood Marshall.* Boston: Little, Brown, 1993.

Safire, William. *Before the Fall: An Inside View of the Pre-Watergate White House.* New York: Doubleday, 1975.

Schattschneider, E. E. *The Semisovereign People.* New York: Holt, Rinehart and Winston, 1960.

Schell, Jonathan. *The Time of Illusion.* New York: Knopf, 1976.

Schlesinger, Arthur, Jr. *A Thousand Days: John F. Kennedy in the White House.* Boston: Houghton Mifflin Co., 1965.

Schwartz, Bernard. *Super Chief: Earl Warren and His Supreme Court—A Judicial Biography.* New York: New York University Press, 1983.

Scigliano, Robert. *The Supreme Court and the Presidency.* New York: Free Press, 1971.

Sheldon, Charles H. and Linda S. Maule. *Choosing Justice: The Recruitment of State and Federal Judges.* Pullman: Washington State University Press, 1997.

Shogan, Robert. *A Question of Judgment: The Fortas Case and the Struggle for the Supreme Court.* Indianapolis: Bobbs-Merrill, 1971.

Sidey, Hugh. *John F. Kennedy, President.* New York: Atheneum, 1964.

Silverman, David. *The Theory of Organizations.* New York: Basic Books, 1971.

Silverstein, Mark. *Judicious Choices.* New York: Norton, 1993.

Smith, William French. *Law and Justice in the Reagan Administration: The Memoirs of an Attorney General.* Palo Alto, Cal.: Hoover Institution Press, 1991.

Sorenson, Theodore. *Kennedy.* New York: Harper and Row, 1965.

Strober, Gerald, and Deborah Strober, eds. *Nixon: An Oral History of His Presidency.* New York: HarperCollins, 1994.

Tanzer, Lester, ed. *The Kennedy Circle.* Washington, D.C.: Luce, 1961.

Twentieth Century Fund. *Judicial Roulette: Report of the Twentieth Century Fund Task Force on Judicial Selection.* New York: Priority Press, 1988.

Warner, Hoyt. *The Life of Mr. Justice Clark: A Testament to the Power of Liberal Dissent in America.* Cleveland: Western Reserve University Press, 1959.

Watson, George L., and John A. Stookey. *Shaping America: The Politics of Supreme Court Appointments.* New York: HarperCollins, 1995.

Watson, Richard, and Rondal Downing. *The Politics of the Bench and Bar.* New York: Wiley and Sons, 1969.

White, G. Edward. *Earl Warren, A Public Life.* New York: Oxford University Press, 1982.

Wicker, Tom. *One of Us: Richard Nixon and the American Dream.* New York: Random House, 1991.

Woodward, Bob, and Scott Armstrong. *The Brethren.* New York: Simon and Schuster, 1979.

Yarbrough, Tinsley E. *John Marshall Harlan: Great Dissenter of the Warren Court.* New York: Oxford University Press, 1992.

———. *Judicial Enigma: The First Justice Harlan.* New York: Oxford University Press, 1995.

Yoder, Edwin. *The Unmaking of a Whig and Other Essays in Self-Definition.* Washington, D.C.: Georgetown University Press, 1990.

DISSERTATIONS, THESES, AND PAPERS

Ashby, John B. "Supreme Court Appointments since 1937." Ph.D. diss., Notre Dame, 1972.

Atkinson, David M. "Mr. Justice Minton and the Supreme Court." Ph.D. diss., University of Iowa, 1969.

Cole, Judith. "Mr. Justice Charles Evans Whittaker: A Case Study in Judicial Recruitment and Behavior." Master's thesis, University of Missouri, Kansas City, 1972.

Davis, Richard. "The Ginsburg Nomination: The Role of the Press, Interest Groups and the Public in the Selection of a Supreme Court Nominee." Paper presented at the annual meeting of the American Political Science Association, New York, 1994.

McHargue, Daniel S. "Factors Influencing the Selection and Appointment of Members of the United States Supreme Court." Ph.D. diss., UCLA, 1949.

Marquardt, R. G. "The Judicial Justice: Mr. Justice Burton and the Supreme Court, 1949–1956." Ph.D. diss., University of Wisconsin, 1973.

Rubin, Eva Redfield. "The Judicial Apprenticeship of Arthur J. Goldberg, 1962–1965." Ph.D. diss., Johns Hopkins University, 1967.

ARTICLES

———. "Brethren Gets First Sister." *Time*, 20 July 1981, 11.

———. "Carswell Supports Legal Precedents." *Washington Post*, 20 January 1970, A6.

———. "Kennedy and Bayh Assail Nixon's Way of Filling Court Vacancies." *New York Times*, 16 October 1971, 28.

———. "Party Chiefs Urge Republican be Named Roberts' Successor." *Washington Post*, 31 July 1945, 9.

———. "Phillips Says He's 'In Dark' on Supreme Court Chances." *Washington Evening Star*, 18 September 1953, A3.

———. "Warren Leads in Speculation on Justice Vinson's Successor." *Washington Evening Star*, 8 September 1953, A1.

Alsop, Joseph, and Stewart Alsop. "Truman in Dilemma Choosing Chief Justice." *New York Herald Tribune*, 18 May 1946.

Belair, Felix, Jr. "Vinson Named Chief Justice; Snyder to Head Treasury; Truman to Let OWMR Lapse." *New York Times*, 7 June 1946, 1.

Berke, Richard. "Hatch Assails Idea of a Justice Babbitt." *New York Times*, 9 June 1993, A17.

Berman, Daniel M. "Mr. Justice Whittaker: A Preliminary Appraisal." *Missouri Law Review* 24 (1959): 1.

Denniston, Lyle. "Will Ford Name a Woman to Douglas Post?" *Washington Star*, 13 November 1975, A1.

Dewar, Helen, and Ruth Marcus, "Mitchell Turns Down Supreme Court Offer." *Washington Post*, 13 April 1994, A1.

Evans, Rowland, and Robert Novak. "Nixon and Material for the Court." *Washington Post*, 18 October 1971, A23.

———. "Why Did He Choose Her?" *Washington Post,* 10 July 1981, A23.

Fish, Peter. "Spite Nominations to the United States Supreme Court: Herbert C. Hoover, Owen J. Roberts and the Politics of Presidential Vengeance in Retrospect." *Kentucky Law Journal* 77 (1988–89): 548.

Folliard, Edward T. "President's Choice Leaves Burton as Only Republican on High Court." *Washington Post,* 7 June 1946, 1.

Frank, John P. "The Appointment of Supreme Court Justices: Prestige, Principle and Politics." *Wisconsin Law Review* (1941): 172.

Frankfurter, Felix. "The Supreme Court in the Mirror of Justices." *University of Pennsylvania Law Review* 105 (1958): 781.

Friedman, Thomas. "Latest Version of Supreme Court List: Babbitt in Lead, 2 Judges Close Behind." *New York Times,* 9 June 1993, A17.

Garraty, John A. "Holmes' Appointment to the Supreme Court." *New England Quarterly* 22 (1949): 291.

Goshko, John, and John MacKenzie. "Douglas' Successor's Nomination Expected in Two Weeks." *Washington Post,* 14 November 1975, A2.

Graham, Fred. "Ramsey Clark Nominated to Be Attorney General; Father to Quit High Court." *New York Times,* 1 March 1967, 1.

Graham, Fred. "Stewart Tells of Barring His Elevation." *New York Times,* 28 May 1969, 36.

Hoffman, David. "Justice White Discussed as Possible FBI Director." *Washington Post,* 19 March 1987, A1.

Ifill, Gwenn. "Choosing a Supreme Court Nominee: Quick and Easy? Forget it." *New York Times,* 16 April 1994, 1.

Kamen, Al, and Ruth Marcus. "Ginsburg Withdraws as Nominee to the Supreme Court." *Washington Post,* 8 November 1987, A1.

Kilpatrick, James J. "Term's End." *National Review,* 25 July 1967, 805.

Kramer, Victor. "The Case of Justice Stevens: How to Select, Nominate and Confirm a Justice of the United States Supreme Court." *Constitutional Commentary* 7 (1990): 325.

Krock, Arthur. "A Game That Nothing Can Discourage." *New York Times,* 25 April 1946, 20.

———. "New Truman Nominees Classed as 'Sound' Men." *New York Times,* 9 June 1946, sec. 4, p. 3.

———. "Supreme Court Choice to Show Truman Policy." *New York Times,* 8 July 1945, sec. 4, p. 3.

Labaton, Stephen. "Shifting List of Prospects to Be Justice." *New York Times,* 9 May 1993, 22.

Lewis, Anthony. "Ohioan Is Chosen for Burton's Post on Supreme Court." *New York Times,* 7 October 1958, 1.

———. "Warren Firm on Retiring; Leaves Date Up to Nixon." *New York Times,* 15 November 1968, 6.

McHargue, Daniel S. "One of Nine—Mr. Justice Burton's Appointment to the Supreme Court." *Western Reserve Law Review* (winter 1953): 129.

MacKenzie, John P. "Rights Leaders Set to Oppose Poff for Court." *Washington Post,* 22 September 1971, A4.

————. "Ramsey Clark Named Attorney General." *Washington Post,* 1 March 1967, A8.

Marcus, Ruth. "Blackmun Set to Leave Court." *Washington Post,* 6 April 1994, A1.

Montgomery, Ruth. "Truman Picks Clark for Supreme Court; Atty. General Post Offered Sen. McGrath." *Washington Times Herald,* 29 July 1949, 1.

Myers, Lisa. "Politics Played Major Role in Selecting Justice." *Washington Star,* 8 July 1981, A6.

Oelsmer, Lesley. "Woman Reported on New Court List." *New York Times,* 20 November 1975, 16.

Paull, Joseph. "Govs. Dewey, Warren Lead for Court Job." *Washington Post-Times Herald,* 9 September 1953, 1.

Perry, Barbara A. "The Life and Death of the 'Catholic Seat' on the United States Supreme Court." *Journal of Law and Politics* 6 (fall 1989): 55.

Perry, Barbara A., and Henry J. Abraham. "A 'Representative' Supreme Court? The Thomas, Ginsburg and Breyer Appointments." *Judicature* 81 (1998): 158–65.

Rich, Spencer. "Southern Nominees Ruled Out by Nixon." *Washington Post-Times Herald,* 10 April 1970, A1.

Roberts, Steven V. "Ginsburg Choice Renews Tension between Factions in White House." *New York Times,* 31 October 1987, A1.

————. "Reagan Vows New Appointment as Upsetting to His Foes as Bork's." *New York Times,* 14 October 1987, A1.

Rosen, Jeffrey. "Annals of Law: The Agonizer." *New Yorker,* 11 November 1996, 83.

Rowland, C. K., Donald R. Songer, and Robert A. Carp. "Presidential Effects on Criminal Justice in the Lower Federal Courts: The Reagan Judges." *Law and Social Review* 22 (1988): 191.

Sack, Kevin. "Clinton and 'Justice Cuomo': The Real Thing or Just Talk?" *New York Times,* 20 March 1993, 9.

Segal, Jeffrey, and Albert Cover. "Ideological Values and the Votes of Supreme Court Justices." *American Political Science Review* 83 (1989): 557.

Segal, Jeffrey, Lee Epstein, Charles Cameron, and Harold Spaeth. "Ideological Values and the Votes of U.S. Supreme Court Justices Revisited." *Journal of Policy* 57 (1985): 812.

Semple, Robert. "Nixon Condemns Senators Who Barred Two Judges; Will Pick Non-Southerner." *New York Times,* 10 April 1970, 1.

————. "Nixon Influenced by Fortas Affair in Court Choices." *New York Times,* 23 May 1969, 1.

————. "Southerner Named to Supreme Court; Carswell, 50, Viewed as Conservative." *New York Times,* 20 January 1970, 20.

————. "Warren Burger Named Chief Justice by Nixon; Now on Appeals Bench." *New York Times,* 22 May 1969, 1.

Shenon, Philip. "Meese and His New Vision of the Constitution." *New York Times,* 17 October 1985, B10.

Sigelman, Lee, and James S. Todd. "Clarence Thomas, Black Pluralism, and Civil Rights Policy." *Political Science Quarterly* 107 (1992): 231–48.

Spargo, Mary. "Gov. Dewey Suggested For Roberts' Seat." *Washington Post,* 18 July 1945, 1.

Steele, John L. "Haynesworth v. U.S. Senate (1969)." *Fortune,* March 1970, 91.

Taft, William H. "Mr. Wilson and the Campaign." *Yale Review* 10 (October 1920): 1.

Tate, C. Neal, and Roger Handberg. "Time Binding and Theory Building in Personal Attribute Models of Supreme Court Behavior, 1916–88." *American Journal of Political Science* 35 (1991): 460.

Totenberg, Nina. "The Confirmation Process and the Public: To Know or Not to Know." *Harvard Law Review* 101 (1988): 1213.

Wermiel, Stephen J. "Changes on High Court Are Likely to Increase Conservatives' Clout." *Wall Street Journal,* 18 June 1986, 1.

———. "Reagan Selects Woman, an Arizona Judge, for Supreme Court." *New York Times,* 8 July 1981, A12.

———. "The Nomination of Justice Brennan: Eisenhower's Mistake? A Look at The Historical Record." *Constitutional Commentary* 11 (1994–95): 515.

Index

282   INDEX

Bennett, Douglas, 129, 255n. 175
Bentsen, Lloyd, 124
Berman, Daniel M., 230n. 121
Beveridge, Albert, 226n. 54
Biddle, Francis, 215n. 2, 216n. 18
Biden, Joseph R., Jr., 158–61
Biggs, John, Jr., 22, 215n. 2
Bischof, Gunther, 43, 225n. 42
Black, Hugo, 36; chief justiceship
  and, 29, 218n. 49; Eisenhower and,
  43; ideology of, 27–28, 33–34, 48,
  63, 79, 89, 219n. 59, 239n. 100;
  retirement of, 114, 248n. 93,
  250n. 110
Blackmun, Harold, 101, 112–14, 143,
  177, 179, 202, 205, 214n. 48,
  248nn. 84, 86, 88, 262n. 91
"black seat" tradition, of Supreme
  Court, 75, 193, 195, 206, 235n.
  36
Bland, Randall, 87
Blough, Roger, 73
Boldt, George, 65–66, 231n. 126
Bork, Robert: controversies regarding,
  vii, 2, 5, 171–72, 266n. 2; Ford consideration of, 127–28, 130, 256n.
  187; interpretivist views of, 146–47;
  Reagan nomination of, 137–38, 144,
  146–48, 150–53, 155–56, 158–61,
  171–72, 175–77, 180, 185–86,
  261n. 81; "Saturday Night Massacre" and, 146, 152, 156, 256n. 187,
  266n. 2; Senate Judiciary Committee
  rating of, 16, 172, 214nn. 48, 49;
  Senate rejection of, 2, 5, 16, 161,
  180, 189–90, 207, 209n. 1
Boskey, Bennett, 127
Bowman, Pasco, 158, 161
Brandeis, Louis, 9–10, 15, 79, 104,
  245n. 41
Brant, Irving, 29, 215n. 10
Bratton, Sam G., 22, 32, 215n. 2
Breitel, Charles, 84, 245n. 39
Brennan, William Joseph, 72; aging of,
  155; Eisenhower appointment of, 50,
  55–61, 63, 67, 69, 177, 179, 228–
  29nn. 94, 95, 98, 241n. 127; ideology of, 63, 65, 68, 143, 149, 259n.
  53, 262n. 91; Judiciary Committee
  questioning of, 67; retirement of,
  191; Senate Judiciary Committee rat-

ing of, 214n. 48; Vanderbilt's support of, 59–60
Brewer, David, 10, 215n. 53
Breyer, Stephen, 188, 198–201, 203–5,
  214n. 48
Bricker, John, 66
Brown, John R., 99, 230n. 111
Brown v. Board of Education, 56, 67, 86,
  153, 249n. 100
Brownell, Herbert, viii, 45, 213n. 47,
  223n. 24; as attorney general, 223n.
  22; Brennan appointment and, 55–
  61, 228–29n. 95; Burger and, 101–
  4, 253–54nn. 17–19; Eisenhower
  consideration of, 41–42, 66–67,
  134, 179, 184, 231–32n. 135; experience of, 242n. 3; Harlan appointment and, 52–55, 226n. 62, 227nn.
  71, 76; Nixon consideration of, 100,
  242nn. 10, 11; Rogers as deputy attorney general and, 44, 58, 223n.
  21, 231n. 123; Warren appointment
  and, 44–49, 51, 223nn. 17, 24,
  225nn. 38, 39; Whittaker appointment and, 61–63, 184
Bryan, Patricia M., 156
Buchanan, Pat, 103, 115–18, 132, 185,
  244n. 27, 245n. 41
Buchen, Philip, 132, 255n. 176
Buckley, James, 162, 248n. 91
Buckner, Emory, 52
Bundshu, Henry A., 215n. 2
Bundy, McGeorge, 79, 236nn. 48, 49
Burger, Warren Earl, 115; Blackmun
  and, 113; Brownell and, 101–4,
  253–54nn. 17–19; Carswell and,
  109; Constitution bicentennial commission and, 150, 263n. 103; Eisenhower consideration of, 64, 66,
  230n. 111; experience of, 101, 262n.
  88; female justice seat and, 119; Friday and Lillie nominations and, 123,
  253n. 149; ideology of, 101, 243n.
  17; Nixon appointment of, 99, 101–
  4, 170, 177, 244n. 29, 244–45n. 33;
  O'Connor and, 136–38; Lewis Powell and, 123–24; retirement of, 142–
  43, 150, 262–63nn. 101, 102; Senate Judiciary Committee rating of,
  214n. 48; Stewart as possible chief
  justiceship and, 102, 244n. 21

288   INDEX

Jordan, Barbara, 255n. 175
Jordan, Emma C., 135
Judiciary Act of 1789, 9
Justice Department, 9, 12–13, 18–19,
42, 212n. 19, 213n. 47, 222n. 9

Katzenbach, Nicholas, viii; Fortas candidacy and, 83–85; Goldberg candidacy and, 80; Hastie consideration
and, 76, 235nn. 34, 35; Kennedy advisor role of, 72, 75, 236n. 46; Kennedy consideration of, 74; lower
court nominations and, 74, 85,
214n. 47, 241n. 118; Marshall candidacy and, 86–87, 89, 239n. 92;
Nixon advisor role of, 250–51n.
116; as undersecretary of state, 88;
White candidacy and, 76, 78–79,
235n. 33
Katzenbach v. McClung, 247n. 70
Kaye, Judith, 267n. 11
Kearse, Amalya E., 136–37, 157, 198,
203–4
Keenan, Joseph B., 34, 36, 233n. 12
Kefauver, Estes, 249n. 100
Keisler, Peter, 156
Kelly, Florence, 255n. 175
Kenison, Frank, 84
Kennedy, Anthony: ideology of, 2–3,
145–46, 152, 165, 210–11nn. 3, 4,
260–61nn. 67, 69, 71, 265n. 158;
Reagan appointment of, 2–3, 144–
46, 152, 156, 159, 161–65, 177,
180; Senate Judiciary Committee rat-
ing of, 214n. 48
Kennedy, Cornelia, 118–20, 129, 136–
37, 170, 255n. 175
Kennedy, Edward M., 122–23, 141,
154, 160, 198, 205
Kennedy, John F., 72, 232–33nn. 5, 6.
See also Kennedy administration
Kennedy, Robert: as attorney general,
72, 106, 233n. 10; Goldberg appointment and, 80–81; Hastie consideration and, 77–79, 236n. 44; J. Kennedy advisor role of, 71–81, 175,
184, 235n. 36; as Senate subcommittee chief counsel, 232n. 5; White appointment and, 79–80
Kennedy administration, 169; 1960 election and, 72, 75, 77, 234n. 29; black

justice issue and, 75, 78, 235n. 36;
"Catholic seat" issue and, 75; Johnson and, 240–41n. 117; labor issues
and, 72–73, 80–81, 232–33nn. 5, 6,
10, 12, 15, 17; lower federal court
appointments and, viii, 73–74, 213n.
47, 233–34n. 19; patronage policy
of, 70, 98; voting rights issues and,
77, 235n. 37
Kennedy administration, advisors in: Dolan, 74–75, 78–79, 234nn. 29, 31;
Katzenbach, 72, 75–76, 78–80, 83–
85, 235nn. 33–35, 236n. 46; Robert
Kennedy, 71–81, 175, 184, 233n.
10, 235n. 36, 236n. 44; Sorenson,
13, 74–77, 74
Kennedy administration, candidates considered by: Freund, 74, 75–79, 95,
175, 184, 235n. 39, 236nn. 48, 49;
Goldberg appointment, 70, 72–75,
74, 81–82, 95–96, 175–77, 232–
33nn. 5, 6, 10, 12, 236n. 52; Hastie,
74, 75–76, 78–79, 175, 235nn. 34–
36, 42; Levi, 74, 76, 78; Schaefer,
74, 76, 78–79; Traynor, 74, 76, 78–
79; White appointment, 16, 74, 75–
80, 95, 174–75, 234nn. 28, 29, 31
Kenyon, Dorothy, 215n. 2
Kilberg, Barbara Greene, 129
Killough v. United States, 243n. 17
Kilpatrick, James J., 105
Kissinger, Henry, 116, 250n. 110
Klain, Ron, 199–201
Klein, Joan Dempsey, 1, 137
Klein, Joel, 202–3
Kleindienst, Richard, 100, 102, 119
Kloeb, Frank L., 215n. 2
Koelsch, Oliver, 99
Kovachevich, Elizabeth, 255n. 175
Kristol, Irving, 117–18
Krock, Arthur, 28–29, 218n. 45
Krogh, Egil "Bud," 110, 115–16, 123,
132, 185
Kurland, Philip B., 127, 137

Lader, Philip, 202–3
Lafontant, Jewel, 118
Landrum-Griffin bill, 232nn. 5, 6,
233n. 12
Lasky, Victor, 80, 232n. 5
Laxalt, Paul A., 137–38

Sumter, Thomas, 10
Sununu, John, Bush advisor role of,
191–92, 194–95, 206
Supreme Court: "black seat" tradition
of, 75, 193, 195, 206, 235n. 36; calendar terms of, 211n. 15; "Catholic
seat" tradition of, 34–37, 39, 54–55,
57–60, 75, 221n. 81, 228n. 80,
229n. 96; conflict among members
of, 27–30, 32–33, 39–40, 217n. 36,
218nn. 42, 44, 45, 49, 218–19n. 53;
Hispanic seat issue and, 194–95,
204; "Jewish seat" tradition and, 84,
86, 104–5, 193, 201, 245nn. 41, 42,
250n. 110; political presence of, 17–
18; rights-based agenda of, 18, 27–
28
Supreme Court nominee consideration
and selection: administration staff
conflicts and, 3, 19–20; Bork rejection, 2, 5, 16, 161, 189–90, 207,
209n. 1; Louis Brandeis appointment, 15; candidates pool, 5–6,
211n. 8; Carswell rejection, 111–12,
121–22, 132, 185, 209n. 1, 247n.
77; Cleveland nominees rejection,
246n. 57; composition of Senate, 4–
5; criteria-driven framework of, 6;
decisionmaking bureaucracy of, 7; divided party government and, 14;
early veto power, 8–9; failed or controversial nominees and, viii, 209–
10n. 3; Harlan nomination, 14;
Haynsworth rejection, 107–8, 185,
209n. 1; impact of, 1–2; judicial politics vs. talents and, 2–3; "open" selection framework of, 6–7, 21; outgoing justice attributes and, 5; Parker
rejection, 209n. 1; presidential nominations and, percentages of, vii–viii,
209n. 1; public approval of the president and, 5; recess appointments
and, 50; rejection percentages and,
viii, 209n. 1; Senate confirmation
percentages and, vii–viii, 209n. 1;
single-candidate-focused framework
of, 6; Stone nomination and, 15; timing of vacancy and, 4. *See also specific
topics and administrations*
Supreme Court nominee consideration
and selection (pre-1945): attorney

general role in, 9–10, 212n. 18; cabinet members' role in, 11; geographical diversity and, 10–11; political advisors' role in, 10; sitting and former
justices' role in, 11–12, 213nn. 35,
36
Supreme Court nominee consideration
and selection (post-1945, factors affecting): federal court policymaking
and, 13–14; federal courts influence
and, 13–14; interest group participation in, 16–17; Justice Department
bureaucratization and, 12–13, 18–
19; legal research technology and,
17; media attention and, 17, 214n.
53; organized bar and, power in, 15–
16, 213–14nn. 47–49; party representation and, 14, 23, 27, 213n. 41,
216nn. 13, 14; political life and, Supreme Court role in, 17–18; public
disclosure and, 14–15, 213nn. 44;
White House bureaucratization and,
13, 18
Supreme Court nominee consideration
and selection (post-1945, patterns
and problems in): ABA Standing
Committee and, 170–71, 266n. 3;
advisors conflict and, 172, 178, 180–
87; "closed" selection mechanism
and, 175–77, *176;* computer research technology and, 169, 186;
consensus building and, 168;
"criteria-driven" approach to, 172,
177–80, *178,* 187; current/past/
present reaction and, 169–70; depiction of, *173, 174, 176, 178;* executive
branch resources and, 168–69; judicial experience requirement and,
169–72, 265–66nn. 1–3; "judicial
transactions" concept and, 173; media attention and, 168; modern developments in, 186–87; "open" decisionmaking framework and, 173–75,
174; organized interests and, 168;
"outcome optimism" concept and,
182–84; personal vs. policy vs. partisan goals of, 180–81; pool of candidates and, expansion of, 169, 178,
186; Senate "benefactors" and,
266n. 3. *See also specific administrations*